THE *Patterns of WAR* since the *Eighteenth Century*

Larry H. Addington

INDIANA UNIVERSITY PRESS
BLOOMINGTON

FOR

Amanda AND *Catherine*

Manufactured in the United States of America

Library of Congress Cataloging in Publication Data

Addington, Larry H.
The patterns of war since the eighteenth century.

Bibliography: p.
Includes index.
1. Military history, Modern—18th century. 2. Military history, Modern—19th century. 3. Military history, Modern—20th century. I. Title.
U39.A33 1984 355'.009'03 83-48902
ISBN 0-253-34305-4
1 2 3 4 5 88 87 86 85 84

CONTENTS

Maps

Diagrams

Illustrations

Preface

I have attempted in this book to present, in a narrative form, a synthesis of the many changes in war that have taken place from the late eighteenth century to the present. The book is not intended to be a complete history of warfare or of wars in that crowded era, but I hope that I have suggested some themes and interpretations which will prove valuable to the student. In addition, I have tried to introduce as many useful facts as possible within a concise form. My underlying assumption in writing this book is that the history of warfare is best understood as a process of change in war's social-political, technological, and organizational aspects. My information was mostly drawn from published sources, but a complete list of the works consulted would be too lengthy to include. I have therefore appended a list of selected sources which may be used as a recommended reading list for the student who wishes to delve further into any aspect of the subject. Finally, I acknowledge my debt to those scholars upon whose published work this book rests; without their labors no book of synthesis would be possible.

Perhaps my first debt of gratitude for help with this book is owed to Theodore Ropp, Professor Emeritus of History, Duke University, who taught me many years ago the importance of synthesizing history, and who kindly read and criticized much of the manuscript upon which this book is based. I also owe a great debt to Professor Gunther E. Rothenberg, Professor of History, Purdue Undiversity, who not only read most of the manuscript but who urged its publication on Indiana University Press. John S. Coussons, Professor and Chairman of the History Department, The Citadel, made every effort to secure for me reduced teaching duties so that I might find time to complete the project, and I owe him much for his splendid cooperation. The Citadel Development Foundation provided funds for the research and the writing of the book, and I express here my gratitude for that assistance. So many of my colleagues in the History Department at The Citadel have suggested themes and ideas for this book that I hesitate to mention any lest I do an injustice to others. However, John W. Gordon deserves to be named as one with whom it is always a pleasure to have intellectual exchanges. My wife, Amanda, reviewed the manuscript for style and errors of grammar and spelling, and, as always, provided the loving support and faith in the project that every author should be so fortunate to have from a spouse. My daughter, Catherine, typed and retyped much of the manuscript, and I am also grateful for her efforts to serve a perhaps too demanding father. And finally, I hope that Roger Bender, Professor Emeritus of Physics, The Citadel, will recognize through these pages that his encouragement to a younger colleague many years ago was not wasted.

March 1984
Charleston, SC

THE *Patterns of WAR* since the *Eighteenth Century*

1

From Dynastic to National Warfare, 1775–1815

In the forty years between 1775 and 1815 occurred a revolution in Western warfare that coincided with the American and the French revolutions, and with the coming of the age of Napoleon. This revolution swept away the traditional forms of dynastic warfare that had evolved in the European world for three hundred years previously, and began an era of national warfare that persists to this day. The study of the patterns of war since the eighteenth century begins appropriately then with an examination of this process of change between 1775 and 1815, an approach which also allows the setting of a bench-mark from which all further changes in warfare may be usefully measured. Although navies were less affected than armies by change in this period, they too will be examined in order to establish the background for understanding the tremendous impact of technological change over the course of the nineteenth century. Still, the central theme of this chapter is how warfare on land was transformed from conflicts between monarchs to great struggles between peoples, the essence of national warfare.

I. Dynastic Warfare

A. Armies. Between the close of the Middle Ages and the last quarter of the eighteenth century, European armies developed coeval with the rise of the centralized monarchy in states in which dynastic identification predominated over national identity. In the earliest part of the period, royal armies were temporary combinations of feudal and mercenary forces assembled only on the eve of war. As royal finances improved, the permanently-assembled or standing army became the rule. Because royal armies identified with dynastic interests and included many foreign troops, the early Western army was not a national institution. Armies of this type reached the peak of their development in the first three-quarters of the eighteenth century, when the great military states of the age were Bourbon France, Hapsburg Austria, Hohenzollern Prussia and Romanov Russia. Of these four, Prussia and Russia were the most lately arrived. Prussia became a recognized major military power with the outcomes of the War of the Austrian Succession (1740–1748) and the Seven Years' War (1756–1763). Russia under Tsar Peter II (the Great) replaced Vasa Sweden as the outcome of the Great Northern War (1702–1721).

Except for Prussia, the major military states of Europe in the late eighteenth century had populations varying between 20 and 30 million people each. Prussia never had a population exceeding 6 million, and it is something of a marvel that this relatively small German state (of many in the so-called Holy Roman Empire) counted for so much in the European balance of power. It did so in part because it maintained a standing army equal at times to as much as 3 percent of its population, whereas the other great powers, with larger populations, usually did not maintain armies in excess of one percent of their respective populations. Still, in absolute numbers, the largest royal army before the French Revolution appeared early in the eighteenth century. Under Louix XIV, the celebrated "Sun King," the French army reached a peak strength of 400,000 troops during the War of the Spanish Succession (1702–1713). Only the French Revolutionary army would exceed that figure, and then not before 1794.

Royal dynastic armies were much alike in their social composition, excepting perhaps to a degree the British and Russian armies. The hereditary nobility held most of the commissioned positions, and the commissioned officer without noble patent might face arbitrary limits on his promotion and branch assignment. The country gentry dominated the officer corps of the British army, only about fifty thousand in a country whose home population was nine million just before the outbreak of the American Revolution. But whereas the buying of officer commissions had faded out on the continent of Europe, the so-called Purchase System in the infantry and cavalry branches of the British army flourished below the general ranks. Accordingly, few British officers ever reached the rank of colonel without private means or a wealthy patron. It was also customary for retired officers to live off the proceeds from the sale of their commissions. In Russia, Tsar Peter II had completely reorganized society early in the eighteenth century so that important positions were filled not on the basis of hereditary privilege, but on the basis of trust. Even in his time, a kind of new nobility had grown up based on service to the throne. Peter imported so many foreign officers, and they in turn founded so many aristocratic military families, that almost two hundred years after Peter's passing the general officer lists of the Russian army were studded with German names. Under Frederick-William II of Prussia, the Junker nobility served as officers, not as a privilege but as compulsory duty.

If officers were mostly drawn from the upper classes of society, enlisted men were drawn from the bottom. Landless peasants, the unemployed of the cities, and vagabonds and drifters were either voluntarily recruited into armies or forced into service by the "press gang," that peculiar institution of eighteenth-century conscription. The sergeants and corporals (the noncommissioned officers chosen from among the old soldiers) disciplined and trained new recruits with close-order drill, the manual of arms, and physical punishments as necessary. The aim of such training was to make of the private soldier an obedient "walking musket," one who would perform his duties without question and with the mechanical precision bred of long practice. Desertion in peacetime was discouraged by housing troops in barracks, and in wartime by close supervision of camps in the field.

The infantry branch was the most numerous in all armies, and the infantry battalion was the basic building-block of any army. A battalion might have a typical strength of eight hundred officers and men, divided among six companies of the line and two so-called flank companies. Infantry of the line usually fought in three close-packed ranks, their smoothbore, muzzle-loading flintlock muskets capable of being fired and reloaded at the rate of about two rounds per minute. Firing was done in volleys by platoons, the sections of a company. One of the flank companies might be composed of light infantry, soldiers trained to fight as skirmishers and sometimes armed with rifles. (The rifle was a musket with grooves in the bore which gave the ball a spin that insured greater range and accuracy than that of a smoothbore musket.) Whereas volleys fired by smoothbores had an effective range not exceeding a hundred yards, aimed rifle fire could be dangerous to twice that distance. On the other hand, rifles took about twice as long to load because the ball had to be worked down the barrel against the resistance of the rifling. Because of its loading problems and greater cost of manufacture, the rifle remained a specialist weapon down to the mid-nineteenth century. The grenadier companies, composed of the largest men in the battalion, were often used to lead bayonet charges, the bayonet being the ordinary soldier's only weapon for hand-to-hand fighting in the late eighteenth century.

Infantry battalions were combined in regiments, and regiments were combined in brigades. When deployed on the battlefield, these formations of infantry were supported by batteries of artillery (a battery was composed of two to six guns) and squadrons of cavalry. (A cavalry squadron was roughly equivalent to a small infantry battalion in size, and was subdivided into "troops," or the equivalents of companies.) When combined with siege and supply trains for mobile warfare, all these forces constituted a field army. In the Seven Years' War (1756–63) in Europe, field armies averaged about forty-seven thousand men. Unless it was the monarch himself, the commander-in-chief of a field army bore the rank of marshal, field-marshal, colonel-general, or lieutenant-general. The practice varied from country to country. Whatever his official rank, the commanding general was assisted in his staff work by an adjutant-general and a quartermaster-general, and in the command of his forces, by one or more major-generals. Brigadier-generals, of course, commanded brigades. Colonels, assisted by lieutenant-colonels, commanded regiments, while majors usually commanded battalions. Captains commanded companies, and lieutenants, the lowest-ranking of commissioned officers, commanded platoons.

On the battlefield, an eighteenth-century army presented a colorful spectacle, since the uniforms were gaudy by current standards, and cover and concealment played no significant role in combat for troops drawn up in large formations and who, as a practical matter, had to stand erect in order to load and fire their weapons efficiently. The artillery pieces were dragged into position by draft animals driven by civilian drivers who, once fighting was about to begin, hurriedly retired to a safe distance in the rear. All guns, except those light enough to be wheeled by hand, had to remain stationary throughout the battle. When forming for battle, each infantry battalion approached the space in the army's line of battle which it was assigned to fill, in a column at right angles to the line. (See Diagram 1.) Then it wheeled to march across the space until it was filled up. By making a half turn to left or right, it faced the enemy line, usually about 300–400 yards away. All this marching and wheeling about took time and required careful judgment on the part of the officers. The cavalry screened the army until it was formed for battle, then guarded its flanks or retired to the rear. Cavalry was rarely committed to action except against other cavalry or broken infantry formations. To repel cavalry, infantry battalions usually formed hollow "squares" (actually diamond-shaped), six ranks to a side and artillery at the corners.

The biggest tactical problems facing infantry in the eighteenth century were the time-consuming delay in forming the line of battle and the inflexibility of the line once formed. With each battalion front 150–200 yards in length, the line of battle tended to weave and to develop gaps when advancing, and frequent halts were required in order to redress the line. Until the middle of the eighteenth century, the common wisdom in armies was that troops could not keep good order if they moved faster than 90 paces per minute. Then, when Prussian infantry introduced the Quick Step (120 paces per minute) without jumbling up their ranks, they were judged the wonder of the age. Eventually other

DIAGRAM 1. Hypothetical Battalion forming from Column into Line of Battle. Each line represents a company of 90 men drawn up in three ranks. Each company has a frontage of 25 yards and a depth of 9 yards.

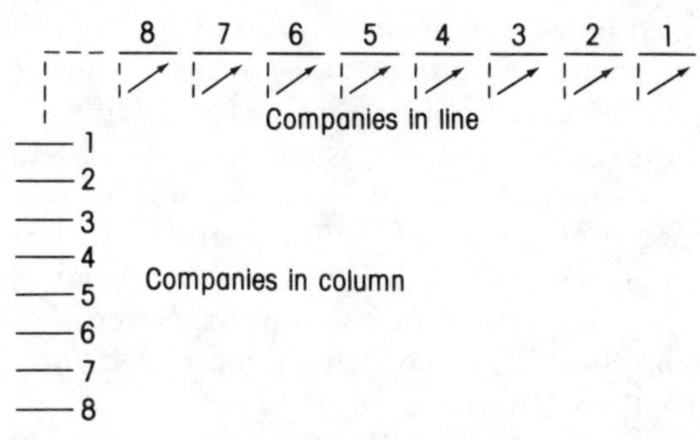

Once the companies were in line and allowing 3 yards between companies, the battalion frontage would be 221 yards, or more than two modern football fields laid end-to-end. Battalions with fewer men and tighter intervals might reduce the length of the line to about 150 yards. In some armies, No. 1 Company would be composed of grenadiers and No. 8 Company composed of light infantry.

armies mastered the Quick Step (today's standard marching cadence), but that improvement did not solve the basic problem of finding better formations for maneuver. The slow, parade-ground-like movements of eighteenth-century armies on the battlefield survived down to the time of the French Revolution.

The strategic movement of armies before 1789 was as slow and deliberate as their movements on the battlefield. Operations in Europe were mounted from large fortresses on the frontiers or from fortified cities where supplies had been accumulated in magazines. Horse-drawn wagons hauled ammunition and food for the troops, and fodder for the animals. But since hay and oats are especially bulky items, and a typical horse ate at least twenty pounds of fodder per day, a supply train could usually meet the needs of a field army for only a five-day march (about seventy miles). Then, food and fodder had to be replenished either by staging supplies from the fortress-magazine, or by drawing resources from the local countryside. In practice, relying on local resources was more practical, though this necessitated long delays at intervals in order for contractors to make arrangements to buy and collect food and fodder, or, if in enemy territory, for troops to take them by force. For logistical reasons, the mark of good generalship in the eighteenth century was a careful regard for supply and a conservation of resources, material and human.

Perhaps the most outstanding practitioner of dynastic warfare was

Frederick the Great, King of Prussia from 1740 to 1786. Frederick-William II, his father, was actually responsible for creating the fourth largest army in Europe at a time when the Prussian population was thirteenth. He was also responsible for making the Junker nobility serve as officers out of duty as well as privilege, and for compelling them to allow short-term training for their peasant-serfs, who were then returned to their owners. Still, up to a quarter of the Prussian army was recruited from outside the country's boundaries. Frederick the Great invested his father's military capital in the War of the Austrian Succession (1740–48), emerging not only with the province of Silesia and the means to expand his army to 163,000 troops by 1756, but with a practical fund of experience that served him well in the Seven Years' War. With generous financial subsidies from Britain, he managed to fight off the attacks of France, Russia, and Austria.

As already mentioned, Britain's royal army was small by continental European standards, and it was scattered over an extensive colonial empire overseas. In addition, after the English Civil War (1642–48) and then a Cromwellian military dictatorship, power over the army under the restored monarchy ended up divided between crown and parliament. Parliament was suspicious of large standing forces which might be converted into engines of royal tyranny, and it preferred to rely on the navy and a militia for defense of the home islands. The colony of India was actually the private possession of the East India Trading Company, which at mid-century organized a company army to protect its holdings in the subcontinent and to combat its French rivals. In the final decade of the eighteenth century, the company army numbered 150,000 troops. The company commissioned its own officers and promoted them on the basis of seniority. The regiments were a mixture of European and native units, the native soldiers being known as sepoys. The Indian army, as a private organization, lasted down to the Great Mutiny of 1857, the subsequent abolition of the company, and the conversion of India to the status of a crown colony.

In summary, the eighteenth-century royal armies were dynastic institutions rather than national institutions. Their social structures reflected the intense hierarchial nature of European society, while their weapons and equipment were merely improvements on those used over the previous two centuries. Eighteenth-century military organization was also a refinement of earlier managerial arrangements. Tactical and strategic thinking emphasized form and caution. Eighteenth-century armies were usually employed to make good dynastic claims, to seize border provinces or overseas colonies, and by their very natures they were best suited to such limited objectives. While these armies also served as forces for internal security, as the events of the American and French revolutions would demonstrate, they were not well suited for the suppression of mass revolt. Accordingly, when major social change stirred the European world toward the end of the eighteenth century, the resultant political upheavals began to sweep away the old military forms and to prepare the way for national warfare.

B. Navies. Navies, like armies, were mostly instruments of monarchy in the late eighteenth century; but, being a form of transportation as well, they were even more dominated by technological considerations. The long naval rivalries among France, Spain, Holland, and England reached their climax with the Anglo-Dutch victory over the French fleet in the Battle of Cape de la Hogue in 1692, and thereafter Britain became unassailably the dominant naval power in Europe and in the world. The British fleet was often the equal in size to the other European navies combined. Britain maintained her naval advantage because of certain unique factors: (1) the insularity of the home islands allowed Britain to concentrate her resources on a navy rather than on a large army; (2) the other naval powers found it difficult to overcome Britain's numerical advantage in ships in an age when there was little technical obsolescence and well-built vessels might last for decades; (3) Britain's great seafaring population provided an abundance of able seamen to the British navy; and (4) Britain's favorable geographical position off the western coasts of Europe made it relatively easy for the British navy to blockade enemy ports in time of war.

The dominant warship of the eighteenth century was the ship-of-the-line-of-battle (shortened to ship-of-the-line or even to battleship). A ship-of-the-line had at least two gun decks and sixty guns, and a large ship might have three gun decks and 120 guns. Even a few larger ships were built. The "first-rate," the most powerful of the type, was defined as a ship-of-the-line carrying a hundred guns or more, and was manned by eight hundred to a thousand officers and men. Such a ship might displace 3,500 tons. More common was the "74-gunner," a vessel manned by six hundred men and displacing 2,000 tons.

The main types of vessels below-the-line were the frigate and the sloop-of-war. Until the 1790s, the typical frigate carried between thirty-two and thirty-eight guns, had one gun deck, and was manned by about 350 men. Some American frigates built in the 1790s were designed to outfight anything they could not outrun, and might carry fifty guns or more. Sloops-of-war carried about twenty guns on the weather deck, and were the only war vessels with two rather than three or four masts. Frigates scouted for the battle line, chased enemy commerce raiders, supported amphibious operations, and, along with sloops-of-war, carried out any other naval missions for which ships-of-the-line were unsuited or were unnecessary.

The naval strategies available in the Age of Sail were three: (1) Grand

A late eighteenth-century British frigate and two ships of the line.

SOURCE: Michael Glover, *The Napoleonic Wars: An Illustrated History* (New York: Hippocrene Books, 1981).

War; (2) Fleet-in Being; and (3) *guerre de course* or commerce-raiding. Grand War involved seeking out the enemy's battle fleet and destroying it in order to have command of the sea. Command of the sea may be defined as the ability to use the sea for one's purposes while denying that privilege to the enemy. With command of the sea, a navy could blockade enemy battle fleets and commercial ports, support invasions and raids into enemy territory, and bombard the enemy coastline to the limit of the range of the guns. Without command of the sea, a belligerent was thrown almost entirely on the strategic defensive. Clearly, only ships-of-the-line mattered much for Grand War, and the side with the greater number had the advantage. Accordingly, after 1692 Britain's favored strategy against France, Spain, and Holland was Grand War.

The strategies of Fleet-in-Being and *guerre de course* were the options open to relatively weaker navies. Under Fleet-in-Being, the object was to conserve the battle fleet in port until opportunities appeared for gaining temporary or local command of the sea for ulterior purposes. *Guerre de course* or commerce-raiding had the advantage that a battle fleet was not a requirement. Ships below-the-line and even armed merchant ships could be sent out to raid the enemy's shipping lanes. Governments sometimes issued Letters of Marque to privately owned vessels to wage a kind of legalized piracy, such vessels being known as "privateers." But in the Sailing Age, even the powers most dependent on the sea for economic reasons—such as Britain—were still so self-sufficient in basic resources that even a highly successful *guerre de course* against them could hardly have decisive results. The usual effect of *guerre de course* was to drive up the cost of doing business by increasing insurance rates and placing financial pressure on the business class. It sometimes forced trade to seek the protection of neutral flags. Still, *guerre de course* was a useful alternative for weak naval powers in the Sailing Age.

When battle fleets fought for command of the sea, their tactics were as formal as those of armies on shore. The stronger fleet normally formed line-ahead in the weather-gauge (i.e., upwind of the enemy), from whence it was easier to attack. The opposing fleet formed in the lee. In the British navy, the "Formalist School" preferred to engage in "conterminous line," but the more adventurous "Melée School" preferred daring maneuvers such as Massing, Doubling, and Breaking. (See Diagram 2.) Before 1783 the British *Fighting Instructions* made it difficult for admirals to signal for melée maneuvers. Revised instructions after 1783 and improved signaling systems paved the way for Horatio Nelson, the greatest admiral of the Sailing Age, to win his three famous victories at the Nile (1798), Copenhagen (1801), and Cape Trafalgar (1805).

The largest naval gun carried in broadside on a ship-of-the-line was the 32-pounder, a piece that with its truck weighed three tons and re-

DIAGRAM 2. Fleet Tactics in the Age of Sail.

A. Fleet "A" forming a conterminous line with fleet "B."

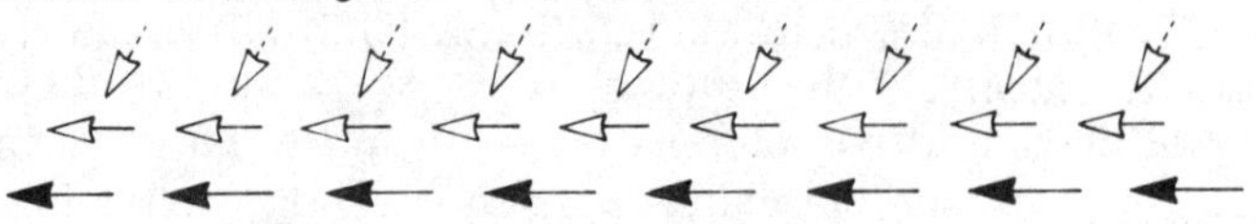

B. Fleet "A" massing on rear division of fleet "B."

C. Fleet "A" doubling on rear division of fleet "B."

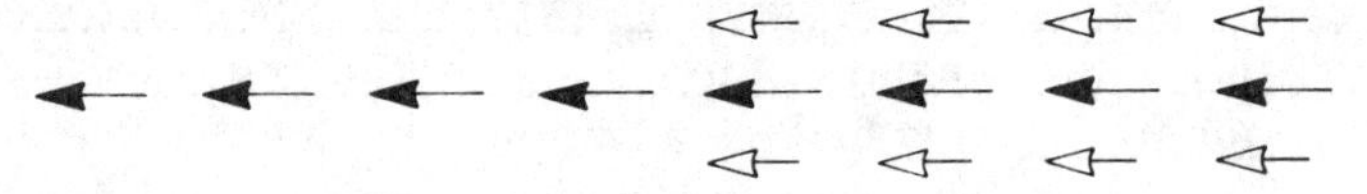

D. Fleet "A" breaking the line of fleet "B."

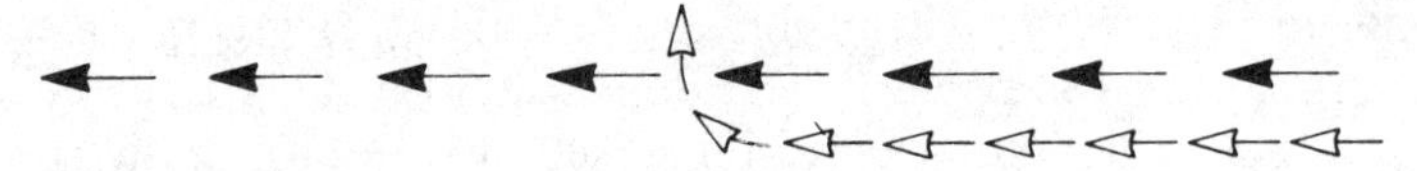

E. Nelson's use of two columns at the Battle of Trafalgar.

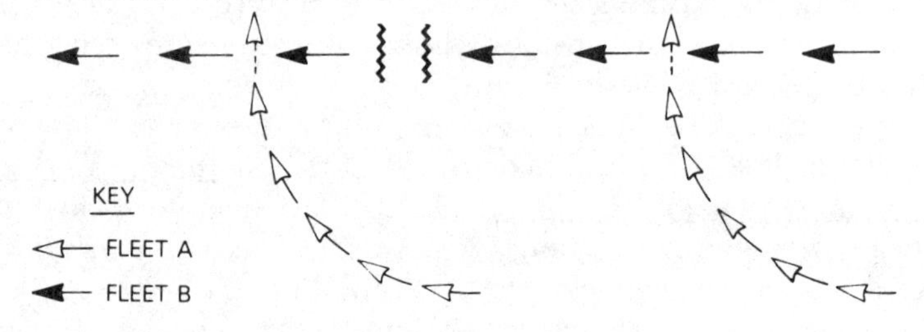

quired nine men to work efficiently. The other typical muzzle-loaders were the 24- and 18-pounders. Rapid rate of fire was prized over precision of aim in an age in which most naval battles were fought at relatively close quarters. Solid shot (cannon balls) and langrage (small balls and chains) were favored for ship-to-ship actions. Exploding shell was so dangerous until after 1815 that it was normally restricted to short-barreled mortars mounted in specially-constructed bomb-ketches and used only for coast bombardments. Duels between masonry forts ashore and fleets at sea were unpredictable in outcome because the gun ashore enjoyed a more stable platform and was better protected, yet a fleet could bring many more guns to bear than found in most forts. Naval fire could only dismount guns, however; in order to make a breach in fortress walls, guns had to be taken ashore where they could be fired with greater accuracy than from the rolling decks of a ship. The bomb-shells fired by bomb-ketches were mostly dangerous to fortress guns without overhead cover *(en barbette)* since they followed a high trajectory. Guns in protected casemates could only be silenced by direct hits on their embrasures. Because of engineering problems, few forts, before the early nineteenth century, had more than two tiers of guns in casemate and one tier *en barbette.*

Naval officer corps in the eighteenth century were less dominated by the hereditary aristocracy than officers corps in armies, perhaps because fewer nobles were interested in the demanding life at sea. In the British navy, officer-candidates—called "midshipmen" for the area in which they were berthed—usually entered service in their early teens through royal appointment ("King's Letter Boys") or upon recommendation of a ship captain. The midshipman served several years as an apprentice while learning ship-handling, navigation, and gunnery. After passing a formal examination, he was commissioned a lieutenant. As a senior lieutenant, he might be given command of a sloop-of-war or other small craft and designated as a "lieutenant-commanding" (probably the origin of the modern ranks of lieutenant-commander and commander). If he was promoted to the rank of captain, he might command a frigate and eventually a ship-of-the-line. A rear admiral originally commanded the rear division of a battle line. The admiral and vice admiral commanded the other divisions, and the admiral, of course, the whole force.

Enlisted men in navies of the Sailing Age were ordinary mariners who either signed on for a hitch or who were impressed in time of war. Enlistment was for service in a particular ship, the terms varying according to circumstance and the convenience of the captain and government. At the conclusion of hostilities, crews were laid off wholesale and the ships laid up "in ordinary" (i.e., the fleet reserve). Recruits and able seamen aboard ship were supervised and, when necessary, punished by the petty officers, the counterparts of sergeants and corporals in armies.

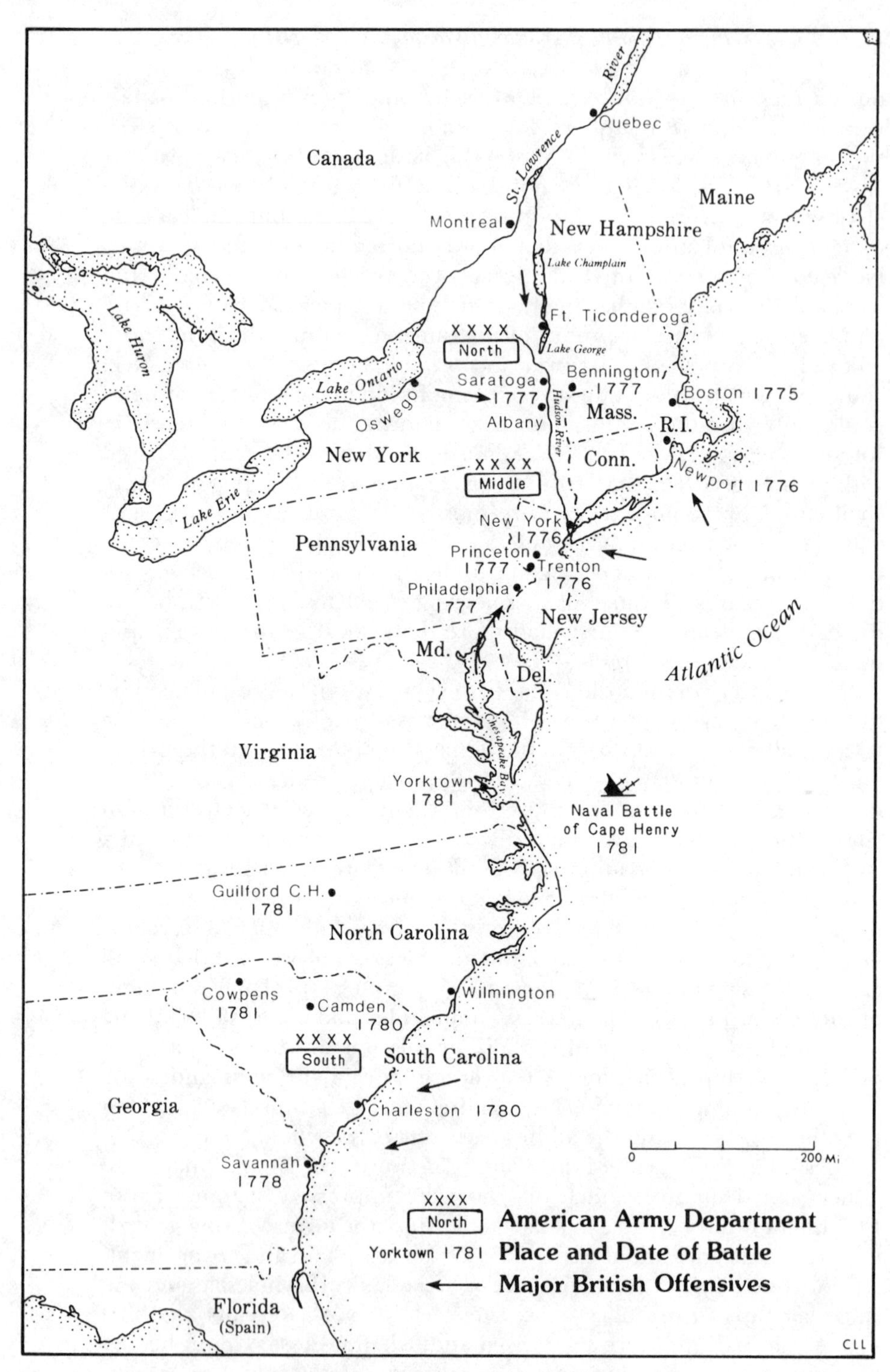

The American Revolution, 1775–1781

Sailors slept in hammocks suspended from the overhead on the gun decks, and their diet consisted of unleavened bread (hardtack), salted beef, pork and fish (known as junk). Water was mixed with rum in a concoction know as "grog" (whence we get the word "groggy") in order to slow the process of spoilage. Accordingly, alcholism was a chronic affliction of navies. Officers enjoyed better food and accomodations than enlisted men, but life at sea was hard for all hands.

II. The War of the American Revolution, 1775–83

Though the War of the American Revolution may be considered as the first of modern national wars, the size of the conflict in North America was small even by dynastic eighteenth-century standards. No more than 35,000 Americans were ever under arms at one time, and not more than 20,000 of them in one place. Usually, the forces on hand were smaller. The Continental Army, the American regular force, never had more than about 17,000 soldiers at a time in its ranks. The majority of Americans who bore arms did so as part-time soldiers of the militia, hence the total of 100,000 American veterans or higher sometimes given in textbooks is somewhat misleading. Nor was the American army strictly national. The Continental Congress commissioned a number of foreign officers to help George Washington fill the need for good general officers. Among the best of the foreign generals were the Marquis de la Fayette (a captain on leave from the French army), Johann de Kalb (a retired French major), and Friedrich Steuben (a retired major from the army of Frederick the Great). Of the thirteen general officers commissioned by Congress in 1775 to serve under Washington, only three had previously held commissions in the British army and none in a rank higher than lieutenant-colonel. Still, some of the native generals had seen service in the French and Indian War as officers of the militia (as was the case with Washington himself) and were therefore not completely devoid of military experience.

When the clashes outside Boston at Lexington and Concord between Massachusetts militia and British red-coats in April, 1775, ignited the war, Britain had only 8,500 troops in the whole of North America. With slight reinforcements, these forces were only able to defend Canada from invasion during the winter of 1775–1776 and to hold Boston until March, 1776. By the summer of 1776, Britain was mobilizing an army of 95,000 men, but only 50,000 of them were sent to the colonies that year, including 30,000 German mercenaries whom the Americans called "Hessians." Britain never had as large a force in North America again for the rest of the war. Although a Loyalist population of half a million whites may have lived in the colonies, the British recruited only 20,000 individuals for their forces, and no more than 11,000 at any one time. The base of the "patriot" population was about 1.5 million whites, although about 5,000 black men served with the American army and an unknown number served with the British. The whole population of the thirteen colonies came to 2.5 million people, that of the British home islands to about 9 million. Obviously, neither side ever fully exploited its potential manpower for the war, not surprising on the British side with its dynastic traditions.

American supply problems might have been overwhelming had not France lent a hand. The monarchy arranged to smuggle $8 million worth of arms and equipment to the colonies even before it became a formal ally in February, 1778. About 90 percent of all American gunpowder came from French sources. In addition, in 1775 the Americans found three hundred stored British cannon at Ft. Ticonderoga. A few armed ships, commissioned by Washington while his army was laying siege to Boston during 1775–76, captured a British vessel loaded with powder and ball. In the fall of 1775, Congress founded a Continental Navy and Marine Corps, but by July, 1776, the aggregate of the Continental and state navies came to only twenty-seven converted merchantmen armed with an average of twenty guns apiece. Such a force was only good for *guerre de course,* not for command of the seas, and even in that role the several hundred privateers sailing under letters of marque captured twice as many British merchantmen as the Continental and state navies put together. Congress tried to create more regular naval forces, approving the building of five ships-of-the-line and eighteen frigates, but only one of the ships-of-the-line—the 74-gun *America*—was ever finished (and it was given to the Frency navy), and only six of the frigates ever got to sea. (One of the six, and a frigate given by France, survived the war.) France converted a few old merchantmen to serve as American raiders from European ports, the most famous being John Paul Jones's *Bon Homme Richard.*

In contrast to the American naval effort, Britain commissioned 123 ships-of-the-line and 222 frigates and sloops-of-war, the whole manned by 100,000 sailors and marines. The real challenge to Britain at sea came with the French intervention in 1778 with 80 ships-of-the-line, with the Spanish intervention in 1779 with 60 of-the-line, and the Dutch intervention in 1780 with 20 of-the-line. Britain's fleets were spread increasingly thin as the war expanded to include European waters and even the seas off India as well as the North American and Caribbean waters. Britain did well to prevent any superior combination at the Channel and to get Gibraltar through the longest siege in its history (1779–1781). It succeeded mostly in the Mediterranean and in the Carribean. The fatal British defeat at Yorktown in 1781 was the result, in part, of a local failure of British sea power and must be viewed against a background of a conflict that had spread to three continents. Nor was the conflict entirely naval beyond North America. Late in the Revolution, a native revolt in India under Prince Hyder Ali added to the British problems of overextension. Viewed in a wider context, the War of the American Revolution might be seen as one in which the British empire was besieged.

American battlefield tactics were not as un-European as is widely supposed. The Continentals usually fought in line, though usually in two ranks rather than in three. Militia, like all irregular troops, fought best from behind natural or man-made cover. Some backwoodsmen were capital skirmishers, especially those armed with the "Kentucky rifle" (actually the Pennsylvania rifle), but militia caught in the open were no match for charging redcoats. On more occasions than the Americans cared to remember, fleeing militia brought on near-disasters for the Continental Army. On the other hand, they provided important "flesh" to the "skeleton" of the Continental Army, and even on the formal battlefield they could fight well if the local American commander understood their strengths and weaknesses. The trick was in choosing the right tactics for combining Continentals and militia. General Horatio Gates failed to do so at Camden, S.C., in August, 1780, and his whole army was routed. Daniel Morgan used the right tactics at Cowpens, S.C., in January, 1781, and won a smashing victory. Using the same tactics at Guilford Courthouse, N.C., in March, 1781, Nathaniel Greene inflicted almost fatal losses on a British army even though his army was compelled to give up the field. Still, Americans usually did better on tactical defense, where less maneuvering was required and cover could offset their other deficiencies.

Understandably, the British troops did best in coastal areas, where the Royal Navy could assist them. This was not because the British army was not used to the forested terrain of the backcountry—it had experienced much of that in the French and Indian War (1754–1763)—but because logistics were such a nightmare away from navigable water. General John Burgoyne's expedition in 1777 from Canada down lakes Champlain and George into upper New York is a case in point. It ran into trouble when its way was blocked by Americans behind earthworks north of Albany, and it could not supply itself either from the lakes or from the surrounding countryside. (Militia wiped out a large foraging expedition at Bennington, Vermont.) It waited too long to begin a retreat, allowing militia time to bring Horatio Gates's army up to a strength of 20,000 men. When his army was finally trapped on Saratoga Heights, Burgoyne ordered his remaining 5,800 troops to lay down their arms on October 17. Saratoga was the biggest unassisted American victory of the war. On the other hand, the biggest British victory was at Charleston,

S.C., in May, 1780, when General Sir Henry Clinton's army and the British fleet compelled the surrender of the entire Army of the Southern Department—5,500 men—and forced the scuttling of most of the Continental Navy.

Save Boston, which the British abandoned in March, 1776, and never recovered, all of the major American cities were seized by the British at one time or another during the war. All of them were accessible from the sea, and none was successfully defended at any time except Charleston in June, 1776. Philadelphia, the largest, with forty thousand people, was occupied in September, 1777, by forces moving through Chesapeake Bay. New York City and Newport, R.I., like Boston with populations of around twenty thousand apiece, were both occupied in 1776. Charleston, the largest city in the southern colonies with twelve thousand people (half of them black) fell in May, 1780. Savannah and Wilmington, each with about half of Charleston's population, were also occupied during the war. But in order to occupy Charleston in 1780, the British were forced to abandon Newport, and when a small French army and fleet occupied the place in July, 1780, the main British force had to be transferred back to the defense of New York City. General Charles, Lord Cornwallis, left in command in the south, launched an offensive into the hinterland that was short on manpower and harassed by partisans. His losses were so severe in the Battle of Guilford Courthouse, N.C., in March, 1781, that his army was compelled to withdraw to Wilmington on the coast. General Nathaniel Greene's American forces were then able to overrun and hold the Carolina and Georgia backcountry, and to confine the British south of Virginia to the ports of Wilmington, Charleston, and Savannah.

The *coup de grâce* to the British effort in North America came after Cornwallis made his base at Yorktown, Va., near Chesapeake Bay, in the late summer of 1781. Upon learning that Admiral Comte de Grasse was coming north with the French Carribean fleet, Washington and General Comte de Rochambeau united their forces on the Hudson River and started south for Virginia. While they were on their way, De Grasse's fleet severed Cornwallis's sea communications, then defeated an effort by the British fleet to reopen them in the Battle of Cape Henry on September 5. When Washington and Rochambeau's forces arrived before Yorktown, Washington—as Allied commander-in-chief—opened a formal siege on September 30. He never had a greater force at his disposal: 38 French ships-of-the-line, 15,000 French sailors and marines, 7,800 French troops and 9,000 American troops (3,500 of them militia). Cornwallis's 6,500 troops stacked arms on October 19 when he dispaired of relief. The war dragged on until the Peace of Paris in January, 1783, but Yorktown was the last straw for the British in North America. Of the total of 35,000 American casualties during the war, 25,000 were fatalities. If as few as 100,000 men served during the war with American forces (as some historians believe), then one out of every three was a casualty, and one out of every four was a fatality.

III. The French Revolution and Napoleon, 1789–1815

If the American Revolution may be said to have given birth to national warfare, however much on a limited scale, then the Wars of the French Revolution and Napoleon may be said to have brought national warfare to full development. The French Revolution of 1789 took place among a people of 25 million, or ten times the American population at the time of the American Revolution, and the second largest in Europe after the Russian. When royal powers threatened the Revolution beginning in 1792, France was able to go far beyond the United States in its measures to wage war. The adoption of the *levée en masse* in 1793, and a centrally directed war economy, produced the first mass army in modern history. When that army became a tool of expansion under Napoleon Bonaparte, for a time it seemed almost irresistable. Indeed, the traditional dynasties were forced to remodel their armies in a more national direction in order to survive, and the old forms of war never fully recovered from the events between 1792 and 1815. As the military philosopher Carl von Clausewitz observed, it was as if war itself had been lecturing.

A. Ideas Borrowed from the Armée Ancien *before 1789.* The power of the Revolutionary army was not alone due to the numbers and enthusiasm released by the upheaval generated in 1789. It was also due to the intelligent application of ideas borrowed from innovators in the old royal army who could never apply them with the same force in the *armée de métier.* In summary form, these ideas called for: (1) infantry tactics based on the column for rapid maneuver and deployment; (2) the exploitation of improved artillery for quick concentration against a hostile line; (3) and the organization of armies into "divisions" for greater strategic flexibility, surprise, and ease of foraging.

The improved infantry tactics were based on the Comte de Guibert's proposals for a battalion "column-of-divisions" (the companies of a battalion drawn up one behind the next with short intervals or "divisions" between companies) in order to move rapidly toward the enemy line behind a screen of skirmishers and then either to deploy quickly into a firing line or to close with the bayonet. The rapid deployment into line was accomplished simply by the first company standing fast and the others forming on its right and left. (See Diagram 3.) The advantage of the column lay in its speed and flexibility, and the elimination of the time-consuming formal movements used by traditional armies in forming line.

French Revolutionary generals applied many variations of the column-of-divisions. In order to speed up the transition from column into line on the battlefield, they deployed the battalion column on a two-company front and thus reduced its depth. (See Diagram 4.) During the Napoleonic Wars (1803–1815), the French generals experimented with forming regiments, brigades, and even whole divisions into columns-of-divisions. The trend had gone too far when, at Waterloo, one French division was formed into a column two hundred files wide and twenty-six ranks deep. This unwieldy phalanx of 5,200 infantrymen was shot to pieces before it could either close with the bayonet or deploy into line for firing. Used on the battalion-level, however, the column-of-divisions greatly improved the infantry's speed and flexibility on the battlefield, and the French system eventually became copied in nearly all armies but the British.

General Jean de Gribeauval, the French Inspector of Artillery before the Revolution, greatly improved the technical qualities of field guns by 1789. The French 12-pounder gun and its carriage were so reduced in weight that two teams of horses could pull the piece at a trot. Accordingly, the firepower of guns began to be less hobbled by a lack of mobility. Baron du Teil, head of the Artillery School of Practice at Auxonne, and his brother (and artillerist) the Chevalier du Teil, were among the first European officers to stress tactical mobility with guns. The young French artillery officers at Auxonne just before 1789, among them Napoleon Bonaparte, were trained to think in terms of rapid concentrations of guns in order to create gaps in the enemy's line which could be

DIAGRAM 3. Guibert's Proposed Battalion Column-of-Divisions on a One-Company Front. (Each company is assumed to have 90 men in three ranks with a breadth of 25 yards and a depth of 9 yards. Diagram not to scale.)

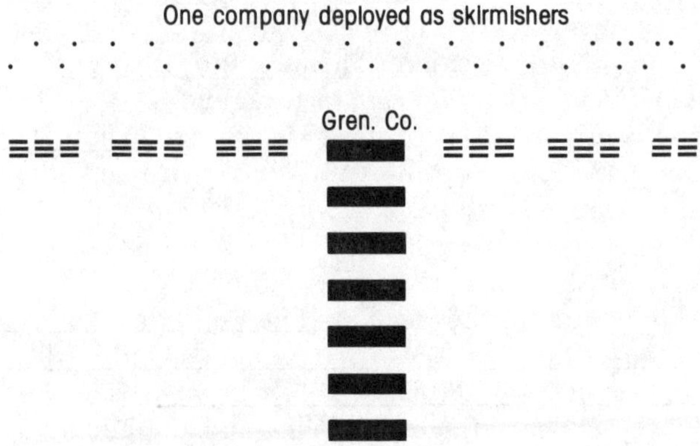

One company deployed as skirmishers

Gren. Co.

DIAGRAM 4. French Battalion of Column-of-Divisions on a Two-Company Front. Proportions are the same as in Diagram 3. Diagram not drawn to scale.

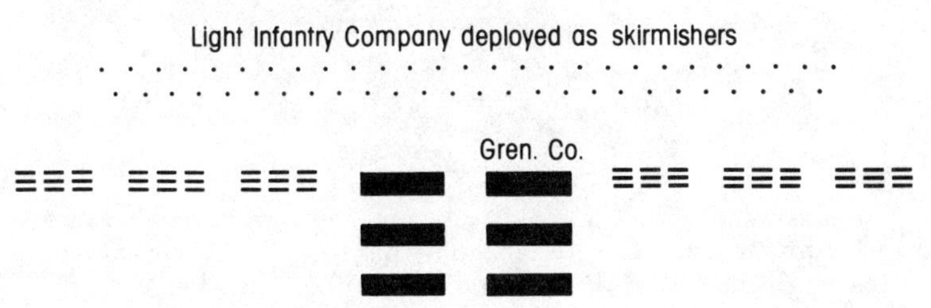

exploited by French infantry or cavalry. Later, General Bonaparte's preference for massed artillery reflected his training as well as his experience. Bonaparte made his own original contributions to French artillery as well, as for instance his use of soldiers to replace civilian teamsters in 1800. The mobility of his artillery on the battlefield became as legendary as its firepower.

Another idea drawn from the old army was that of dividing field armies into self-contained "divisions" which, for a limited time, could both march and fight independently. The idea was probably original with Colonel Pierre de Bourcet at mid-century, and the Marshal de Brogley even experimented in a small way with divisions in the Seven Years' War, but the idea was not really practical until many more and better parallel highways were built in the late eighteenth century. Then, when the French Revolution produced the mass army, it became both natural and necessary to divide field forces into divisions in order to move and supply armies efficiently. The fanlike spread of several divisions advancing over several parallel roads could forage locally much more efficiently than a concentrated force, and they could also be maneuvered to concentrate against an enemy force from several directions at once. The French army division—essentially a miniature field army, often numbering ten thousand men—permitted a flexibility in strategy previously unknown. And when too many divisions produced a problem of span-of-control for the army commander, Napoleon solved it, in 1800, by inventing the army corps, two-to-four divisions under an army corps commander who saw to the coordination of their movements before and during battle. The corps system worked so well that in 1805 Napoleon transferred all cavalry and part of the artillery in every corps to the corps reserve under the direct control of the corps commander. The army corps, varying from twenty to forty thousand men, then became Napoleon's principal element of maneuver. Much of Napoleon's reputation rests on his uncanny ability to maneuver numerous corps and divisions in the approach in ways that confused the enemy, and then to unite them in a kind of net with which he crushed the enemy army. It

DIAGRAM 5. Napoleonic Strategy.

A. Approach Phase. Divisions or corps are deployed on a wide front to locate main enemy force.

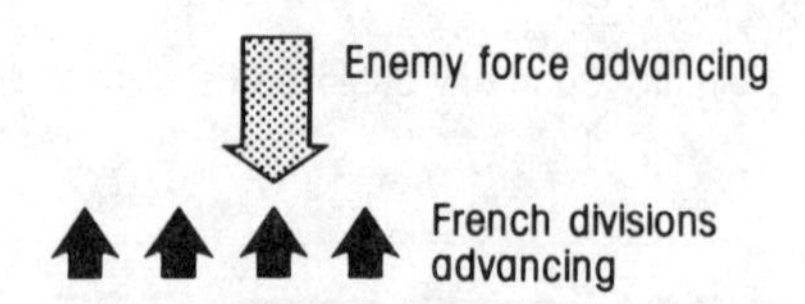

B. Concentration Phase. Some divisions make contact and attack in order to force the enemy to deploy his forces. Other divisions "march to the sound of the guns" to reinforce divisions already engaged or to turn the enemy's flank.

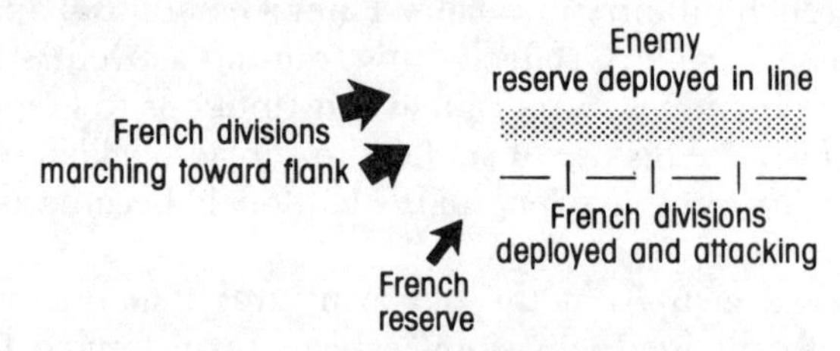

C. Deployment of the Reserve. Here deployed opposite the junction between the enemy's front and his refused flank. Artillery concentration to prepare for a breakthrough.

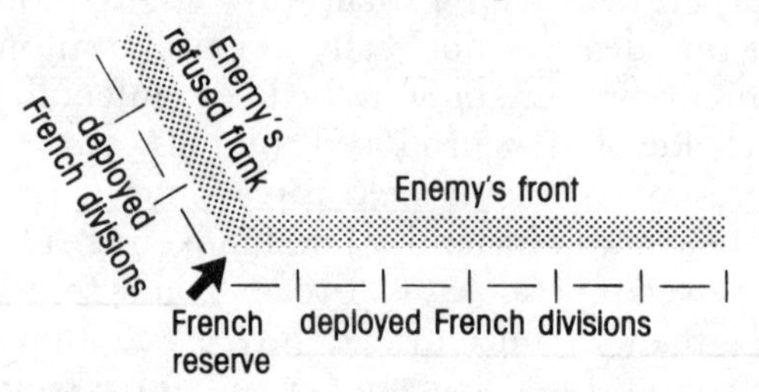

D. Breakthrough and Exploitation. The enemy's line is severed and cavalry sweep into the rear of his regiments. As his forces disintegrate, vigorous pursuit is carried out to prevent a rally and to inflict maximum casualties.

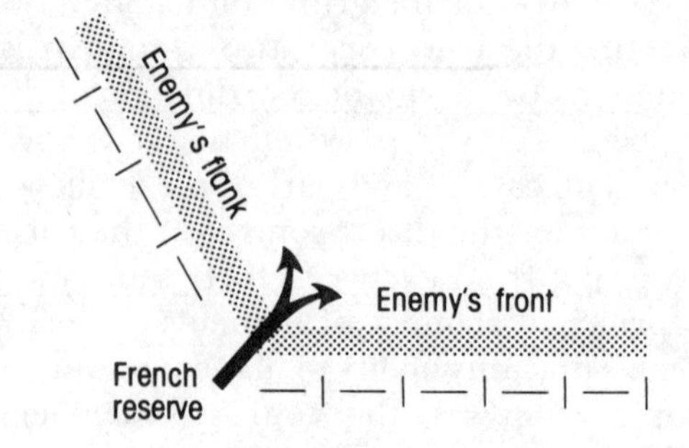

hardly goes too far to say that, through the use of division and corps, Napoleon revolutionized the whole technique of strategic movement. (See Diagram 5.)

B. The Wars of the French Revolution and the Rise of Napoleon Bonaparte, 1789–1802. The national revolt in France in 1789 resulted in the transfer of many royal powers to an elected National Assembly, the abolition of the last vestiges of feudalism, and the formation of a citizen-militia called the National Guard. After Louis XVI tried unsuccessfully to leave France in 1791, the National Assembly required a new oath of every officer to the French nation. Those who refused were discharged and supporters of the Revolution appointed to their places. When Prussia and Austria threatened France with an expeditionary force of one hundred thousand troops under the Prussian Duke of Brunswick in the spring of 1792, the National Assembly declared a state of war and strengthened the regular army by adding "demi-brigades" of volunteer citizen-soldiers serving under their own officers. Under General Charles Dumouriez, fifty thousand troops of this regular-volunteer combination turned back thirty-five thousand of Brunswick's troops in the Battle of Valmy, forty miles east of Paris, on September 20, and subsequently Brunswick withdrew his expedition from France. The National Convention, which had replaced the National Assembly, declared France a republic and ordered its armies to carry the war into the Austrian Netherlands (Belgium) and into the German Rhineland. In January, 1793, it sent Louis XVI to the guillotine.

The execution of Louis XVI inflamed much of royal Europe against the Revolution, and, in the spring of 1793, Britain, the Dutch Netherlands, Spain, Prussia, Austria, and lesser powers formed the First Coalition. They sent four hundred thousand troops into the field, and by summer the Allied armied had expelled the French armies from Belgium and the German Rhineland. Dumouriez had deserted to the Allied side, as had the Marquis de la Fayette, the first commander of the National Guard. In order to save the Revolution, the National Convention turned to drastic measures. It conferred extraordinary executive powers on a Committee of Public Safety headed by Maximilien Robespierre, and sent deputies-on-mission to all army headquarters to insure the loyalty of the generals and to supervise the political indoctrination of the troops. But for our study of the patterns of war, its most important measure was to proclaim a *levée en masse* in August, 1793, that made all able-bodied French males liable to military conscription until the soil of the republic was secure. In addition, its measures of "war socialism" placed all the economic resources of France, including its civilian labor, at the disposal of the government for waging war. By December, 1794, a million Frenchmen were under arms and Paris had become the largest arms-producing center in the world. The "Organizer of Victory" was Lazare Carnot, a former captain of Royal Engineers, who as a revolutionary general both advised the Committee of Public Safety and, after Robespierre's fall from power in the summer of 1794, served as minister of war under the Directory. Carnot organized a prototype of a centralized "general staff" with which he provided overall central direction to the French field armies, at one time numbering fourteen including one devoted to suppressing a peasant revolt in the Vendée. Never before in modern history had one government commanded so much military power or had the revolutionary idea so kindled fires in the minds of men.

The revitalized French armies carried the war again into Belgium and overran the Dutch Netherlands. They also occupied the Rhineland. In 1794, Prussia made a separate peace with France, and Spain switched sides. By 1796, only Britain and Austria, among the major powers, were still at war with France. In the midst of these events, Napoleon Bonaparte rose to prominence. Promoted from captain to brigadier-general in 1793 for his work at the siege of Toulon (he was just twenty-four years old), he served with the garrison at Paris, helped to suppress a royalist-inspired revolt against the Directory in 1795, and in the spring of 1796 was appointed by Carnot to command the "Army of Italy" on the Italian Riviera. Bonaparte's first major command turned out to be forty thousand ragged and hungry troops who were outnumbered by the Austrian and Piedmontese armies in northern Italy, yet he managed to lead this unpromising force to victory over Piedmont and to expel the Austrians from northern Italy. With a larger army in 1797, he advanced to within eighty miles of Vienna and then dictated terms of peace to the Hapsburg envoys. By the time Napoleon returned to Paris, he was the most popular as well as one of the youngest of the French generals.

When the Directory had no better ideas for bringing Britain to terms, it approved Bonaparte's plan to lead an army to Egypt, establish a French base there, and then to march all the way to India where he would overthrow British rule. Bonaparte and twenty-five thousand troops sailed from Toulon in May, 1798, evaded the British fleet in the Mediterranean commanded by Admiral Horatio Nelson, and, after occupying Malta on the way, arrived at Alexandria in July. After capturing Alexandria, the "Army of the East" marched up the Nile, defeated the Egyptian army at Omm-Dinar (the Battle of the Pyramids), and occupied Cairo. In August, Nelson's fleet destroyed the French fleet at Aboukir Bay (the Battle of the Nile) in an all-night battle. But Bonaparte, undeterred by the fact that Nelson had cut his communications to France, led thirteen thousand troops into Turkish Palestine in February, 1799, and defeated all opposition until his way was blocked by the seacoast fortress-city of Acre (Beirut). When his army could neither

Admiral Horatio Nelson

SOURCE: Geoffrey Bennett, *Nelson the Commander* (New York: Charles Scribner's Sons, 1972).

take the fortress by assault from its Anglo-Turkish defenders nor starve its garrison into submission, Bonaparte was forced to lead his army—greatly reduced by disease and wounds—back to Egypt. Though the French beat off a British landing at Abukir Bay in July, Bonaparte realized that it was only a matter of time until his trapped army would be destroyed.

In August, 1799, Bonaparte and a few selected officers secretly boarded two frigates at Alexandria and set out for France, leaving the "Army of the East" to fend for itself. (In 1801, it was compelled to surrender to the British.) By the time Bonaparte's vessel had evaded the British fleet in the Mediterranean and reached the southern coast of France in October, the Directory had lost prestige as the result of early defeats at the hands of a new Second Coalition composed in the main of Britain, Austria, and Russia. Carnot had fled to Switzerland in 1798, after an unsuccessful coup against the Directors, who, by 1799, were plotting against each other. Bonaparte threw in his lot with a faction and wound up as its leader. His coup in November, 1799, toppled the Directory and brought the Consulate to power.

As First Consul, Bonaparte became general-in-chief of French armies. He personally commanded one of them in northern Italy against the Austrians, narrowly winning the Battle of Marengo in June, 1800. After Austrian defeats in Germany, Bonaparte dictated terms of peace again to the Hapsburg emperor in 1801. His scheme for forming a League of Armed Neutrality among the Baltic states, aimed at Britain, miscarried the same year, when Nelson's fleet destroyed the Danish fleet at Copenhagen; but by 1802 even Britain was ready for a compromise peace. The Peace of Amiens in March, 1802, officially brought the Wars of the French Revolution to a close. But war between Britain and France broke out again in May, 1803, and in 1804 Bonaparte crowned himself as Napoleon I, Emperor of the French. The republic had become the French Empire.

C. Napoleon and the Imperial Army at Zenith, 1804–1807. Napoleon retained the Directory's law of 1798 which allowed resort to the *levée en masse* only when the republic was threatened, and otherwise provided men to the army through a system of volunteering and choosing by lot. Under lottery conscription, men with the "bad numbers" faced up to seven years of service; but married men were usually excused, and single men could provide substitutes. In 1804, Napoleon revived the rank of marshal and established patents of nobility for service to the empire. In addition, the Imperial Guard, also founded in 1804, included soldiers who had distinguished themselves in earlier campaigns, and Napoleon later added the "Middle Guard" and the

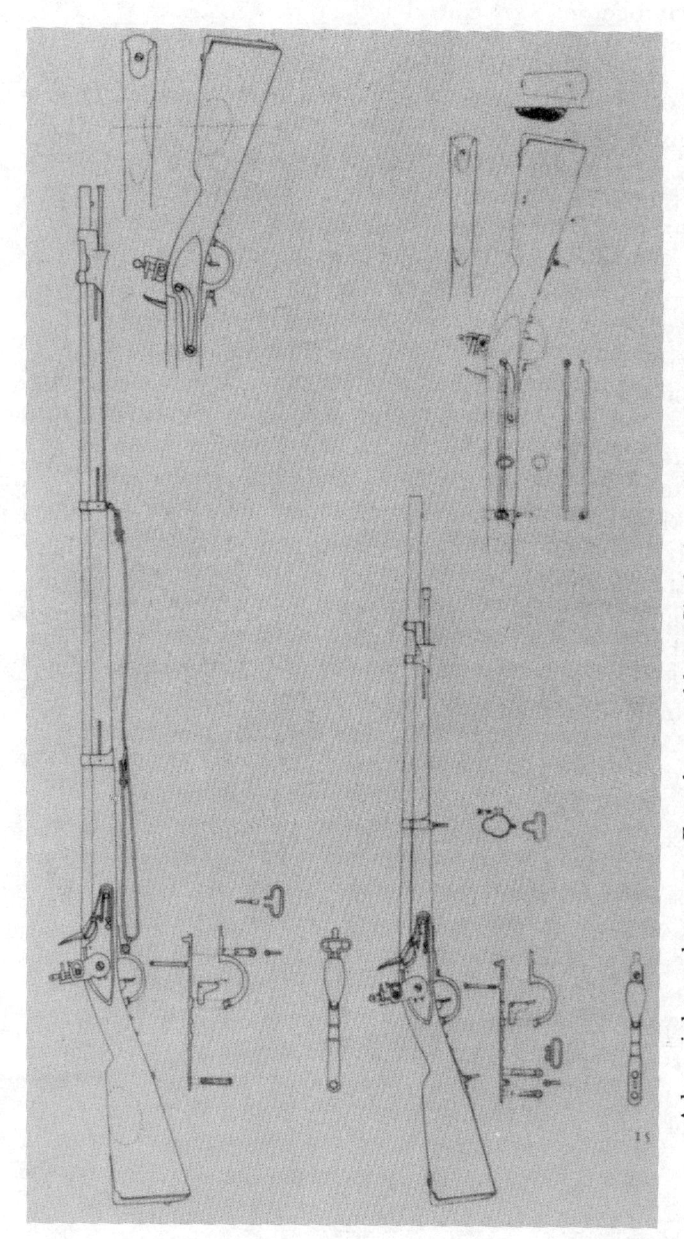

A late eighteenth-century French smoothbore flintlock musket and a carbine.

SOURCE: Michael Glover, *The Napoleonic Wars: An Illustrated History* (New York: Hippocrene Books, 1981).

"Young Guard." By 1815, at least 100,000 soldiers had served in various guard units which together were considered a *corps d'élite*.

At the beginning of the Napoleonic Wars (1803–1815), the French army had about 750,000 troops and was a thoroughly national force. The *Grande Armée* (Main Army) of 1805–1807 gave Napoleon victories over Austria, Prussia, and Russia, making him master of most of Europe from the English Channel to the Russian frontier. But rising casualties and the need to find new sources of manpower led Napoleon to expand membership in his forces to foreigners. No less than a quarter of the 1.3 million men who entered the French army between 1800 and 1812 were born outside the 1792 frontiers of France, and included Belgians, Dutch, Germans, Italians, and Poles. While many of these foreign troops served well, their presence tended to dilute the national quality of his army just when other armies were trying to increase national homogeneity. By 1812, only the rewards of conquest united all of Napoleon's soldiers, and the original values of the French Revolution were increasingly subordinated to objectives of French domination over Europe and a reward-system that rested at heart on military aggression.

When war with Britain broke out in May, 1803, Napoleon tried to limit the conflict by scheming for an early invasion of the British Isles before other powers could intervene on the British side. Napoleon induced Spain to enter the war on the French side in December, 1804, and in March, 1805, a Franco-Spanish Combined Fleet under Admiral Pierre Villeneuve left the Mediterranean for the West Indies in hopes of drawing the British Channel fleet away long enough for an "Army of England"—two hundred thousand of Napoleon's best troops camped at Boulogne—to invade England. But Nelson's Mediterranean fleet, not the Channel fleet, followed Villeneuve to the West Indies and then relentlessly tracked his fleet back across the Atlantic late in the summer. In August, Napoleon scrapped his plans for an invasion of England when he learned that Austria and Russia had signed an alliance with Britain and that Allied armies were on the march across central Europe. Villeneuve's fleet put in at Cadiz until October, when it made a dash for the Straits of Gibraltar. Nelson's fleet caught up with it off Cape Trafalgar on October 21, and, in a brilliant mélee action, thoroughly demolished it. For the British, the action was only marred by Nelson's death in victory. Napoleon's naval power was effectively finished for the duration of the wars.

The "Army of England," rechristened the *Grande Armée* in August, 1805, was the finest field force that Napoleon ever led. All of its marshals and generals wre experienced yet had lost none of their vigor, while the troops were either veteran soldiers or well-trained recruits. The phenomenal speed of the march from the Channel to the Rhine wrecked Allied plans for concentrating on the French borders before Napoleon could act, and in late September the *Grande Armée* swept into southern Germany on a front of seventy miles. Marshal Karl Mack's Austrian army was encircled and the last of its troops compelled to surrender at Ulm on October 20, the day before Nelson's victory at Trafalgar. Having left detachments to hold southern Germany and to sever Allied communications with northern Italy, Napoleon marched with the rest of the *Grande Armée* down the Danube to capture Vienna and then into Bohemia (now western Czechoslovakia) in order to engage an Austro-Russian army. Though the enemy slightly outnumbered his forces (eighty-five thousand Austrian and Russian troops to seventy-two thousand French), Napoleon won a smashing victory at the Battle of Austerlitz early in December. Before the month was out, Emperor Francis signed a peace that took Austria out of the war, and the Russian army retired to its own territory in order to recover from its defeat.

The *Grande Armée* wintered in southern Germany, warily watching Prussia, while Napoleon's relations with Frederick-William III moved toward the breaking point. In the late summer of 1806, the Prussian king summoned up his courage and declared war. But as his old-style army moved cautiously toward French communications to the Rhine, the *Grande Armée* swept north to sever the Prussian army's communications with Berlin. As the Prussian army retreated in divided forces, Napoleon brought it to battle on October 14 and crushed it at the twin battles of Jena and Auerstädt. After those victories, the *Grande Armée* overran most of Prussia, forcing Frederick-William to flee to the protection of the Tsar. The Russian army tried to defend East Prussia, and, on a snow-covered battlefield, even fought the French to a draw at Prussian Eylau in February, 1807. Napoleon then withdrew his army to a winter camp in Poland and awaited better weather. Finally, he had his revenge when he cornered the Russian army under General Levin Bennigsen at Friedland and severely mauled it before it retreated into Russian territory in June. On July 7, Tsar Alexander agreed to the terms of the Peace of Tilsit, which left Napoleon in control of most of Europe between the Channel and the Russian frontier, and left Prussia in the status of a French vassal state. Never had Hohenzollern fortunes fallen so low.

D. The Decline of French Fortunes in the West, 1808–14, and the Anglo-American War of 1812. Napoleon's victories of July, 1807, left him again to face the problem of how to bring Britain to terms. An invasion of the British Isles was out of the question after Trafalgar, and another voyage to Egypt seemed impractical. But as early as his occupation of Berlin in December, 1806, Napoleon believed that he had an answer. The issuance of the Berlin Decree inaugurated the so-called Continental System, or a European-wide boycott of trade with Britain. Though the boycott worked some hardship on continental Europe,

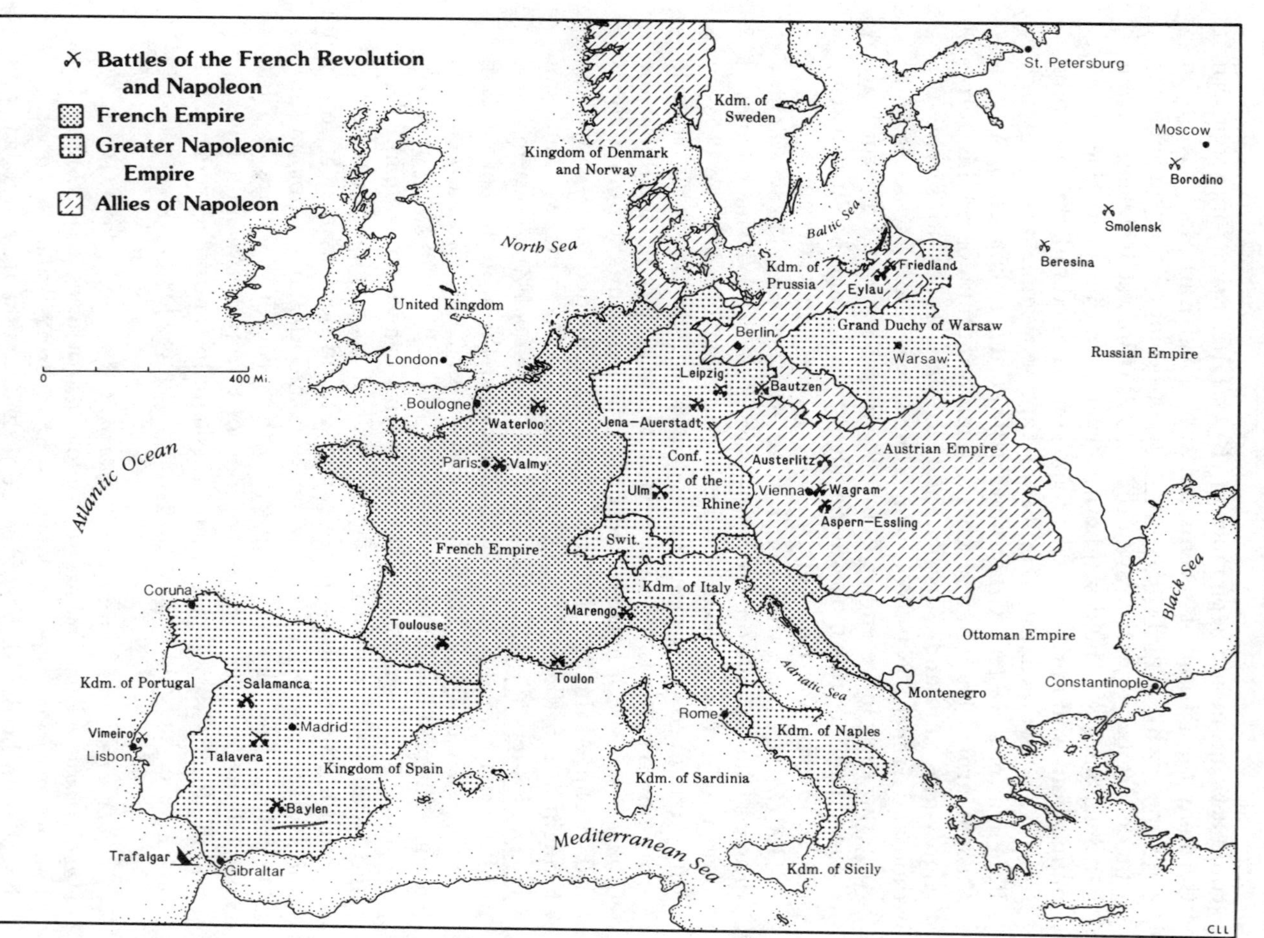

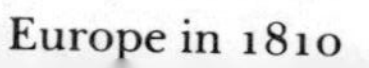
Europe in 1810

Napoleon calculated that most trade with Britain had been in luxury items and that more expensive continental substitutes, such as sugar beets for cane suger, would meet the need in most cases. Where necessary, exceptions to the boycott could be made. With Tsarist Russia committed to cooperate with the Continental System, Napoleon believed that such stress would be brought to the pocket books of Britain's "nation of shopkeepers" that they would pressure their government to make peace and leave Napoleon a free hand on the continent.

But the Continental System, to be effective, had to leave no big holes in its dike, and Portugal, a long-time trading partner with Britain, was still beyond Napoleon's grasp. In addition, British goods landed in Portugal were sometimes smuggled into Spain and even into France itself. Accordingly, in the fall of 1807, Napoleon pressured Charles IV of Spain to allow a French army under General Jean Andoche Junot to pass through his country on the way to Portugal. Subsequently, Junot's army had no difficulty in defeating the royal Portuguese army, occupying the capital at Lisbon, and forcing the Portuguese royal family to flee into exile in Brazil. Then, under the pretence of maintaining Junot's lines-of-communication across Spain and of aiding the Spanish authorities in stopping the smuggling of illicit goods, Napoleon poured two hundred thousand troops into Spain in the spring of 1808. Charles IV and his heir Ferdinand wre summoned to Bayonne where they were forced to abdicate the Spanish throne in favor of Napoleon's brother Joseph. Napoleon presented the Spanish people with a *fait accompli* and expected their subservience.

Instead, a major revolt began against the French on May 4 in Madrid, and spread to the whole country. French troops found themselves under attack by both Spanish troops and civilians, and, in July, an entire French corps was trapped and compelled to surrender at Bailen. Napoleon and two hundred thousand additional troops came to Joseph's assistance after his forces had withdrawn behind the river Ebro, and in November the regular Spanish army was decisively defeated. After Joseph was reseated on his throne at Madrid, Napoleon returned to Paris in December, 1808. But a Spanish junta held out in the port of Cadiz, and peasants in the mountainous interior of Spain waged *guerrilla* ("little war") against the French. Spain had been conquered, but not subdued.

Meanwhile, Britain had sent two armies to assist Spain and Portugal respectively. The army sent to Spain under General Sir John Moore was caught up in the Spanish army's defeat on the Ebro in November, 1808, but, after a gruelling march over the mountains, it reached the safety of Corunna and was evacuated by the British fleet in January, 1809. Moore, however, was killed. Another British army of twenty-five thousand troops commanded by General Arthur Wellesley was more successful. Wellesley's army defeated Junot's army at Vimeiro and subsequently occupied Lisbon. In 1809, Wellesley's army drove the French forces from the rest of Portugal and even made a sortie into Spain, where it defeated a French army under Jean-Baptiste Jourdan at Talavera. Though superior French forces forced a subsequent British retreat into Portugal, Wellesley was rewarded for his victory on Spanish soil with the title of Viscount Wellington. (He was raised to the Duke of Wellington in 1814.) Wellington rapidly proved to be the ablest of the British commanders in the field.

Though Wellington never had more than sixty thousand Anglo-Portuguese troops during his six years in the Iberian peninsula, his service in India had accustomed him to the command of multinational armies in difficult country. When Marshal Nicolas Soult's 110,000 French troops invaded Portugal in 1810, Wellington's smaller army slowly gave ground before them, inflicted a repulse when they attacked at Busaco, then retired behind earthworks built across the Lisbon peninsula (the Lines of Torres Vedras). Soult had not known that the lines existed, and, finding them impregnable, he finally led his starving army back to Spain, after losing forty thousand men to no purpose. Wellington's losses in the campaign came to four thousand men.

The French marshals were also baffled by Wellington's tactical methods. His favorite tactic was to occupy high ground, deploy his main line in two ranks behind its crest, and deploy skirmishers (including the green-uniformed sharpshooters of the Rifle Corps) on the forward slope. The main line was protected by the crest from French artillery, the skirmishers on the forward slope fended off French skirmishers, and when French columns tried to rush the crest, they were crushed by volleys from the British main line before they could either close with the bayonet or form into line. But Wellington was capable of sudden counteroffensives as well. When Marshal Auguste de Marmont's forty thousand troops tried to turn Wellington's flank at Salamanca in 1812 and were careless about their security, Wellington's unexpected counterattack sent them flying.

Despite Wellington's skill as a general and the Spanish guerrilla harassment, the French did not completely lose their grip on Spain until Napoleon's disastrous invasion of Russia in 1812. In his effort to build a new army in Germany, Napolean ordered Joseph to send him reinforcements from the French army in Spain. Wellington was quick to exploit the weakened enemy position, carrying out a brilliant strategic march across northern Spain, and finally routing Jourdan's army at Vitoria in June, 1813. During the fall of 1813, Wellington's forces crossed the Pyrenees into France; and in April, 1814, Wellington decisively defeated Marshal Soult's army at Toulouse. He was on the point of launching a drive deeper into France when he received news of Napoleon's abdication. The Peninsular War cost the French four hundred thousand

Duke of Wellington

SOURCE: David Howarth, *Waterloo: Day of Battle* (New York: Atheneum, 1968).

casualties over the course of six years, or nearly as many men as Napoleon lost in Russia in six months in 1812. Thus, the "Spanish ulcer" ultimately did about as much damage to the Imperial Army as the gaping Russian wound.

The Anglo-American War of 1812 was a side-show of the Napoleonic Wars. Only seven thousand regulars were in Canada when the United States—provoked by British interference with American trade, supposed incitement of the Indians, and the impressment of American seamen—declared war in June, 1812. A botched American mobilization and incompetently led forces saved Canada until British reinforcements began to arrive. Generals Jacob Brown and Winfield Scott were among the few capable American leaders, but the invasion of Canada in 1814 was also eventually turned back. Meanwhile, the Royal Navy carried out raids along the American coasts and hunted down or blockaded in port the handful of American frigates that attempted to wage *guerre de course.* American privateers were more successful, but their operations merely drove up the British expense for conducting the war. The worst American defeat of the war came at Bladensburg in August, 1814, just before the British burned the new capital at Washington, D.C. In September, the British attack on Baltimore was turned back by the defense of Ft. McHenry, and an American flotilla turned back a British drive down Lake Champlain. General Andrew Jackson's repulse of the British attack on New Orleans in January 1815, came after the signing of the Peace of Ghent in Europe, but before the news had crossed the Atlantic. A total of seven thousand Americans died in the line of duty during the War of 1812.

The British army in the Napoleonic Wars may be described as seminational in character. Parliament never adopted the equivalent of the French *levée en masse,* but by various inducements it encouraged militia to volunteer for service overseas in the regular army. At its peak strength in 1812, the army had 220,000 men, a respectable performance for a country which also had 330,000 sailors and marines.

E. The Decline of Napoleon's Fortunes in Eastern Europe, the First Abdication, and the Return of the Hundred Days, 1808–15. In the wake of Austria's defeat in 1805, the Hapsburg monarchy made efforts toward a more national army, though the polyglot nature of the empire made the task difficult. Still, in the spring of 1809, an seminational army of 300,000 Austrian troops took the field in hopes of exploiting the French preoccupation with Spain and Portugal. Commanded by the Archduke Charles, the Austrian troops fought Napoleon's "Army of Germany" to a bloody draw at the Battle of Aspern-Essling in May; Jean Lannes was to be the first French marshal to die in action. Napoleon finally defeated the Austrians decisively at the Battle of Wagram in July, but only by

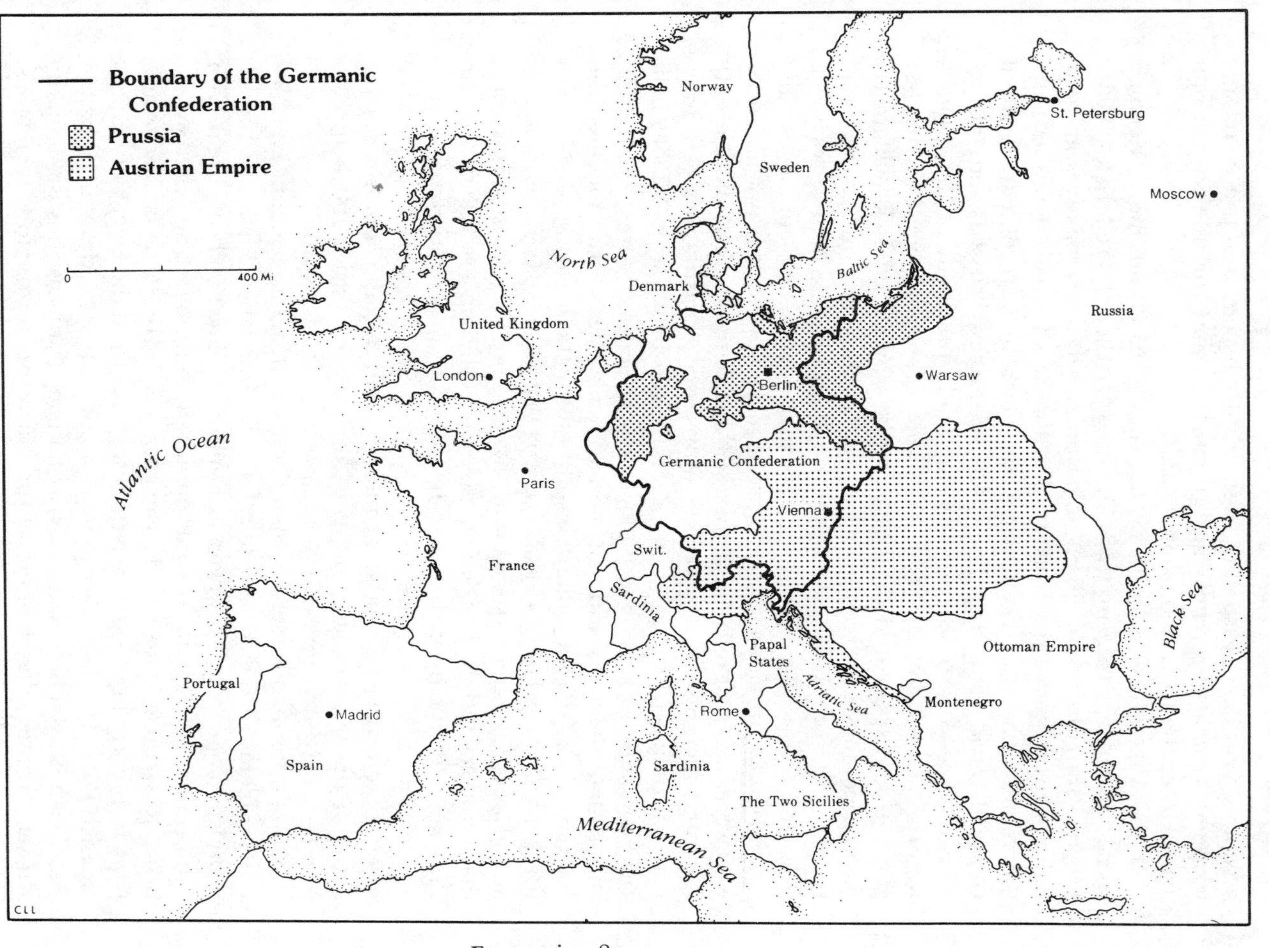

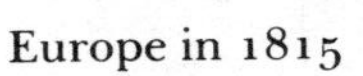

Europe in 1815

accepting very heavy casualties. Significantly, his terms of peace not only stripped Austria of territory and population, they forbade an Austrian army larger than 150,000 troops.

In the wake of its defeat in 1806, Prussia carried out more sweeping social and military reforms than Austria, even though Frederick-William III was not enthusiastic about abandoning royal prerogatives and the military privileges of the Junkers. Serfdom was partially abolished, and the middle class was given a greater voice in government. General Gerhard David von Scharnhorst, one of the few Prussian generals before 1806 who favored reforms, was made president of the Military Reform Commission. It cashiered numerous incompetent or overage generals and sponsored the legislation by which Frederick-William III offered commissions to the sons of the middle class on a more equal footing with the Junkers. In order to get around the limit of forty-two thousand troops placed on the Prussian army by Napoleon, a so-called *Krümpersystem* provided for the short-term training of civilian volunteers, who were then sent into the army reserve. The reserve had about twenty thousand men by 1812. Napoleon suppressed Scharnhorst's plan for a national militia *(Landwehr)*, but after Prussia broke with Napoleon in 1813 and launched the War of Liberation, the *Landwehr* was organized to supplement the army and its reserve. Finally, the reforms included the founding in 1810 of a military institution for the higher study of war, a forerunner of the later *Kriegsakademie* or War College. Officers chosen to attend were prepared systematically to carry out the duties of high command and staff work. In 1812, Napoleon insisted on a sizable part of the Prussian army being included in his forces to invade Russia that year, and many of the reform-minded officers either resigned, retired, or offered their services to other armies opposed to Napoleon. But in 1813 many of the same officers returned to Prussia's service and helped to lead her army to victory over Napoleon.

Though his involvement in Spain and Portugal had brought him serious problems, Napoleon made a fatal decision when he decided to invade Russia in 1812. However, he could not allow the Tsar's break with the Continental System to go unpunished, and he saw no other way to bring Russia back into line. In the spring of 1812, he assembled a new *Grande Armée* of 600,000 troops in East Prussia and the Duchy of Warsaw (French Poland), about twice as many soldiers as Tsar Alexander I had in European Russia. His plan was to launch a surprise invasion of the Russian frontier, destroy most of the Tsar's forces close to French bases, and then to follow the survivors to either St. Petersburg or Moscow. At either place, he expected to dictate terms of peace to a penitent Tsar.

Napoleon's strategy began to go wrong almost from the moment that the *Grande Armée* began crossing the Russian frontier on June 22. There was no surprise. The Tsar had been expecting an attack for weeks. Still

General Gerhard von Scharnhorst

SOURCE: Walter Goerlitz, *History of the German General Staff, 1657–1945*, trans. Brian Battershaw (New York and London: Frederick Praeger, 1953).

worse, the Russian army, about 250,000 men, retreated instead of fighting, drawing the French on toward Moscow and through some of the worst agricultural land in western Russia. Napoleon's plans to supply his army from the rear broke down, and the troops in the lead of his column consumed what food and forage were available, leaving little to those who followed. Over 100,000 of his troops had been lost to the effects of hunger, thirst, typhus, and heat by the time the *Grande Armée* reached Smolensk. Napoleon cancelled plans to bring replacements into Russia; the country could not sustain them. On September 7, at the insistence of the Tsar, old Marshal Mikhail Kutuzov ordered the Russian army to make a stand at the village of Borodino, seventy miles west of Moscow. The battle which followed was sanguinary—40,000 Russian and 30,000 French casualties—but indecisive. The Russian army resumed its retreat after nightfall, and again Napoleon had no choice but to follow.

By the time Napoleon reached Moscow a week after Borodino, about 250,000 troops were still with him. The city was deserted. The Moscovite population of half a million people had joined the Russian army in its migration further east. Worse, fires broke out in the largely wooden city as the French were entering, and within a few days the *Grande Armée* found itself occupying a burned-out shell, devoid of food and shelter against the approach of winter. Napoleon waited in the Kremlin in the vain hope that Alexander would negotiate with him, then on October 19 ordered the *Grande Armée* to begin a withdrawal toward Poland. But Kutusov adroitly maneuvered the Russian army to block that route through unused country, and forced the *Grand Armée* to retrace its steps over the plundered route to East Prussia. By late November, when it crossed the Beresina river, the *Grande Armée* was down to 50,000 men. The rest had fallen victim to incessant attacks by the Russian army, the assaults by guerrillas, hunger, cold, and despair. Napoleon turned over command of the survivors to Marshal Michel Ney, and rushed on to Paris in order to prepare public opinion and to mobilize new forces. Ney finally got 30,000 men back to East Prussia in December. All told, of the 500,000 Napoleonic troops who entered Russia 250,000 died of wounds, disease, hunger, or exposure, and 100,000 troops were taken prisoner. The rest, exclusive of those who escaped with Ney, apparently deserted.

In the wake of Napoleon's disaster in 1812, Russia, Sweden, Prussia, and Britain, among the major powers, formed the Fourth Coalition. Upon Prussia's mobilization in March, 1813, Frederick-William III entrusted command of the Prussian army to old Marshal Gebhard von Blücher, who in turn appointed Scharnhorst as his chief-of-staff. August von Gneisenau, a disciple of Scharnhorst, served as chief of operations until Scharnhorst's mortal wound at the Battle of Lützen in May, then replaced him as chief-of-staff. Many of the officers who served in key positions in the Prussian army were products of advanced military schooling. After Prussia adopted general conscription, her forces swelled to 300,000 troops by the fall of 1813. Meanwhile, a Swedish army entered the field under Prince Bernadotte, formerly one of Napoleon's marshals. After Kutuzov's health broke in April, 1813, he was replaced in command of the Russian army by General Prince Ludwig Wittgenstein.

Allied delays in the spring of 1813 allowed Napoleon to form 250,000 troops into a new "Army of the Elbe," and, in May, to launch an offensive to recover eastern Germany. In rapid succession that month he inflicted sharp defeats on the Allied forces at the battles of Lützen and Bautzen. In June, the eastern Allies and Napoleon agreed to Austria's offer of mediation, and until August a general armistice was in effect. Napoleon used the time to build up the strength of the "Army of the Elbe" to 440,000 troops, but the Allies used the lull to even greater advantage. They not only raised the strength of their armies to 500,000 men, they convinced Austria to join the Fourth Coalition. They reorganized their armies into three international forces commanded, respectively, by Bernadotte, Blücher and the Austrian Prince Felix von Schwarzenberg. None of the top Allied commanders was the equal of Napoleon, but all were about as good as his marshals.

When the armistice collapsed in August, the Allies frustrated Napoleon's attempt at a quick victory at Dresden and managed to drag out the German campaign until mid-October. Then at the four-day Battle of Leipzig (October 16–19), 195,000 French troops battled 257,000 Allied troops in the greatest battle of the Napoleonic Wars. In this "Battle of the Nations," Napoleon came close to victory at one point, but the mistakes of subordinates almost caused his army to be encircled. Though a hasty retreat prevented the worst disaster, Napoleon lost 68,000 men while inflicting 57,000 casualties on his enemies. By December, when it retreated across the Rhine into France, the "Army of the Elbe" was down to 100,000 men.

Napoleon tried to arrange a new armistice in order to buy time in which to mobilize reinforcements, but the Allies were not interested. About 450,000 Allied troops crossed the Rhine into France and the Low Countries in January, 1814. In a series of dazzling maneuvers, Napoleon fended them away from Paris until the end of March, but even his wizardry had its limits. The Prussian army finally entered Paris unopposed. Down to 60,000 troops, Napoleon made a new capital at Fontainebleu, but it was only a matter of time before his dwindling forces would be crushed between the armies of the eastern Allies and Wellington's army in the south. In mid-April, Napoleon accepted Allied peace terms in the Treaty of Fontainebleu. He exchanged the throne of France for one on the island of Elba and a pension for life. The Allies placed

Louis XVIII on the French throne, and on April 28 he signed the so-called First Peace of Paris, returning France to her frontiers of 1792. The division of Napoleon's empire outside France was to be made at the Congress of Vienna, scheduled to open in September, 1814.

Napoleon's Reign of the Hundred Days (March 20–June 22, 1815) and the campaign that led to Waterloo were anticlimactic, but may be briefly summarized. At the beginning of March, Napoleon landed on the southern coast of France and appealed to the French people and his former soldiers to rally to him. As he marched on Paris, Ney (who had transferred loyalties) and his troops deserted to him, and the French royal family fled the country. Napoleon resumed his rule on March 20, but on March 25 the Allied powers declared war. Wellington and Blücher began assembling troops in Belgium (then part of the Dutch Netherlands). Napoleon assembled 124,000 of his old veterans in an "Army of the North," and on June 15 advanced into Belgium to catch the Allied armies while still divided. On June 16, he defeated Blücher's army at Ligny and caused it to retreat, but failed to send Marshal Emmanuel Grouchy and thirty thousand troops after the Prussians until the next morning. Ney had meanwhile fended off Wellington's attempt to join Blücher in an action at Quatres Bras on June 16, but that night Wellington's army began withdrawing towards Brussels. Napoleon and Ney, with seventy-two thousand troops between them, pursued on June 17, only to find Wellington's army camped on the heights of Mont Saint Jean, a mile south of the village of Waterloo and twelve miles south of Brussels.

Napoleon resolved to attack the next day. Early on June 18, he learned that Prussian forces were twelve miles away at Wavre to the east, but he counted on Grouchy's forces to keep them from interfering in his battle with Wellington's, sixty-four thousand British, Hanovarian, Dutch and Belgian soldiers. He made a natural but fatal mistake when he decided to delay opening the battle until the ground had dried out from an all-night rain. Wellington's army just managed to fend off French attacks all afternoon, while Blücher, who had left a corps at Wavre to contain Grouchy's forces, was marching with three corps to Wellington's assistance. When late in the day the Prussian attack struck the French flank and Wellington's army counterattacked against the French front, the "Army of the North" was swept by panic and fled the field. Napoleon got away to Paris, but public support had vanished. He abdicated his throne on June 22 and fled to the coast, where he finally surrendered himself to Admiral Sir Henry Hotham, commanding the naval blockade at Rochefort. The British subsequently transported Napoleon to an island-exile on St. Helena in the South Atlantic, where he died in May, 1821. All the Reign of the Hundred Days and the Waterloo campaign accomplished was to add fifty thousand more casualties to the list of 2 million since 1792.

2

The Nineteenth Century, 1815–71

I. Armies

A. The Long Peace and Military Thought. No wars occurred among the five major European powers for almost forty years after Waterloo. The armed violence of the period before 1850 was mostly internal and associated with liberal revolts or with the early social effects of the Industrial Revolution. The great powers usually settled their differences through the "congress system" adopted at Vienna, and in the 1820s Russia, Austria, and France concerted their efforts to crush insurgencies in Spain and Italy. Britain made common cause with Russia and France in order to aid the Greek fight for independence from the Turkish Empire. An international fleet under a British admiral fought the last great fleet action under sail when it destroyed a Turko-Egyptian fleet off Navarino in October, 1827.

In 1830, a middle-class revolt toppled Charles X, the last Bourbon ever to rule France, and replaced him with Louis Philippe of the Orleans dynasty, a liberal monarch. Begrudgingly, the conservative governments accepted the legitimacy of the "July Monarchy." Belgium's secession from the Kingdom of the Netherlands in 1830 almost set off an international war, but British diplomacy finally secured international recognition of Belgian independence. In 1839, Britain, France, and Prussia signed a treaty to observe Belgium's independence and neutrality, and the pact remained unbroken until the outbreak of World War I. The Revolutions of 1848 hit all the major powers except Britain and Russia, but were finally successful nowhere but in France, where the "July Monarchy" was replaced by a republic under Louis Napoleon Bonaparte, a nephew of Napoleon I. Tsar Nicholas I was prepared to honor the terms of the Quadruple Alliance signed in November, 1815, and to wage war for Louis Napoleon's overthrow, but again British diplomacy maintained the peace when the Second Republic pledged to respect the frontiers set in 1815. In December, 1851, Louis Napoleon overthrew the republic with the help of the army, and in December, 1852, he proclaimed himself Napoleon III, Emperor of the French. The Second Empire lasted until 1870 and Napoleon III's defeat in the Franco-Prussian War.

Excepting Prussia, after 1815 the continental powers returned to the *armée de métier,* the long-service, professional army, though even professional armies were more national in character than those before the French Revolution. Officer corps were less exclusively aristocratic, especially in the French army, though in most armies the old nobility still tended to dominate the higher ranks. Enlisted men were more commonly recruited from within their countries' national boundaries. Foreign soldiers were usually confined to special units such as the French Foreign Legion, founded in 1831 for service in Algeria. Except in Russia, conscription was handled in such a way that the better-off classes could escape service either by providing substitutes or paying a special "blood tax." In practice, the main burden fell on the peasant class. In Russia, where serfdom was not abolished until 1861, peasants summoned to the colors served for life. In the French and Austrian armies, they faced only a seven-to-twelve year stretch. With 880,000 troops, the Tsar's army was numerically the largest in Europe, but qualitatively the poorest. The 500,000 troops of the Austrian army were beset by minority problems. The French Army, 350,000 troops in metropolitan France, was considered qualitatively the best of the continental armies, at least among those of the *armée de métier* type. Only the British army relied entirely on volunteers, men signing up for twenty-year hitches and serving mostly in overseas outposts. Exclusive of the troops in India, until 1854 the British army numbered about 140,000 men.

Again except for Prussia, the military states of Europe looked to France as the model for military thought until 1870, a reflection of the prestige of the French army under Napoleon I even after defeat in 1815. The French army, in turn, was dominated by a school of ideas associated with the writings of General Antoine, Baron de Jomini (1779–1869). Jomini had the distinction of having served as a general officer under both Napoleon I and Alexander I, having switched sides in 1813, and being Swiss into the bargain. A prolific writer, Jomini's most influential book on the theory of war was the *Précis de l'Art de la Guerre* or *Summary of the Art of War* (1836). The *Précis* became a model for European military textbooks, and was widely used for the teaching of military theory in the plethora of military academies which sprouted up over the Western world between 1800 and 1850. Jomini's approach was to concentrate on the conduct of military campaigns, claiming that all the great soldiers of history, including Napoleon, had been successful through observing certain unalterable principles. The essence of war, according to Jomini, was to master the lines-of-communication within a given theater of war, utilizing them in such a way that first strategic superiority, then tactical superiority, is obtained. Jomini believed that the great art of war lay in seizing the communications of the enemy without exposing one's own, and that when that goal was accomplished the outcome of the resulting battle was practically decided. In so many words, Jomini was saying that superior strategy insures a numerical and material advantage on the battlefield.

Because Jomini's approach to war was so geometrical, some critics have held that his real idol was not Napoleon but Frederick the Great. They accuse him of being too abstract and too willing to separate the conduct of a particular war from its unique technological, organizational, and social-political underpinnings. On the other hand, practically all commentators have given Jomini credit for distinguishing more clearly than any previous military writer among the factors of strategy, tactics, and logistics, and their relevant roles in the systematic waging of war. Jomini's influence is still found in the very term "military science" and the emphasis on the teaching of "military principles" in the contemporary military colleges of our day. In Jomini's own time, of course, such an abstract approach had great appeal in politically conservative countries, which had no reason to celebrate the idea of revolutionary warfare. Still, it must be admitted that Jomini's influence also served to fix the student's attention on the permanent operating factors of war and not on the element of change which might affect them. This was particularly unfortunate in the rapidly changing circumstances of the mid-nineteenth century.

The other principal military writer of the first half of the nineteenth century was Carl von Clausewitz (1780–1831), but the impact of his ideas outside of Prussia were really felt only after 1871. A disciple of Scharnhorst, Clausewitz served as a junior officer in the disastrous Jena campaign of 1806 and then in 1807 as secretary of the Prussian Military Reform Commission. When Prussia was dragooned into supporting Napoleon's invasion of Russia in 1812, Clausewitz offered his services to the Tsar. Between 1813 and 1814 he served as a liaison officer between the Prussian and Russian armies. As a brigadier-general, he served as chief-of-staff of the Prussian corps that fought at Wavre during the Waterloo campaign in 1815. Until a short time before his death from cholera in 1831, he spent the final years of his career as head of the Prussian War College, writing in his spare time a philosophical treatise that after his death was published in 1832 under the title *Vom Kriege (On War)*.

In *Vom Kriege,* Clausewitz treats war as a political act distinguished from other political acts by the violence of its means. In theory, he wrote, war is violence unrestrained. In real life, all sorts of conventions and

General Carl von Clausewitz

SOURCE: Walter Goerlitz, *History of the German General Staff, 1657–1945*, trans. Brian Battershaw (New York and London: Frederick Praeger, 1953).

considerations prevent war from being in practice what it is in theory. Still, with the coming of the Wars of the French Revolution and Napoleon, war in practice had approached that in theory, and what had caused the great change was the eventual involvement of whole peoples emotionally as well as physically. Such national passions were aroused, Clausewitz believed, that the population not only supported, but also demanded, the goal of total victory. Clausewitz believed that in the wake of the "peoples wars" of the early nineteenth century it would be harder to restrain the degree of violence employed in future, especially when the issues in any particular war caught the popular imagination. Accordingly, Clausewitz believed that Prussia, and by implication every great power, must prepare in time of peace for a total effort in time of war. He wrote that the "bloody solution" is the "first-born son of war," and that even limited wars may escalate unexpectedly to full-blown struggles. The state must not be left to defend itself with a "dress rapier" if the enemy takes up a "sharp sword."

Unlike Jomini, Clausewitz had little use for universal rules for the waging of war. In his view, every war had its own set of rules resulting from its political causes, the technology then in use, and, of course, the degree to which it involved the public. In addition, the waging of war could not be separated from the factors of luck and circumstance, and, when a general of Napoleon's stature appeared, even from the influence of genius. While Clausewitz believed that a familiarity with the history of war was essential for the student-soldier, for guides to action in any particular war he preferred empirical observation and common sense. Insofar as land warfare was concerned, he argued that the three great objectives always boiled down to destroying or disarming the enemy's armed forces, invading the most vital parts of his territory, and finally breaking his will to resist. Since all three of these goals could be achieved only by combat, or the threat of combat, war remained in essence a phenomenon of violence.

The influence of *Vom Kriege* is not easy to measure precisely even in the Prussian army, where it was studied even before 1871; but, in general, Prussia's preparations for, and the waging of, the German wars of unification in the mid-nineteenth century conformed to the Clausewitzian prescription. Certainly, Helmuth von Moltke, chief of the Prussian General Staff and the great architect of Prussia's victories in those years, shared the Clausewitzian views. In other armies down to the eve of World War I, Clausewitz's great work was usually read in translation and often with an incomplete understanding of its admittedly difficult and sometimes metaphysical language. For the most part, and whether Clausewitz ever intended to have such an effect or not, such reading of *Vom Kriege* promoted a faith in maximum violence as the surest road to victory, and a belief that moderation in war is imbecility.

B. The Technological Revolution in Mid-Nineteenth Century Warfare on Land. The warfare of the French Revolution and Napoleon was mostly a revolution in the social, political, and organizational nature of armies, and only secondarily one of technology. The reverse was true of developments after 1815 and especially beginning about the middle of the nineteenth century. The military changes in technology reflected the facets of the early Industrial Revolution: steam power, the factory system, mass production, as well as discoveries in metallurgy, chemistry, and physics. The first products of the Industrial Revolution to affect war on land were: (1) the steam railroad; (2) the electric telegraph; and (3) the mass-produced, rifled musket. The first two developments changed strategy and logistics. The last changed tactics.

The steam locomotive marked the greatest revolution in land transportation since the invention of the wheel. As railways were rapidly built across Europe in the 1830s and '40s, military men gradually began to appreciate their military potential. The railroad could move troops and their supplies fifteen times as fast as their marching speed, conserving the energies of men and animals into the bargain. On the other hand, beyond the railhead, soldiers still marched and draft animals still drew supply wagons. Accordingly, military logistics of the mid-nineteenth century became an amalgam of the new and the old. The railhead replaced the fortress-magazine as the collection point for supplies, and local forage remained important to armies beyond a certain distance from the railhead. Railroads in enemy territory had to be repaired and protected as invading armies advanced, and the logistical "trail" tended to increase as communications had to be maintained with the nearest railhead. Thus the layout of rail systems in a particular country began to assume the role of the "bones" of strategy. Similarly, the telegraph permitted instantaneous transmission of messages over hundreds of miles between headquarters, but on the battlefield itself the soldiers still depended on signaling with drums, bugles, and flags. Captain Claude Minié's invention of the "expandable, cylindro-conoidal-shaped bullet" in 1848 made the loading of rifled muskets as quick as that of smoothbores. With percussion-cap ignition (perfected by Joshua Shaw), the "cap-and-ball rifle" had an accurate range up to five times as far as that of the smoothbore. The percussion cap cut down the number of misfires by seventy-five percent. The new weapon transferred the tactical advantage to the defenders who, if they were wise enough to protect themselves behind earthworks, could with relative impunity pour a withering fire into the traditional massed formations used in the attack. As a result of a fairly simple set of inventions, rifle fire accounted for ninety percent of the casualties suffered on American Civil War battlefields. By 1865 a sixth of the Union soldiers had been reequipped with the even deadlier breech-loading rifle and a few with repeating breech-loaders.

Land-artillery development generally lagged behind progress in shoulder-arms until after 1871. Half the cannon in American Civil War armies were muzzle-loading smoothbores, and most of the rifled guns had to be loaded at the muzzle. Rifled shells carried further than spherical-shaped shells from smoothbores, but they lacked reliable fuses and high explosive. Alfred Nobel tamed nitroglycerine with sawdust in 1867, turning it into dynamite, but even dynamite was too sensitive to be employed in artillery shells. In the Civil War, if guns were advanced close enough to enemy lines to use cannister *à la* Napoleon, their crews were likely to be mowed down by rifle fire. If the guns remained out of range of rifle fire, they were not effective supporting weapons on the attack. For a time, effective artillery fire was restricted largely to the defensive. As related below, only the Prussian army really mastered the technique of combining an offensive strategy with defensive tactics, the effectiveness of the famed Krupp breech-loading guns being as much due to better Prussian tactics as to the technical qualities of the guns themselves.

The Prussian army aside, military men of the mid-nineteenth century tended to cling to Napoleonic tactical methods long after they were outmoded by developments in rifled arms. This "cultural lag" was due in part to the rapidity with which the wars of the mid-nineteenth century came in succession, giving even the reflective soldier little time to assess their lessons, and to the fact that no other army of the time but the Prussian had an organization well suited for the study and application of lessons learned from experience. Except for the Crimean War and the American Civil War, the conflicts of the mid-nineteenth century were relatively brief. The Americans learned the hard way through a four-year ordeal, their armies paying a dreadful price in blood and suffering for their generals's education. In contrast, Prussia's victories were engineered with a remarkable economy of time and effort, none of the German wars of unification lasting as long as a year.

C. The Prussian General Staff, the Nation-in-Arms, *and the* Kesselschlacht *Doctrine.* Scharnhorst and his disciples laid the foundations of the modern Prussian general staff system as early as the Napoleonic Wars, and, after 1815, the Prussian Great General Staff assumed responsibility for developing army doctrine and preparing contingency war plans. It did not, however, have direct control over operations in the field until after the middle of the nineteenth century. The extension of its authority was coeval with the rising influence of Helmuth von Moltke the Elder, chief of the General Staff from 1857 to 1888. Under his leadership, the General Staff's authority began to

Count Helmuth von Moltke, the Elder

SOURCE: Walter Goerlitz, *History of the German General Staff, 1657–1945*, trans. Brian Battershaw (New York and London: Frederick Praeger, 1953).

widen in 1864 when King William I was impressed with Moltke's advice during the Danish War. On the eve of the Austro-Prussian War in 1866, the king empowered Moltke to issue orders directly to field commanders in the royal name. The successes of the Prussian army in the Austro-Prussian War of 1866, and again in the Franco-Prussian War of 1870–1871, confirmed the supremacy of the General Staff in control of field operations. After the founding of the *Kaiserheer* (the Imperial German Army) in 1871, the Prussian General Staff widened its responsibilities to include all the land forces of the Second Reich.

The excellence of the Prussian General Staff has been traced to three factors: (1) all its members were the best products of the *Kriegsakademie*, the like of which was found nowhere else in Europe until after 1871, and much superior to any other school of higher military education; (2) the General Staff officer periodically rotated between duties at general headquarters and service with the headquarters of field armies, corps, and divisions, thus avoiding isolation from the rest of the army; and (3) the separation of duties between the Ministry of War and the General Staff, allowed the latter to avoid routine military administration and to concentrate on its missions of revising doctrine and dissimenating it, making contingency war plans, and preparing its officers to execute those plans in time of war. In comparison, the general staffs of other powers before 1871 were deficient in one or more of these facets.

An officer could take a qualifying examination for entry to the War College beginning in his tenth year of commissioned service, usually when he was a captain or major. No more than one hundred fifty officers a year were admitted, and each officer faced a rigorous three-year curriculum which delt with all aspects of military operations on the division, army corps, and field army levels. The most promising students at the end of the three-year curriculum were then taken on an annual staff ride under the supervision of the chief of the General Staff himself. At the ride's conclusion, the chief chose three or four students to become General Staff probationers. The rest of the War College graduates returned to line duties. Once the probationers donned the distinctive trouser-stripe of the General Staff officer, they rotated periodically among the sections of the General Staff at general headquarters until they were considered fully qualified. Thereafter, they rotated between duties at general headquarters and those on the staffs of commanders of divisions, corps, and field armies. The chiefs-of-staff of field commanders bore the same relation to them as the chief of the Great General Staff bore to the Prussian king, constitutionally the army's commander-in-chief. Accordingly, their advice was highly valued and bore the authority of the chief of the General Staff himself. They also served to insure dissemination of changes of doctrine and adherence to war plans. By tradition, General Staff officers maintained a relative anonymity, yet their status and authority within the army was enormous.

The organization of the Prussian army as a *Nation-in-Arms* was unique in the middle of the nineteenth century, as was the Prussian general staff system. After the Napoleonic Wars, Prussia had retained the practice of using short-service conscripts as a major part of the army. The process began in 1818 when General Leopold von Boyen, then minister of war and another of Scharnhorst's disciples, secured the king's assent to a military system which imposed three years of compulsory military service on all able-bodied males when they reached age twenty, and then their rotation to the army reserve for a further two years, followed by varying periods of service in the Prussian *Landwehr* or militia. Middle-class sons could volunteer for one year's service as officer candidates, to be followed by commissioning in the *Landwehr.* In the event of war, regiments of the active army, the army reserve, and the *Landwehr* were to be brigaded together as they had been in the 1813 War of National Liberation. The peacetime strength of the army was set at 125,000 troops, which could be doubled upon mobilization of the army reserve and *Landwehr.* In 1834 compulsory active-duty service in the army was reduced to two years.

In the 1850s, General Albrecht von Roon, minister of war, reformed the Boyen System at the behest of King William I. Compulsory service had not been strictly imposed for two decades, and the strength of the army no longer represented the growing Prussian population. Accordingly, Roon raised the annual number of conscripts from forty thousand men to sixty-three thousand men, increased compulsory service to three years on active duty and four years in the army reserve, and reduced the status of the *Landwehr* to that of a second-line reserve of older men. Liberals in the *Landtag,* Prussia's parliament, opposed these changes because they decreased middle-class influence in the army, increased the importance of the professional and mostly aristocratic officer corps, and cost too much money. When the Liberal majority in the *Landtag* blocked further appropriations for army reform, William I appointed Otto von Bismarck, a Junker and a career diplomat, to assume the duties of prime minister in September, 1862. Bismarck broke the impasse by claiming that the Constitution of 1850 allowed the government to continue to collect taxes under the old budget whenever the monarch and the *Landtag* could not agree on a new one. The Liberals railed at Bismarck's parliamentary maneuvers, but the Prussian victories in 1864 and 1866 made the army so popular that the *Landtag* saw fit to approve Bismarck's budget manipulations retroactively and to grant the army still more monies. By 1870, Prussia could mobilize half a million combat troops in two weeks, half of them reservists.

Prussia's heavy reliance on trained civilian reservists made a swift and efficient mobilization system vital to her military success, and Moltke gave much attention to this problem. All contingency war plans had an accompanying set of railroad timetables, and by sending out a single coded order by telegraph the General Staff could put into motion overnight a highly complex process with speed and precision. Because every unit knew its assigned role according to the contingency plan indicated, even without knowing all the details of the plan, it could assemble at the prearranged rail station and be ready for movement to any of Prussia's frontiers. The Prussian railroad authorities worked closely with the Railway Section of the Great General Staff in peacetime as well as in time of war, and individual components of the plans were rehearsed many times until all obstacles to a speedy mobilization were removed. Thus when the real mobilization began, hundreds of troop-trains were instantly available, and within hours thousands of troops and animals were pouring toward the frontier indicated, eventually arriving as fully organized armies ready to take the field. No other country in Europe prior to 1871 had such carefully developed plans for mobilization, not to mention large numbers of reservists to mobilize. Advocates of the *armée de métier* failed to realize that the Prussian system combined large numbers with speed.

Characteristically, Moltke gave as much attention to the details of tactical doctrine as he did to those of organization and mobilization. His first experience with the new defensive fire came at Düppel during the Danish War in 1864, and he quickly surmised that the day of massed frontal attack was over. After the war the Prussian doctrine was revised to emphasize the avoidance of frontal attacks where possible, while seeking to turn the enemy's flanks instead. The revised doctrine was employed with qualified success against Austria in 1866, and the experience brought about further changes in Prussian methods, culminating in the doctrine of the *Kesselschlacht* or the planned battle of encirclement and annihilation. The object of the new doctrine was to use strategic maneuvers in order to encircle large enemy forces, then the tactical defensive in order to allow firepower to destroy the enemy as he strove to break out of the ring. The new doctrine had its greatest success under Moltke at Sedan in September, 1870, where an entire French army was trapped, its efforts to escape were repelled with terrible loss, and it was finally compelled to surrender. After Sedan, the *Kesselschlacht* doctrine had a special place in German military thought down through the Second World War.

II. Navies

Ships being machines, navies even more than armies were technologically transformed between 1815 and 1871. The steam engine began the revolution by gradually replacing sail as the primary means of propulsion, though the process was retarded by the vulnerability of the paddle-wheel to enemy fire and the inefficient fuel-consumption of the early steam engines. Better engines eventually appeared, and the screw-propellor located underwater at the stern of the ship solved the vulnerability problem. The first screw-propelled warship was the USS *Princeton* (1842), designed by the Swedish-American inventor John Ericsson. Ocean-going ships still required sails as late as the American Civil War because of range factors; still, steam power freed the warship to maneuver in battle independently of the wind and to move more safely in and out of port. On balance then, steam improved warships in a tactical sense but robbed them of their former unlimited range-in-space. During the American Civil War, the Union navy discovered that it took three times as many steam-and-sail hybrids to maintain the same blockade as sailing ships because steam vessels had to go back and forth to refuel with coal or wood. But the speed of the steamship made the interception of blockade-runners easier, unless the blockade-runner was also steam propelled. The steam blockade-runner not only had speed, it was both independent of the wind and less reliant on the tide than the pure sailing ship. The experience of the American Civil War suggested that on balance, steam had made naval blockades harder to enforce.

The science of naval gun-making improved tremendously after Nelson's day, and by the mid-nineteenth century guns with bores as large as twelve inches had become practical. Such weapons might weigh forty tons. The tendency was to mount fewer but larger guns on the big warships, a practice that gradually abolished the old distinction between ships-of-the-line and ships-below-the-line based on the number of guns carried. Around 1870, the most powerfully gunned ships afloat began to be called "battleships." As guns grew in size, their lethality was increased through the use of contact-fused shells, harnassing fulminate of mercury.

Shell fire put an end to the unprotected wooden hull in warships. At the Battle of Sinope (1853) on the Black Sea, a Russian fleet using shell-guns utterly demolished seven Turkish frigates, killing or wounding three thousand Turkish sailors. No armored warships appeared in time for the Crimean War (1854–1856), but in 1859 France launched the *Gloire*, the first wooden vessel protected with iron plates and a true "ironclad." The plates were 4½-inches thick and proof against existing shell-guns. The *Gloire*, a steam-and-sail hybrid, was ocean-going and displaced five thousand tons. In 1860, Britain went France one better when it launched the *Warrior*. It had an iron frame, an iron hull, and armored plate over the hull as thick as that of the *Gloire*. The *Warrior* displaced nine thousand tons, almost as much as a World War II heavy cruiser. Both the *Monitor* and the *Virginia (née Merrimack)* of Civil War fame were entirely steam propelled and the first American armored ships, but both

La Gloire, 1859, the first iron-clad warship.

Source: Peter Padfield, *The Battleship Era* (New York: David McKay, 1972).

HMS *Black Prince,* c. 1862, similar to HMS *Warrior,* the British iron-clad riposte to *La Gloire.*

Source: Peter Padfield, *The Battleship Era* (New York: David McKay, 1972).

HMS *Inflexible,* 1881, the last of a type of sail and steam battleship.
SOURCE: Peter Padfield, *The Battleship Era* (New York: David McKay, 1972).

HMS *Devastation,* 1871, the first ocean-going battleship propelled entirely by steam engines.
SOURCE: Peter Padfield, *The Battleship Era* (New York: David McKay, 1972).

had very low freeboards and shallow drafts in order to operate in river and harbor waters. Neither was designed to operate on the high seas. Still, their engagement at Hampton Roads, Virginia, in March, 1862, was the first combat between armored vessels in modern times. The *Virginia* was a converted Union frigate with an improvised armored casemate made from railroad tracks. The *Monitor,* designed by John Ericsson, was new from the keel up and featured the first revolving gun turret. It contained two 11-inch smoothbore guns. The *Monitor* and the *Virginia* had so much trouble penetrating each other's armor that they resorted to ramming as a tactic. The Union built seventy-four armored warships during the war. The Confederacy converted, or began work on, fifteen "iron-clads," though not all were ever operational.

But armor and the large naval gun did not have uncontested sway in the mid-nineteenth century. They were challenged by the torpedo, both stationary (the mine) and mobile. The torpedo had its greatest effect in this period in the defense of harbors and coastal waters. Fulminate of mercury fuses made the contact mine practical, while the invention of the wet-cell electric storage battery led to the command mine set off from shore by an observer. Even the crude Confederate "keg-mines" (converted wooden barrels) could be dangerous when a ship brushed their detonators. The Confederates pioneered the mobile torpedo as an explosive device carried on the end of a spar and designed to be rammed below the water-line of an enemy ship, and used by the class of semisubmersibles called *Davids.* The CSS *Hunley,* a true submersible, sank the USS *Housatonic* in 1863 off Charleston, S.C., with either a spar torpedo or a towed torpedo, though the *Hunley* never returned from its mission. Propelled by a hand-cranked-screw, it had previously drowned several crews and its inventors in tests. The Englishman Robert Whitehead, while working for the Austrian navy, invented the first self-propelled torpedo in 1870. Originally launched from shore, the Whitehead torpedo had a maximum speed of eighteen knots and a range of four hundred yards. Compressed air turned its screw, and its "soft launch" allowed a warhead of dynamite. An ingenius depth-regulator prevented it from either plunging or broaching during its run. But the story of the automotive torpedo really belongs to the period after 1871.

The future of *guerre de course* was left especially clouded by the experiences of the mid-nineteenth century wars. The international Declaration of Paris, made in 1856 at the conference which ended the Crimean War, outlawed the old practice of "privateering," for which reason it was not much used by the Confederacy during the Civil War. In addition, even state-owned, steam-propelled commerce-raiders were more tied to their bases and restricted in range than raiders in the sailing age. Still, a dozen Confederate steam-and-sail raiders inflicted considerable damage to the

Union merchant fleet during the Civil War. They so impressed the British government that it sought to discourage the building of such raiders by neutral governments for belligerents by accepting financial responsibility for the damage done by the CSS *Alabama,* a raider built in a British port and sold to the Confederacy.

III. The Mid-Nineteenth Century Wars before 1861

The effects of the Industrial Revolution were little felt in the mid-nineteenth century wars before 1861. The Mexican War (1846–1848) was both too early and fought in an undeveloped region of North America. The Crimean War (1854–1856), the first great war of the period, was also fought in a remote region, and was only brushed by the effects of the Industrial Revolution. The Great Sepoy Mutiny (1857) is mostly important for the organizational changes it helped to bring about in the British army. The Franco-Austrian War of 1859 was the first in which the infantry of both sides were armed with the cap-and-ball rifle, and in which on the French side large numbers of troops were moved by rail, but the war lasted only four months and involved only two major battles. After 1859, the wars of Italian unification to 1861 have little to teach about the patterns of war. Nevertheless, brief examinations of the wars before 1861 provide useful background for understanding the American Civil War (1861–1865) and the German wars of unification (1864–1871).

The Mexican War began with disputes between Mexico and the United States over the southern border of Texas after the latter was admitted to the Union. Texas had been a republic after winning a war for independence in 1836, but Mexico had never recognized that independence formally or the Rio Grande as the southern boundary of Texas with Mexico. After both the United States and Mexico sent troops into the disputed territory just north of the Rio Grande in the spring of 1846, armed clashes occurred at Palo Alto and Resacca del Palma in April. The U.S. Congress declared a state of war on May 11, and simultaneously approved the raising of state volunteer regiments to supplement the small regular army of 8,500 troops. The United States then had a population of 20 million. The Mexican army numbered about 20,000 men, and Mexico had a population of about 7 million.

In the aftermath of the little American victories north of the Rio Grande, General Zachary Taylor and 4,000 American regular troops invaded northern Mexico. The arid, desertlike nature of the country created more problems than did enemy resistance, and by the time Taylor captured Monterrey in September, his force was only two hundred miles south of its starting point. Early in 1847, Taylor and 5,000 Ameri-

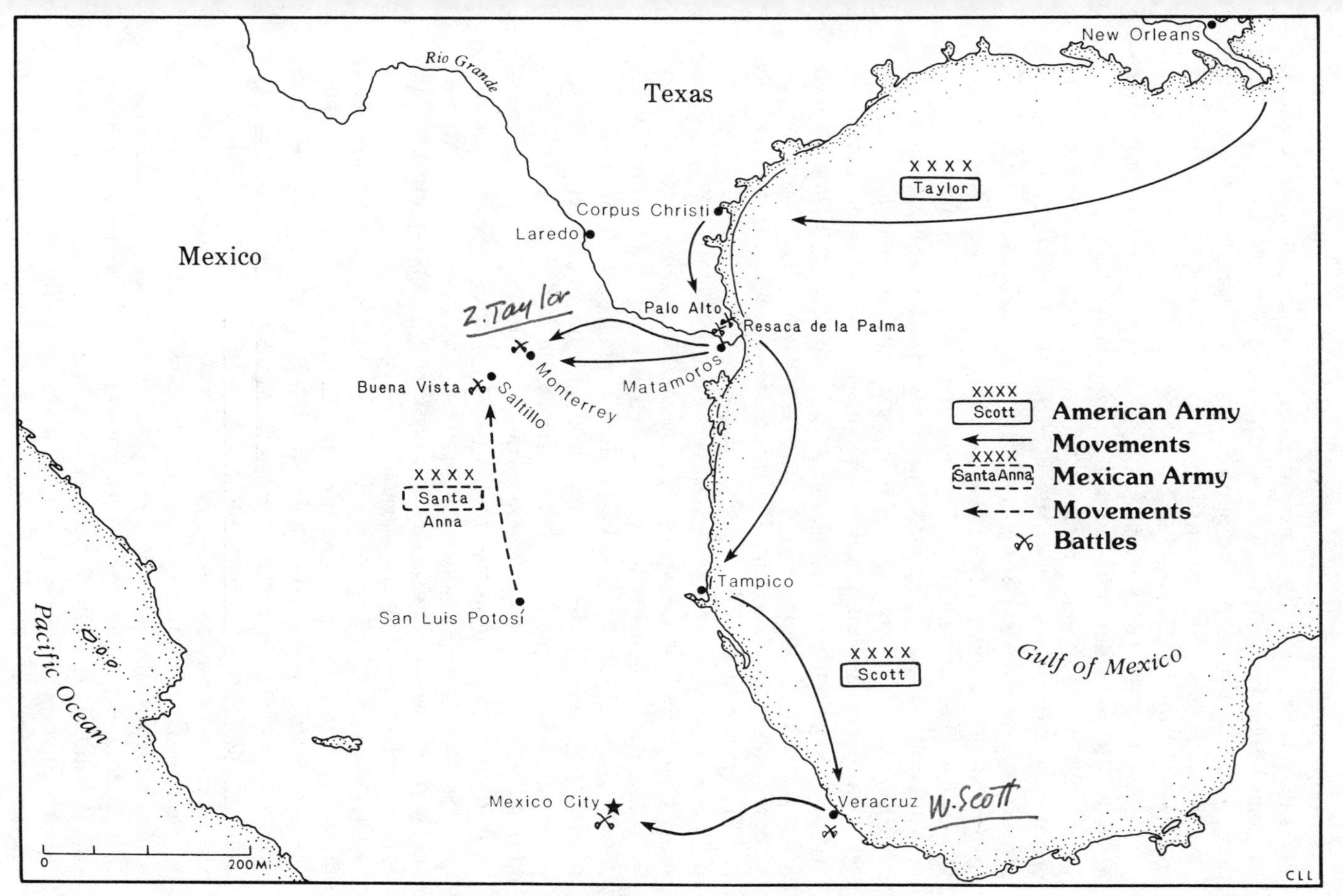

The Mexican War, 1846–1848: Principal Operations

can troops finally got as far south as Buena Vista, where they were attacked in February by a Mexican army of 15,000 troops under General Antonio Lopez Santa Anna. The Americans fended off the attack, but they made no further penetration of Mexico from the north. Instead, Taylor's army spent the rest of the war on the defensive and screening the border at the Rio Grande.

Meanwhile, another American army of 14,000 troops was assembling in New Orleans under command of General Winfield Scott. In the absence of a Mexican navy (unless two small converted steamers are counted), the small U.S. Navy had command of the sea. In March, 1847, Scott's army was landed just south of Vera Cruz on the Gulf of Mexico in the first large amphibious assault in the history of United States armed forces. After capturing Vera Cruz, Scott dropped his communications to the Gulf and made a daring march inland toward Mexico City, about two hundred miles away. Halfway to his objective, the enlistments of his one-year volunteers ran out, however, and with only half of his former army, Scott had to linger between the coast and Mexico City until late summer when his strength had been raised by replacements to 10,000 troops. With this force, Scott assaulted the approaches to Mexico City and finally captured it in September.

The capture of Mexico City, however, did not lead to a quick conclusion of the war. The Mexican government did not come to terms until February, 1848, when it finally signed the Peace of Guadaloupe Hidalgo. The treaty recognized the Rio Grande boundary with Texas, and for a sum of $15 million ceded territories that later became all or part of the states of California, Arizona, New Mexico, Utah, and Nevada. This land-grab cost the lives of 14,000 Americans in uniform, but only 2,000 of them died as the result of wounds received on the battlefield. Disease and misadventures accounted for the rest. Another 16,000 Americans survived wounds or illness. Mexican losses are uncertain, but probably exceeded the American casualties.

The Mexican War was a limited war on both sides, for the United States because it had no need for more than a limited effort, and for Mexico because of governmental incapacity and lack of resources. Both Taylor and Scott conducted their campaigns in order to occupy key places rather than to destroy the Mexican army. Partisan resistance to the American invasion was minor in contrast to the Mexican guerrilla war waged against an invading French army of 35,000 troops in the 1860s, which finally toppled the regime of the Archduke Maximilian. Scott, perhaps the ablest of the American generals between the American Revolution and the American Civil War, remained commanding general of the U.S. Army until November, 1861. Taylor, whom the defensive victories at Palo Alto, Resacca del Palma, and Buena Vista had made famous, went on to the White House.

The Crimean War was a much larger affair than the Mexican War, and was also the only major amphibious war in Europe of the mid-nineteenth century. Its origins lay in a quarrel between Tsar Nicholas I of Russia and the Sultan of the Turkish Empire as to the administration of the Christian holy places in Palestine. When the Tsar demanded the right to protect Orthodox Christians within the Sultan's empire, he was refused. He then ordered Russian troops to invade the Turkish provinces of Moldavia and Wallachia (now constituting much of present Rumania) in the Balkans, and Turkish territory in the Caucasus. Turkey retaliated with a declaration of war on Russia. In November, 1853, the Russian Black Sea fleet engaged and destroyed the Turkish fleet off Sinope. The governments of Napoleon III and Queen Victoria protested Russian actions, and, after fruitless negotiations, both Britain and France declared war on Russia in March, 1854.

When the Anglo-French fleets entered the Black Sea, the Russian fleet hastily retreated to the safety of its base at the fortress-city of Sevastopol in the Crimean peninsula. Allied troops were then landed at Varna (now in Bulgaria) in order to assist the Turks in driving the Russians from the Balkans, but in the summer of 1854 the Tsar ordered a withdrawal of his troops from Moldavia and Wallachia. Instead of leaving well enough alone, the Allied governments decided to teach the Tsar a lesson by capturing Sevastopol and occupying the Russian Crimea. That decision led unexpectedly to a long and costly war that focused most of its action in a struggle for the control of Sevastopol and the Crimean peninsula.

Well over a year after the Tsar had first sent troops into the Balkans, an Allied expeditionary force of fifty-thousand troops, about half British and half French, landed across open beaches near Eupatoria, north of Sevastopol, in September, 1854. Lord Raglan, the British commander-in-chief, was an amiable but bumbling soldier who had last seen action at Waterloo, almost forty years earlier. He was devoted to the memory of the Duke of Wellington, who had died in 1852, but seems to have had no ideas of his own. French Marshal Armand Saint-Arnaud had made a reputation fighting natives in Algeria, but he was riddled with cancer and died ten days after the campaign began. Marshal François Canrobert, his successor, was competent but unenthusiastic about the whole enterprise.

The Allied advance southward toward Sevastopol soon encountered the Russian army, about as large as the Allied, under General Prince Menshikov on the heights above the river Alma. On September 20, the French bungled a turning movement to catch the Russians in the flank, and the British engaged the Russian front in a bloody action that cost them heavily before the Russians finally withdrew. The exhausted Allies were so slow in pursuing that the Russian army had ample time to detach a garrison to hold Sevastopol before withdrawing into the interior of the

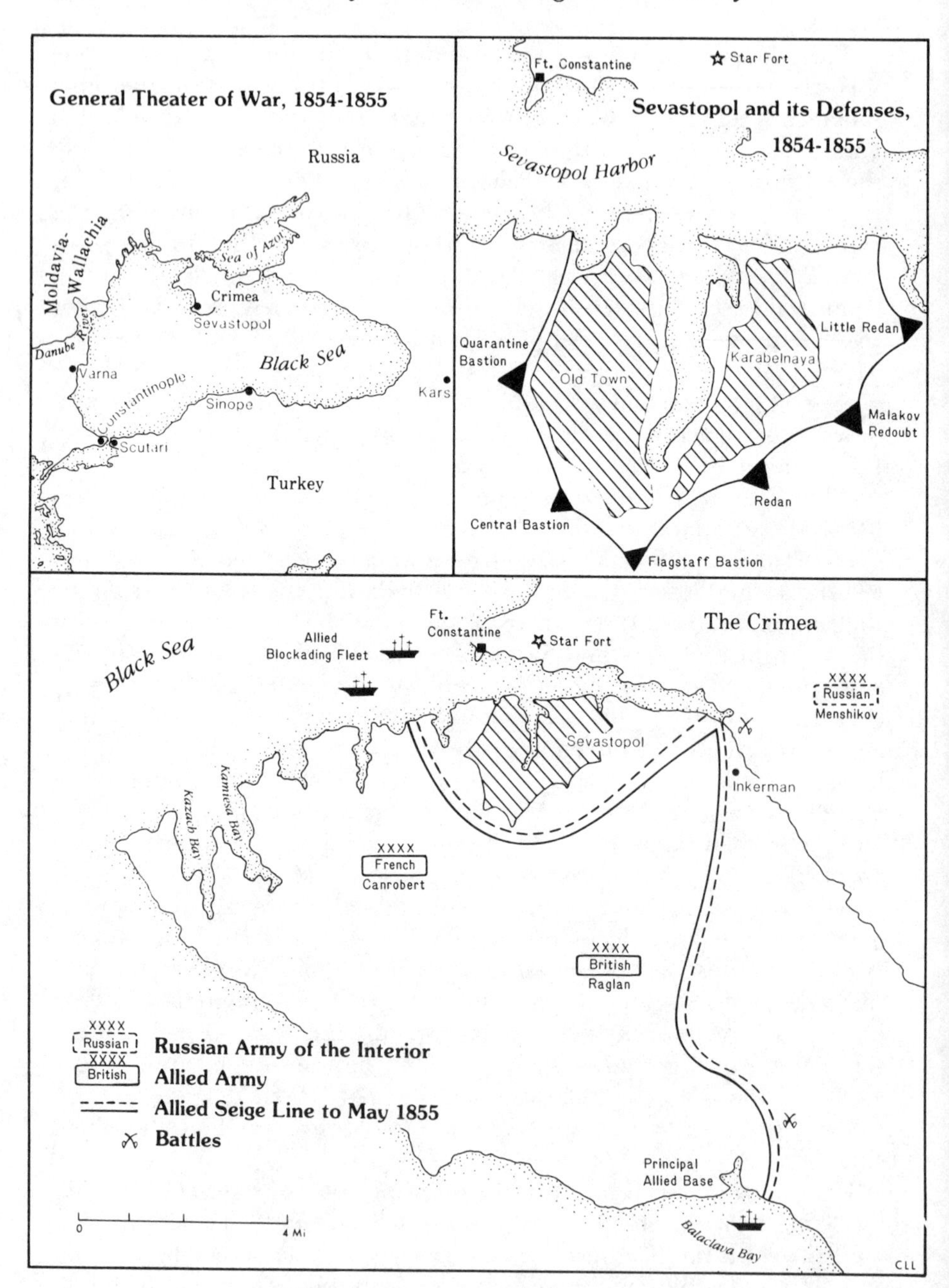

The Crimean War, 1854–1856

Crimea. After establishing a base at the Bay of Balaclava, twelve miles south of Sevastopol, the Allied armies began a siege of Sevastopol that would last a year.

The siege was far from watertight. The Allies lacked enough men to invest Sevastopol completely around its landside, and not even Allied command of the sea prevented reinforcements and supplies from reaching the garrison periodically. The Russians had taken guns from ships before they were sunk to block the harbor mouth in order to strengthen the earthworks facing inland. Colonel Franz Todleben, the chief Russian engineer, designed rifle pits to cover the intervals between redoubts. Then there was the threat from the Russian army in the interior. The Allies nearly lost their base at Balaclava to its attack on October 25, but managed to fend it off despite the British blunder known as the "Charge of the Light Brigade." After the Russian garrison inside Sevastopol, 120,000-strong counting Russian sailors, failed in its attack on the Allied lines at Inkerman on November 5, both sides settled down to a war of attrition. At the beginning of winter, the Allied forces consisted of 40,000 French troops, 25,000 British troops and 12,000 Turkish troops.

That winter more men on both sides died from disease, bad food, and exposure than from bullets. The French came through the best, but scarcely 11,000 British troops were alive and fit for duty by the spring of 1855. After reinforcements arrived, Raglan and the new French commander-in-chief, Marshal Aimable Pélissier, launched an assault on the defenses of Sevastopol in June, only to see it bloodily repulsed. Later that month, the despondent Raglan died of dysentery. He was succeeded by General Colin Simpson, a competent if not outstanding soldier.

Over the summer of 1855, Allied strength in the Crimea was raised to 150,000 troops, Sevastopol was more tightly invested (though never completely cut off from outside contact), and the muddled supply and medical situation was improved. On September 8, the Allies launched a second major assault. Where the British attacked, they were wholly repelled, but the French took the key Malakov Redoubt and resisted all Russian attempts to retake it. A total of 23,000 Allied troops had been killed or wounded. Still, Prince Gortschkov judged the further defense of Sevastopol as hopeless, and his army withdrew to the north. The war then dragged on to March, 1856, when the new Tsar Alexander II (Nicholas had died in March, 1855) agreed to the terms of the Peace of Paris. Russia withdrew her claims on Turkey, was forbidden a naval base or a fleet on the Black Sea, and returned Kars in the Caucasus to Turkey. The Danube River was internationalized. The first great European war since 1815 was over.

Over the whole of the Crimean War, the Allied powers (finally Britain, France, Turkey, and the north Italian state of Piedmont) committed 597,000 troops, of which 309,000 were French, 98,000 were British,

165,000 were Turkish, and 25,000 were Piedmontese. Russia committed 600,000 troops and would have sent more except the lack of railroads to the Crimea made it difficult to supply even the men who were there. About 440,000 Russians were finally casualties, while the French and Turkish armies each lost 100,000 men, the British 25,000, and the Piedmontese 5,000. Four-fifths of these casualties were due to disease and exposure. Though essentially an old-fashioned war, the Crimean conflict had some modern touches. Most of the Russian infantry lacked rifles, but those who did inflicted frightful execution on attacking troops. Todleben's rifle pits foreshadowed the hasty entrenchments of the American Civil War. William Howard Russell's dispatches to the *Times* went by the Mediterranean submarine electric-cable to London where newspaper readers could, for the first time, follow military events almost as soon as they happened and through other than self-serving official accounts. Russell's revelations about British supply and medical failures influenced Florence Nightingale—the proprietor of a nursing home—to organize a dozen female nurses for service in the British hospital at Scutari where lay thousands of wretched wounded and ill. Nightingale and her lady-nurses not only cut the death rate at Scutari by 40 percent through simple measures of hygiene and common sense, their example prodded the British army medical corps to mend its ways. Nightingale's activities also foreshadowed the work of Clara Barton and the United States Sanitary Commission in the American Civil War.

Indirectly, the Crimean War contributed to the coming of the Great Sepoy Mutiny in India in 1857. Many regiments of the British regular army were stationed in India as well as the troops of the various armies of the East India Company until the outbreak of the Crimean War. Then most of the British regulars were siphoned off to the Crimea, and not many returned. In consequence, there were only 23,000 European soldiers among the 151,000 troops in India when the rebellion broke out, adding to the British difficulties in suppressing it. Historians still debate the precise reasons for the revolt, though they certainly involved some mixture of religious and national resentment of British rule. In any case, many sepoy regiments turned against their British officers, and whole areas of northern India passed out of control for months on end. The worst of the revolt took place in the company's Bengal Army, and most of the sepoys in the other two armies remained loyal. Still, it required the services of 40,000 European reinforcements before complete order was restored.

In the aftermath of the Great Mutiny, the East India Company and its army were abolished, and henceforth India became a crown colony, whose defense was entrusted to an Indian Army composed of regiments of regular British troops and native regiments. About half of the army was composed of European troops. Down to World War I, the strength of the Indian Army hovered around 200,000 troops, hardly too many to police and defend a subcontinent with a population of 250 million. No serious disloyalties appeared among the native regiments down to World War II, and they were to serve as the core of the Indian Army after India's independence in 1947.

The Crimean War and the Great Mutiny, taken together, had consequences that led to other army reforms between 1868 and 1872, while Lord Cardwell was secretary of state for war. In this period, the regular enlistment was reduced from twenty to twelve years, and six of those could be served in the army's reserve. By the 1880s, two-thirds of the British soldiers on their first hitches were under the shorter enlistment. Cardwell also introduced the linked-battalion system whereby regiments kept one battalion in the British Isles as a recruiting and training unit to send replacements to the battalion stationed overseas. In addition, the home battalion was assigned up to three battalions of militia for training, from which it could draw volunteers in time of war. Cardwell managed to get parliamentary abolition of the Purchase System in 1872, and thereafter most young officers entering service were products of the royal military college at Sandhurst (infantry and cavalry) or the one at Woolwich (artillery and engineering). Promotion was based on seniority and merit. Aside from still being entirely a voluntary organization, the remaining chief weaknesses of the British army after 1872 lay in the lack of an organized expeditionary force in the home islands for the rapid reinforcement of forces overseas, and in an old-fashioned command and staff system.

The Franco-Austrian War of 1859 was the first of the wars which led to the unification of Italy in 1861. Count Camillo di Cavour, prime minister of Piedmont, had sought to curry favor with Napoleon III by bringing his country into the Crimean War on the side of France. After the war, he pressed for French support in expelling Austrian control from the Italian provinces of Lombardy and Venetia, awarded the Hapsburg government by the Congress of Vienna in 1815. Cavour's original aim was to unite all northern Italy under King Victor-Emannuel of the Savoy dynasty. When Piedmont provoked war with Austria in the spring of 1859, a total of 128,000 French troops were transported to northern Italy by rail, the first large-scale wartime railroad movement of troops in history. Once in Piedmont, they joined with 35,000 Piedmontese troops to take on about 150,000 Austrian soldiers in Lombardy. Both sides were armed with cap-and-ball rifles, but the French artillery was in advance of the Austrian by having muzzle-loading rifled cannon as well.

Both the battles of Magenta and Solferino were fought in June, 1859, the first being a confused meeting battle that led to an Austrian retreat to the other side of Lombardy, and the second almost turning into a bloody stalemate until the French artillery weakened the exposed Austrian line to the point where it could be penetrated with a bayonet charge. But French losses were very heavy at Solferino, and a third of the Piedmontese troops were killed or wounded. After Prussia threatened to enter the war on the side of Austria, Napoleon III settled for a hasty peace at Villafranca in July by which Austria ceded Lombardy to Piedmont but kept Venetia. Several other northern Italian states then joined Piedmont in forming the Kingdom of Upper Italy. Between 1859 and 1861, Giuseppe Garibaldi, the famous Italian patriot and guerrilla fighter, joined forces with Piedmont to bring about the formation of the Kingdom of Italy (save Rome and Venetia), but France was not directly involved in those conflicts.

The War of 1859 cost France 24,600 casualties, most of them suffered in just a month of fighting. Just after the Battle of Solferino, the French medical corps was so swamped with casualties that some injured men lay on the field for two days before they received attention. Jean Henri Dunant, a Swiss observer who visited the stricken field just after the battle, was so appalled that he returned to Switzerland and wrote *Un Souvenir de Solferino,* which shocked European sensibilities. Dunant was later instrumental in the founding of the Red Cross organization and the Geneva Convention in 1864. The contemporary concern for the war-wounded and ill, prisoners-of-war, and the rights of noncombatants in war zones, dates from that time.

IV. The American Civil War, 1861–65

A. The Opposing Sides. The eleven states of the Confederacy in 1861 possessed a land-area equal to Western Europe; but only 9 million people lived within its bounds, and only 5.5 million of them were white. The Confederate "garrison" was really too small for the "fortress" it had to defend. Confederate conscription was adopted in 1862, and about 900,000 individual males served in Confederate gray during the war, but only about a third of this number were brought in by the draft. Many Southerners secured exemptions on grounds that they were slave-overseers (plantations were allowed one overseer for every twenty slaves), newspaper editors, or schoolteachers. The draft law was tightened up in 1864. The Confederate forces reached a peak strength of 600,000 men in 1863, but shrank to no more than 150,000 men by April, 1865. Perhaps 200,000 Confederate soldiers died in the war, and another 100,000 men survived wounds or illness.

The states loyal to the Union had a combined population of 22 million people, and the Federal government did not resort to conscription until 1863. The use of substitution and commutation (payment of taxes in lieu of military service) promoted such class resentments in the North that the draft was widely evaded and even openly resisted. Draft riots in New York City in the summer of 1863 required 20,000 Federal troops to suppress, a number equal to Union casualties in the Battle of Gettysburg. Although about 2 million individuals wore Union blue sometime during the war, only 42,000 of them were conscripts. As a consequence, less than a third of the North's abundant manpower was tapped during the war. About 370,000 Union soldiers died during the war, and some 230,000 survived wounds or illness.

The Southern economy was dominated by a cash-crop agriculture, mainly cotton and tobacco, and for most manufactured goods during the war the South had to depend on trade with Europe. What little heavy industry the Confederacy possessed was heavily concentrated at Richmond, Va., only a hundred miles from Washington, D.C., and the *de facto* frontier at the Potomac River. The Tredegar Iron Works and associated industries at Richmond constituted a "Confederate Ruhr," which, like the Ruhr in Germany, was almost on the border. Even if the Confederate capital had not been shifted from Montgomery, Ala., to Richmond after Virginia's secession, the city would have been defended at all costs.

The Confederacy did surprisingly well in arming its forces throughout the war. In 1861, 300,000 muskets and rifles were in the hands of the Southern militia, and 110,000 stands of arms were in Federal armories in the South. With machinery captured at Harper's Ferry, Md., at the begining of the war and moved to Richmond and Fayetteville, N.C., many of the smoothbores were converted to rifles. Confederates captured 120,000 rifles on the battlefield, and 200,000 more were imported from overseas. Three hundred heavy naval guns were captured with the Norfolk navy yard in 1861, and over the course of the war the Tredegar Iron Works turned out 1,099 cannon, more than any single Union supplier in the North. Ammunition production, if not lavish, was at least adequate. In sum, the Confederacy was never fatally deficient in the number or the quality of its armaments. Even toward the end of the war, the Confederate army was running out of men more rapidly than arms.

The effects of the Union blockade on the outcome of the war is surprisingly hard to measure precisely. By mid-1862, ten out of thirteen Confederate ports with rail connections had been captured or effectively neutralized, and the naval blockade of the remaining three—Wilmington, N.C., Charleston, S.C., and Mobile, Ala.—should have been relatively easy. Still, 80 percent of the cargoes dispatched from overseas to the Confederacy reached one or another of the Southern ports. But the blockade forced goods to be shipped on vessels chosen for speed rather than carrying capacity, and the average cargo delivered was about four hundred tons. In addition, the failure of the Confederate government to regulate cargoes until 1864 resulted in much of the imported materials being useless for the war effort. Often, the privately owned blockade-runners, with an eye to profit, brought in luxury items. Even when cargoes had military value, the breakdown of Southern railroads as the war progressed made it impossible to deliver them where needed. Perhaps the classic example is Robert E. Lee's hungry and ragged troops in the trenches before Richmond in the winter of 1864–1865, when two hundred miles away the warehouses of Wilmington were filled with idle supplies. Perhaps the breakdown of the Southern rail system was as important as the blockade in bringing the Confederacy to the breaking point, though clearly the two factors reinforced each other.

About 16,000 officers and men were serving in the U.S. Army at the beginning of 1861. Few of the men, but many of the officers, were Southerners. Fully a third of the 1000 officers defected to the Confederacy. Few of the 8,000 officers and men in the U.S. Navy and Marine Corps went south. The Navy had 42 warships in April, 1861, most of them small. By December, it had raised the number to 264 vessels by converting civilian craft. Still, by the end of the war, the Union navy boasted 50,000 sailors and marines, and 671 vessels mounting some 5,000 guns. The majority of the craft were designed to operate in Southern rivers and coastal waters, and the number of "iron-clads" in this force—only about 70—was relatively small compared to the whole. Few of the American "iron-clads" were ocean-going when Britain had 40 and France had about 35. Much has been made of the fact that the U.S. Navy was the largest in the world in 1865, but it was a very specialized navy.

B. Tactics on land in the Civil War. The generals of the Civil War were, for the most part, products of the "Jominian school," and as such they tended to cling through much of the war to traditional Napoleonic methods and assumptions regarding tactics. Almost none of them had foreseen the tactical implications of rifled firearms, and most persisted for far too long in committing regiments and brigades *en masse* in the assault. A favorite assault formation was a brigade of four regiments, each drawn up behind the next in a column-of-divisions, with intervals of 50 to 150 yards between regiments. Civil war regiments were nearly always deployed in two ranks. Two companies out of the ten in every regiment were deployed before the brigade as skirmishers. In theory, the fire of the skirmishers, and that of the leading regiment, would prepare the way for a breakthrough with the bayonet; in practice, such a formation was woefully vulnerable to defending rifle-fire, which often mowed down the attacking "waves" of infantry or forced them to take cover. When defending infantry protected themselves with earthen breastworks or trenches, they were almost invulnerable to frontal attack, even when bombarded by artillery.

The history of the Civil War is replete with examples of costly and usually futile frontal assaults. Robert E. Lee's Army of Northern Vir-

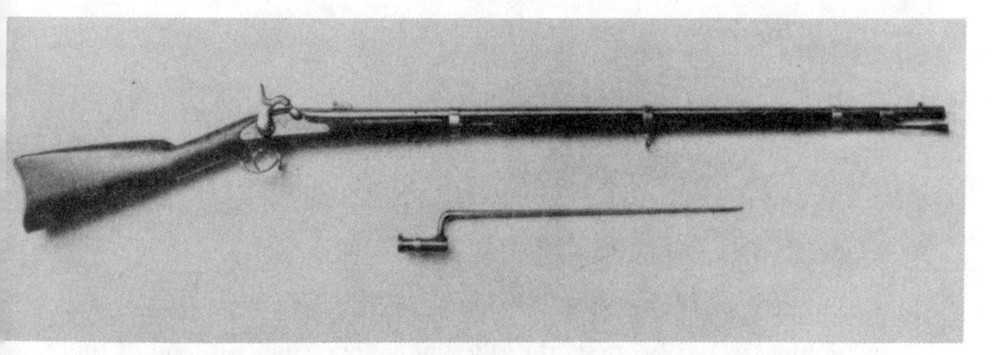

Rifled musket and bayonet, U.S. Civil War.

SOURCE: Bell I. Wiley and Hollis D. Milhollen, *They Who Fought Here* (New York: Bonanza, 1959).

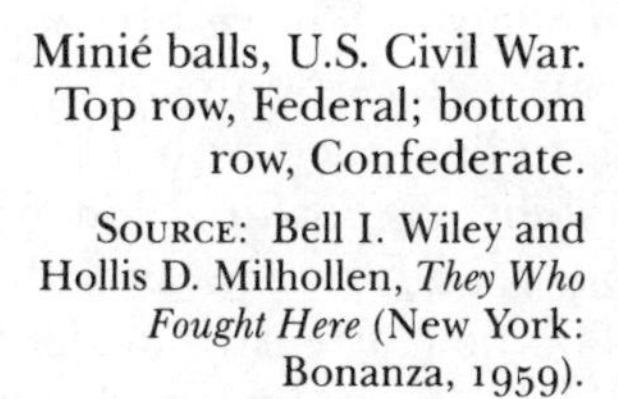

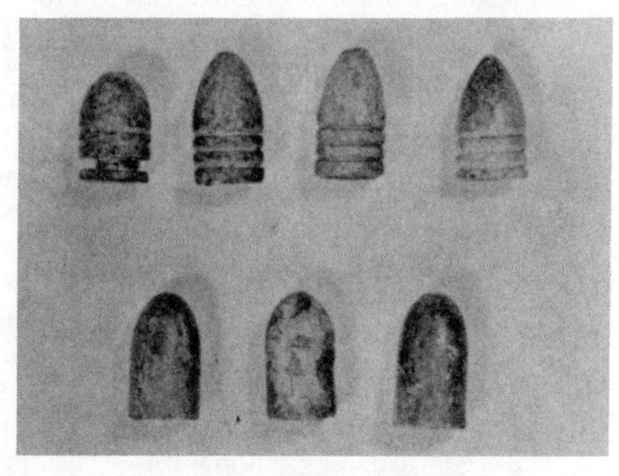

Minié balls, U.S. Civil War. Top row, Federal; bottom row, Confederate.

SOURCE: Bell I. Wiley and Hollis D. Milhollen, *They Who Fought Here* (New York: Bonanza, 1959).

ginia launched a frontal attack at Malvern Hill on July 1, 1862, which cost it five thousand casualties in two hours of fighting without significant gain. The casualties at Malvern Hill amounted to a quarter of all those suffered over the whole of the Seven Days' Battle. In the earlier fighting, Lee had relied on flanking attacks. Lee did not repeat his mistake at Malvern Hill until a year later at Gettysburg. Then "Pickett's Charge" with fifteen thousand troops against the Union center on Cemetery Ridge cost seventy-five hundred casualties in less than an hour, or about a third of the casualties suffered by Lee's army over the three days of Gettysburg. U. S. Grant had his own version of "Pickett's Charge" at Cold Harbor in 1864, when he lost six thousand men in a frontal assault, and William T. Sherman lost three thousand men in a similar fashion at Kenesaw Mountain in the same year. Union troops stormed Missionary Ridge at the Battle of Chattanooga in 1863, but in that case the Confederates had dug their rifle pits too far from the forward slope and the attacking troops used the cover of "dead" ground until they were on top of their adversaries.

Flanking attacks were much more likely than frontal attacks to be successful under Civil War conditions, cases in point being Lee's attack at Second Bull Run (or Second Manassas) in 1862 and Thomas J. "Stonewall" Jackson's turning movement at Chancellorsville in 1863. However, against an alert and skillful enemy, turning or flanking movements were not always possible. The main hindrance to a successful frontal attack was, of course, the rifle bullet. The chief surgeon of the Union Army of the Potomac reported that in a few days in May, 1864, his doctors treated a wound from a sword, 14 bayonet wounds, 749 wounds caused by artillery, but 8,218 wounds caused by rifle bullets. Moreover, an examination of the dead on the battlefield revealed that the large majority were victims of rifle fire. Still, the vulnerability of attacking troops to rifle fire varied much with the particular formation they chose. At the Battle of Antietam in 1862, 54 percent of the men of the Sixth Wisconsin Regiment who attacked in a close column-of-divisions were casualties, but only 5 percent of the men deployed as skirmishers were hit. Toward the end of the war, the more experienced soldiers learned to break up their column-of-division into small groups of men, some advancing while others provided covering fire, and all seeking to reinforce the skirmish line. If enemy defensive fire proved too intense, the soldier resorted to pick or spade to throw up an earthen wall of protection. If he was lucky enough to be armed with a breech-loading rifle, he could reduce his vulnerability by loading and firing from a kneeling or prone position. The tactical advantage lay with the defender to the end of the war, but by 1865 new offensive tactics had reduced casualties among the attackers and largely ended the mass slaughters so common through most of the Civil War. Nor were American Civil War armies the only ones in the mid-nineteenth century bedeviled by the problem of defensive fire.

C. Naval Tactics and Coast Defense. As the only tactical actions on water in the Civil War were mélees between river and harbor flotillas, the power of the individual ship counted for more than formation. Generally having the better "iron-clads" and more of them, the Northern flotillas usually had the advantage in such combats. Except for reviving the old tactic of ramming, the Civil War broke no new ground in the art of conducting fleet actions. On the other hand, new ground was broken by the Union navy in the art of dealing with coastal defenses. Early in the war, wooden steamships successfully ran by coastal batteries to sever Confederate communications or by-pass them, a classic example

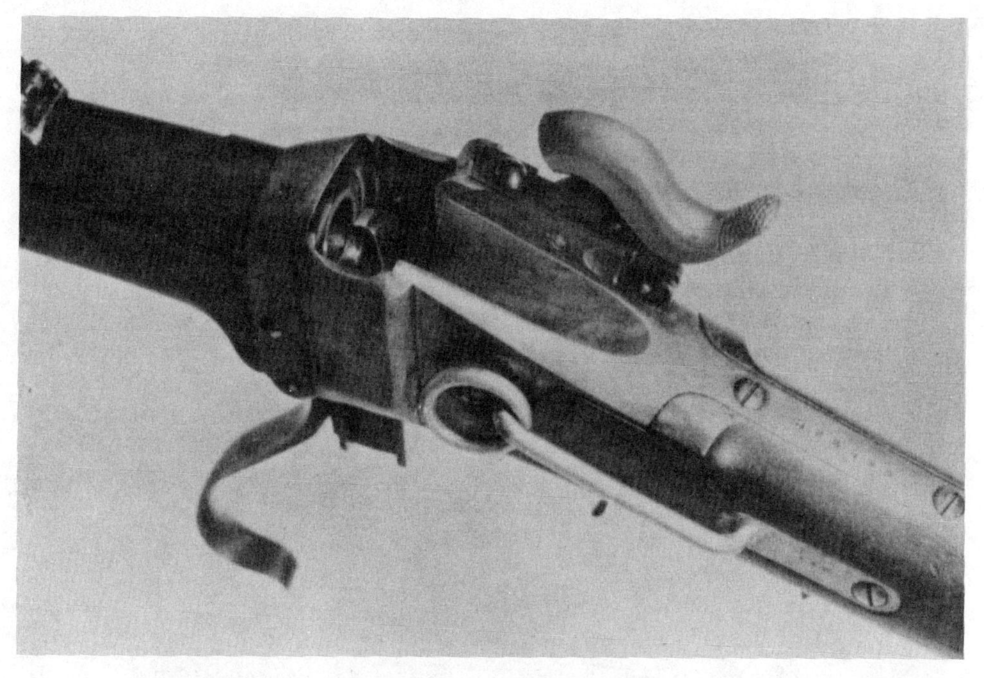

Sharps breech-loading rifle, U.S. Civil War.

SOURCE: Bell I. Wiley and Hollis D. Milhollen, *They Who Fought Here* (New York: Bonanza, 1959).

Open breech of the Prussian Dreyse, or "needle gun," mid-nineteenth century.

SOURCE: Harold L. Peterson, *The Treasury of the Gun* (New York: Ridge Press/Golden Press, 1962).

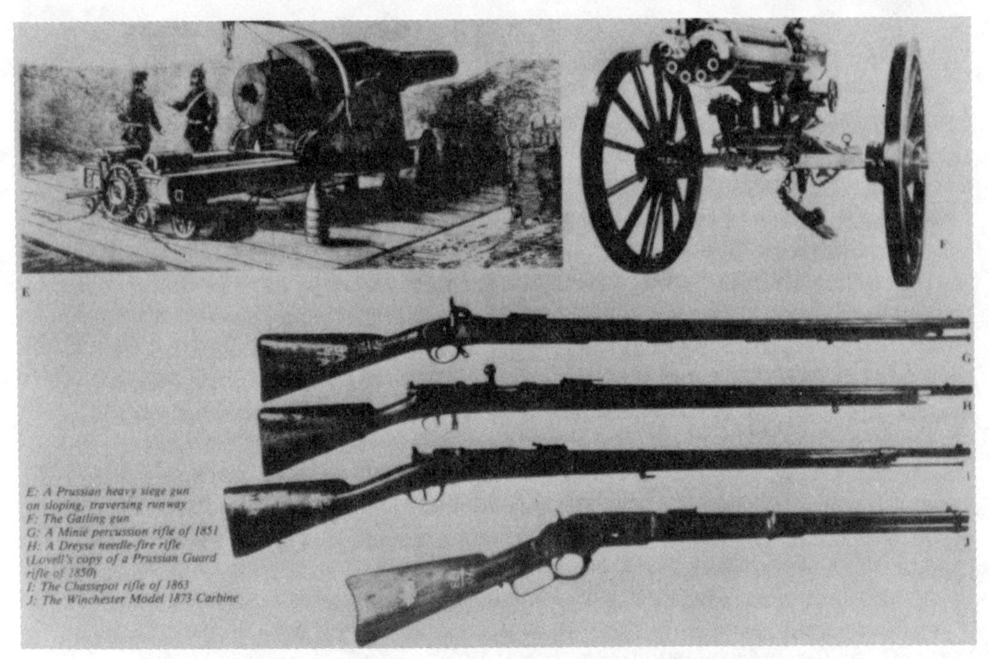

Siege gun, gatling gun, and small arms, mid-nineteenth century.

SOURCE: David G. Chandler, *Atlas of Military Strategy* (New York: Free Press, 1980).

British Artillery Types, 1850-80

Decade	Category	Horse	Field	Mountain	Heavy
1850s	Smooth-bore, muzzle loading	6pdr. gun 12pdr. gun	9pdr. gun 24 pdr. howitzer	3pdr. gun 12pdr. howitzer	18pdr. gun 8in. mortar
1860s	Rifled, breech loading	9pdr. gun	12pdr. gun	6pdr. gun	40pdr. gun 8in. mortar
1870s	Rifled, muzzle loading	9pdr. gun	9pdr. gun 16pdr. gun	7pdr. gun	40pdr. gun 6.3in. howitzer

Mid-nineteenth-century developments in artillery: the Whitworth breech-loader.

SOURCE: David G. Chandler, *Atlas of Military Strategy* (New York: Free Press, 1980).

Confederate 12-pounder howitzer, complete with limber, U.S. Civil War.

SOURCE: Bell I. Wiley and Hollis D. Milhollen, *They Who Fought Here* (New York: Bonanza, 1959).

20-pounder rifled Parrott gun, U.S. Civil War.

SOURCE: Bell I. Wiley and Hollis D. Milhollen, *They Who Fought Here* (New York: Bonanza, 1959).

Imported Confederate breech-loading gun, U.S. Civil War.

SOURCE: Bell I. Wiley and Hollis D. Milhollen, *They Who Fought Here* (New York: Bonanza, 1959).

being that of Commodore David Farragut's Gulf Squadron and its by-passing of Confederate forts at the mouth of the Mississippi in April, 1862. Farragut relied on darkness, a well-directed fire, speed, and the harassment of mortar bombs from barges. After by-passing the forts, his ships moved ninety miles up the river to capture almost-defenseless New Orleans, with 180,000 people the largest city in the South. On the other hand, if a fort had to be reduced, rifled guns taken ashore were more than a match for brickwork. The classic case was the swift reduction of Ft. Pulaski, near the mouth of the Savannah river, in 1862.

But the Northern advantage over Confederate coast defenses soon faded. The Confederates countered rifled bolts and shells with earthen mounds to absorb their impact before they could reach brick, and purely earthen forts proved formidable as well. The Confederates sowed mines at the mouths of harbors and improved the aiming technique used against moving ships. In 1863, when Admiral Samuel Du Pont's fleet tried to break-through the entrance of the harbor at Charleston, it met with a hurricane of fire as well as a mine field. The attack failed and the new "iron-clad" *Keokuk* was pierced by shot and shell ninety times before it sank. In August, 1864, Farragut's squadron "damned" the torpedoes in order to run by Ft. Morgan, but one of the Confederate mines sank the "iron-clad" *Tacumseh* within three minutes after exploding. Had the other Confederate mines worked as well, Farragut's daring would have resulted in a massacre of Union ships. Perhaps the most striking example of the effectiveness of Confederate coast defense was the resistance of earthen Ft. Fisher near the mouth of the Cape Fear River near Wilmington. It repeatedly beat off the attack of superior forces. When it finally fell in January, 1865, about twenty-five hundred soldiers and seventy-five guns had held out for three days against a hundred warships (including twenty-three "iron-clads") and eight thousand Union troops. The assembly of ships under Commodore David Porter was the largest seen under the flag of the United States during the whole of the nineteenth century. Charleston, of course, never yielded to attack from the sea. The port was abandoned after Sherman's army had cut its land communications and threatened its garrison with encirclement.

D. Geography and Strategy in the Civil War. The Appalachian mountains divided the Confederacy into two major theaters of war, the East and the West. The Eastern theater was essentially a great coastal shelf which, for the most part, lay between the Atlantic seaboard and the Appalachians. Where the mountains dwindled out in northern Georgia, the Eastern theater merged with the Western theater. South of Virginia, the coasts of the Carolinas and Georgia consisted mostly of swamps and marshes, skirted by barrier islands. Inland, coastal railroads allowed the swift movement of defending troops to any threatened point, thus preventing the easy outflanking of ports such as the British had accomplished during the American Revolution. The Union found easy only the capture of the barrier-islands, such as Hilton Head, S.C., the largest island off the Atlantic coast south of Long Island, N.Y.

In northern Virginia, the coastal shelf narrowed between Chesapeake Bay and the mountains to the west. Richmond was located in this funnel, appearing deceptively vulnerable because of its proximity to Washington and to the Potomac River, effectively the northern boundary of the Eastern Confederacy. Actually, Richmond was not geographically vulnerable at all. The hundred-mile long corridor from Richmond to Washington was crisscrossed with ridge-lines, forests and rivers, and was well-adapted to defense. Southeast of Richmond, the York and the James flowed to the Chesapeake, but in their upper courses passed through swamps and forests. When all these barriers were defended by the strongest army in the Confederacy, they were quite formidable. In addition, Union forces moving down the Shenandoah valley to the west were moving away from rather than toward, Richmond. Confederate forces going in the other direction potentially threatened Washington's communications.

Beyond the Appalachians, the Western Confederacy stretched to the

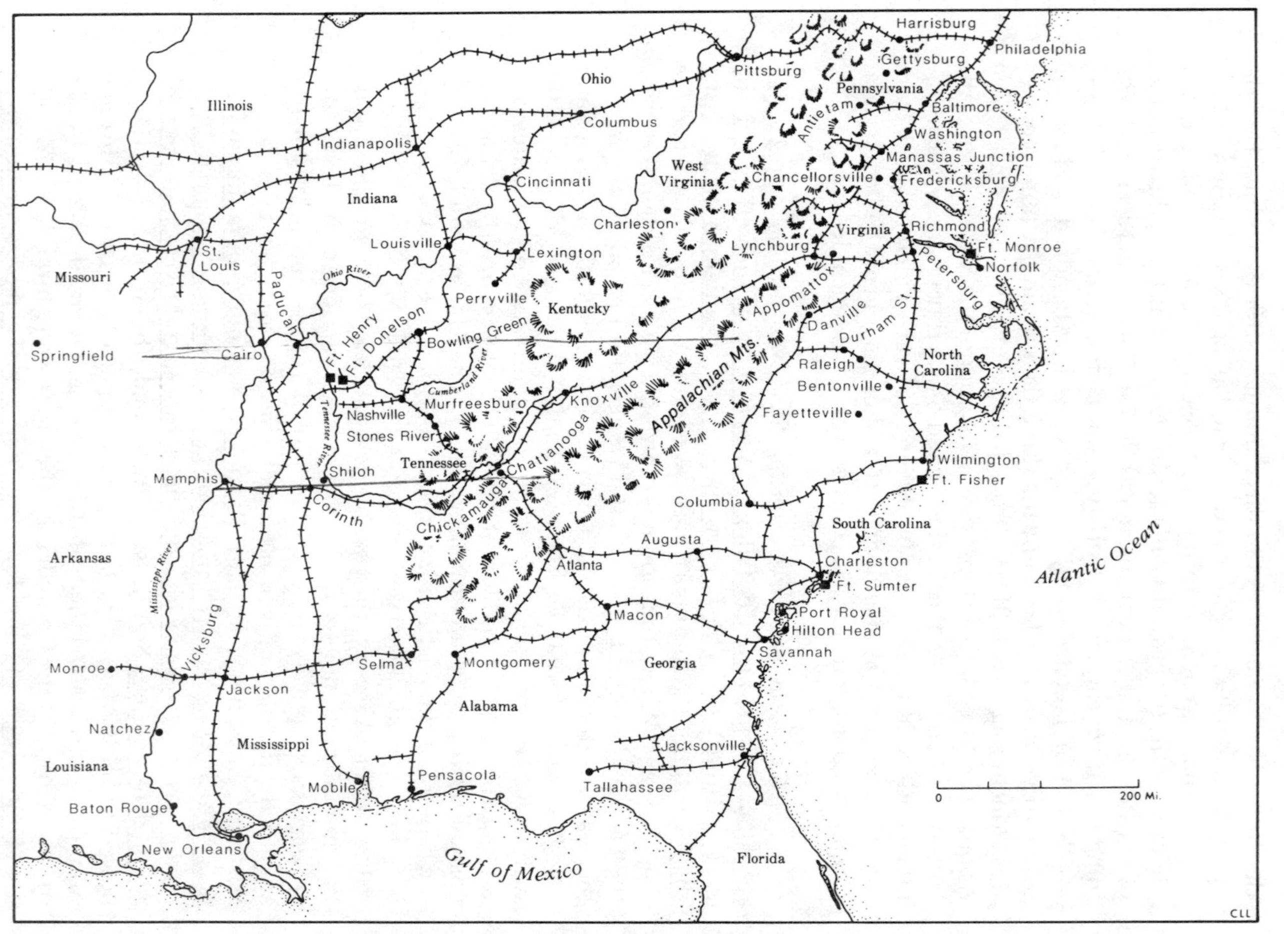

The American Civil War: The Eastern and Western Theaters

Mississippi River valley. Its Gulf coast, like the Atlantic coast of the Eastern Confederacy, was not easily penetrable except perhaps at the mouth of the Mississippi River. But unlike the rivers in the Eastern Confederacy, the major rivers in the West served the invader better than the defender, especially so when Union forces got footholds south of the Ohio. From the south bank of the Ohio, Union amphibious forces could move up the Cumberland River to Nashville, Tenn. Going up the Tennessee, they could reach Pittsburg Landing, only twenty miles from Corinth Junction, Miss., on the only continuous railroad in the South from the Atlantic coast to the Mississippi River (the Charleston-to-Memphis line). And, of course, if Union forces could ever control the Mississippi over its length, they could split the Confederacy in half and isolate the Trans-Mississippi South. The relatively fragile nature of the Western Confederacy, compared to the Eastern Confederacy, explains in part why some of the earliest Union victories were scored there, and why Union leaders gradually grasped that the solution to the Eastern Confederacy lay not in its front door in Virginia, but in its back door in Georgia. A drive from Chattanooga, also on the Charleston-to-Memphis line, to Atlanta and thence to Savannah or Charleston, would split the South still again.

E. The Strategic Direction of the Civil War. Given the Confederacy's limited resources, President Jefferson Davis believed that the goal of Southern independence was best served by a strategy which conserved those resources as much as possible and at the same time encouraged foreign intervention. His strategic thinking was, therefore, similar to that of George Washington in the American Revolution. Davis called for an active defense of Confederate territory and an embargo on cotton shipments to Britain and France. The textile industries of both countries were heavily dependent on Southern cotton (about twenty percent of the British population drew its revenue from textiles), and Davis believed that one or both countries would intervene on behalf of the Confederacy in order to secure that supply. With the consent of the Confederate Congress, Davis embargoed cotton shipments for the first year of the war, but without results. Britain and France had an eighteen-month supply of cotton when the war broke out, and they found alternative sources of supply in both Egypt and India. While Britain, especially, was willing to trade with the Confederacy after the embargo was lifted—and a thriving business developed with blockade-runners at Nassau in the British Bahamas (only 550 miles from Charleston)—the embargo only served to delay that trade a year when the Union blockade was at its weakest.

Robert E. Lee represented the other principal school of Confederate strategy. In command of the most important of the Confederate armies

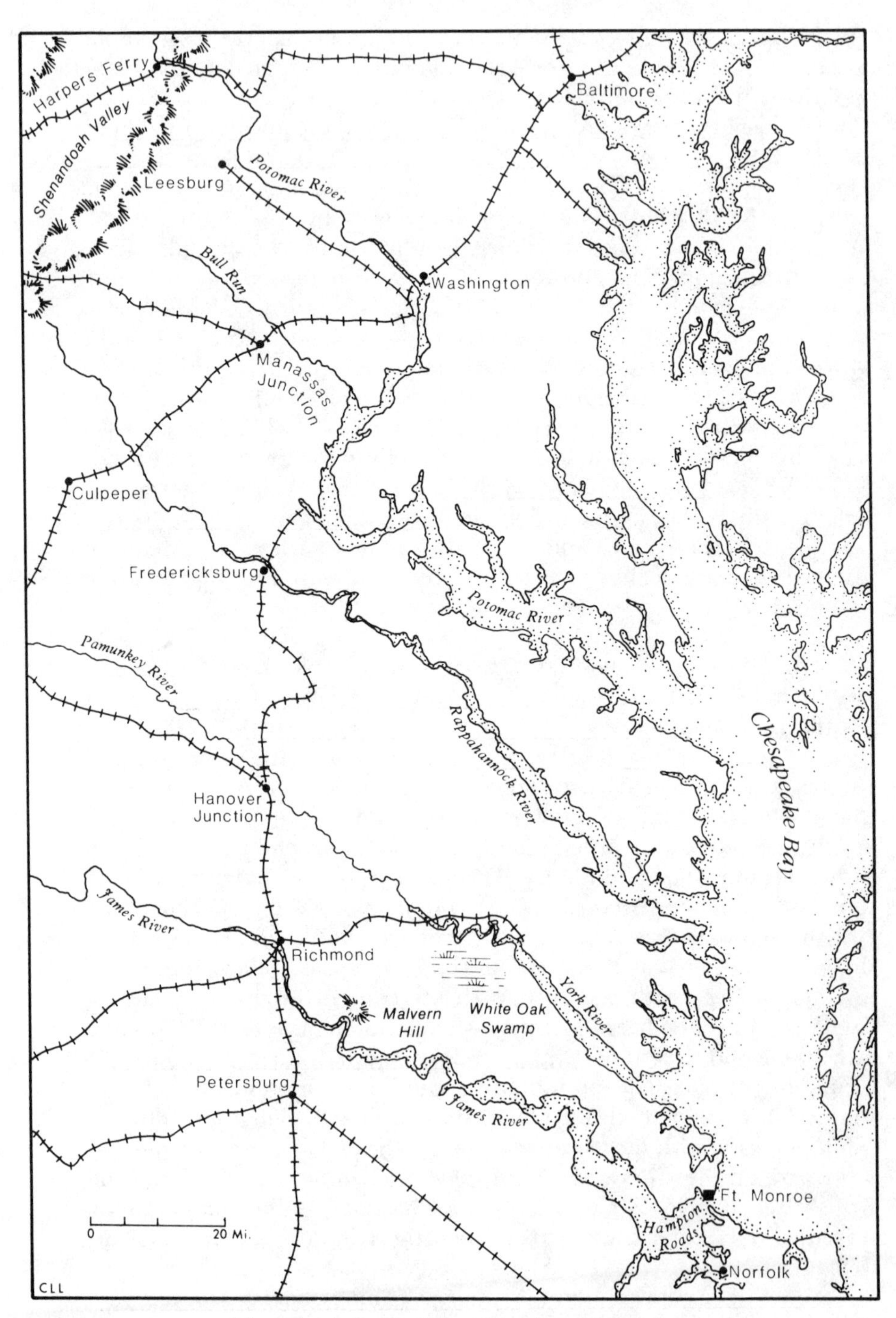

The American Civil War: Northern Virginia

after June 1, 1862, Lee had no faith in either foreign intervention or an active defense of Southern territory. He believed that the war could only be won by carrying it to the soil of the North and there winning Napoleonic victories over the Union armies. His ultimate objective was to break the Northern will to continue the war. But Lee's strategy did not accord with the tactical trends of the time. In his two great forays into the North—the first leading to Antietam in 1862 and the second to Gettysburg in 1863—the results in both cases were tactically indecisive, while almost ruinous to the Confederate army in their human cost. After Gettysburg, Lee abandoned his earlier strategy and returned to an active defense of Confederate territory, one that he knew was likely to fail eventually if the Union managed its resources well and was willing to pay a high price for the extinction of Southern independence. Perhaps there was no good Southern strategy, given the circumstances of the mid-nineteenth century, although Southern valor and determination managed to drag out the war for four years.

The North did not lack for strategic options at the beginning of the war, but it lacked a management for an effective central direction of the war effort. Old General Winfield Scott, technically commanding general until his retirement in November, 1861, wisely urged the buildup of very strong forces and then a concentration of effort against only the most vital areas of the South. But Scott's scheme was largely ignored, and the early Union efforts went after too many things at once and often with unprepared forces. From November 1861, to February, 1862, General George McClellan tried to command an army in the field and serve as general-in-chief at one time. Then, until August, 1862, Lincoln and Edwin M. Stanton, Lincoln's secretary of war, tried to function collectively as the Union high command without success. General Henry W. Halleck was brought in from the West to serve as general-in-chief, but while Halleck proved to be a good administrator, he did not turn out to be the strong strategist that Lincoln needed. The problem was only solved in March, 1864, when Lincoln appointed General U. S. Grant to the post of general-in-chief. In little over a year after that appointment, concerted Union operations brought about the final fall of the Confederacy. Had an effective Union high command existed early in the war, it might have been shortened by years.

F. The Eastern Theater to May, 1864. In July, 1861 35,000 inexperienced Federal troops under General Irving McDowell tried to seize Richmond by an overland drive from Washington, only to be routed on the banks of Bull Run just twenty miles southwest of Washington by a like number of Confederate soldiers under General Joseph E. Johnston. In the aftermath, General George McClellan assumed command of the Army of the Potomac, the most important of the Union armies in the

East. In early 1862, McClellan moved 90,000 troops to Ft. Monroe at the tip of the peninsula between the York and James rivers, and tried to approach Richmond from the southeast. Johnston, with only 60,000 troops, fought delaying actions until McClellan's army was quite close to Richmond. Then on May 31, at Fair Oaks, the Confederate army attacked only to be repelled with heavy loss. Johnston was seriously wounded into the bargain. On June 1, 1862, Robert E. Lee succeeded to the command of the Army of Northern Virginia.

In the wake of the Battle of Fair Oaks (or Seven Pines), Lee fortified Richmond and called up reinforcements. McClellan decided to wait until his army could be reinforced before making his final attack on Richmond. Meanwhile, a detached Confederate corps in the Shenandoah valley under General Thomas J. "Stonewall" Jackson had inflicted several defeats on small Union forces entering the valley, finally causing President Lincoln to divert reinforcements there instead of to McClellan. Jackson's corps then moved by rail to join Lee's army at Richmond. By June 25, Lee stood at the head of 80,000 troops, the largest army he was ever to command and only marginally smaller than McClellan's army.

In the Seven Days' Battle (June 26–July 1, 1862), the Lee-Jackson team outmaneuvered McClellan every day but the last, and forced his army to withdraw down the James River to a position dominated by Malvern Hill. Then, with no Union flank to turn, Lee tried to smash through the Union center, losing 5,000 men to no purpose. The campaign was at a stalemate, but Richmond was secure. A frustrated Lincoln then ordered the troops in the Shenandoah Valley assembled at Manassas Junction, two miles south of Bull Run, under General John Pope. Pope's 60,000 men were to approach Richmond from the north while McClellan kept Lee's army tied to the James. When Pope's army began to move in August, Lee detached Jackson's corps to deal with the threat. Jackson's corps managed to turn the western flank of Pope's army as it groped its way south, then to get into its rear and to burn its base at Manassas Junction. Lincoln was so alarmed that he ordered McClellan to bring his army back to Washington by way of the Chesapeake in order to aid Pope. But McClellan's withdrawal freed Lee's army to come to Jackson's aid, and his army could move faster by rail overland part of the way than McClellan's could move by water. The result was that as Pope's army finally cornered Jackson's corps in a railway cut on the old Bull Run battlefield, it was struck in the flank and rear by Lee's arriving troops. The Union forces were badly defeated at Second Bull Run (August 30–31), and McClellan's army only arrived in time to cover Pope's retreat into Washington.

With the initiative passed to the Confederates, Lee led 57,000 troops across the Potomac west of the Blue Ridge and into the Cumberland

Valley in September, 1862. His aim was to recross the mountains further north, sever Washington's communications, and force McClellan's army into the open for a final battle. But faulty Confederate security allowed McClellan to divine Lee's intentions and the fact that he had temporarily divided his army. With unusual vigor for him, McClellan pushed his troops across the mountains and cornered part of Lee's army near Sharpsburg, Md., on the banks of Antietam Creek. There, on September 17 occurred the bloodiest single-day's battle of the war. Lee's army, 47,000 men against 90,000 Union troops, barely managed to hold until Jackson's corps arrived from Harper's Ferry. The battle ended a tactical draw, with 12,000 Confederate casualties to 15,000 Union casualties. The next night Lee ordered his army to begin withdrawing to Virginia. Five days after the Battle of Antietam, a Union strategic victory, Lincoln issued the Emancipation Proclamation, effective January 1, 1863.

Lee withdrew his army to a defensive position at Fredericksburg, Va., on the Rappahannock River, equally distant between Richmond and Washington. Ambrose Burnside relieved McClellan of command, and in December, 1862, his army tried to bull its way across the river at Fredericksburg only to fail and to lose 13,000 men in the process. Joseph Hooker replaced Burnside, and in April, 1863, his army tried to turn Lee's position at Fredericksburg by crossing the Rappahannock upstream at Chancellorsville. Hooker managed to get his army south of the river and dug-in facing in the direction of Fredericksburg before Lee's army could arrive, but he had left his right flank unprotected in the woods. On May 2, Jackson's corps worked its way around the Union flank and late in the day launched an attack that nearly drove Hooker's army into the Rappahannock. But in fading light, Jackson was fired on by his own men by mistake, and in the confusion of a change in command, Hooker managed to avert the worst disaster. On May 4, however, he withdrew his army north of the river, having lost 17,000 men to Lee's 13,000. The critically wounded Jackson died on May 10. No other Confederate general serving under Lee proved as able.

The climax of the war in the East approached when Lee assembled 75,000 troops and launched his second invasion north of the Potomac. As in 1862, his army marched up the Cumberland Valley, this time reaching southern Pennsylvania before recrossing the mountains to the east. Five days before the pivotal battle of the Civil War, Hooker resigned after a quarrel with Lincoln over strategy. Lincoln appointed George Meade, a corps commander, as his replacement. Some of Lee's troops ran into Union soldiers just outside the crossroads town of Gettysburg on July 1. The Union troops were driven back to heights behind the town by nightfall. By July 2, both armies were assembled. Meade's 90,000 troops remained on defense. For two days running, Lee attacked the left, right, and center of the Union position, with only the loss of

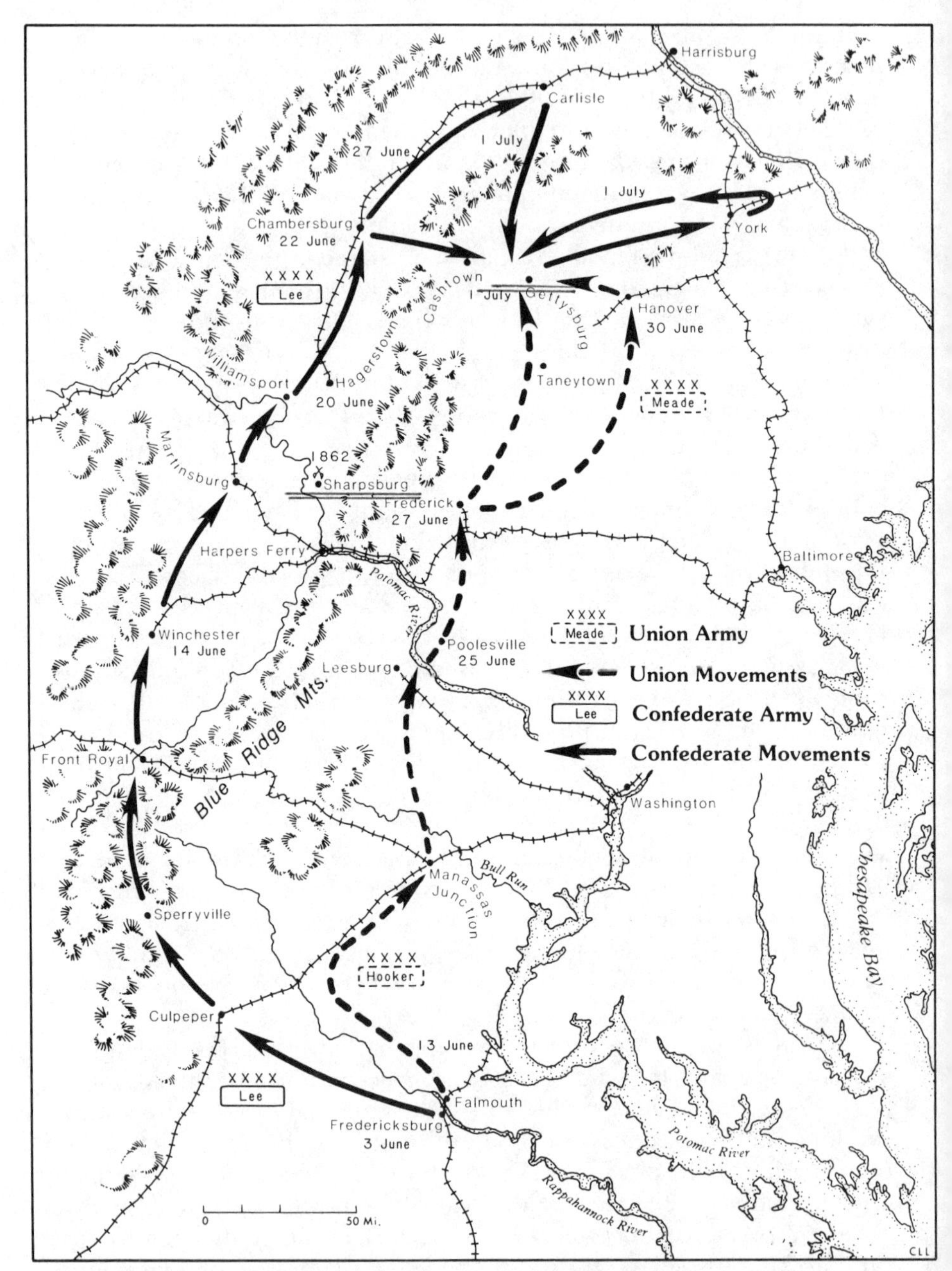

The American Civil War: The Gettysburg Campaign, 1863

23,000 men to show for his pains. Meade had lost 20,000 men, but he could more easily replace them. The battle lulled on July 4, and that night Lee's army began its retreat to Virginia. The greatest of the Confederate commanders had failed to find that Napoleonic victory which he had hoped would end the war and bring about Southern independence. Meade, grateful for his defensive victory, cautiously followed Lee, still a formidable adversary.

Gettysburg
July '63

Gettysburg, like Antietam, was a tactical draw but a strategic victory for the Union. Its detrimental effects on the Army of Northern Virginia were long-lasting. Lee's army, shorn of much of its strength, took up its old defensive position at Fredericksburg, where it was still strong enough to block the way to Richmond, but not strong enough to launch any more offensives into northern territory. Meade's army, which soon made up its losses, camped north of the Rappahannock but made no effort to force its way across until May, 1864. Thus, after Gettysburg, a long lull settled over the front in northern Virginia. Lincoln put no pressure on Meade to act. By then it was becoming clear to him that the war was being won in the West, and the fate of the Eastern Confederacy would finally hinge on that outcome. Both Lee and Meade sent reinforcements to the West in the fall of 1863, but the pendulum there swung ever further in the Union favor. Lee would continue to fight resolutely at the front door of the Confederate mansion to the end of the war, but its rooms were being destroyed one by one in his rear. When the front door finally collapsed in the spring of 1865, there was little left intact behind it.

G. The Western Theater to May, 1864. In 1861, General Albert S. Johnston, Confederate commander-in-chief of the Western Confederacy, tried to guard against Union invasions from the Ohio Valley and down the Mississippi by creating a chain of forts and camps along the major waterways and railroads leading into the South. But a cordon-defense is only as strong as its weakest link. In February, 1862, Ft. Henry on the Tennessee River was flooded and was thus easily captured by 40,000 Union troops, under General U. S. Grant, when they came upstream on steamers. Grant's army then marched the twelve miles to the rear of Ft. Donelson on the Cumberland River and, in concert with Union gunboats, captured the fort and 12,000 Confederates in March. Another Union army of 40,000 troops, under General Don Carlos Buell, moved by the Cumberland and the railroad from Louisville, Ky., to occupy Nashville, Tenn. Grant's army went back to the Tennessee and then up the river as far as Pittsburgh Landing, only twenty miles from the vital rail junctin at Corinth, Miss. He went no further, on orders from General Henry Halleck, then Grant's superior, that his army should wait to seize Corinth until it was reinforced by Buell's army from Nashville.

The Union delay allowed Johnston time in which to concentrate 35,000 Confederate soldiers at Corinth and to prepare an offensive against Grant's army before Buell's army could arrive at Pittsburg Landing from Nashville. Johnston's plan almost worked. At dawn on April 6, his army caught Grant's army by surprise, while it was camped around Shiloh Church, and in the absence of its commander, who was down river on an errand. The Confederate assault almost drove the leaderless Federal troops into the Tennessee River, but Johnston was mortally wounded early in the fighting, and there was a Confederate delay while P.G.T. Beauregard assumed command. On the Union side, William T. Sherman assumed the chief command. The Federal forces then managed to maintain a foothold on the Tennessee River until nightfall, and Grant's return. Later that evening, Buell's army arrived on the other bank and was transferred across the river. The Union attack on April 7 recovered part of Grant's camp, but both armies were exhausted by the end of the day. That night Beauregard ordered a Confederate retirement to Corinth, and the Battle of Shiloh came to its end. The Confederates had lost 10,000 troops to a Union loss of 13,000 men, but Buell's arrival had more than offset Grant's losses.

The super-cautious Halleck delayed the final push on Corinth until 110,000 Federal soldiers had been assembled, and Beauregard gave up the rail junction without a fight on May 31. After the fall of Memphis to Union forces coming down the Mississippi, and the fall of New Orleans to Farragut's fleet on May 1, the only remaining Confederate links to the Trans-Mississippi South were at Vicksburg and Port Hudson. Their rapid capture might have been accomplished in 1862 had the Union forces remained concentrated, but Buell's army went back to Nashville when a new Confederate army assembled at Chattanooga under General Braxton Bragg. Buell's victory at Perryville, Ky., in September narrowly averted a severing of his communications to Louisville when Bragg launched an offensive through eastern Tennessee and into Kentucky, but Lincoln relieved Buell of command and replaced him with General William S. Rosecrans. Bragg's army retired to a defensive position at Stones River near Murfreesboro, Tenn., where it could cover the approaches to Chattanooga. At the turn of the year, Rosecran's attempt to drive Bragg from that position led to such a bloody battle that both armies were incapable of offensive operations for months after. In effect, a stalemate settled over the war in central Tennessee.

Grant's repeated efforts to get at Vicksburg in 1862 and in early 1863 all failed. Then, in April, part of his army marched down the west bank of the Mississippi below Vicksburg, and was transported to the other side after transports ran by the Vicksburg batteries by night. Instead of attacking Vicksburg from the south, as General John C. Pemberton, the Confederate commander, expected, Grant took a leaf out of Scott's book, dropped his communications to the river, and struck out for Jackson, Miss., a rail junction and Vicksburg's supply center. His sudden arrival there enabled his troops to capture the supplies they needed, and Grant's army beat off Pemberton's attempt to reestablish his communications at the Battle of Champion's Hill. The Vicksburg garrison was forced back into its works, Grant reestablished contact with his forces on the Mississippi, and the Union forces imposed a tight siege on Vicksburg. Pemberton surrendered the twenty thousand men of his starving garrison on July 4, the night on which Lee began his retreat from Gettysburg. Four days later Port Hudson fell, and the entire length of the Mississippi River was in Union hands.

In September, 1863, Rosecrans maneuvered Bragg out of Chattanooga, and the Confederate army withdrew over the state line into Georgia. But the arrival of James Longstreet's corps from Lee's army enabled Bragg to defeat the advancing Rosecrans at Chickamauga Creek and to pursue his shaken force to Chattanooga. Thanks to a rear-guard action by General George Thomas, Rosecrans were able to man the city's defenses and to deny Bragg entry, but his army was soon under siege. The fate of the garrison in Chattanooga seemed likely to be that of the garrison in Vicksburg.

Lincoln dealt with the crisis by appointing Grant to command an army of relief assembled from forces in the West and reinforcements sent by Meade from the East. Grant managed to arrange a line of supply and reinforcement to the Union army inside Chattanooga, and to replace Rosecrans with Thomas as its commander. While the army inside Chattanooga was increasing in strength, Bragg weakened his army by sending off Longstreet's corps to Knoxville to besiege another Union army. The scene was set for a Confederate disaster. In the three-day Battle of Chattanooga, in late November, 1863, the army that Grant had assembled inside the city broke through Bragg's weak lines and forced his army to make a hasty withdrawal into Georgia. The relief of Chattanooga set Lincoln's stamp of approval on Grant.

H. The Final Campaigns, May 1864–April 1865. After the turn of the year, Grant was appointed as general-in-chief of Union armies and promoted to the rank of lieutenant-general. He made his headquarters with Meade's Army of the Potomac, leaving the chief command in the West to Sherman. His plan for ending the war was both simple and sensible. Meade's army, then 134,000-men strong, would attempt to drive Lee's army back on Richmond and prevent any transfers of its forces to the West. Sherman's army, 100,000 troops, would launch a drive from Chattanooga to Atlanta, and thence to either Charleston or

Savannah. If successful, his drive would split the South in half again and permit Sherman's army to threaten the Carolinas and southern Virginia. At some point, Grant reasoned, Confederate resistance would collapse.

Within the same twenty-four-hour period in early May, 1864, both Meade's and Sherman's offensives got underway, while lesser Union forces maintained pressure wherever they could. After terrible battles in the Wilderness, at Spottsylvania Courthouse and Cold Harbor, Meade's army had lost sixty thousand men but had driven Lee's army behind the defenses of Richmond again for the first time since June, 1862. In the fighting, Lee had lost a third of his sixty thousand troops. The fighting had also taken Meade's army to the vicinity of the old Seven Days' Battlefield in a month's time, and Grant ordered it to try to outflank Lee's army by a jump south of the James and a rush to seize the rail junction of Petersburg. Lee's army narrowly blocked the move on Petersburg, and in July the Union offensive settled down to a siege of the Richmond-Petersburg lines. Jubal Early's diversion in the Shenandoah valley did not shake Grant's determination to maintain his grip on Richmond. That fall, a Union army under General Philip Sheridan ran Early's force to ground, destroyed it, and then devastated the Shenandoah valley. Though Grant could not take Richmond for months, Meade's efforts had prevented Lee from sending help to the West as in 1863.

Joseph Johnston and sixty thousand Confederate troops skillfully resisted Sherman's drive on Atlanta during the spring and summer of 1864. As they gradually fell back on the defenses of Atlanta, they inflicted a bloody repulse on Sherman's attack at Kennesaw Mountain. But Jefferson Davis relieved Johnston of command and replaced him with John Bell Hood. Hood rashly took up the offensive, and his attacks on Sherman's army nearly gutted his own. When his force was reduced to twenty thousand men by the end of August, Hood withdrew it to eastern Alabama. Sherman's army occupied Atlanta on September 1. Subsequently, Hood tried to threaten Sherman's communications in Tennessee, but Sherman sent Thomas and forty thousand troops to deal with the threat. Hood was first rebuffed at Franklin, and then his army was effectively destroyed at the Battle of Nashville in December. In November, Sherman and sixty thousand troops dropped their communications and launched a drive across central Georgia, foraging and devastating the countryside until they reached Savannah in December. By the end of 1864, Georgia was effectively out of the war and the Confederacy had been cut in half again. Having presented Savannah to Lincoln as a symbolic "Christmas present," Sherman resupplied his forces from the sea and turned to the task of removing the Carolinas from the war by a northward drive.

In January, 1865, Sherman's army headed north into South Carolina, but by a route that took it to Columbia, the state capital. After burning

Columbia in February, Sherman's army moved toward Fayetteville, N.C. As in Georgia, it destroyed as it went and so completely severed the communications of the garrison defending Charleston that the Confederacy was forced to abandon the port which had defied attack from the sea for almost four years. Wilmington had fallen to other Union forces in January, and as Sherman's army marched to link up with those forces at Goldsboro in eastern North Carolina, the last organized major resistance it was to encounter took place at Bentonville in mid-March. There twenty thousand Confederate troops under Johnston fought for two days before withdrawing further north. Having resupplied and strengthened his army at Goldsboro, Sherman moved on to occupy Raleigh, the state capital, and he was preparing for a drive into southern Virginia when, in early April, the Union attacks at Richmond finally broke Lee's lines. Lee withdrew the remains of his army toward Lynchburg and a cache of supplies, but its way was finally blocked by Sheridan's cavalry at Appomattox Courthouse. Lee surrendered his remaining twenty-six thousand men to Grant on April 9. Later that month, Johnston surrendered his command to Sherman at Durham Station, N.C. By the time of the two surrenders, there was little left in the South to defend.

V. The Wars of German Unification, 1864–71

The final wars of the mid-nineteenth century were associated with the process of unification of the states of Germany under the monarchy of Hohenzollern Prussia. None of the three conflicts lasted as long as a year, even though those of 1866 and 1870 opposed major powers. During the Austro-Prussian War (1866) occurred the greatest battle of the nineteenth century—Königgrätz or Sadowa—in which more men fought than even at Leipzig, the greatest battle of the Napoleonic Wars. The number was more than twice the number of men who fought at Gettysburg, the greatest battle of the American Civil War. The chief reasons for these quick German victories were the excellence of the Prussian General Staff, the soundness of the Prusso-German *Nation-in-Arms,* and the comparative mediocrity of opposing armies.

A. The Danish War and the Austro-Prussian Wars, 1864 and 1866. When the King of Denmark refused to allow the provinces of Schleswig and Holstein, his personal possessions since the Congress of Vienna, to become members of the Germanic Confederation, the Confederation declared war on Denmark, and both Prussia and Austria put armies into the field. The small Danish army, armed with cap-and-ball rifles, put up a brave resistance in a fortified position at Düppel on the

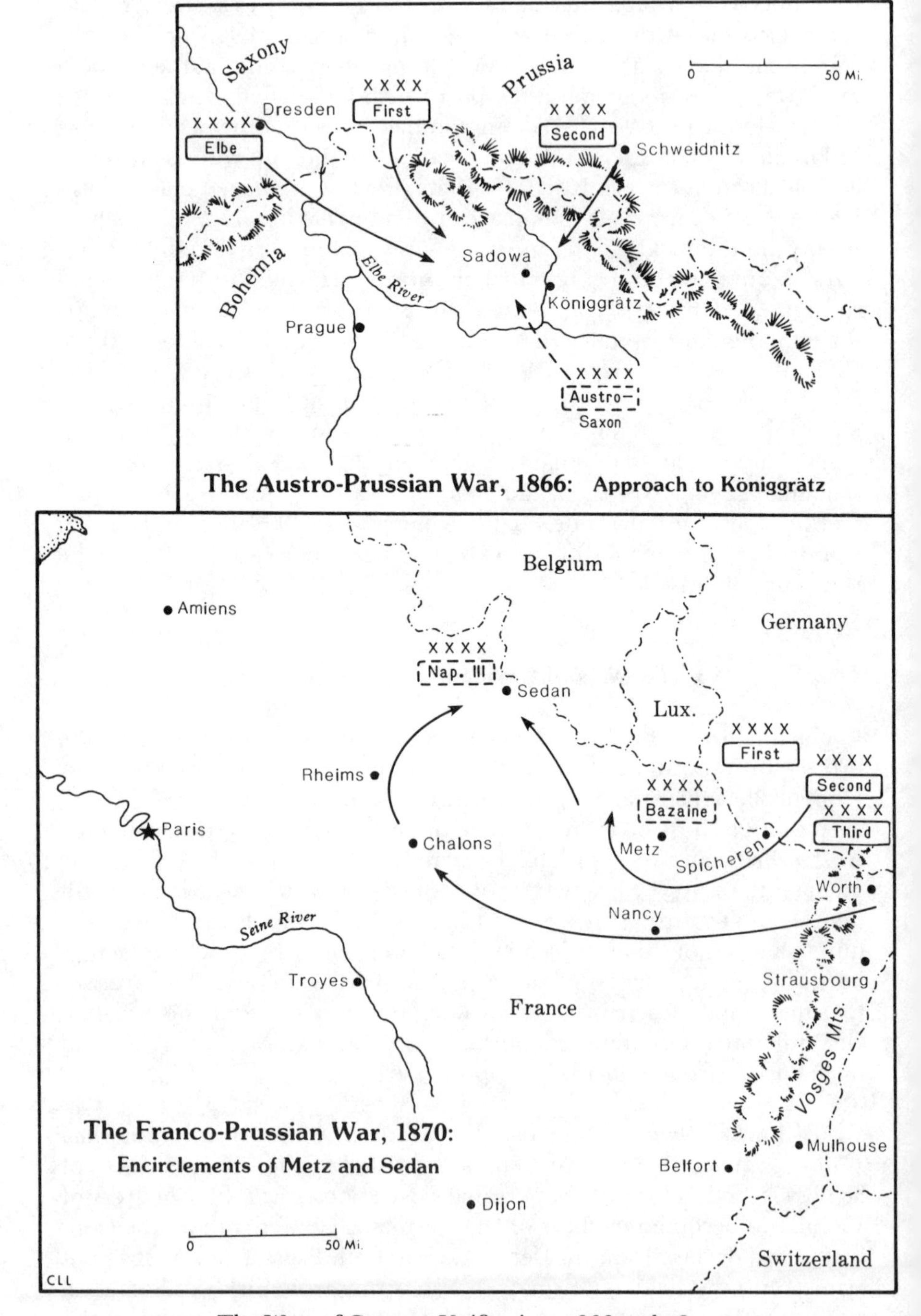

The Wars of German Unification, 1866 and 1870

Jutland peninsula, and, as mentioned earlier, it was from that experience that Helmuth von Moltke, chief of the Prussian General Staff, first gained insight regarding the effects of the new firepower on tactics. The combined armed strength of the Austro-Prussian powers proved too much for Denmark, however, and the Danish king was compelled to accept the inclusion of Schleswig and Holstein in the Germanic Confederation under the administration of Prussia and Austria.

By 1866, Otto von Bismarck was ready to risk war in order to expel Austria from the Germanic Confederation, a first step in extending Prussian domination over Germany. Bismarck manufactured a quarrel with Austria over the administration of Schleswig-Holstein, and so provoked the Hapsburg government that in June the other German states sided with Austria in declaring war on Prussia. France and Russia declared their neutralities as the result of Bismarckian diplomacy, but the new Kingdom of Italy lined up with Prussia, in hopes of gaining the province of Venetia from Austria as an outcome of the war. Superficially, the Austrian and Prussian armies seemed well matched, each being able to mobilize about 500,000 troops initially. Austria's artillery was nearly all rifled, if muzzle-loading, while about half the Prussian guns were muzzle-loading smoothbores and the other half were Krupp-made rifled breech-loading guns. Austrian infantry were armed with the muzzle-loading Lorenz cap-and-ball rifle, the Prussian infantry with the Dreyse breech-loading rifle (the so-called needle gun, for its long firing-pin). The Lorenz had superior range and accuracy, but the Dreyse could be fired by troops lying down or kneeling. Austrian cavalry was generally considered to be better than the Prussian. Taken in all, Prussia did not have a great technological advantage over Austria. Her advantages were rather her *Nation-in-Arms*, an excellent General Staff, a sound doctrine of war, and the fact that Bismarck's diplomacy insured that Austria would have to fight on two fronts at once and with only weak support from her German allies.

The Prussian General Staff implemented its contingency plan at the outbreak of war. Three field armies, totaling two hundred fifty thousand troops, took the field against Austria, while the rest of the Prussian forces overawed other German states and stood guard against foreign intervention. In contrast to the smooth Prussian mobilization, the Austrian mobilization was disorderly, and confused by the Italian declaration of war. Lieutenant-Field-Marshal Ludwig von Benedek was belatedly appointed to command the Northern Army assembling in Bohemia, about two hundred thirty thousand troops. It was still not ready for action when, on June 16, the Prussian Army of the Elbe invaded the territory of the King of Saxony, by then Austria's most reliable German ally, and forced his army of 32,000 troops to retreat into Bohemia. Benedek hastened to join his forces with the Saxons near

Königgrätz, a city and a key rail junction fifty miles south of the Prussian border. Meanwhile, the Prussian First Army absorbed the Army of the Elbe as it advanced across the low mountains shielding Bohemia and approached Königgrätz from the northwest. The Prussian Second Army approached from the northeast. Benedek deployed his combined forces of 262,000 troops around the village of Sadowa and west of the river Elbe, rather than east as Moltke had expected. On the morning of July 3, exactly three years after the Battle of Gettysburg, the First Army under Prince Frederick-Charles unexpectedly collided with the front of the Austrian army in a heavy fog and commenced a major battle. Though outnumbered, the First Army managed to hold out for most of the day, until the Second Army arrived to inflict a fatal thrust into the flank of the Austro-Saxon forces. Benedek managed to cover the retreat of his army across the Elbe with cavalry charges, but he had lost 44,000 men and his army was too dispirited to fight again. The Prussian losses came to just 9,000 men. Within a few days, the Hapsburg government asked for an armistice, and the Peace of Prague, ending the so-called Seven Weeks' War, was signed in August.

On the Italian front, the Austrians had hurled back all invasions of Venetia, but the province was lost to Italy under the terms of peace. The most interesting combat between Italians and Austrians was not on land, but at sea. On July 20, Admiral Wilhelm von Tegetthoff's Austrian fleet engaged the Italian fleet of Admiral Count Carlo di Persano off the island of Lissa in the Adriatic Sea. Tegetthoff formed his seven inferior "iron-clad" warships and fourteen wooden warships in a "V" formation and charged the center of the Italian line at right angles to the Austrian fleet. In the confused mélée which followed, the large Italian armored ship *Re d'Italia* was rammed and sunk, and Austrian gunfire fatally damaged two smaller Italian "iron-clads." A total of 667 Italian sailors were killed and another 39 were injured. Tegetthoff lost no ships, and his casualties were limited to 38 Austrian sailors killed and 138 wounded. In the absence of a more recent fleet engagement to study until 1893, both naval tacticians and architects were influenced by the Battle of Lissa in their provision for ramming tactics and the inclusion of rams in the bows of ships long after the prospect of getting close enough to ram had passed. But Lissa was the last fleet action on the high seas of the mid-nineteenth century and, except for the American Civil War, the value of command of the sea was brought into question by the outcomes of both the Austro-Prussian and the Franco-Prussian wars.

The Peace of Prague dissolved the Germanic Confederation created in 1815 and excluded Austria henceforth from German affairs. The Protestant German states north of the Main River were brought into union with Prussia as the North German Confederation in 1867, a union headed by King William I of Prussia. The Catholic German states south of the Main signed treaties of defensive alliance with the North German Confederation. Also in 1867, in order to appease the Magyars of Hungary, Emperor Francis-Joseph was forced to reorganize the Hapsburg domains into the Dual Monarchy of the Austro-Hungarian Empire. The two halves of the empire were joined only in the person of the monarch, a common army, and a common foreign office. Down to the early twentieth century, the agitation of other minorities within the empire for more autonomy further weakened the military potential of Austria-Hungary. In contrast, first the union of the north German states under Prussia in 1867, and then the unification of all Germany under the Hohenzollern dynasty in 1871, confirmed the fact that the seat of power in Central Europe had shifted from Vienna to Berlin. Indeed, Imperial Germany was to emerge as the single strongest military state in Europe.

B. The Franco-Prussian War, 1870–71. Napoleon III was deeply troubled, first by the outcome of the Austro-Prussian or Seven Weeks' War, and then by the union of the north German states under Prussia in 1867. In effect, a new and powerful German political unit had emerged on the eastern frontier of France. Accordingly, Napoleon directed a reform of his military forces, accepting a proposal for a larger and more nationalized army from Marshal Adolphe Niel, the minister of war, in 1868. Under the laws passed to implement Niel's plan, the number of annual conscripts would be greatly increased, a four-year active-duty obligation being imposed on some and a five-month active-duty stint, followed by a long period in the army reserve, being imposed on others. Men who secured exemption from either of the other two forms of obligatory service were required to enroll in a *Garde Nationale Mobile,* a semi-trained militia which was supposed to be somewhat like the German *Landwehr.* Had the reform gone as Napoleon intended, and had war not come sooner, by 1875 the Imperial Army would have consisted of a mobilizable force of 800,000 troops, backed by a *Garde Mobile* of 500,000 men. In practice, the reform had scarcely got underway when war came, and both the mobilizations of the reserve and the *Garde Mobile* were botched. In reality, at the outbreak of the Franco-Prussian War, the only French force that counted was a relatively small *armée de métier* of 350,000 troops.

Napoleon III also tried to reform French armaments. By 1870 French infantry had been issued the Chassepot rifle, a better breech-loader than the Prussian Dreyse. France was also producing the *mitrailleuse,* an early machine-gun mounted on an artillery carriage, and similar to the Gatling gun of the American Civil War. But the *mitrailleuse* was kept so secret that few French commanders had any idea as to how to get the most out of it; while, in contrast to the Prussian artillery which by 1870 was entirely equipped with steel Krupp breech-loading guns, French artillery was still armed with the rifled, muzzle-loading guns with which it had confronted the Austrians in 1859. But the areas of fatal French inferiority to Prussia-Germany were not primarily technological. They were, in fact, an inferior command and staff system, a flawed system of mobilization, and an unsuitable doctrine of war.

In contrast to the fumbling French efforts toward military reform before 1870, the Prussian General Staff worked effectively to apply the lessons from the experiences of 1866. Besides a reform of the Prussian artillery by 1870, in 1867 the revised *Kesselschlacht* doctrine was issued, a sound doctrine, as it turned out, against the French in 1870. By 1870, Moltke could mobilize 500,000 German troops in the Rhineland in a little over two weeks, and the army of the North German Confederation could be tripled within six months. The standards of Prussian staff work were passed on to the rest of the German army. Perhaps it is not surprising that when Bismarck asked Moltke how favorable were the odds on the eve of the Franco-Prussian War, Moltke replied that they were 80 percent in the German favor.

The genesis of the Franco-Prussian War was a quarrel between Napoleon III and William I over the candidacy of William's cousin to the then-vacant throne of Spain. In July, 1870, when pressed by Napoleon's ambassador to withdraw the candidacy, William agreed, but he refused a second demand to make his dynasty forever ineligible. Bad feelings had been aroused in both France and Germany over the issue and, his second demand refused, Napoleon apparently believed that he had no choice but to declare war or lose face with the French people. The French declaration of war on July 19, however, not only made France appear as the aggressor, and thereby reduced the chances of foreign intervention on the side of France, it also served to trigger the defensive alliances between the North German Confederation and the German states south of the Main. The wave of nationalism which swept over Germans in the summer of 1870 would enable Bismarck to move forward swiftly with the final steps toward political unification of Germany under the house of Hohenzollern.

By the end of the first week in August, 1870, Moltke had assembled 500,000 German troops in three armies on the French frontier. In contrast, only two French army corps had reached the frontier area, and they were divided by the line of the Vosges mountains. Further west, Marshal François Bazaine was laboriously cobbling together an army at Metz from 180,000 troops. Between Metz and Paris, another 124,000 troops were being gradually assembled into an army. Moltke grasped the opportunity to seize the initiative. Two German armies promptly attacked the lone French corps on Spicheren Heights, overlooking Saarbrücken, while a third German army attacked the French corps on the other side of the Vosges at Wörth (Fröschwiller), both offensives beginning on August 6. As the outnumbered French corps retreated, two German armies penetrated the Lorraine Gap and wheeled south of Metz. They severed Bazaine's line of retreat, beat back his attempts to withdraw from Metz at the battles of Mars-la-Tour and Gravelotte, and imposed a siege on his army. The third German army probed further west. Napoleon III, mortified by the defeats at the frontier and the encirclement of Metz, took personal command of his 124,000 troops at Chalons-sur-Marne, and, with the assistance of Marshal Patrice MacMahon, tried to bring Bazaine relief by approaching from the direction of the Belgian border. The third German army promptly followed the French army north, while a German army at Metz peeled off in order to close on the French front. About 250,000 German troops finally composed the force that encircled Napoleon's army on September 1 in a perfect *Kesselschlacht* near the small town of Sedan. A total of 20,000 French soldiers were mowed down by Prussian artillery and small-arms fire, while vainly attempting to break out of the ring, and on September 2 Napoleon surrendered himself and the remaining 104,000 troops under his command. The surrender was the largest in the field in modern times.

Following their victory at Sedan, the German forces not occupied in besieging Metz began an advance on Paris. While they were on their way, a revolution in the French capital toppled the headless Second Empire and established the Third Republic and a Government of National Defense. General Louis Trochu, formerly one of Napoleon's generals, was prevailed upon to head the new republic, but its real driving force was Leon Gambetta, the minister of the interior. He encouraged Trochu to defend Paris with its regular garrison, the forts surrounding the city, and the Parisian National Guard. Meanwhile, a delegation of the government would be sent to Tours in order to direct a *levée en masse* and the building of new armies. France still had her ports; her navy was intact; and she could import new weapons and other items of war. It was vital, however, that the defense of Metz and Paris tie down so many German troops that Moltke could not attempt to occupy the rest of France for a few months.

In fact, Moltke was alarmed by the new French strategy. Though he staged artillery bombardments of Paris in order to placate Bismarck, who feared that if the war went on too long other powers might get involved, Moltke knew that the only sure means was starvation. With troops also besieging Metz, he lacked the means to take Paris, a city of 2 million people in 1870, by storm. In addition, the only functioning railroad from Germany to Paris (via Strasbourg) was barely able to meet the German need in munitions. For food and fodder, the German troops had to live off the country. Fortunately for the Germans, Bazaine surrendered his 180,000 troops at Metz on October 31, months before a surrender was expected. By November, the Germans had regrouped to beat off the attacks of the new French armies in the south and the west, and also to repel a sortie by the French garrison in Paris. In December, the logistical situation eased, and Moltke was able to concentrate a million German soldiers on French soil. By then, too, it was becoming clear that the German *Nation-in-Arms* had been more than a match for either the French *armée de métier* or the French *levée en masse*.

On January 17, 1871, William I of Prussia was crowned *Kaiser* (Emperor) of Germany at Versailles, and the Second Reich was born. Paris surrendered ten days later, and a general armistice went into effect on January 30. A French National Convention meeting in Bordeaux approved a new government led by Adolphe Thiers and empowered it to make peace with the Second Reich. Just after the Germans vacated Paris in early March, radicals seized control of the Paris Commune (city government) and refused to recognize the new French government, seated at Versailles, or any peace it might make with Germany. Bismarck consented to French troops resorting to force in order to restore the French government's authority in the capital, and subsequently more Frenchmen died in the suppression of the Commune than during the German siege of Paris. The last vestiges of resistance were still being stamped out when the Peace of Frankfurt was signed on May 10, 1871. Under its terms, France lost the provinces of Alsace-Lorraine to Germany, had to pay off a large war indemnity, and had to submit to German occupation of fortresses in eastern France until the indemnity was paid. The last German soldier left French soil in 1873. In addition, the war had cost France 238,000 casualties. The German losses came to 133,750 men.

3

The March toward World War, 1871–1914

I. Armies

A. The Spread of the German System and the Technology of Land Warfare. In the years after 1871, France, Italy, Austria-Hungary, and Russia followed Germany in adopting the *Nation-in-Arms* and the German-style war college and general staff. The size of the major European armies kept pace with the growing populations and national budgets. Defense expenditures also provided for the training, arming, and equipping of the reserves. As the proficiency of the general staffs increased across Europe, ever larger numbers of men could be mobilized in less time. The mobilization plans dovetailed with the initial offensive plans of each army in such a way that the early movements were foreordained. Their complexity was such that, once mobilization was begun, it could not be stopped or altered extensively without risking chaos. Long before 1914, European governments had come to view the very act of general mobilization as tantamount to an act of war, and thus in any diplomatic crisis there was always the danger that one side or the other might "panic forward."

France made a heroic effort to keep up with German military development before 1914. In 1872, the Third Republic imposed universal liability to compulsory military service on all Frenchmen of military age, and by 1880 most of them were required to perform three years of service in the army, followed by four years in the army's reserve. In the 1890s, the size of the French and German mobilizable armies was about the same, a million men apiece, but after the turn of the century the German edge in population (60 million Germans to 44 million French after 1914) made it impossible for France to keep up in total numbers even with extraordinary measures. In 1905, France reduced active service to two years in order to speed up the formation of the reserve, and by 1914 four out of every five eligible young French males were being called up for service in the army. In contrast, Germany summoned only half of its eligible manpower pool, leaving the rest—the *Ersatz Reserve*—to be trained in event of war. In August, 1914, France mobilized 1,650,000 troops and sixty-two infantry divisions, while Germany mobilized 1,850,000 troops and eighty-seven infantry divisions. But whereas Germany had a large, if untrained, *Ersatz Reserve* for further army expansion, France had few more young men to call up. Heavy losses would affect not only the strength but the quality of the French army.

With a population of 150 million by 1914, Tsarist Russia had no difficulty in finding enough men for the army, but training them, arming them, and mobilizing them was another matter. Despite French loans, Russia remained industrially backward compared with the other great powers, while Russian distances and lack of enough railroads forced the army to take up to forty days in order to mobilize all of its 3 million troops and 114 infantry divisions. Even then, not all of these forces could be concentrated in European Russia, and they did not compare with the German or French troops in the quality of their arms and equipment. The Austro-Hungarian and Italian armies could field 1.25 million men apiece by 1914, and, like the German and the French armies, they could mobilize in about two weeks. But the Austro-Hungarian army was plagued with ethnic divisions, and the Italian army had never shown much military prowess since Italy's unification. Still, the total mobilizable strength of the five largest armies in Europe came to about 9.5 million men in 1914, easily the largest number in history to that time.

In the 1880s, European infantry began to reequip with the repeating, magazine rifle and smokeless-powder ammunition. By 1914 the typical bolt-action, repeating rifle held three-to-nine rounds in its magazine, and by working the bolt the soldier could jack a fresh cartridge into the chamber once every three seconds. The insertion of rounds into the magazine was a matter of only a few seconds. Under conditions of good visibility, the army rifle was dangerous up to a thousand yards. Even more dramatic in its effect on firepower was Hiram Maxim's water-cooled machine-gun. The Maxim gun could fire four hundred rounds a minute, using belts of ammunition, yet was light enough that a crew of three men could carry its parts and ammunition from place to place, and fire it from a prone or sitting position. Though the Maxim gun and its imitators were too heavy for easy use on offense by 1914, they made ideal defensive weapons for infantry.

In the period between 1871 and 1914, artillery made great strides. Nitrocellulose (gun cotton) replaced black powder as the propellant, and trinitrophenol (picric acid) and trinitrotuolene (TNT) were excellent high explosives. The invention of the field telephone made it possible for forward observers to exploit the increasing range of the guns, now measured in miles, and to site gun batteries well in the rear. The first field gun with a recoil piston was the French 75-mm, introduced in 1897. It could fire as many as seven 18-pound shells in sixty seconds and hit targets up to seven miles away. The caliber of siege guns rose dramatically. "Big Bertha," the giant siege howitzer unveiled by the Germans in 1914, had a caliber of 420 mm (16.8 inches) and could hurl a 2,200 lb. shell up to nine miles in order to smash concrete forts. Advances in artillery by 1914 had increased the depth as well as the devastation of the battlefield.

The hot-air balloon had been used for observation as far back as the wars of the French Revolution, but the free balloon could not be steered and the tethered balloon had severe limits. The situation changed at the beginning of the twentieth century with the advent of both the dirigible (a steerable lighter-than-air craft using hydrogen gas for inflation and gasoline engines for power), and the gasoline-engine airplane. Count Ferdinand von Zeppelin's work put Germany first in the world in dirigibles by 1914, and by then most armies had a few airplanes. In the 1911–1912 Italian invasion of Turkish Libya, a few planes were even used as platforms from which to hurl grenades on enemy forces below, but not very effectively. Similar experiments were carried out with airplanes in the Balkan Wars of 1912–1913. Still, down to 1914, no army saw the real potential in airpower for war.

The greatest weaknesses of the mass army by 1914 were in logistics and signal communications. Beyond the railhead, the troops still had to march, and horse-drawn wagons still had to be used to move supplies. The automobile and the motor truck had appeared, but both were still in their infancies. The mobilized German army in 1914 used 726,670 horses but fewer than 5,000 automobiles and motor trucks. The animals consumed 14,533,400 pounds of fodder per day, or enough to fill up 581 railroad boxcars or 7,266 horse-drawn wagons. The need for ammunition competed for space in supply columns with food and fodder to a degree unprecedented in warfare, and as a consequence no army in motion could meet all its needs further than fifty miles from the nearest railhead. Huge numbers of men and horses also found it more difficult to meet needs for food and fodder locally, especially if they could not camp for an extended period. (If they camped too long, of course, they would exhaust local forage.)

The telephone joined the telegraph as an instrument of strategic control from a central headquarters, but both telegraph and telephone are dependent on vulnerable land-lines. Wireless telegraphy was short-ranged and unreliable in 1914, and voice-radio was not perfected until after World War I. In consequence, mass armies on the move were often harder to control from the rear, possessing a kind of slow but irresistable momentum of their own. Like the fictional Dr. Frankenstein, the general staffs of Europe had created monsters that they could scarcely control and whose movements at a distance were more difficult to gauge.

B. The Alliance Systems and Contingency War Plans. One of the significant developments after 1871 was the development of alliance systems to bolster the security of the great powers. Military alliances were nothing new to European history, of course, but in the past they had been short-term and for specific objectives. The new alliances were indefinite in duration and amounted to mutual defense pacts. The process was begun in 1879, when Germany and Austria-Hungary concluded the Dual Alliance. The pact was expanded to include Italy in 1881 with the formation of the Triple Alliance, but subsequent quarrels between Italy and Austria-Hungary over their Adriatic frontier robbed the addition of much vitality long before 1914. Bismarck's diplomacy kept Russia and France apart until his retirement in 1890, but in 1894 the autocratic empire and the democratic republic became unlikely allies against attack by the Central Powers. Britain remained aloof officially from either alliance system down to the turn of the century, but the growth in German naval power and rising German overseas imperialism left her increasingly uneasy. In 1904, Britain settled her colonial differences with France under the *Entente Cordiale,* and thereafter Britain and France engaged in joint defense planning for the contingency that Britain might intervene in a Franco-German War. In effect, Britain had become an unofficial member of the Dual Entente (France and Russia).

All of the alliance systems were defensive in purpose, but their existence made it more likely that a local quarrel might gestate into a general European war. Under the direction of Helmuth von Moltke, the German General Staff drew up contingency plans for a two-front war with Russia and France as early as 1879. Upon Moltke's retirement in 1888, General Graf von Waldersee succeeded Moltke at the head of the General Staff, and Waldersee retained Moltke's scheme for a concentration of German forces in East Prussia to execute a *Kesselschlacht* in Russian Poland in conjunction with Austro-Hungarian forces. Neither Moltke nor Waldersee intended to follow up a maiming of the Tsar's armies in Poland with an invasion of Russia proper. Instead, both intended to switch the German armies to the West in order to deal with the French threat which, they hoped, would be contained in the meantime by German frontier defenses and a minority of the German army. Moltke and Waldersee were agreed that in the face of the French frontier defenses and a mobilized *Nation-in-Arms* a quick offensive victory over France was not likely, and both believed that the war with Russia and France would be ended with a compromise peace. The main objective of German war plans was to insure the safety of the Reich and to provide its diplomats with good bargaining chips at the peace table.

A main shift in German strategy came in 1891 with the retirement of Waldersee and William II's appointment of General Alfred von Schlieffen to replace him as chief of the General Staff. The young, headstrong

Count Alfred von Schlieffen

SOURCE: Walter Goerlitz, *History of the German General Staff, 1657–1945*, trans. Brian Battershaw (New York and London: Frederick Praeger, 1953).

Schlieffen

Kaiser had fired both Bismarck and Waldersee in the first three years of his reign, and Schlieffen found himself free to depart from the more cautious policies of his predecessors. Schlieffen sought a strategy which might insure the total defeat of at least France, and such a strategy required that the initial German concentration must be in the West. In the face of France's border defenses and the French army, there was little prospect of a decisive success by attacking from Alsace-Lorraine, hence Schlieffen examined other possibilities. He finally concluded that the best chance for a quick German victory over France before Russia could come to her aid was to strike through Luxembourg, Belgium, and Holland in order to outflank and encircle the French armies at the frontier. If the French *Nation-in-Arms* could be destroyed in a *Kesselschlacht* within forty days of the outbreak of war, the victorious German forces could then be transferred to the Eastern front to assist the Austro-Hungarian armies in dealing with the Russians. Schlieffen knew that the invasion of Belgium might provoke Britain into entering the war in order to uphold the Treaty of 1839, but he also knew that the British land forces sent to the continent at the start of the war were bound to be small. Accordingly, he expected an expeditionary force would either be swept up in the encirclement which destroyed the French armies, or it would be penned up helplessly somewhere on the coast. He did not expect effective resistance from the armies of the Low Countries.

In the final version of Schlieffen's plan, passed on at his retirement in January, 1906, a mobilized German army of ninety infantry divisions was called for, or twelve more divisions than the army possessed in 1906. Ten divisions would be assigned to an army in East Prussia as a hedge against an unexpected early Russian offensive, but eighty divisions in seven armies were to be sent to the West. Two armies, composed of ten divisions, were to stand on the defensive in Alsace-Lorraine, while the German right wing, composed of seventy divisions in five armies, would make the thrust through the Low Countries and northern France, spreading its front until it reached all the way to the English Channel. The Schlieffen Plan was inherited by Helmuth von Molkte the Younger, nephew and namesake of the first Moltke, and chief of the General Staff through the opening campaign of World War I.

The younger Moltke accepted the Schlieffen Plan in principle, and he achieved an expansion of the army to eighty-seven infantry divisions by 1914, almost as many as Schlieffen had called for. But Moltke also made important changes in Schlieffen's plan. He allocated nine divisions to the army in East Prussia, twenty divisions to the two armies in Alsace-Lorraine, and only fifty-eight divisions to the five German armies on the right wing in the West. The ratio of forces between right and left wings in the West was changed from seven-to-one to less than three-to-one. In addition, Moltke cancelled the planned invasion of the Dutch Nether-

Count Helmuth von Moltke, the Younger

SOURCE: Walter Goerlitz, *History of the German General Staff, 1657–1945*, trans. Brian Battershaw (New York and London: Frederick Praeger, 1953).

	Rus	Fr.(Als.-Lor)	Low Lands	Tot
Schlieffen	10 DIV	10 DIV	70 DIV	90 DIV (1906 plan)
Moltke	9 DIV	20 "	58 DIV	87 DIV (1914)

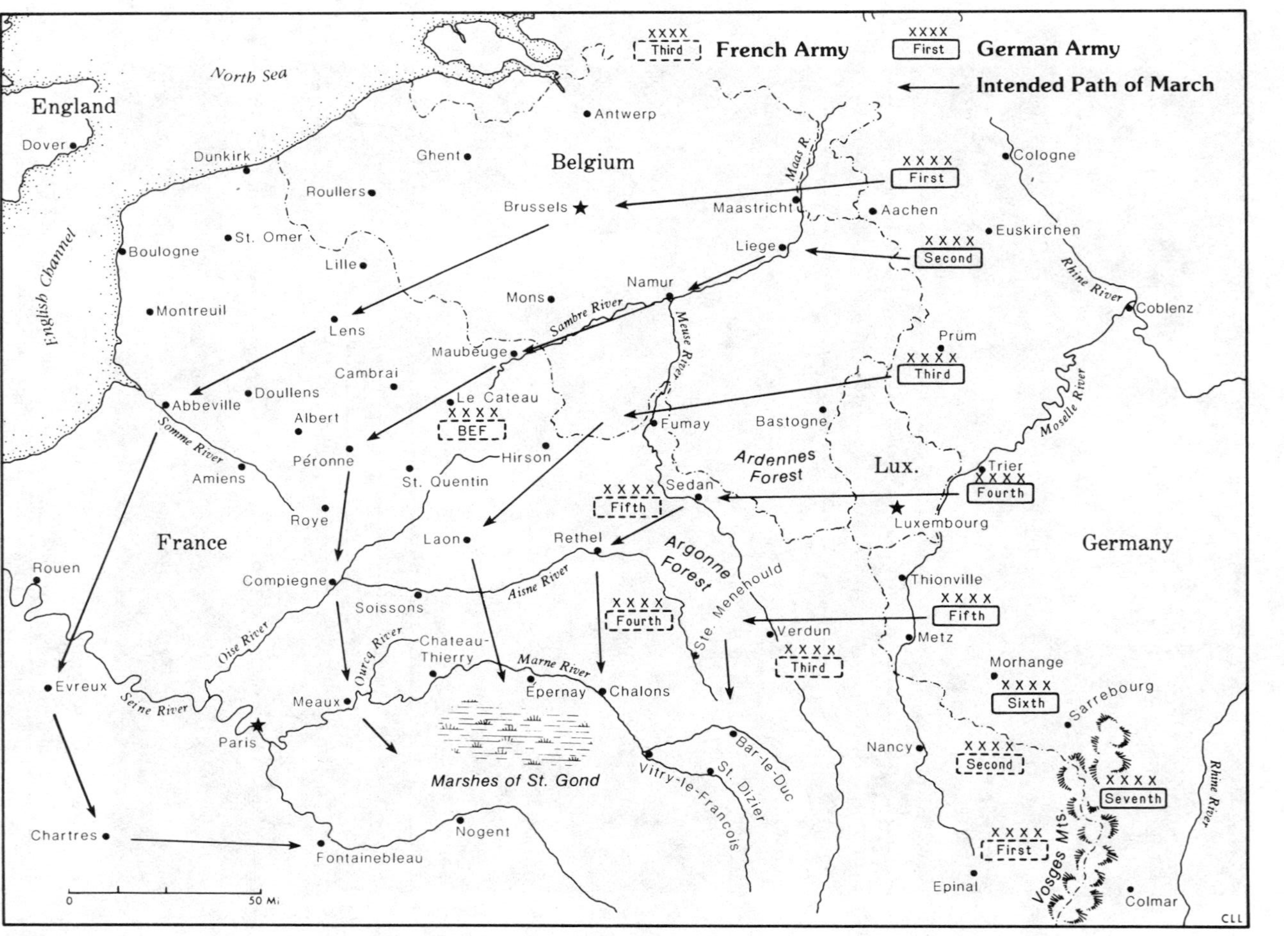

The Schlieffen Plan of 1905 and the French Plan XVII

lands, a change that caused three of the five armies on the right wing in 1914 to crowd together at the Liège Gap in order not to violate the neutrality of the so-called Maastricht Appendix. Yet when these armies deployed in the plains of Belgium, their front was barely broad enough to envelop Paris, much less to reach the Channel.

Since World War I, critics have tended to fasten blame for the failure of the Schlieffen Plan on the changes made by Moltke, but in reality any version of the plan was risky. The combined French, British, and Belgian armies had almost as many divisions as the Germans in the West, while the Germans quite underestimated the logistical difficulties their armies west of the Meuse would face. The Germans never expected that the French would be able to correct the error in the original deployment of their forces in the time it took for the German armies to enter northern France, yet they accomplished that very thing in 1914. When the German armies closed in for the final battle, they encountered the enemy's front, not his rear. True, had seventy divisions borne down on that line which extended no further west than Paris, they might have outflanked it, but it is also true that German logistics in 1914 were not even adequate to support the fewer than sixty divisions on the right wing. Indeed, had the campaign not taken place in August–September, 1914, when there was an abundance of local forage in the plains of Belgium, German logistics might have faltered sooner than they did.

Whatever the faults of the Schlieffen Plan, it was superior in imagination to the French Plan XVII adopted after 1911. The plan was a product of the French prewar obsession with the offensive, and its underlying assumptions were in part derived from misapplied lessons from Ardant du Picq's *Battle Studies.* This book, published after its author was killed in the Franco-Prussian War, was based on questionnaires filled out by combat veterans. From those answers to probing questions about the nature of combat, du Picq concluded that the morale factor was dominant in the success or failure in battle. A later generation of French officers convinced themselves that high morale was associated with seizing the offensive, while Ferdinand Foch, professor at the French war college, developed syllogistic arguments which tried to prove that improvements in firepower benefitted offense over defense. By 1914 French heads and field manuals were chock-full of aphorisms praising the offensive and denigrating defense.

The French obsession with seizing the offensive from the beginning of the war did not, however, blind the French General Staff to the danger of a German flanking attack through Belgium, but the debate boiled down to whether the Germans would strip their frontier of troops in order to risk a wide envelopment west of the river Meuse, or whether they would follow a more cautious course and use fewer troops to carry out a narrow envelopment through the Belgian Ardennes and Luxembourg. General August Michel, the French commander-in-chief-designate in 1911, believed that the Germans would gamble everything on a wide envelopment and that, in such a case, the French army should deploy many of its forces on the Belgian frontier. The "Young Turks" on the General Staff argued to the contrary that only a narrow envelopment would be risked and that the danger could be averted without abandoning plans for an early invasion of German territory. The "Young Turks" won out, General Joseph Joffre replaced Michel as commander-in-chief, and the details of Plan XVII were worked out in the final years before World War I.

Plan XVII called for the rapid mobilization of fifty divisions in five armies, four of which were to invade German-held Alsace-Lorraine and the German Rhineland beyond. The fifth army was to stand guard against a flanking movement through Luxembourg and the Belgian Ardennes. Only twelve divisions, formed from older reservists, were held back at Paris as a general reserve. By accident, the same divisions, and reinforcements from North Africa, were the first forces available to Joffre when France was faced with a wide-front envelopment from Belgium in 1914. On that account, and because the French offensive into Alsace-Lorraine smashed itself to pieces on German fortifications and defensive fire, the Schlieffen Plan might have worked after all if its logistics had not been faulty and the French General Staff had not carried out a miracle of redeployment after defeat at the frontier.

The Russian war plan was predicated on the French need for early action in the East in order to draw off as many German divisions as possible. The *Stafka* (or high command) showed great powers of self-sacrifice in agreeing that a Russian offensive aimed at German soil would be launched within two weeks of mobilization. Two armies composed of twenty divisions would attempt to encircle the German forces in East Prussia. Within a month of the beginning of mobilization, the Russians would launch forty divisions in four armies against the Austro-Hungarian frontier. But forty days from the beginning of mobilization would pass before all of Russia's 114 infantry divisions could be deployed. The early Russian offensives in 1914 did help to insure France's survival, but the Tsar's armies never fully recovered from the effects of the defeats resulting from them.

General Field Marshal Conrad von Hötzendorff, the ambitious chief of the Austro-Hungarian General Staff, planned to concentrate fifty infantry divisions in Galicia for Austria-Hungary's part in the *Kesselschlacht* in Poland, unaware that his German ally had cancelled that plan long before. But other Austro-Hungarian plans called for a different deployment in event of war with the Balkan state of Serbia on Austria-Hungary's southern border or in event of war with Italy. As matters turned out, in 1914 the Austro-Hungarian army started to concentrate against Serbia, then had to carry out a hasty deployment against the Russian danger from Poland. It too never fully recovered from the effects of the battles of 1914. As Italy declared her neutrality in 1914, and then entered the war on the Allied side of 1915, her war plan will not be considered here except to say that it was as unrealistic as any of the others.

Until 1911 the British were unsure whether to commit an expeditionary force to the continent independently of the French, or to send it to fight alongside the French armies. Advocates of the "Blue Water" strategy argued that the British Expeditionary Force (BEF) would have more effect as an amphibious force-of-distraction on either the Belgian coast or perhaps even the German Baltic coast. But most army leaders favored the view of the French General Staff that it was vital for the BEF to join the French armies in eastern France for the opening battles. This "Continental" school of strategy finally won out over the "Blue Water" school, and the French General Staff assigned the BEF (six infrantry divisions and a cavalry division in 1914) to a position just west of the river Meuse on the flank of the French Fifth Army watching the Ardennes. If the Germans tried an envelopment through the Ardennes as the French expected, they would find themselves blocked to the front by the Fifth Army and outflanked to the west by the BEF. In reality, of course, the BEF's position put it squarely astride the path from Belgium that three German armies would take in 1914.

C. The Anglo-American Military Experience to 1914. The United States and Britain were unique among the great powers of the world by 1914 in that neither imposed compulsory military service nor maintained a *Nation-in-Arms.* Until 1890 the United States was preoccupied with westward expansion across the North American continent and final conquest of Indian territory, a task safely left to a small professional army. In the 1880s, Congress approved the Endicott Plan for repairing America's crumbling seacoast fortifications, but so little money was actually appropriated that not much was accomplished in that regard down to the outbreak of the Spanish-American War in 1898. At the war's outbreak, the U.S. Army numbered only twenty-six thousand officers and men, and the militia of the several states—its only uniformed reserve—was understrength and poorly prepared for war. The wartime army had to be improvised by taking in volunteers into the regiments of the regular army and adding volunteer regiments under their own officers. The mobilization process was so confused and hectic that it served as a major impetus for the first major American military reform since the Civil War.

The chief architect of American military reform at the turn of the century was Elihu Root, Secretary of War from 1899 to 1904. The Root Reforms included: (1) a quadrupling of the authorized strength of the peacetime army to one hundred thousand officers and men; (2) an Army War College and modernized War Department General Staff; and (3) federal aid to the state militias—now called the National Guard—in hopes that they might serve as the school of the volunteer soldier in peacetime. The Root Reforms were, in certain respects, an attempt to compromise the views of the regular military establishment and the defenders of the National Guard. The former's views had been influenced many years before by Brevet Major-General Emory Upton's *The Military Policy of the United States,* which, among other recommendations, had advocated the largest possible cadre of professional soldiers in skeletonized regiments into which wartime volunteers could be poured. The leaders of the National Guard preferred the creation of independent volunteer regiments drawn from the Guard and volunteers straight out of civilian life to fight alongside the regulars. Actually, neither the regular army nor the Guard had a good solution to the problem of getting civilians to train in peacetime, however they might be mobilized in time of war. In *laissez faire* America, compulsory military service in any form was quite out of the question. The army's biggest progress after the Root Reforms was in completing a modern system of seacoast fortifications at home and overseas, and in creating separate field and coast artilleries for more effective specialization.

The British army remained largely unchanged from the time of the Cardwell Reforms down to the Second Anglo-Boer War (1899–1902). Problems of rapid expansion and heavy initial defeats in South Africa signaled the need for change as soon as the war was over. The Haldane-Esher Reforms, the counterpart to the Root Reforms for the American army, included: (1) the creation of a British Expeditionary Force in the home islands for quick deployment overseas in future emergencies; (2) the consolidation of the militia and other voluntary military bodies into the Territorials, an organization somewhat similar to the American National Guard but assigned to regiments of the British regular army for training and mobilization; and (3) the establishment of an Imperial General Staff and a modern war college system. Britain, like America, rejected any form of compulsory peacetime service, but by 1914 the Territorials provided the seven divisions of the BEF with a backup force of fifteen partially trained and equipped reserve divisions. Moreover, unlike the American National Guard down to 1916, Territorials could be compelled to serve overseas in time of war. But beyond the Territorials and a small army reserve, the army's expansion in wartime called for taking volunteers straight out of civilian life. Even in World War I the British did not adopt general conscription until 1916.

II. Navies

A. The Challenge of the Jeune École *to 1889*. From 1871 to 1889, the most formidable challenge to the old concepts of sea power was presented by the *Jeune École* ("Young School") of the French navy. Led by Admiral Theophile Aube, this school of thought predicted that mines and automotive torpedoes would make effective blockade impossible in future, and would rob the battleship of its traditional value as the chief means of commanding the sea. The *Jeune École* believed that *guerre de course* would take on unprecedented effectiveness under these conditions, a development that would aid continental countries such as France but which would make Britain very vulnerable. The *Jeune École*'s arguments were persuasive to a French government already saddled with the expense of maintaining a *Nation-in-Arms* and which saw little value in a navy except for a war with Britain. France could hardly expect to rival Britain in battleships while carrying the burden of great land armaments; and a fleet built around torpedo-boats, mines, coast defenses, and commerce raiders would be much less expensive than one created around battleships. The high point for the *Jeune École* in France came in January, 1886, when Aube was appointed Minister of Marine and stopped all battleship building in favor of a navy built for *guerre de course.*

The claims of the *Jeune École* alarmed even the British Admiralty and raised the question whether command-of-the-sea based on the battleship was going out of date. In 1885 some members of the naval establishment admitted that the battleships then under construction might be the last ever to join the British navy. Between 1885 and 1888, however, the Admiralty carried out extensive studies and tests and, in the latter year, concluded that, while the fleet must be extensively redesigned and strengthened, the battleship remained the *sine qua non* of naval supremacy. The British Naval Defense Act of 1889 reflected both renewed confidence in the battleship and the fact that only a "balanced fleet" could meet a variety of threats satisfactorily. Huge sums of money were provided to restore the "Two-Power Standard," whereby the British navy was to be kept at least as large as the next two naval powers combined (at the time France and Russia), and the new battleships were to be completely steam propelled and their large guns supplemented with numerous smaller-caliber quick-firing (QF) guns suitable for defense against torpedo-boats. In addition, a new class of "torpedo-boat-destroyers" armed with QF guns and torpedoes was to be constructed to screen larger ships. When the first British destroyer was commissioned in 1893, it set off a wave of destroyer-building in other navies. Finally, the problem of commerce raiders was to be dealt with by constructing numerous armored cruisers, fast enough to run down enemy ships and with more than enough power and armor to destroy them. Altogether, the Naval Defense Act of 1889 provided for the construction of seventy ships in five years.

British faith in the battleship and in a "balanced fleet" served to influence other navies to follow suit. Even the French navy moved in that direction after Aube left office. Moreover, the French strategic position changed. The last crisis between Britain and France occurred over rival claims to the Sudan in 1898, but after the French backed down in order to curry British favor, Anglo-French relations began to improve. The last outstanding colonial differences were amicably settled under the *Entente Cordiale* of 1904, following which the French and British began joint defense planning. Well before 1914 the French navy could afford to leave the problem of an ever-increasing German navy to the British, and it concentrated on naval supremacy in the Mediterranean Sea over Italy and Austria-Hungary. By the outbreak of World War I, the ideas of the *Jeune École* seemed largely irrelevant even to the French fleet.

B. The Mahanite School of Naval Power, 1890–1914. Next to Britain's example, perhaps the writings of Captain Alfred Mahan of the United States Navy did more than anything else to encourage navies to return to traditional concepts of sea power. While serving as a professor at the U.S. Naval War College, founded in 1884, Mahan published his lectures in book form in 1890 under the title *The Influence of Sea Power Upon History, 1660–1783,* and thereby put himself on the way to be proclaimed as a "Jomini of the sea." The central theme in Mahan's book, and in the other books by his hand which followed, was that unchanging principles govern the conduct of war at sea as much as on land, and that certain natural factors largely determine the fitness of a state to be a sea power. These natural factors, according to Mahan, were a state's geographical position, its physical conformation, the extent of its territory, both the size and character of its population, and the character of its government. Britain's rise to naval predominance was no accident according to Mahan, but almost the inevitable result of the natural factors being more favorable in her case than in the cases of her rivals. The force of these factors manifested themselves in the case of Britain by an unceasing urge for overseas empire, a merchant fleet to link that empire's trade with the mother country, and a great battle fleet which supported, and was supported by, the wealth of that empire. In Mahan's view, overseas imperialism and great sea power were concomitants.

Mahan's drawing of a connection between sea power and overseas imperialism could not have been better timed. The forty years after 1871 saw the greatest Western overseas expansion since the eighteenth century, and most of its thrust was aimed at undeveloped regions in Africa and Asia, where the prospects of markets and sources of raw materials served to lure the industrial powers of Europe. Mahan's thesis that great navies and imperialism combine to produce, rather than to consume, great wealth helped to produce "navalism," or the uncritical demand for naval power. Mahan's writing influenced even continental European countries, none more so than Imperial Germany. Kaiser William II was so enamoured with Mahan's first book that he caused translated copies to be placed in every ship of his navy. He was so conditioned that by the turn of the century he had fallen under the influence of the wily Admiral Alfred von Tirpitz, who served successively as chief of staff of the Supreme Naval Command (1892), secretary of state for naval affairs (1897), and admiral of the fleet (1911–1916). Aided by the preachments of Mahan and by the Kaiser's own visions of Germany as a world power, Tirpitz had little difficulty in convincing William that the German navy should be placed on the same secure financial basis as the army. Navalist propaganda by the Navy League and imperialist associations helped to lobby the German people in favor of a High Seas Fleet. The Fleet Laws of 1898 and 1900 marked the passage of Germany to the status of a great naval power.

Once Germany committed a substantial part of her national wealth to her navy, the German battle line soon exceeded in size that of any other naval power in Europe, save the British. But there is also irony in the fact that with her resources divided between a great army and a great navy, Germany was never likely to overtake Britain's naval lead. Tirpitz rationalized his so-called Risk Theory in order to justify the second-best navy. Strict naval equality with Britain was unnecessary, he maintained, because Britain's much larger overseas empire forced a greater dispersion of her fleet over the globe. Should Britain try and succeed in destroying the rising navy of her new rival, she could do so only at the risk of such naval losses as would make her vulnerable to the attack of other naval powers. Germany's new and elaborate coastal defenses on the North Sea would make a direct British attack and close blockade of the German High Seas Fleet extremely hazardous. Britain would therefore be more respectful of Germany's ambitions overseas in time of peace, and less effective against Germany in time of war.

Tirpitz's "Risk Theory" proved as hollow as any other prewar military rationalization. Britain solved the problem of concentrating most of her fleet on the North Sea by reaching diplomatic agreements with potential overseas rivals. Agreement with the United States over the Caribbean Sea and the right of the United States to build an isthmian canal across Central America opened the way for the British West Indian fleet to be withdrawn to home waters. The Anglo-Japanese Treaty of 1902 protected British interests in the Far East against the rising power of Japan. And deals struck with France in 1904 and Russia in 1907 removed still other obstacles to "bringing the legions home." By 1914 most of Britain's battleship strength was based only three hundred miles from Germany's

North Sea coasts. Moreover, the peculiar geography of the North Sea eliminated British need for a close blockade of German ports. By controlling the Channel at one end and the passage between Scotland and Norway at the other, the British navy could impose a "distant blockade" far from Germany's coastal defenses. The final result of William's big-navy policy was a fleet large enough to antagonize Britain but too small to make her respectful in peace or vulnerable in war. Perhaps a more careful reading of Mahan's work would have revealed to the Kaiser that no other European power since the seventeenth century had successfully competed with Britain for naval supremacy.

Outside Europe, however, the naval picture was indeed changing. The United States and Japan were respectable—and still growing—naval powers at the turn of the century. As early as 1890 the United States had become the world's leading industrial power. In 1898 she annexed the Hawaiian islands, two thousand miles from her Pacific shores, and acquired the Philippines in the Far East from Spain at the end of the Spanish-American War. President Theodore Roosevelt was no less a big-navy man than the Kaiser, and, as a close friend of Mahan, Roosevelt steadily pushed the expansion of the American fleet. By 1914 the American navy was third largest in the world after the British and German. Japan rose to fourth place after knocking Russia out of the lists in the Russo-Japanese War (1904–1905). The rise of the United States and Japan as naval powers was the principal reason that Britain abandoned the Two-Power Standard before 1914 to concentrate on naval supremacy over Germany.

C. Technical Developments in Navies, 1890–1914. The British battleships built under the Naval Defense Act of 1889 displaced 13,000 tons, carried four 12-inch guns in two large turrets, and were armed with as many as ten 6-inch and 4-inch QF guns as secondary batteries. Armor thickness at belt-line was up to 24 inches. The largest guns could hit a target 6,000 yards distant, or six times further than the range of existing torpedoes. The first torpedo-boat-destroyer was launched by Britain in 1893. It displaced only 420 tons and carried two 3-inch QF guns as well as torpedoes. By 1914 the average destroyer's displacement had risen to 1,000 tons, the newer destroyers carried four 4-inch guns and 21-inch torpedo tubes. Destroyers might do up to 35 knots, and their mission had been expanded to attacking large ships whenever they could get within torpedo range. Armored cruisers, typically carrying 8-inch and 6-inch guns, completed the most important ships of the fleet.

In 1906, a revolution in battleship design occurred when Britain launched HMS *Dreadnought*, the first of the "all big-gun ships." Thanks to new methods of fire-control, large guns could lay down an accurate fire to 13,000 yards (6.5 nautical miles). The *Dreadnought*'s designers had

HMS *Dreadnought,* 1906, the first "all big-gun battleship."
SOURCE: Peter Padfield, *The Battleship Era* (New York: David McKay, 1972).

dispensed with secondary batteries in favor of arming her with ten 12-inch guns in five turrets. Any conventional battleship would have been overwhelmed by the *Dreadnought*'s salvoes even before it could get within range to reply. The *Dreadnought* also had oil-fired burners instead of coal furnaces, and steam-turbine engines in place of piston-driven engines. Despite her 13 inches of armor at belt-line and a total displacement of 17,800 tons, she reached a speed of 21.5 knots on her trials, 6 knots faster than existing battleships. In short, the advent of the *Dreadnought* design made all previous battleships obsolete.

Admiral Sir John ("Jackie") Fisher, First Sea Lord at the time of the launching of the *Dreadnought,* was the person most responsible for her development. A naval officer with an unconquerable faith in big ships and big guns, Fisher also pushed the development of the battle cruiser, a ship with the same firepower as a dreadnought battleship but achieving greater speed and range through reduced armor. The first pair of British battle cruisers were launched in 1907. Remote fire-control centers were subsequently located high in ship's masts in order to extend the range of observed fire to 20,000 yards (10 nautical miles). By 1914, HMS *Queen Elizabeth* displaced 27,000 tons, carried eight 15-inch guns, and had a speed of 25 knots. Each 15-inch shell from her guns weighed almost a ton.

Britain did not retain a monopoly on dreadnought design for long. Germany and other naval powers began laying down both dreadnought battleships and battle cruisers. A so-called dreadnought race developed between Germany and Britain in the years just before World War I, and until 1914 the British and German admirals thought of little else but big ships and big guns. At the end of the peacetime race in August, 1914, Britain had twenty-two dreadnought battleships and battle cruisers in commission and thirteen building. Germany had fourteen dreadnought battleships and battle cruisers in service, and seven more were under construction. On the average, the British ships carried slightly larger guns than the German, but the German ships were better armored. Still, with the numerical advantage lying with the British fleet, the German High Seas Fleet had no choice but to adopt a Fleet-in-Being strategy at the beginning of World War I.

The naval obsession with dreadnoughts before 1914 obscured important improvements in the submarine, still considered a kind of "thinking mine" and useful only for coast defense. The French *Gymnote,* launched in 1888, was the first submarine commissioned in any European navy, but the great breakthrough in submarine development came with the inventions of the gyro compass and periscope for underwater navigation, and the diesel engine for surface propulsion. The diesel was more efficient than existing gasoline engines, far safer, and could be used to charge the electric storage batteries which powered the electric motors used underwater. Britain did not commission a submarine until 1902, but with ninety-seven of the craft in 1914, the British submarine fleet led the world on the eve of World War I. The average British submarine displaced 540 tons when submerged. France, the United States, and Russia, in descending order, had the next largest number of submarines. Germany, the fifth-ranked submarine power in 1914, had forty-five of the craft, but fewer than half were designed to operate beyond the North Sea. Only by accident of circumstance after the outbreak of war did the German navy discover that the submarine's true vocation was *guerre de course.* Before World War I was over, the submarine in that role had upset many Mahanite assumptions about the nature of naval power and the command of the sea.

III. The Wars, 1871–1914

Most of the wars of this period were connected with Western imperial expansion. Some of them were waged against older empires such as the Ottoman Turkish, the Chinese, and the Spanish, while still others were

"Profit, Prophecy & Prestige"

aimed at the primitive or less developed societies in Africa and Asia. The motivation for Western imperialism in this period has been attributed to "Gold, God and Glory," or economic, missionary, and prestige factors. Thanks to steam power, preserved foods, and advances in medicine—as well as to superior arms, equipment, and organization—the Western countries could project their power into regions heretofore almost inaccessible. In 1870, 90 percent of the great continent of Africa was still unknown to Europe. By 1914 all of Africa was European-controlled except for the black states of Liberia and Ethiopia. The story was similar in Southeast Asia where only Thailand (Siam) escaped Western domination before 1914.

A. The Russo-Turkish War and Tensions among the Great Powers, 1877–78. Complaints by Christians of Turkish abuse in the Balkans gave Tsar Alexander II an excuse to launch still another Russo-Turkish war in 1877. Though the Russian armies out-classed the Turkish, they were brought up short by repeating rifles in the siege of Plevna, where they required months of effort and heavy casualties in order to break Turkish resistance. The Russian Black Sea fleet, revived after 1870, claimed to be the first to sink an enemy warship with a Whitehead torpedo, though the first confirmed sinking with a Whitehead did not take place until 1891 when a Chilean torpedo-boat sank the "iron-clad" *Blanca Encalada* after it was seized by mutineers. The Russian victory over the Turks in the Balkans almost set off a new "Crimean War" among the great powers until Bismarck hosted an international conference at Berlin in order to settle the matter peacefully.

The Congress of Berlin in 1878 created an independent Rumania (which ceded the province of Bessarabia to Russia), Bulgaria, and Montenegro, while requiring Turkey further to grant full independence to autonomous Serbia. But the Tsar was angered when the Congress awarded administrative control over the provinces of Bosnia and Herzegovina to Austria-Hungary, and thereby made the Hapsburgs rivals of the Romanovs for influence in the Balkans. Because the Tsar blamed Bismarck personally for this outcome, tensions between Germany and Russia increased to the point where Berlin and Vienna found it prudent to conclude the Dual Alliance of 1879. But Bismarck had no intention of tying Germany's interests to Austria-Hungary's ventures in the Balkans, or of allowing Russia to drift into the arms of France. He worked diligently to improve relations among Germany, Russia, and Austria-Hungary through the Three Emperors League and ultimately a secret Reinsurance Treaty with Russia which guaranteed that Germany would never support Austria-Hungary in an offensive war against Russia. Bismarck was largely successful in his diplomacy until William II came to the throne in 1888, but the Reinsurance Treaty was allowed to lapse after

William compelled Bismarck to retire in 1890. Four years later, Russia concluded a defensive alliance with France.

B. The Overseas Colonial Wars. Britain and France waged more overseas colonial wars than any other powers before 1914, though Italy and Germany were involved in some lesser conflicts in Africa and Asia. Often the native armies or tribal hosts were superior in numbers to the invading Western armies, but they were usually inferior in weapons and organization. The essential problem for Western forces was to bring about native subordination at the lowest possible cost and in a manner likely to insure permanent pacification.

In general, Western armies were best at set-piece battles, where their superior firepower made short work of attacking hordes armed with spears or primitive flintlocks, but this was not always the case. The Zulu host in South Africa proved to be brave, numerous, and well led. In 1879, when General Lord Chelmsford invaded Zululand with 8,500 British and Kaffir (native) troops, 20,000 Zulu warriors outmaneuvered his army, isolated a detachment of 1,800 troops at Isandhlwana, and overwhelmed it, leaving only 50 of the Europeans and 300 of the Kaffirs alive. Nearly all the Zulu warriors had no arm more deadly than the *assegai* (throwing spear). In comparison, in 1876 perhaps 1,800 Sioux Indians wiped out fewer than 300 cavalrymen under George Custer at the Battle of the Little Big Horn, the biggest victory of the Plains Indians in North America, and at least some of the Indians were armed with repeating rifles. Chelmsford's army was compelled to retreat after Isandhlwana, but six months later it defeated the Zulu host decisively at the Battle of Ulundi, and the power of the Zulu nation never recovered.

The British also had their share of trouble in North Africa after they established a protectorate over Egypt in 1882 in order to protect their interests in the Suez Canal, opened in 1869, and to collect debts owed by the Khedive of Egypt. They inherited Egypt's war with the Dervishes of the Sudan, and in 1883 an Egyptian army advised by British general William Hicks invaded the Sudan, only to be wiped out in the sands of the Khordufan desert. The Dervishes laid siege to the Egyptian garrison at Khartoum, commanded by British general Charles "Chinese" Gordon, and, after 317 days, broke through Khartoum's defenses to massacre the garrison and its commander in 1885. The British abandoned the Sudan for thirteen years after the fall of Khartoum, but in 1898 an Anglo-Egyptian army of 25,000 troops under General Hubert Horatio Kitchener drove up the Nile to crush a Dervish host of 40,000 men at the Battle of Omdurman. An Italian army of 15,000 troops invading Ethiopia in 1896 had not been so lucky. It was routed at Adowa by Abyssinian tribesmen in the worst defeat suffered by any Western colonial army before 1914.

Among the ablest of the British imperial generals were Garnet Wolseley and Frederick Roberts. Wolseley won a reputation in the Ashanti Wars of West Africa in the 1870s, and he commanded the expedition to Egypt in 1882 with brilliance. Roberts came from the other end of the social scale, rising from private soldier to field marshal, a remarkable feat in the Victorian army. He first won fame in the Second Afghan War when, in 1880, he led a relief expedition to besieged Kandahar. In the Second Anglo-Boer War (1899–1902), he was to rally a defeated army and lead it forward to victory. Perhaps the best of the French colonial generals were Joseph Galliéni and Louis Lyautey. Galliéni is best remembered for his vital role as military governor of Paris in the crisis of 1914, but he first achieved reputation as a colonial soldier and administrator in Tonkin China (northern Vietnam) in the 1890s. Lyautey also served in the construction of the French colony of Indochina (Vietnam, Laos, and Cambodia), in Madagascar, and was the dominant figure in the French conquest of Morocco in 1912. The greatest of the German colonial commanders was General Lettow von Vorbeck, whose operations with black troops in German East Africa (Kenya) during World War I repeatedly confounded the best efforts of the British.

No colonial foe proved more difficult for the British to defeat than the white South Africans known as the Boers. This hardy people were descended from the Dutch who settled Cape Colony in the seventeenth century and who found themselves under British rule there after the Napoleonic Wars. After the British parliament outlawed black slavery throughout the empire, many Boers trekked into Natal where they defeated the Zulu chieftain Dingaan at the Battle of Blood River in 1838. When Britain annexed Natal in 1843, Boers migrated over the Drakensberg range to found the Orange and Transvaal republics. These farming republics were threatened again when gold and diamonds were discovered on their territory and a host of British prospectors and mineral companies rushed to the Rand. In 1881, Boer militia, well armed with modern rifles, beat back the invasion of a small British army under General Sir George Colley in the First Anglo-Boer War. The defeat at Majuba Hill, in which Colley lost his life, was the first successful white colonial resistance to British regulars since the American Revolution a century earlier.

The Second Anglo-Boer War (1899–1902) broke out when negotiations between President Paul Krueger and the British governor of Cape Colony collapsed in October, 1899. Rather than await British invasion of their territories, the Boer militia—45,000-strong—invaded British Rhodesia, Natal, and Cape Colony, imposing sieges on the British garrisons at Mafaeking, Ladysmith, and Kimberley. No more than 15,000 British troops were in South Africa at the beginning of the war. When 47,000 British reinforcements arrived in South Africa under General

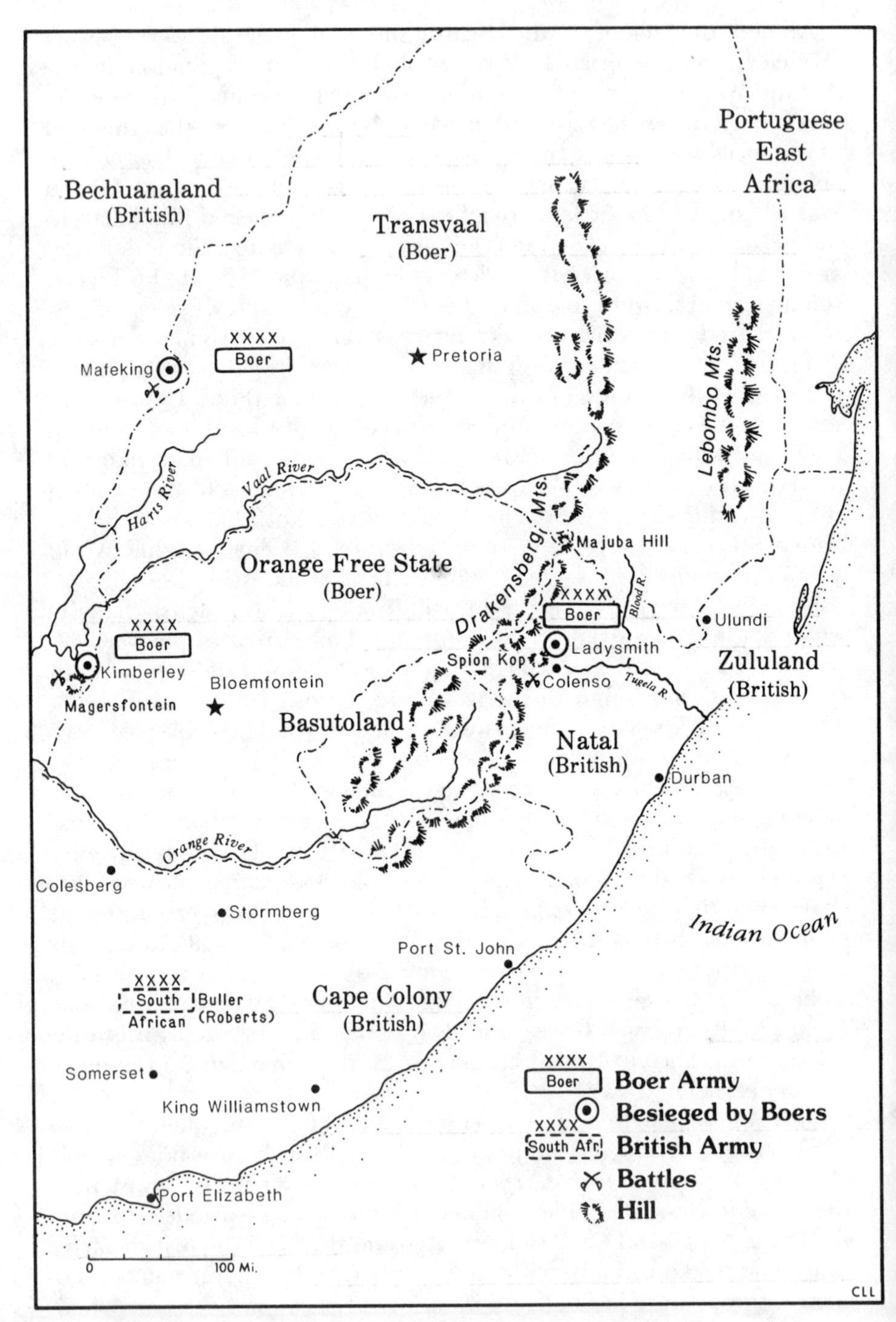

The South African Theater of War, 1899–1902

Redvers Buller, they were heavily defeated in their attempts to raise the sieges of Kimberley and Ladysmith at the battles of Magersfontein, Colenso, and Spion Kop (December, 1899–January, 1900). Roberts then relieved Buller of command, and his forces were eventually raised to a strength of 250,000 troops. During 1900, Roberts relieved Kimberley, Ladysmith, and Mafaeking, and went on to capture the Boer capitals at Bloemfontein and Pretoria. After the Boer armies had been broken up, Roberts passed his command to Kitchener and returned to Britain in January, 1901, where he was personally decorated by Queen Victoria a few weeks before her death.

But the Boer War was not over. Boer commandos launched a hit-and-run guerrilla war by horseback that required the better part of two years for the British to suppress. Kitchener resorted to the very un-Victorian methods of burning Boer farms, imprisoning Boer populations in concentration camps, and crisscrossing the open veldt with block houses and barbed wire. His systematic sweeps through Boer country foreshadowed the American "Search and Destroy" tactics used in the Vietnam War nearly seventy years later. A fifth of the Boer population in the concentration camps died from disease, bad food, and poor sanitation. By the time the last commandos surrendered, the war had cost the lives of 25,000 Boers (in a population of less than a million), 22,000 Britons, and 12,000 black Africans.

The regular side of the Boer War revealed once again that in the face of modern rifled arms, armies must practice dispersion, avoid frontal attacks where possible, and employ cover and concealment. The British army shifted to the khaki-colored uniform and learned to blend in with the countryside like its Boer enemy. The early British defeats were attributable to outdated assault formations, which even included the movement of artillery to within range of Boer marksmen. The British were so impressed with Boer shooting that, after the war, British infantry were given the most intensive training with small arms of any army in Europe. As a result, the accuracy of British rifle fire in 1914 was second to none, something the Germans learned to their cost on more than one occasion. The war had also demonstrated the need for centralized imperial war planning and thus contributed to the creation of an Imperial General Staff as well as to all the other Haldane-Esher reforms already discussed.

Coincident with the Boer War was the Philippine Insurrection against American rule, just after the Spanish-American War. Led by Emilio Aguinaldo, the Filipinos offered such resistance that eventually the Americans had to employ 65,000 regular troops and 35,000 short-term volunteers to put it down. By the time President Theodore Roosevelt declared the insurrection at an end on July 4, 1902, the Americans had suffered 10,000 casualties, or twice as many as in the Spanish-American

War. American troops joined those of other powers for the first time since the American Revolution in relieving the besieged legations at Peking during the Boxer Rebellion (1900), and some remained as part of a larger international force to garrison the Tientsin-Peking railroad until 1938. The American acquisition of the Philippines and the Boxer Rebellion had the effect of making the United States a new power in the Far East, with great consequences for itself and the Pacific region.

C. The Spanish-American War, 1898. American involvement in the Far East came about by the unlikely route of conflict with Spain over its island territory of Cuba. American interest in the Carribean was connected with prospects of Latin American trade and the need for an isthmian canal across Central America, but American attention was drawn to Cuba by a long revolt there against Spanish rule and the Spanish measures for crushing it. Americans were horrified by newspaper accounts of the Spanish policy of *reconcentrado* (herding the population into concentration camps so it could not aid the guerrillas), though the Spanish measures were no more cruel than some to be used by the British in the Boer War or by the Americans themselves during the Philippine Insurrection. The tensions produced by "Yellow Journalism," especially by the competing Pulitzer and Hearst newspaper syndicates, were heightened in February, 1898, with the mysterious explosion that sank the U.S. battleship *Maine* while on a visit to Havana, and by the De Lome Letter episode, in which the Spanish minister to Washington seemed to insult President William McKinley. McKinley ordered Admiral William T. Sampson's North Atlantic Squadron to begin a blockade of Cuban ports on April 21, and on April 25 Congress declared a state of war with Spain.

The United States had all the advantage at the outbreak of war. The U.S. Navy boasted six battleships, two armored cruisers, ten protected (partly armored) cruisers, and a number of gunboats against a Spanish fleet of five cruisers, a few destroyers, and some lesser craft. While the Spanish army had a hundred thousand troops in Cuba and twenty thousand troops in Puerto Rico, they were diseased and harried by guerrillas, as were those in the Spanish Philippines. The U.S. Army of twenty-six thousand officers and men could only serve as the cornerstone of a wartime army, but the principal operations against Cuba would be relatively close to American shores. Spain was far away from all her territories in jeopardy.

Though the war began over the Cuban issue, the first blow was struck far across the Pacific on May 1 at Manila Bay in the Philippines. There Commodore George Dewey's cruiser squadron annihilated the decrepit Spanish fleet in a morning's fighting after steaming from Hong Kong, where it had been on an official visit. The attack was not improvised, but

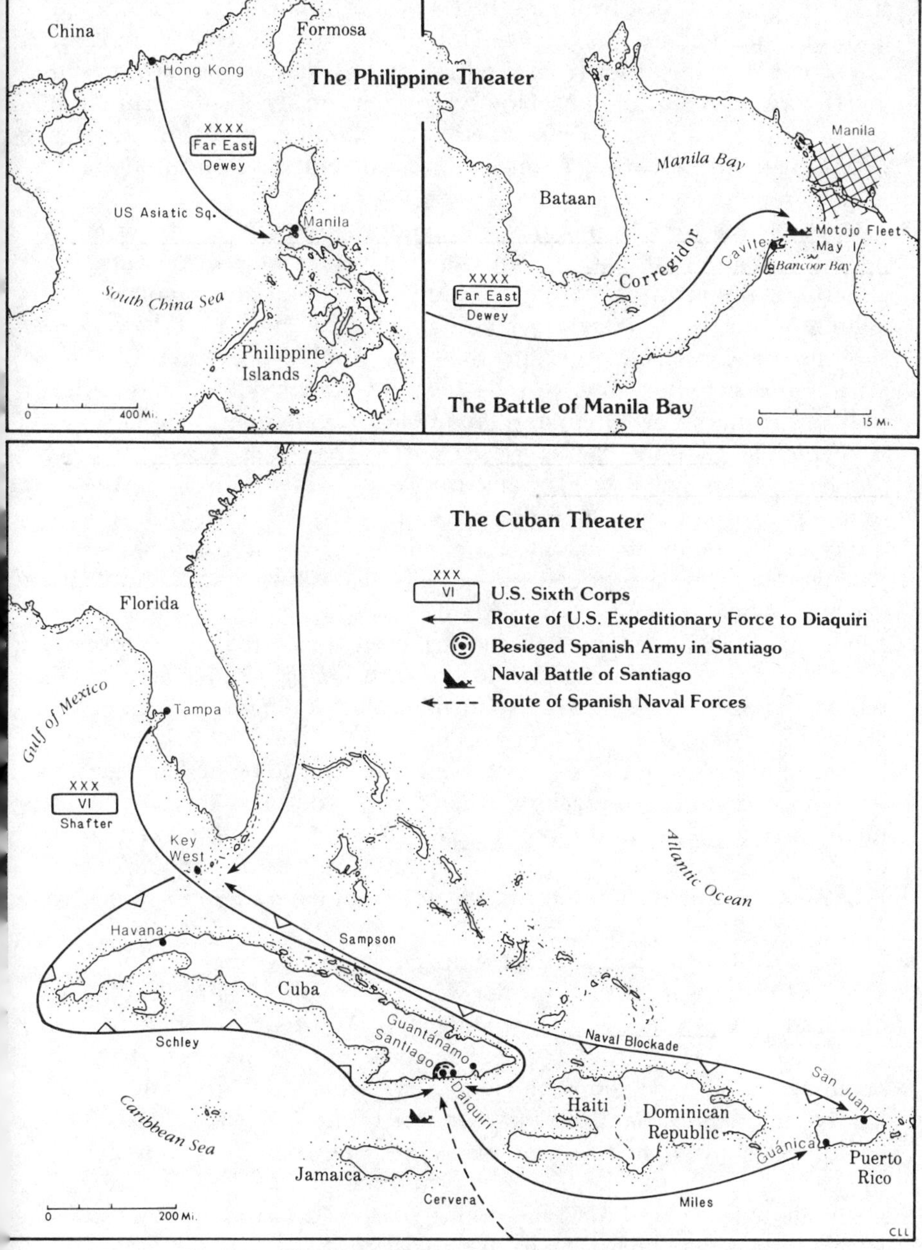

The Spanish-American War, 1898

had been planned in advance in the event war broke out between Spain and the United States, the cable at Hong Kong keeping Dewey apprised of events. A simple order from Washington was all that was necessary to get Dewey's force in motion. However, American troops to occupy the city of Manila did not arrive for another two months, though the cruiser *Charleston*—while escorting a convoy of reinforcements—captured Spanish Guam on the way.

Dewey's attack on Manila Bay was about the only thing that went as intended at the outbreak of war. General Nelson Miles, commanding general of the army, favored preparing eighty thousand regulars and volunteers for tropical warfare, landing them near Havana at the end of the rainy season in October, and following up that operation with the seizure of Puerto Rico. But Russell Alger, the secretary of war, was under pressure from the president and the public to begin operations at once. Accordingly, training camps were hastily erected at Chickamauga, Mobile, and Tampa Bay, Fla., and the hard-pressed War Department sought to arm and equip an influx of volunteers quickly. Amid the growing chaos of the army's mobilization, word was received that Admiral Pascual Cervera's naval squadron had left Spanish waters for the Western hemisphere. Rumors abounded that his purpose was to bombard the American cities along the Atlantic seaboard, protected by crumbling pre-Civil War fortifications. While the army improvised seacoast defenses, the navy formed a fast squadron under Commodore Winfield S. Schley to intercept Cervera's force in the North Atlantic. All this activity proved pointless when Cervera's force turned out to be heading across the South Atlantic, approaching Cuba from a southerly direction, and finally taking shelter in the port of Santiago on Cuba's southwest coast on May 19. Belatedly, Sampson and Schley reunited their squadrons at Key West and finally imposed a blockade on Santiago beginning on May 27.

The arrival of Cervera's fleet at Santiago shaped the further American strategy of the war so far as Cuba was concerned. On June 10, a few hundred U.S. Marines seized Guantanamo in order to provide Sampson's fleet a coaling station near Santiago, and on June 20 the first seventeen thousand troops of General William R. Shafter's V Corps landed at Daiquiri. Santiago's garrison of twenty-five thousand troops withdrew behind their fortifications as the American army approached the rear of the port. The first major land-fighting of the war—indeed about all that occurred in Cuba—took place on July 1, when U.S. troops attacked the outer line of Spanish defenses at San Juan Hill and at El Caney, an action in which Theodore Roosevelt, who had resigned his post as assistant secretary of the navy in order to accept a lieutenant-colonelcy in a volunteer cavalry regiment, was prominent. At the end of the day, the Spanish troops had fallen back on their final line of defense.

On July 3, Cervera's squadron tried to get to sea before Santiago fell; but with four battleships and a cruiser, Commodore Schley made short work of the Spanish force, whose ships were sunk or driven ashore. A fortnight later, the remaining twenty-two thousand Spanish troops in Santiago surrendered to Shafter. Before July was out, General Miles had led an unresisted invasion of Puerto Rico, and in August the Spanish government asked for an armistice. The whole war had cost the United States five thousand casualties, three-fifths of them fatal, and most caused by disease and bad food. Cuba received independence, while Puerto Rico and the Philippines became American territories, as the result of what Roosevelt called "a splendid little war."

D. The Sino-Japanese and Russo-Japanese Wars. Two Far Eastern wars at the turn of the century marked the rise of Japan to great power status, the Sino-Japanese War (1894–1895) and the Russo-Japanese War (1904–1905). As the first Oriental state in recent times to modernize, Japan escaped the fate of China and other Far Eastern states who were being increasingly eroded and overwhelmed by Western imperialism. Before the end of the nineteenth century, Japan had a modest but modern industrial base, a modern army modeled on the German, and a modern navy modeled on the British. But Japan was also eager to share in the spoils of the disintegrating Chinese empire, and in 1894 found a pretext for war through a Japanese-fomented rebellion in Korea, long a client-state of China. When Japanese troops landed in Korea to support a puppet regime, China declared war on August 1.

The war was not much of a contest for Japan. The decrepit Chinese army and navy were speedily defeated—the so-called Naval Battle of the Yalu being the first large fleet action since the Battle of Lissa in 1866—and Japanese troops overran Korea, southern Manchuria, and, across the Yellow Sea, the Shantung peninsula and its port of Weihaiwei. By the spring of 1895, the Japanese government was all set to demand the cessions of these territories and more when a coalition of European powers—jealous of their own interests in the Far East—threatened to intervene unless Japan submitted to a revision of the terms. Thanks to the interference of Russia, Germany, and France, Japan was forced to content herself with the island of Formosa (Taiwan), the nearby Pescadores, and a large war indemnity. Worse still, the Germans subsequently moved into the Shantung peninsula, and, in return for a Russian loan to pay off the Chinese war indemnity to Japan, China granted Russia the right in 1896 to extend her Trans-Siberian railroad to Vladivostok by the most direct route through central Manchuria. In 1897 Russia acquired the right to extend a spur of that line—known as the Chinese-Eastern railroad—from Harbin south to Port Arthur on the end of the Laiotung peninsula. In 1898 Russia acquired a long-term lease on the naval base at

Port Arthur and on the neighboring commercial port of Dairen. By all these moves, Russia had gained a dominating position in Manchuria, warm-water ports on the Yellow Sea, and a good position for further expansion into Korea. Not only was Russia expanding into territory coveted by Japan, her moves threatened the security of the home islands. Korea is about as close to Japan as Cuba is to the United States.

Fortunately for Japan, Britain was also disturbed by Russian Far Eastern expansion and anxious to protect her Far Eastern territories, while shifting more of her naval strength to home waters in order to counterbalance the growing German navy. The Anglo-Japanese Treaty, signed in 1902, guaranteed Japan's respect for British possessions and interests in the Far East in return for Britain's neutrality if Japan became involved in war with another foreign power, and British intervention on the Japanese side if Japan faced two or more enemies. The treaty freed Japan to follow a harder line toward Russia, and she wasted no time in demanding a renegotiation of the Russian position in Manchuria and increased security for Korea. When the negotiations with Russia faltered, Japan resorted to war in early 1904.

On the eve of the Russo-Japanese War, Russia appeared to have the advantage in forces-in-being. Tsar Nicholas II had a million troops on active service and 2.5 million reservists. His navy was then third largest in the world with fifteen battleships, nineteen cruisers, and thirty-eight destroyers. In contrast, the mobilized Japanese army contained eight hundred thousand troops, and the Japanese navy had six battleships, twenty-five cruisers, twenty-one destroyers, and thirty-nine torpedo-boats. Moreover, all of Japan's large ships had been built in foreign ports—mostly British—and she still had no capacity for building battleships or even carrying out extensive repairs. But, as Admiral Mahan was fond of pointing out, geography often vitiates apparent strength. Only three hundred thousand Russian troops were stationed in Manchuria when the war began, and they were dependent on a single-track trans-Siberian railroad, stretching over five thousand miles to European Russia, to bring them supplies and reinforcements. Seven Russian battleships, eleven cruisers, and eight destroyers made up the Russian Far Eastern fleet, but the battleships and destroyers were at Port Arthur, four of the cruisers were at Vladivostok (frozen in until spring), and one cruiser was at Inchon, Korea. By international treaty, the Black Sea fleet could not pass through the Dardanelles, and the Russian Baltic fleet would take months to reach the Far East, if, by chance, it could solve the logistical problems of an eighteen-thousand-mile voyage without overseas coaling bases. Japan had local superiority in land and naval forces, and that counted most.

The war began with a surprise attack by Admiral Heihachiro Togo's Combined Fleet on February 8 against the Russian fleet at anchor in Port Arthur and the Russian cruiser at Inchon. The attack with gunfire and

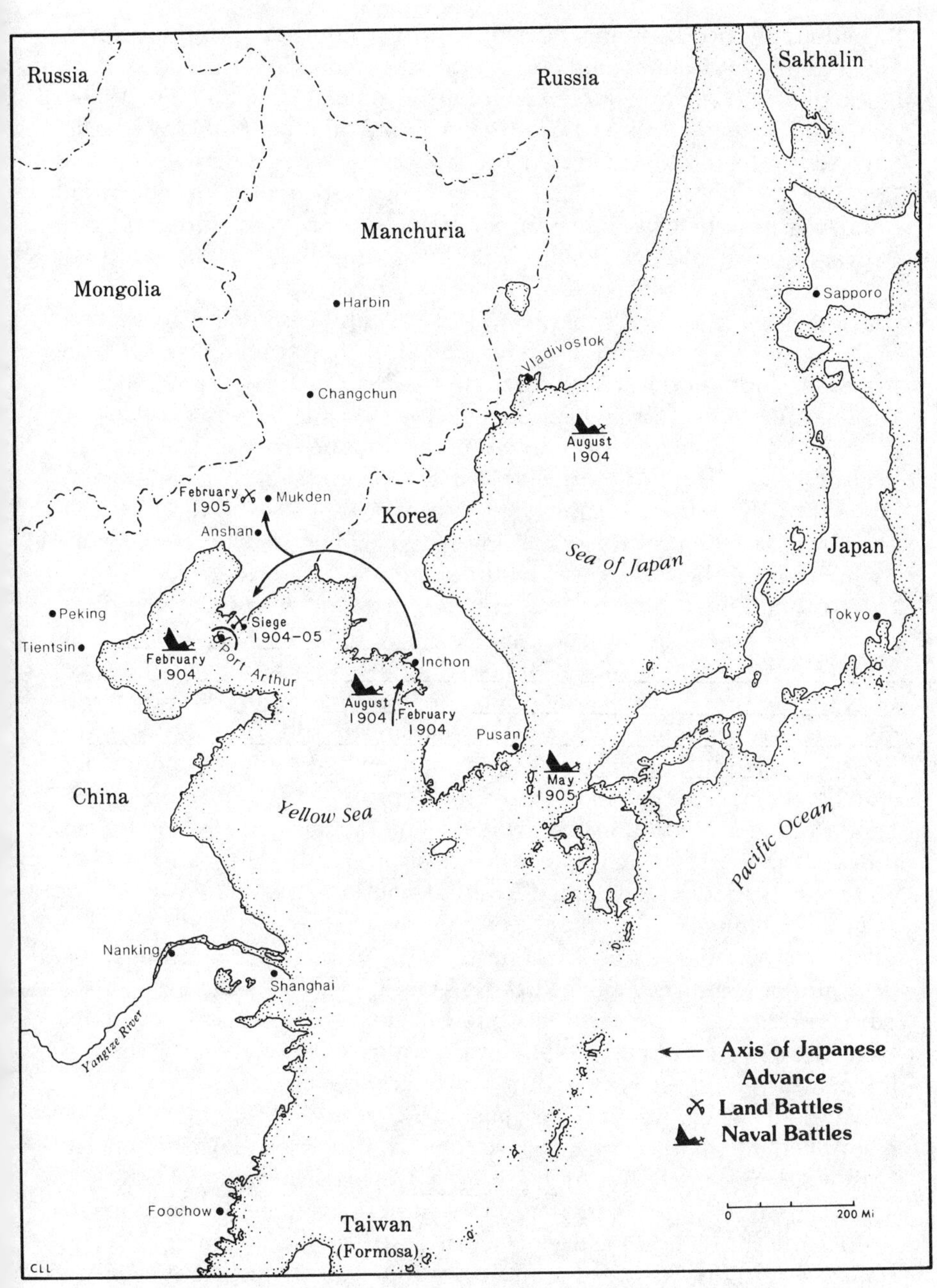

The Russo-Japanese War, 1904–1905

torpedoes put two Russian battleships and a cruiser out of commission at Port Arthur and eliminated the cruiser at Inchon. While Togo's fleet blockaded Port Arthur, Japanese troops invaded Korea and eventually imposed a siege on Port Arthur's rear. Admiral Stephan Makarov led the Port Arthur fleet to sea in March, only to lose his life and his flagship to a Japanese mine. Admiral Vilgelm Vitgeft, his successor, took no action until August, when he led six battleships, four cruisers, and eight destroyers into the Yellow Sea in hopes of getting them to the safety of Vladivostok. Though Togo's fleet had lost two battleships to mines the previous May, it proved superior to the Russian fleet in both speed and in the accuracy of its fire. Vitgeft was killed by shell fragments, and only five battleships, a cruiser, and three destroyers managed to limp back to Port Arthur. Two Russian cruisers which also sortied from Vladivostok in August had been destroyed by a separate Japanese force. The Russian fleet at Port Arthur was surrendered along with the port in January, 1905, though by then Japanese siege guns had destroyed most of it at anchor. About 65,000 Russian soldiers and sailors had defended Port Arthur, half of them casualties by the surrender.

All the attempts of the Russian army in Manchuria to relieve Port Arthur had failed during 1904, and in early 1905 the Japanese massed 300,000 troops near Mukden to take the rail center and drive the Russians further north. In the biggest battle in history before World War I, the Japanese grappled with 350,000 Russian troops for ten days in February on a front that eventually stretched for twenty miles. Both sides employed entrenchments, barbed-wire, repeating rifles, machine-guns, hand-grenades, and rapid-fire artillery. The Japanese finally outflanked the Russian position and forced a withdrawal, but they had suffered 70,000 casualties. The defeated Russians had lost 89,000 men.

The remaining card in the Tsar's hand was the arrival of the Russian Baltic fleet in the Far East. Accompanied by a train of coal colliers, the fleet, under Admiral Zinovi Rozhdestvenski, left the Baltic in October, 1904, and made its way slowly around Europe and Africa with covert aid from the French colonies. While in the Indian Ocean in early 1905, it learned of the fall of Port Arthur. Rozhdestvenski decided to make for Vladivostok when his fleet reached the Far East. After his fleet was resupplied for a final time near Camranh Bay, French Indochina, in May, it steered north toward Tsushima Strait between Japan and Korea. There awaited Togo's Combined Fleet. Superficially, the Russian fleet—eight battleships, seven cruisers, seven destroyers, and four old "ironclads"—was more powerful than Togo's four battleships, eight cruisers, fourteen destroyers, and thirty-nine torpedo-boats; but months at sea had left the Russian vessels fouled and their crews exhausted. The issue was joined on May 27, when Togo, using two columns and superior speed, inflicted a crushing defeat. Five Russian battleships, four cruisers, and two destroyers were sunk or captured. A Russian cruiser and two destroyers got through to Vladivostok, but the remaining Russian ships fled to neutral ports, where they were interned. Of the 13,000 Russian sailors, 4,830 had lost their lives. Togo's losses came to three torpedo-boats, some minor damage to larger vessels, and 117 sailors killed or wounded.

The Russo-Japanese War was formally concluded by the Peace of Portsmouth in September, 1905. Japan acquired Port Arthur, the Laiotung peninsula on which it is located, the Chinese Eastern Railroad as far north as Mukden, the southern half of Sakhalin Island off Russia's Pacific coast, and effective control over Korea (formerly annexed to the Japanese empire in 1910). Russia avoided paying a war indemnity. Military observers concluded from the events of the war that future great conflicts would probably be violent but brief, and the side which attacked first would have the advantage. No conflict as large as the Russo-Japanese War would occur again before 1914, and there was no opportunity to reconsider their verdict.

E. The Final Wars and Crises before 1914. In 1905, Germany's challenge to the Anglo-French having settled on Morocco without consulting Berlin set off the First Moroccan Crisis, but Germany backed down in its demands after Britain firmly supported France at the Algeciras Conference in 1906. In 1908 an even greater threat of war was posed by Austria-Hungary's formal annexation of Bosnia and Herzegovina. The Russian government was outraged, as was that of Serbia, which had dreamed of adding those provinces to a future Yugoslavia ("south Slav state") with Serbia as its hub. But when Germany firmly supported Austria-Hungary, Russia had to back down, and the Bosnian Crisis subsided. In 1911 a new Moroccan Crisis was peacefully settled when France transferred to Germany some minor territory in Africa, but in the same year Italian forces invaded Turkish Libya and achieved an easy victory. The Balkan League (Serbia, Montenegro, Greece, and Bulgaria) were encouraged to attack Turkey's remaining territories in Europe in 1912, but then Bulgaria fell out with the other members of the League over the division of the spoils, and a second Balkan War was fought in 1913. The London Conference established the new state of Albania on the Adriatic Sea as a partial solution, but Serbia was bitter over Austria-Hungary's diplomatic maneuvers to prevent her gaining access to the sea. In turn, the government at Vienna had come to view Serbia as a threat to the integrity of the Slavic parts of its empire. By the beginning of 1914, all of these developments and a strident nationalism surging across Europe made the maintenance of general peace precarious at best. That year the march toward world war reached its destination.

4

The First World War, 1914–18

I. The Outbreak and the Stalemate of 1914

A. The Outbreak of War. The Great War, as the generation between 1914 and 1939 would call it, was precipitated by the assassination of the Archduke Franz-Ferdinand, heir to the Austro-Hungarian throne, on June 28, 1914, while he was making a state visit in Sarajevo, Bosnia. The Austro-Hungarian government placed blame for the plot on Serbia, and succeeded in getting German support for a punitive policy toward the Balkan state. In late July, Vienna dispatched an ultimatum to Belgrade, which threatened Serbia's sovereignty and independence had all its points been agreed to. When the Serbian government refused to comply with all demands in the ultimatum, Austria-Hungary declared a state of war with Serbia on July 28.

The Russian government viewed Austria-Hungary's actions toward Serbia as unjustified, and resented Germany's support of Austro-Hungarian policy. On July 30, Tsar Nicholas ordered general mobilization against both of the Central Powers in support of Serbia. The German government promptly demanded that Russia cease mobilization on pain of war, and inquired of Paris where France would stand in the quarrel. The French government replied that it would consult its own interests, but on the afternoon of August 1 ordered general mobilization. Kaiser William II ordered German mobilization against both France and Russia within the hour. By the night of August 1, a *de facto* state of war existed between two of the Central Powers on one hand, and the Allied Powers on the other. Italy declared her neutrality.

Immediately upon the outbreak of war, the German General Staff, headed by General Helmuth von Moltke, proceeded to implement the revised Schlieffen Plan. On August 2 German troops occupied little Luxembourg, and on August 3 special German units at the frontier launched attacks on the Belgian forts around Liège, the gateway to the Belgian plains. German violation of Belgium's neutrality provoked a strong protest from the British government which, under the Treaty of 1839, was a guarantor of Belgian neutrality and independence. London warned that Britain could not fail to take action if the Germans persisted with their invasion. Berlin rejected the British demand for withdrawal of troops, and pled the excuse of "military necessity." The German government expressed the hope that Britain would not go to war over "a scrap of paper." The tactless German rejection of the British ultimatum did much to stimulate war fever against Germany in the British Isles. At midnight on August 4, Britain declared a state of war with Germany.

B. The Opening Battles and the Stalemate in the West, 1914. Except for the German occupation of Luxembourg and German attacks on Liège, the first two weeks of August, 1914, were taken up in the West with the completion of the mobilizations of both sides. By mid-month France had mobilized 1,060,000 troops in eastern France and divided them into five armies. Three armies composed of 660,000 men prepared to attack over the Franco-German border into Alsace-Lorraine, the Fourth Army of 160,000 men to invade the southern tip of the Ardennes forest in Belgium, and the Fifth Army of 240,000 men to attack down both sides of the Meuse river into the northern Ardennes. General Joseph Joffre, the French general-in-chief, thus intended that his forces on the right would drive toward the German Rhineland, while his forces on the left blocked any German attempt at a narrow-front envelopment through southern Belgium. As a further precaution, the British Expeditionary Force (BEF), under General Sir John French, took position just south of the Belgian border on the western flank of the Fifth Army. On the German side, 1,360,000 men were deployed in the West in seven armies, 320,000 troops in two armies to protect the border with France. Over a million German troops in five armies assembled to carry out the great encirclement of the French forces at the Franco-German border by a wide envelopment through Belgium.

The outcome of the Battle of the Frontiers (August 16–23) was a victory for the Germans. The three French armies trying to break into Alsace-Lorraine were repelled in their attacks, and in a week's time the French army had suffered 300,000 casualties. The French illusions about the irresistability of the attack were wiped out in a trice by withering German defensive fire. Meanwhile, further north, the Belgian army of 115,000 troops was compelled to abandon the defenses of Liège after German monster siege guns had knocked out its concrete forts and German infantry had infiltrated the gaps between them. The Belgian army retreated towards Brussels and Antwerp. After detaching troops to follow the Belgian army, the German First, Second, and Third armies advanced into central Belgium, then pivoted south toward the French frontier to the west of the river Meuse. On the inside of the German

Artillery of the World War I era: the French 75mm gun and the British 18-pounder gun.

SOURCE: John Batchelor and Ian Hogg, *Artillery* (New York: Ballantine, 1972).

Artillery of the World War I era: the German 21cm howitzer.

SOURCE: John Batchelor and Ian Hogg, *Artillery* (New York: Ballantine, 1972).

Artillery of the World War I era: the Austrian Schlancke Emma and the German Big Bertha.

SOURCE: John Batchelor and Ian Hogg, *Artillery* (New York: Ballantine, 1972).

wheel, the Fourth and Fifth armies advanced through the Belgian Ardennes and Luxembourg, respectively, pivoting on the fortified area of Metz-Thionville. At first unaware of the huge size of the German right wing entering Belgium, the French Fourth and Fifth armies, plus the British Expeditionary Force (BEF), advanced headlong into the wall of oncoming German forces and were almost enveloped before they recognized the danger. Then they began a fighting withdrawal to French territory.

The Allied defeat in the Battle of the Frontiers opened Joffre's eyes to the fact that, all French prewar predictions to the contrary, the Germans were attempting a wide-front envelopment of his forces through Belgium. In order to thwart German intentions, a new front of Allied armies had to be formed, facing north, as quickly as possible, while at the same time the Franco-German frontier had to be defended from attacks by the German armies in Alsace-Lorraine. Working with his staff, Joffre ordered the French First and Second armies to man the fixed defenses at the frontier, where they subsequently beat off the attacks of the German Sixth and Seventh armies. He regrouped the Third and Fourth armies between the fortress-city of Verdun and Rheims. With reserves and drafts from other armies, he created a new Ninth Army (so designated to confuse the Germans), under General Ferdinand Foch, to extend the new line further toward Paris. The gap between the Ninth Army and Paris was to be filled by the BEF and the French Fifth Army, as they retreated from Belgium. Finally, the collection of reserve divisions at Paris, and troops arriving there from North Africa, were formed into a new Sixth Army under General Joseph Maunoury and stationed just north of the capital. General Joseph Galliéni, the military governor of Paris, rushed the city's fixed defenses to completion. The new line of Allied forces finally ran from Verdun down the axis of the Marne Valley to Paris, a distance of one hundred fifty miles. Joffre lacked enough forces to extend the line further from Paris to the English Channel, and he could only hope that the Germans lacked the forces for a turning movement west of Paris.

The Allied redeployment took a little over a week to accomplish, and was possible because of at least two factors. The first was the excellent rail network between the Franco-German frontier and the French capital. The second factor was the relative slowness of the German advance through Belgium, hindered as it was by logistical difficulties. A bypassed Belgian garrison at Namur kept the direct rail line from Liège closed until late August, and the same line, where it entered northern France, was shut down again by a French garrison bypassed at Maubeuge. In consequence, the Germans had to forward supplies to their First and Second armies by a rail dog-leg north to Brussels, then south again through Mons and Cambrai. The German First Army, on the outside of the wheel, became so short on food and fodder that at night, instead of resting between marches, troops had to scramble about seeking local supplies. Some of its troops, and some of those of the Second Army next in line on the wheel, would enter the Battle of the Marne having been unfed for two days.

Still, the German armies might have summoned enough strength to swing slightly west of Paris and to envelop Joffre's new line in early September had not other factors intervened. First, there was an unexpected early Russian offensive against East Prussia, which caused Moltke to detach two army corps from his right-wing armies and to send them off to the Eastern Front, where they were to aid the embattled Eighth Army. The detachment forced a contraction of the German front and reduced the chance of outflanking Paris. Second, General Alexander von Klück, commander of the German First Army, caused his troops to veer to the southeast in an effort to trap the BEF before it could withdraw below the Marne. The attempt failed and the new direction insured that the First Army would cross the Marne well east of Paris. Klück was unaware that the French Sixth Army, just north of Paris, even existed, or of the danger that it might attack his army's flank and rear.

Galliéni was first to grasp the significance of the German First Army's change in direction, and accordingly he urged Joffre not to have his armies stand at the Marne, but to withdraw them still further south—except for the Sixth Army near Paris. In this way, the German advance south of the Marne would move the whole line of their right-wing armies into a potential trap. Joffre agreed to the proposal, and the Allied retreat continued south of the Marne in early September, the Germans in hot pursuit. Joffre planned for his line to turn about and offer battle on September 6, when all the German forces would be well into the trap, but Manoury misjudged the position of the German First Army and attacked twenty-four hours too soon. The attack of the French Sixth Army near Paris not only revealed its presence to the startled Klück, it came while two of Klück's four corps were still north of the Marne. Klück promptly wheeled these corps to intercept the French attack and ordered the other two corps to return to their assistance as rapidly as possible. Thus the fighting on the river Ourcq began the action that the next day would continue as the Battle of the Marne, as the other Allied armies came about and also attacked. By the night of September 6, a general action was underway all along the front from Verdun to Paris.

The French Sixth Army's premature attack ruined Joffre's chance to envelop the German right from the direction of Paris, but it opened up another possibility. The concentration of the German First Army against that attack had left a gap between the First Army and the Second Army, the latter heavily engaged with the French forces to its front. As it happened, the gap—about twenty miles in width—was on the axis of the BEF's advance. But General Sir John French, the BEF commander, was not aware of that fact. As his forces probed north, he was puzzled that his troops had failed to make contact with the enemy while the French armies to either side were heavily engaged. His caution increased as his troops neared the Marne, for he feared a German trap. Meanwhile, on the German side, both Klück and General Karl von Bülow, commander of the German Second Army, were acutely aware of the gap and the danger it posed to their forces. To make matters worse for the Germans, both Klück's and Bülow's headquarters had lost contact with Moltke's headquarters (by then in Luxembourg). Moltke, perhaps sensing that something was wrong, had meanwhile dispatched Lieutenant-Colonel Richard Hentsch to their headquarters by automobile, but Hentsch did not arrive until the afternoon of September 8, when the Battle of the Marne was approaching its climax. After conferring with both Bülow and Klück's chief-of-staff, Hentsch appraised the situation. Since there was no time to refer to general headquarters, Hentsch took the decision on his own responsibility to order both the First and Second armies to begin withdrawing if the BEF crossed the Marne the following day. His decision proved crucial for the outcome of the battle. On the morning of

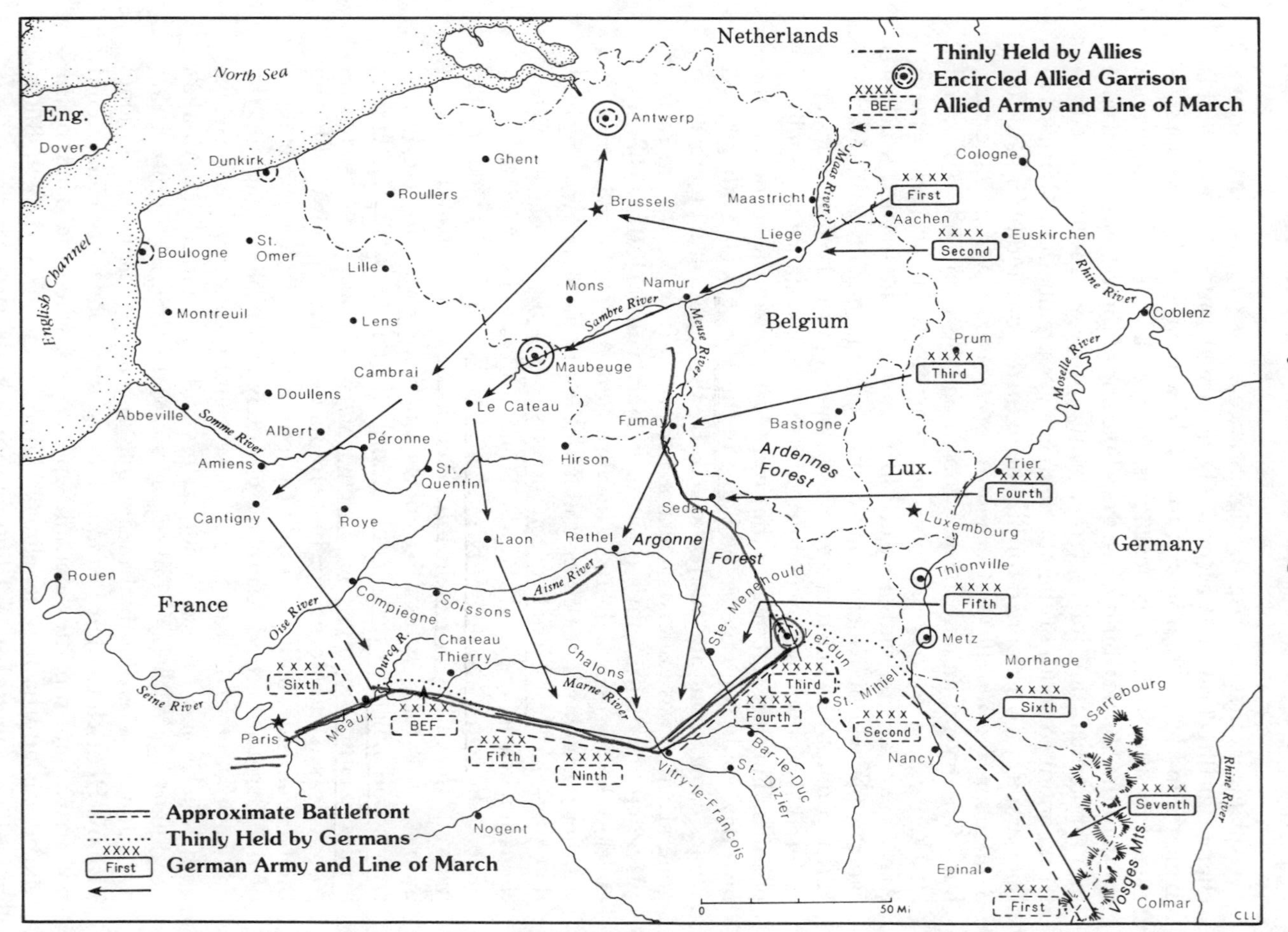

Battle of the Marne: BEF Penetrates Gap between German First and Second Armies, September 9, 1914

September 9, General French sent a few patrols over the Marne and unwittingly decided one of the greatest battles in history. By that afternoon the German First and Second armies had begun breaking off contact with their adversaries, and that night had begun a full-scale retreat. On September 10 the German Third Army, which had nearly gutted the French Ninth Army to its front, was forced to conform. That evening Moltke, who had meanwhile learned of the situation on the right, had sanctioned a general withdrawal to the river Aisne, about forty miles north of the Marne. Gradually it dawned on the French and British commands that somehow they had stopped the German drive and a new phase in the war was beginning. As for Moltke, the news of defeat led to his secret resignation and the appointment of General Erich von Falkenhayn, formerly the minister of war, as the new chief of the General Staff, effective September 14. That day the German First, Second, and Third armies took up defensive positions along the Aisne.

The German armies beat off the Allied attacks on their new position on the Aisne in mid-September, leaving each side the option of digging in part of their forces to hold its line and with the rest to shift toward the west in hopes of outflanking the opposing line. As more men were called up and deployed, the so-called Race to the Sea began. Meanwhile, the Belgian army broke out of its besieged position at Antwerp and made its way down the coast to link up with the BEF which had leap-frogged the French armies on its left. The battling line of armies finally reached the North Sea just north of Nieuport on October 10, and, for the first time in the war, they faced a war without flanks. The Germans then tried to break through the BEF's position at Ypres, but to no avail. When the Germans suspended their last efforts on November 11, it was exactly four years before the armistice of 1918. A deadlocked front stretched from the North Sea some 450 twisting miles to the neutral Swiss frontier. For this result, France paid 950,000 casualties in the first five months of the war. The Germans had lost 700,000 men on the Western front. About two-fifths of the original BEF and the Belgian army were casualties as the result of half a year of fighting.

C. The Opening Battles on the Eastern Front and the Stalemate of 1914. In obedience to its prewar vow to aid the French by launching an early offensive against German territory, the Russian General Staff assembled General Pavel von Rennenkampf's First Russian Army at Vilna and General Alexander Sampsonov's Second Russian Army at Warsaw in the first two weeks of August, 1914. The Russian plan called for the First Army to invade East Prussia from the east in order to hold the attention of the defending German Eighth Army, while the Russian Second Army struck from Poland into its rear. Soon after the Russian First Army crossed the frontier in mid-August, it inflicted a repulse on

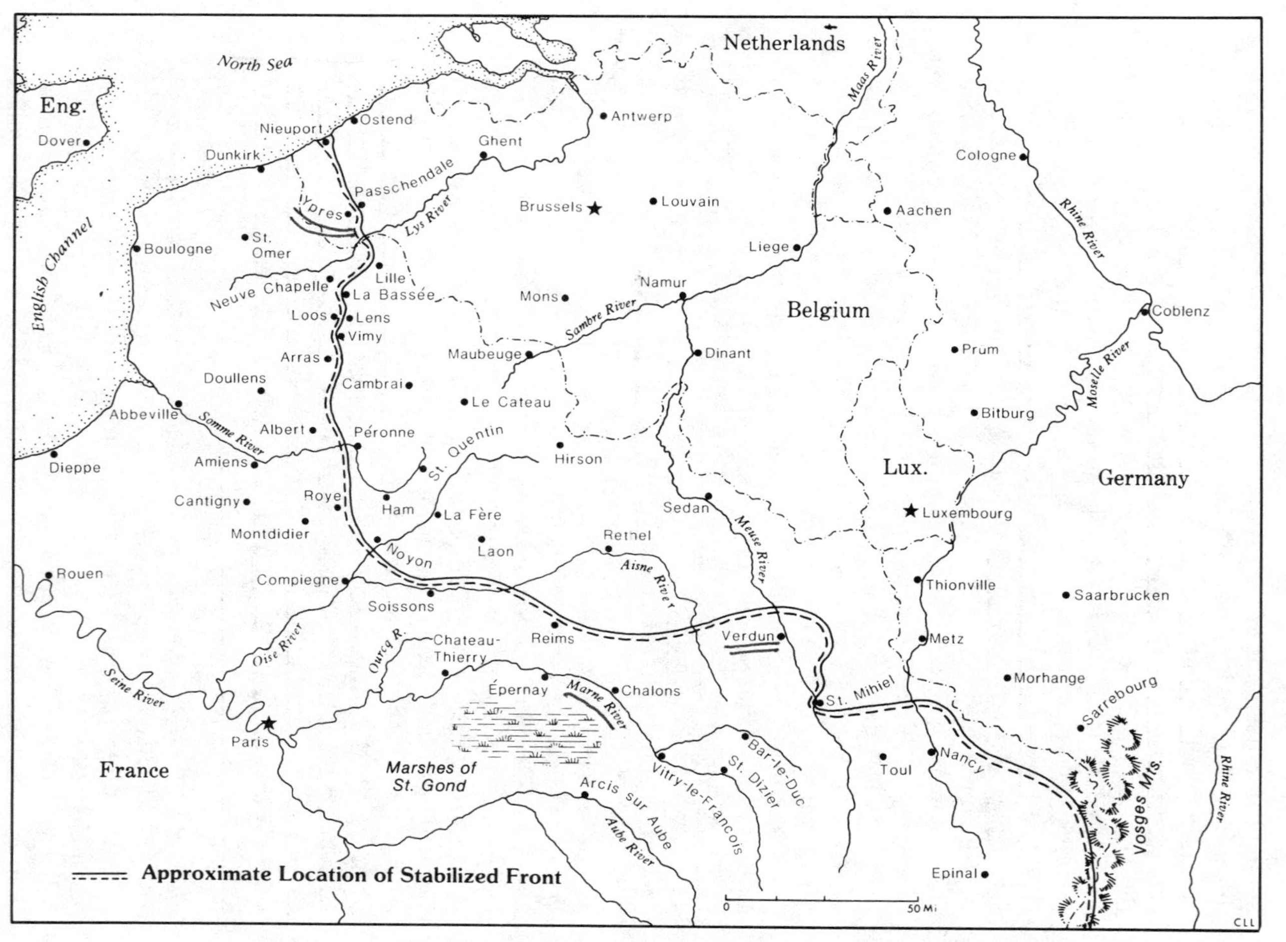

Approximate Location of Stabilized Front

The Western Front, 1915–1916

the Eighth Army at Gumbinnen. When the commander and chief-of-staff of the Eighth Army seemed unable to handle the situation, Moltke relieved them and appointed General Paul von Hindenburg, recalled from the retired list, to command the Eighth Army, and General Erich Ludendorff to serve as his chief-of-staff. The new team arrived at East Prussian headquarters on August 23. By then Colonel Max Hoffmann, the Eighth Army's chief-of-operations, had worked out a plan for the Eighth Army to redeploy rapidly by rail to deal with the threat posed by Sampsonov's army. Hindenburg and Ludendorff, who had a similar idea in mind, quickly approved Hoffman's arrangements. The rapid rail redeployment was not detected by Rennenkampf's army, which remained stationary while working on logistical problems, and Sampsonov was unaware that he was leading his army into a trap when it pushed into East Prussia in late August. The resulting Battle of Tannenberg (August 26–30) was to be the only *Kesselschlacht* of World War I, but it was a brilliant German success. About a hundred thousand Russian troops in ten divisions were encircled and destroyed. Then the Eighth Army redeployed rapidly again by rail against Rennenkampf's army, outflanking it at the Battle of the Masurian Lakes (September 9–12) and forcing it to withdraw to the Russian frontier. The second battle had been won before the German retreat to the Aisne in the West was finished, and Hindenburg and Ludendorff emerged as the first major German heroes of the war.

The Russians had better luck against the Austro-Hungarians. Conrad von Hötzendorff, the Austro-Hungarian chief-of-staff, made the mistake of dividing his forces for an invasion of Serbia, then changing his mind and trying to concentrate on the Polish frontier. As a result, four Russian armies got the better of three Austro-Hungarian armies in the Battle of the Galician Frontier (August 23–September 1). By late September, the Austro-Hungarian armies had been driven back a hundred miles to the line of the Carpathian mountains. The Germans came to their rescue when a new German Ninth Army, under General August von Mackensen, joined the Eighth Army in the East and launched an invasion of Poland. The Russians had to take off pressure from the Austro-Hungarians in order to deal with these attacks, and by the end of 1914 they had lost half of Poland and a million men. The first five months of the war cost the Austro-Hungarian army 750,000 men. The Germans suffered fewer than 200,000 casualties on the Eastern Front in 1914. Still, another deadlocked front stretched for nine hundred and fifty miles from Memel to the neutral Rumanian border. Neither the Russian nor the Austro-Hungarian army ever fully recovered from the effects of the opening battles in 1914, but neither was there any prospect of a quick end to the war in the East.

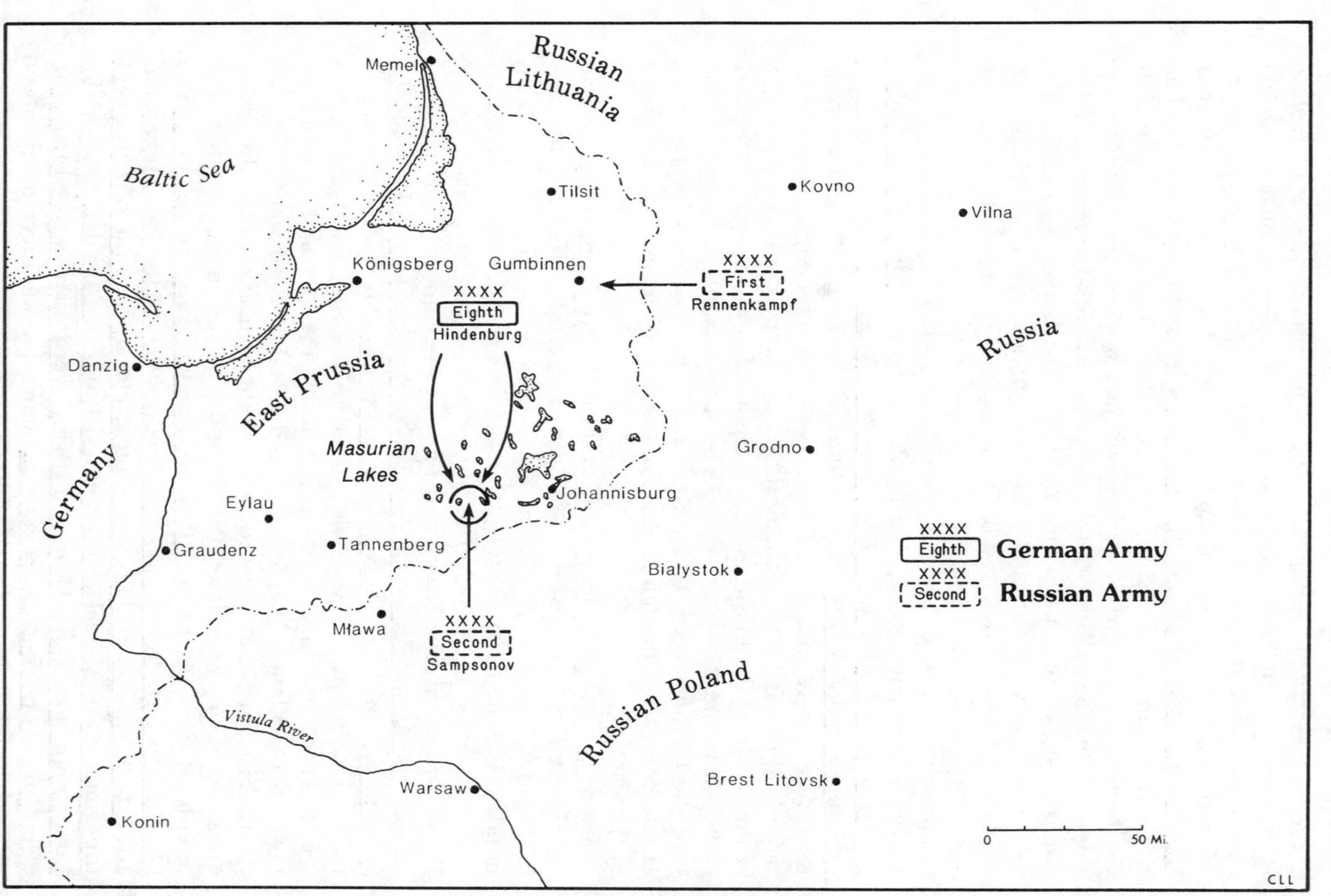

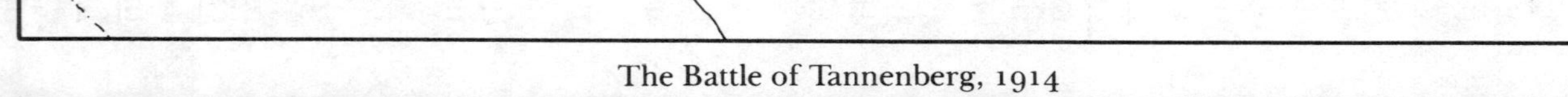
The Battle of Tannenberg, 1914

D. The War at Sea in 1914. The German High Seas Fleet braced itself for a British attack on its anchorages on the North Sea in August-September, 1914, but none came. Admiral Sir John Jellicoe, commander of Britain's Grand Fleet, moved his dreadnoughts to war stations at Rosyth, Scotland, and Scapa Flow in the Orkney islands. The British Channel Fleet, composed of old battleships, closed off the other exit from the North Sea. The British then declared a "War Zone" in the North Sea and a distant blockade on Germany's ports. Only then did Germany's leaders begin to realize how dependent the Second Reich was on foreign raw materials and even food-stuffs. As events were to reveal, Germany had the capacity to last about four years if the blockade was not sooner removed.

The French fleet in the Mediterranean quickly bottled up the Austro-Hungarian navy in the Adriatic with assistance from the British navy, but two German ships—the battle cruiser *Goeben* and the cruiser *Breslau*—cruising in the Mediterranean at the outbreak of war, fled to Constantinople, where they were interned by the Turks. When the Ottoman Empire entered the war on the German side in November, 1914, the two ships, complete with their original German crews, were recommissioned in the Turkish navy. The *Goeben* was more than a match for the five old Russian battleships on the Black Sea. In the Far East, Admiral Graf von Spee led his cruiser squadron from Shantung to the German Marshall and Caroline islands in the Pacific, then launched attacks on Allied shipping along the South American coasts. On November 1, his squadron defeated a pursuing British cruiser force off Coronel, Chile, but in December all his ships but the *Dresden* were sunk by British battle cruisers in the Battle of the Falkland Islands. The *Dresden,* and the *Emden* (earlier detached from Spee's squadron), were run down and destroyed during 1915. Though a few other German surface raiders appeared from time to time during the rest of the war, the submarine was to carry the main burden of German *guerre de course* in World War I.

The German discovery of the submarine's potential for *guerre de course* was accidental. In 1914, the U-boat's greatest achievement was in a coast defense encounter in which the U-9 sank three British cruisers in less than an hour when they came too close to German coasts. But in retaliation for the British "War Zone" proclaimed in the North Sea, the German admiralty declared a "War Zone" around the British Isles and claimed the right of its submarines to attack any Allied vessel there without warning. With only twenty-two U-boats with enough range to operate beyond the North Sea, and only a third of them on station at any one time, the German declaration seemed little more than a gesture. But by the beginning of 1915 that gesture was beginning to have substance when submarines proved unexpectedly effective against slow-moving merchant ships. The German admiralty ordered the building of more, longer-ranged submarines and took a new interest in the heretofore despised *guerre de course.* By the end of the war, Germany had commissioned 345 submarines, manned by 10,000 sailors. The lowly U-boat proved to be one of the most effective weapons in the Kaiser's arsenal.

II. The Search for Victory, 1915–16

A. The Allied Strategy and Operations, 1915. By 1915, British councils had divided between "Easterners" and "Westerners" over the conduct of the war. General French, the BEF commander, favored concentration of Britain's war effort on the Western Front. The "Easterners," led by Winston Churchill, first lord of the admiralty (secretary of the navy), favored operations against the Ottoman Empire and the establishment of new lines of supply to Tsarist Russia, already suffering from a dearth of arms and ammunition. The problem was complicated by unprecedented efforts to expand Britain's land forces as well as equip the volunteer forces of Canada, Australia, and New Zealand. Field Marshal Kitchener was called back from retirement to serve as secretary of state for war, and he promised an army of thirty-seven divisions by the end of 1915. David Lloyd George soon headed a new Ministry of Munitions to deal with the British and Allied ammunition crisis. The final decision was to give priority to the Western Front, but to launch lesser operations in the Middle East, relying heavily on Dominion forces and troops of the Indian Army. Priority was given to opening a new line of supply for the Tsar's hard-pressed armies.

The biggest Allied effort in the Middle East in 1915, and the largest amphibious assault in World War I, turned out to be a disaster. In early 1915, British warships tried to knock out shore batteries blocking the straits of the Dardanelles, preliminary to making contact with the Russians on the Black Sea. When the naval effort failed, an amphibious force composed mostly of Australian and New Zealand troops was sent to occupy the key Gallipoli peninsula. The bungled Allied landings lost the element of surprise, and Turkish troops, advised by German General Liman von Sanders, kept the Allied forces bottled up within their beachheads for months. By the time the Allied troops were withdrawn at the end of the year, they had suffered three hundred thousand casualties. The British and French had lost several old battleships and lesser craft to shore batteries, submarines, and mine fields into the bargain. An Allied effort through Greece to aid Serbia against German, Austro-Hungarian, and Bulgarian invasion came too late. Though the Allied army kept its foothold in Greece, the Germans referred to it as an "armed prisoner-of-war camp." The British beat off a Turkish attack on Egypt from Palestine, but a British drive from the head of the Persian Gulf into

Mesopotamia bogged down. On balance, Allied operations in the Middle East in 1915 accomplished very little.

Allied spirits were encouraged when in May, 1915, Italy entered the war against the Central Powers and launched offensives over the river Isonzo at the head of the Adriatic Sea against the Austro-Hungarian frontier. But the narrow coastal shelf left little room for maneuver and the offensives soon bogged down in the face of defensive firepower. For the next three years, the Italian armies would make repeated efforts to break the stalemate, using up a million men in the process, and, until nearly the end of the war, getting no nearer the objective of Trieste than when they had started. With German stiffening, the Austrians not only held but in 1917 launched a counter-offensive that drove the Italian forces back fifty miles. The Austro-German aerial bombing of small Italian towns behind the front would inspire General Giulio Douhet, the most radical of the postwar advocates of air power, to believe that the destruction of civilian morale might be the key to breaking future stalemates. Certainly Italian morale declined from 1915 on for a variety of reasons in a theater as deadlocked as any in World War I.

Allied performance on the Western front in 1915 was disappointing. General French's offensives at Neuve Chapelle, La Bassée, and Loos gained little ground and almost used up the last of the "Old Contemptibles," the original soldiers of the BEF. The attacks against the German entrenchments also took a large toll of the Territorials and the first of Kitchener's volunteers. Near the end of 1915, General Sir Douglas Haig relieved French of the command of the BEF, but he was to prove to have no more strategic or tactical insight than French, though he held his command to the end of the war. As for France's army, it called up older men in order to expand to 102 divisions during the year, but Joffre squandered much of the new strength in offensives in the Artois and in the Champagne. In point of casualties, 1915 was the worst year of the war for the French: 1,450,000 men killed, wounded, taken prisoner, or missing. In the seventeen months since the war began, the French had suffered a total of 2,400,000 casualties.

B. German Strategy in 1915. Like the British councils, the German leaders divided among "Easterners" and "Westerners." Falkenhayn recognized Russia's material weakness, but he also believed that an extensive invasion of Russia would be a prolonged affair. He therefore favored a concentrated effort to knock France out of the war first. Hindenburg and Ludendorff, in supreme command on the Eastern Front by 1915, favored a concentration against Russia. In early 1915, the Kaiser agreed that four German armies in the East (Eighth, Ninth, Tenth and Eleventh), amounting to sixty-five divisions, would be permitted to try to force Russia from the war by the end of the year. The reduced German forces in the West would launch only local offensives and mainly stand on the defensive. The German drive in the East took Warsaw and nearly all the rest of unoccupied Poland. By October, when the effort was called off, the battle line ran from just west of Dvinsk south through the Pripet Marshes. Still worse for the Russians, they had lost 2 million men during 1915, and the Grand Duke Nicholas had been discredited as the Russian commander-in-chief. Tsar Nicholas II assumed personal command of the Russian armies, though it meant he had to be away from St. Petersburg and near the front most of the time.

With only limited forces left on the Western front in 1915, Falkenhayn confined himself to local offensives about Ypres, including the first use of poison gas in the West on April 22. French Algerian troops fled at the approach of the cloud of chlorine released from cylinders in the German trenches, but Canadian troops nearby filled the gap. The Canadians also withstood a second gas attack on April 24. The small quantity of gas used had not been decisive. By the time the Germans were ready that summer to use gas on a large scale, the Allies were equipping their troops with gas masks and other antigas equipment, and preparing to use poison gas themselves. Gas-filled artillery shells became the favored means of delivery as the war went on, but gas merely made the deadlock worse rather than better. Twelve times as many men were killed by shell-fire as by gas in World War I.

C. The War at Sea, 1915. Sixty-eight new U-boats were added to the Kaiser's submarine fleet during 1915, against the loss of twenty-three. Meanwhile, the U-boats sank an impressive 1 million tons of Allied shipping in the War Zone. But on May 7 a German U-boat sank the trans-Atlantic liner *Lusitania* off the Irish coast, causing the death of over a thousand passengers and crew, including 128 Americans. The unannounced attack was clearly in violation of international law governing the conduct of *guerre de course,* and President Woodrow Wilson strongly denounced the German action. After three more American lives were lost on the *Arabic* in August, diplomatic relations between Germany and the United States seemed on the point of being severed. Then the Kaiser's government made the "Arabic Pledge" that no more liners would be attacked in the War Zone without proper notification. A new crisis arose in 1916 with the sinking of the French steamer *Sussex* and the injury to three Americans, and the Kaiser avoided a break with the United States with the "Sussex Pledge" that German submarine warfare would be carefully restricted in future. Admiral Wilhelm Tirpitz resigned as head of the German navy in protest. Not until early in 1917 did Germany go over to unrestricted submarine warfare again, an act that nearly won the war for her but which made war with the United States inevitable.

D. The War on Land, 1916. Falkenhayn's faith in victory over France was given full sway in February, 1916, when the biggest German offensive of the war to that time was unleashed against French lines around Verdun. Falkenhayn hoped for either a breakthrough or a battle of attrition that would hurt the French army worse than the German. General Henri Pétain, placed in charge of the defense of the threatened sector, pledged "They shall not pass." In August, Falkenhayn admitted his failure to the Kaiser, who appointed Hindenburg to succeed him as chief of the General Staff and Ludendorff to serve as Hindenburg's deputy. The French kept the battle going in order to regain lost ground, and, when it finally ended ten months after its beginning, it had cost the Germans 362,000 men and the French 332,000 men. Joffre was blamed for the near-disaster at Verdun in the battle's early stages and was replaced with General Robert Nivelle as French commander-in-chief. French casualties for the whole of 1916 came to 950,000 troops.

Britain adopted conscription for the first time in her history in January, 1916, and New Zealand followed suit. An Australian referendum on conscription rejected the draft. Canada adopted conscription, but officials were afraid to enforce it vigorously in the French province of Quebec. In any case, British and Dominion conscript armies were not ready for service before 1917, and in the meantime General Haig believed the existing combination of regulars, Territorials, and volunteers could win a decisive victory on the Somme. For a week prior to the attack on July 1, 850 British guns hammered an eighteen-mile stretch of German front. On July 1, 100,000 British troops went forward only to suffer 60,000 casualties before noon, the largest number ever on a single day in the history of the British army. Haig's repeated attacks on the Somme that summer and into the fall, until the drive officially ended on November 14, ran up the total to 400,000 casualties in 140 days of fighting. By then the regular-Territorial-volunteer combination was about used up, and British armies in 1917–1918 were overwhelmingly conscript.

When Nivelle took command of the French army, he was confidentially told that the new levies might represent the "last army of France." By 1917, France had run through about half the young manpower of the country. But Nivelle optimistically prepared a new French offensive on the Aisne for April, 1917. In the East, the Russian offensive, directed by General Aleksi Brussilov, against the Austro-Hungarians was successful and even encouraged Rumania to throw in its lot with the Allies, but a German army under Falkenhayn—who had accepted a field command after his relief as chief of the General Staff—crushed the Rumanian army, and the Russian offensive was contained. By the fall of 1916, German intelligence had indications that the Tsar's armies were close to collapse.

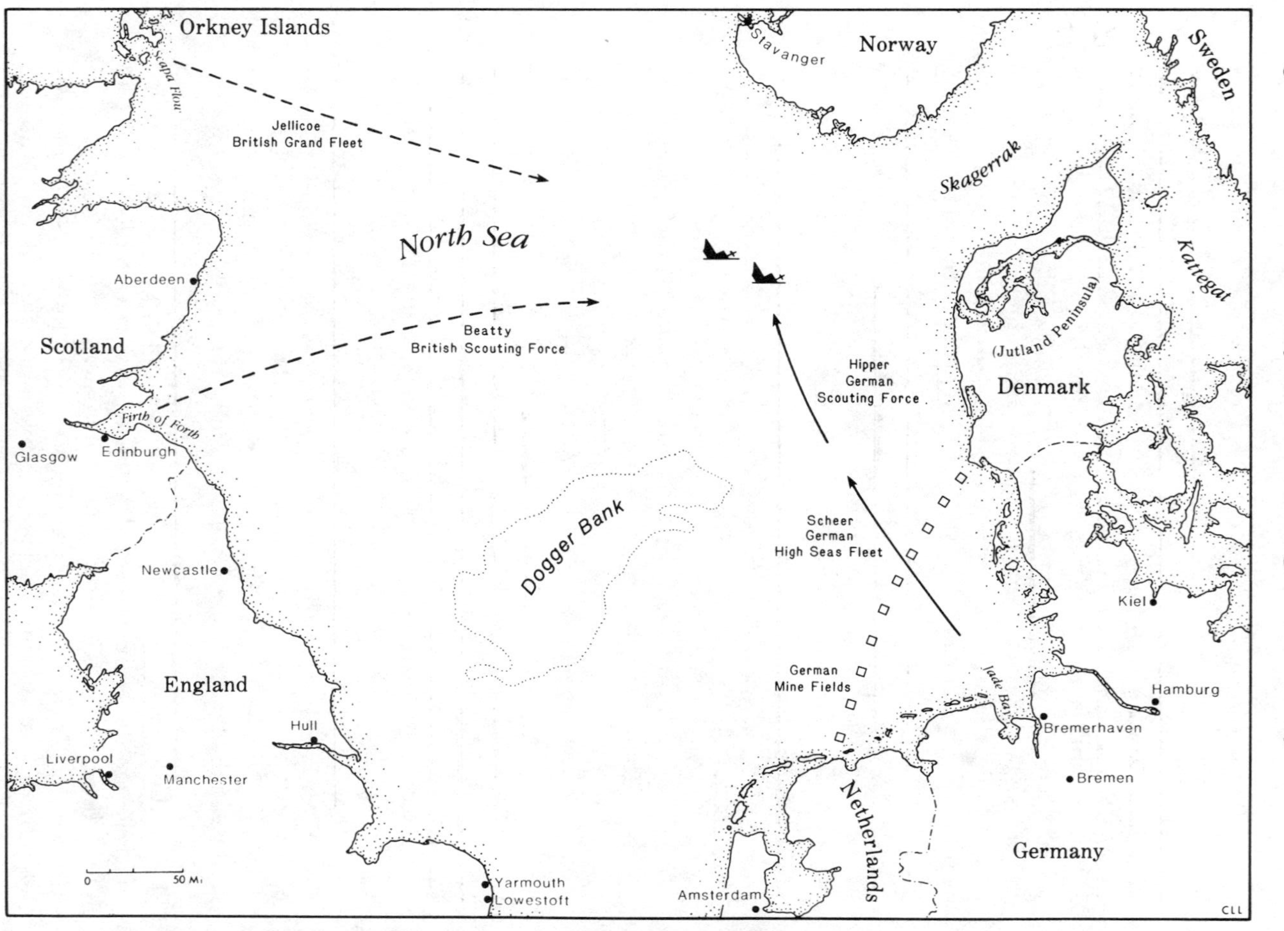

The Naval Battle of Jutland, May 31–June 1, 1916

In the Middle East, 1916 was a mixture of Allied successes and failures. The British had occupied the Sinai desert and were on the borders of Palestine, but the British drive from the Persian Gulf had ended in a humiliating defeat at Kut on the Tigris River, where fourteen thousand Britons were surrendered in April. Still, Major T. E. Lawrence, with his mastery of Arabic, was making some progress in arousing the Arab tribes against their Turkish masters, though it was 1917 before the war in the Arabian desert would begin to have important results.

E. The War at Sea, 1916. German U-boats sank 2 million tons of Allied shipping in 1916, but the great drama of the year was fastened on the one and only sortie of the German High Seas Fleet far into the North Sea during World War I. Admiral Reinhardt von Scheer, commander of the fleet, hoped to court action with Admiral David Beatty's Scouting Force without risking a major fleet action with Jellicoe's forces, but radio intelligence alerted the British admiralty that Scheer's forces were going to sea at the end of May. Late in the afternoon of May 31, on a latitude with the Danish peninsula of Jutland but in the center of the North Sea, the two fleets engaged. In the largest fleet action to its time, Jutland involved 254 ships, displacing 1,600,000 tons. The backbone of Jellicoe's Grand Fleet were 37 dreadnought battleships and battle cruisers; that of Scheer's fleet 21 dreadnought battleships and battle cruisers. In a battle obscured by smoke and falling darkness, the Grand Fleet lost 3 battle cruisers, 3 cruisers, and 8 destroyers (110,980 tons), and 6,784 men. The High Seas Fleet lost a pre-dreadnought battleship, a battle cruiser, 3 cruisers, and 10 destroyers (62,233 tons), and 3,039 men. Much of the British loss was due to defects in magazine protection in the three battle cruisers. Though Scheer claimed a victory on points, Jellicoe was left with command of the sea. Britain's blockade was not affected. After Jutland, it was clear that a German victory at sea—if there was to be one—would have to be accomplished by submarine and *guerre de course.*

F. The Rise of Air Power. Though both the airship and the airplane began their careers in World War I as observation and scouting craft, they made the transition to weapons-platforms in remarkable time. In January, 1915, German zeppelins based in Belgium began a campaign of strategic bombing against the British Isles and especially London. The typical airship could carry 5,000 lbs. of bombs, but accuracy was poor and it was vulnerable to bad weather. In the span of two and a half years, zeppelins made 208 sorties over England, dropped 196 tons of bombs, killed 557 Britons and injured 1,360 more. But 80 zeppelins and 1,600 crewmen were lost in these raids. In June, 1917, twin-engine Gotha and Giant airplanes took over the strategic air war, each plane capable of carrying 1,000 lbs. of bombs apiece. By November 1918, they had dropped 73 tons of bombs on England, killing 860 Britons and injuring 2,060. The main effect of the strategic bombing was to lower civilian morale, already weakened by food shortages and the horrendous casualties on the Western front.

The German air raids on the British Isles had an important influence on British thinking about the organization of air power. Until 1918, Britain had followed the practice of other countries in leaving aviation divided between the army and the navy, but neither the army's Royal Flying Corps (RFC) nor the navy's Royal Naval Air Service (RNAS) was willing to take prime responsibility for defense of Britain's skies. The problem was referred to a special committee, headed by Field Marshal Jan Christian Smuts, which, after studying the problem, concluded that all British aviation should be combined in a single Royal Air Force (RAF) with specialized commands for particular airpower missions. In April, 1918, the RFC and the RNAS were merged in the RAF, and a new Air Ministry was founded. Headed by Hugh Trenchard, former head of the RFC, the RAF assigned pursuit squadrons to the Home Defense Air Force, tactical squadrons to the support of the army and navy, and even created a special force of Handley-Page bombers for the long-range bombardment of Germany from airfields in eastern France. (The war ended before the long-range bombardment could begin.) This rational organization was not imitated outside of Britain until the postwar period, and, in embryo, it foreshadowed the Fighter Command and Bomber Command of World War II.

The pursuit plane was the most glamorous type of aircraft to appear in World War I and was originally a scout plane crudely armed to interfere with the scouting missions of the other side. The pursuit plane came into its own when, in 1915, Anthony Fokker, a Dutch designer working for the Germans, came up with the synchronized aerial machine-gun which could be safely fired through a spinning propeller. The pilot could aim the gun by aiming the plane, thus increasing the probability of hits. After Allied synchronized machine-guns appeared, the age of great aerial "dog-fights" over the Western front began. By 1916, as many as a hundred planes at a time dueled in those skies. As parachutes were absent until nearly the end of the war, pursuit pilots came back with their planes or not at all. "Aces," pilots who had downed five or more enemy planes, were good newspaper copy, and governments were ready to use aerial heroes for propaganda and to keep up morale. But combat flying was extremely hazardous, and there was a tremendous rate of attrition in the airplanes themselves. Assemblies of engines, doped canvas skin, and external struts and wiring, the fragile aircraft of World War I were used up at a great rate. Though some 30,000 airplanes were produced during World War I for combat purposes, only 8,000 Allied and 3,300 German planes were serviceable at the end of the war.

The internal organization of air units was much the same from country to country during World War I. The typical pursuit squadron consisted of 18 planes and 25 pilots, supported by 150 ground personnel. Bomber and observation squadrons often had 25 aircraft and 50 aviators, counting observers and gunners. Squadrons composed groups, groups composed wings, and wings composed air divisions. The authorized strength of the 1918 French air division was 432 pursuit planes and 193 bombers and observation planes. Usually, one or more air divisions were assigned to the support of a field army, but resources were a limiting factor. An air officer assigned to the field army's staff coordinated air operations with the ground forces.

In terms of aircraft performance, the Fokker D-VII pursuit plane, introduced in 1918, had a speed of 118 mph in level flight. The French Nieuport 17, with a maximum speed of 110 mph, was also popular. The Spad, with a speed of 119 mph, was so successful that over 5,000 of them were built. The British Sopwith Camel flew at 115 mph, and 5,490 copies were made for the army and navy. Most of these planes were bi-planes, but the Fokker Dr.I was an excellent tri-wing fighter. All were very small machines by the standards of today's aircraft.

The British Royal Naval Air Service was the largest and best equipped of naval air arms in 1914, with thirty-one seaplanes, forty land-based airplanes, and seven airships. Yet it had no aircraft carriers of any kind and no plans to carry aircraft to sea in warships. Soon after the war began, the British navy converted three small cross-Channel steamers into seaplane carriers, the planes being hoisted over the side for take-offs and being hoisted back aboard after landing on the sea. In December, 1914, these carriers even launched nine Short seaplanes against German naval bases in the Helgoland Bight. Four aircraft were lost, and not much damage was done to the bases. In mid-1915, the *Campania,* the first carrier which could launch aircraft from a flight-deck, joined the fleet. The planes, however, had to land again on the water and be hoisted back aboard. The *Engadine,* sister ship of the *Campania,* served with the fleet during the Jutland campaign, but had no influence on the outcome. The first British carrier which could both launch and recover airplanes from her decks was the *Furious,* a battle cruiser converted in 1917, but the take-off and landing decks were separate. Finally, in August, 1918, *Argus* joined the fleet as the first aircraft carrier which could both launch and recover aircraft from a single flight-deck; it was the prototype of carriers in the Second World War.

G. The Development of Armored Fighting Vehicles. Although a few armies had armored cars propelled by gasoline engines before 1914, the history of the tracked armored fighting vehicle (AFV) began when Colonel Ernest D. Swinton of the British infantry conceived of a "Machine-Gun Destroyer" while watching tractors powered by gasoline engines

The Pfalz D.XII, German pursuit plane, World War I.

SOURCE: John Batchelor et al., *Air Power: A Modern Illustrated Military History* (New York: Exeter Books, 1979, in association with Phoebus Company/BPC Publishing, London).

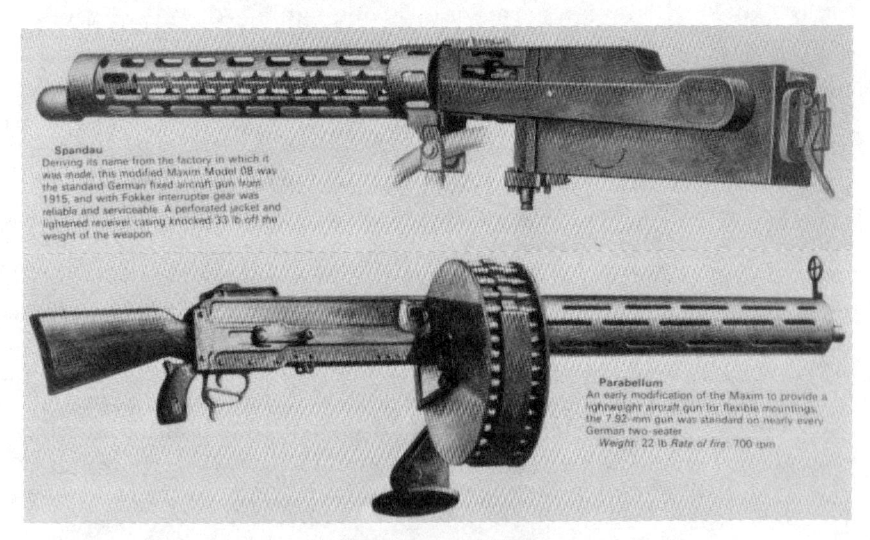

German aerial machine guns, World War I: the fixed-mounted synchronized Maxim-Spandau and the flexibly mounted Maxim-Parabellum.

SOURCE: John Batchelor et al., *Air Power: A Modern Illustrated Military History* (New York: Exeter Books, 1979, in association with Phoebus Company/BPC Publishing, London).

towing heavy artillery behind the Western front early in the war. Swinton imagined a machine with endless treads which could negotiate broken ground, smash through barbed wire, and roll over trenches. It would be protected by armor thick enough to deflect small-arms fire and shell fragments. Swinton offered his idea to the British War Office, but it was preoccupied with problems and paid little attention. Apparently Winston Churchill, the First Lord of the Admiralty, rescued the idea from oblivion by forming a Landships Committee, and, after the army joined the project, Swinton was recalled to become its secretary. In order to protect secrecy, the early landships were covered with tarpaulins when moved on flatcars between factory and proving ground, their covers marked "Water Tank." The term "tank" became a code-word for the new vehicles, and even after landships went into action in September, 1916, the term "tank" stuck to the tracked AFV.

A mechanical test-bed dubbed "Little Willie" was successfully demonstrated in December, 1915, but the first combat model was the "Mother" Mark I of 1916. This, the first true combat tank, had less than half an inch of armor protection, and its 105-horsepower gasoline engine could move it at a maximum speed of four miles per hour. Requiring a crew of nine to man it efficiently, it was armed with two 6-pounder naval guns and four machine-guns. Its rhomboidal shape, so characteristic of many World War I tanks, enabled a track running around the outside of its frame to drag it across trenches and shell-holes up to ten feet in diameter. Because its stated purpose was merely to smash a gap in enemy lines through which conventional forces could advance, this early tank was provided with a range of only twenty-three miles. The Mark I was thirty-two feet in length, almost fourteen feet in width, and was just over eight feet in height.

Unknown to the British, the French also launched a program to develop tracked AFV's. Their first machines were designed to fit a suggestion of Colonel Jean Estienne of the artillery that armored, self-propelled guns should be developed. The French mated existing Holt tractors used for towing guns with armored boxes carrying the French 75-mm. gun. The Schneider CA-1 of this version weighed 14.6 tons, had a 70-hp engine, a speed of 5 mph, and an inch of armor protection. But when first put into action in 1917, it proved to have poor trench-crossing abilities. When the French and British discovered each other's work, they agreed that tanks would not be introduced to battle until large numbers of reliable machines were available, something that would be impossible for either nation before mid-1917.

Unfortunately for the Allies, the secret of the tank was compromised by General Haig in September, 1916, when he ordered the thirty-six Mark Is available to be thrown in, in hopes of reviving his flagging offensive on the Somme. Many of the machines mired down in the

British Mark I, the first type of tank introduced on the Western Front, 1916.

SOURCE: Kenneth Macksey and John H. Batchelor, *Tank: A History of the Armoured Fighting Vehicle* (New York: Charles Scribner's Sons, 1970).

muddy morass produced by weeks of shelling, but the few that reached enemy lines made a powerful impression before they too were put out of action. Many German troops panicked and fled at the sight of the puffing monsters, and Haig was so impressed that he urged the War Office to increase the number on order from 150 to 1,000 tanks. On balance, however, the unveiling of the tank at that stage was a mistake. Attacks with large numbers of tanks were many months away; and by tipping the secret to the Germans, the British allowed them time to develop antitank weapons and techniques that might have been absent otherwise in 1917 and 1918. Among their measures were antitank traps and direct-fire artillery. These by no means completely neutralized the tank, but they may have prevented it from being the war-winning weapon by itself that its designers had hoped for.

The first successful tank attack in history came at Cambrai in November, 1917, where Colonel J. F. C. Fuller, chief-of-staff of the Royal Tank Corps, planned the attack very carefully. He chose a place with hard, chalky ground, he eschewed a preliminary artillery bombardment, lest it alert the Germans, and he employed 371 of the improved Mark IV British tanks. The sudden assault in a thick fog completely unhinged the local German defense, and before the end of the day the British had gained four miles. But by then nearly all of the machines were out of action, and, in any case, the infantry and cavalry had proven unable to keep up.

Fuller was among the few soldiers who looked beyond the tank as a hole-punching device. He envisioned machines capable of rapidly exploiting gaps, not merely creating them. The British Whippet tank, available in large numbers by 1918, was movement in that direction. It weighed only fourteen tons, had twice the speed of the British heavy tanks, and much better range. After still more experience was acquired in the Allied offensives of 1918, Fuller composed a "Plan 1919," which envisaged heavy or battle tanks smashing holes in the enemy's front through which light and fast tanks would plunge deep into the enemy's rear areas in order to overwhelm headquarters and support facilities. Here, in primitive form, lay the use of armored forces twenty years in the future.

By the end of the Great War, Britain had built three thousand tanks of all kinds, and the French had built about two thousand. Though it cannot be said that the tank won the war for the Allies in 1918, it may be said that the tank played an important role in breaking the trench deadlock on the Western front and, in combination with other arms, was a significant factor in the success of the final Allied offensives. It, like the airplane, however, required another two decades of technical and doctrinal development before it came into its own. The Germans entered the field of armored warfare only after the British revealed their secret on the Somme, and in effect much later than the British or the French. By the 1917–1918 period, the British blockade was slowly starving Germany's industries of raw materials, and it was quite impossible for her to produce tanks in large numbers. Moreover, the German A7V was hastily designed and inferior to the British Mark IV, and the Germans never had more than forty tanks that they could put into action at one time. The Germans pursued different avenues in seeking solutions to the deadlocked front, and tanks played no great role in their 1918 offensives which came so close to winning the war on the Western Front.

III. The Years of Decision, 1917–18

A. The 1917 U-Boat Campaign and America's Entry into the War. On February 1, 1917, German submarines operating in the War Zone around the British Isles dropped all restrictions on their operations and began an unprecedented attack on the shipping of belligerents and neutrals alike. This action was bound to lead to war with the United States, but the German government had taken it out of two considerations. The first was the knowledge that unless Britain was beaten and her blockade broken within the next two years, the Central Powers would be defeated in any case. Secondly, only a submarine campaign which included neutral shipping bound for the British Isles could possibly starve Britain out before Britain's surface blockade did the same to Germany. Admiral Henning von Holtzendorff, chief of the U-boat command, was confident that without restrictions Germany's submarines could drive

Britain out of the war within a year and at the same time prevent the United States from affecting its outcome even if it chose to enter on the Allied side. The first savage attacks fell on Allied merchant ships, but on March 12 the American steamer *Algonquin* was torpedoed and sunk near the British coast. A week later three more American merchant vessels were torpedoed and sunk in the War Zone. Wilson, who only a few months before had attempted to mediate a "peace without victors," now declared that the world had to be made safe for democracy. On April 6, 1917, the Congress of the United States declared war on Germany.

Before the United States entered the war, only modest measures had been taken for preparedness. The Wilson administration had adopted a policy of "a navy second to none," but nearly all the new building planned was in battleships and battle cruisers. In April, 1917, the U.S. Navy was weak in destroyers and other antisubmarine craft. Although the navy put the 1916 program on the shelf and switched building-priority to antisubmarine warfare, the main burden for defeating the U-boat offensive fell perforce to the British navy. In the first months of 1917, that navy was clearly failing. Between February 1 and May 31, the German submarines sank 1,175 ships, amounting to over 2.5 million tons, or more than submarines had sunk in all of 1916. Part of the U-boat's effectiveness in this period was, however, due to the refusal of the British admiralty to adopt convoy in place of its "Defense of Routes" strategy. Under the latter strategy, British destroyers and other antisub vessels simply patrolled the sea lanes and attacked any U-boats they chanced to come upon. The admiralty's opposition to the convoy stemmed from the fact that the flow of material and food from overseas would be reduced if merchant ships delayed sailing in order to be collected in groups large enough to justify escorts. Still more delays would be imposed when so many ships arrived at British ports at one time and had to wait in line to be unloaded. Until 1917, the trade-off between sinkings and maintenance of the general flow of trade had been favorable.

Admiral William S. Sims, appointed the commander of the U.S. naval forces operating in European waters, soon joined his voice to those of a minority of British naval officers in the admiralty favoring convoy. Their pressure, and the terrible losses from February through May, 1917, at last convinced the British admiralty to experiment with convoys for ships bound for British ports. Almost magically, the number of sinkings began to decline. The admiralty then extended escort protection to ships leaving ports, and finally to Allied ships in the Mediterranean, and in both cases the German pressure eased. The effectiveness of convoy lay in the fact that it forced the U-boats to attack in the presence of ships designed to destroy them. The knowledge that a swift counterattack was awaiting any transgressor made U-boat commanders more cautious, and the number of U-boat sinkings went up dramatically. Of the 345 German submarines commissioned in World War I, 178 never returned to base. Half of the 10,000 sailors manning the submarines were lost with them. Still, before the German U-boats were finally defeated, they had sunk 11 million tons of Allied shipping and another million tons in Allied warships. The Allies added 13 million tons to their merchant fleets during the war. Because large numbers of American troops did not start out for Europe until after December, 1917, by which time the U-boat menace was under control, no American troop ships were sunk on the trans-Atlantic voyage while loaded, and only three troop ships were sunk on return trips.

Despite the Allied victory over the submarine by the end of 1917, it remained to be seen whether the United States could make a difference in the outcome of the land war in Europe. The National Defense Act of 1916, another part of Wilson's preparedness package to keep the country out of war, defined the land forces of the United States as the regular army, the army's reserve, the National Guard when in federal service, and a so-called National Army to be raised by means to be prescribed by Congress in time of war. On April 6, 1917, the regular army had 108,399 officers and men, the army's reserve had 16,767 officers and men, and the National Guard had 181,620 officers and men. At the time the National Army still existed only on paper. Neither did the United States have stockpiles of arms and equipment with which to prepare a large army if one could be invented.

Newton D. Baker, Wilson's secretary of war, believed that the manpower problem could be solved only by general conscription, and since February, 1917, had a plan drafted by Enoch Crowder, judge advocate general, for making the National Army described in the National Defense Act of 1916 a conscript force. Baker proposed to make the National Army a pool of manpower from which the regular army and the National Guard might draw for expansion, and was in effect a *levée en masse.* Wilson courageously supported the Baker plan before Congress, and that body, encouraged by the country's enthusiasm for the war, enacted the Selective Service Act on May 18. The law, which applied to all males between twenty-one and thirty-five years of age, was administered by local boards of citizens, a feature that may have made it more palatable to the American people. On the whole, compliance was good. Though the Navy and the Marine Corps remained volunteer, the United States Army and the National Guard used conscripts whenever they failed to recruit up to strength. Eventually the United States Army, National Guard, and the National Army were consolidated into the Army of the United States (August, 1918). Approximately 4,000,000 men served in the AUS, of which 2,180,296 entered by way of the draft. Since by the end of the war about 2,000,000 American troops were serving in France, the number of conscripts only slightly exceeded the number who actually served at or near the front. About 800,000 men served in the United States Navy and Marine Corps.

Selective service supplied enough men for a large army, but it could not provide them training or equipment. The United States was the world's leading industrial power, but little had been done prior to April, 1917, to prepare for a conversion of civilian industry to war-time production. The Americans were to learn that it took a year to plan and retool, and still another year before much flowed from the production lines, and in the crisis of the World War the two-year delay would be inadmissible. And with so many raw recruits and so few experienced soldiers to train and lead them, the training problem seemed similarly insurmountable over the short haul.

Fortunately, the United States could fall back on the resources of its Anglo-French allies for solving both problems with relative speed. The United States undertook to provide the American Expeditionary Force (AEF) with most of its small arms and clothing, while Britain and France undertook to meet its needs in heavy arms and in most other items of equipment. The AEF adopted the French 75-mm. gun as its basic field piece, and only a hundred of the 2,250 field guns it used in France were made in the United States. Similarly, though some 5,000 American pilots and other aircrewmen served in forty-five combat squadrons on the Western front, nearly all of the 1,029 airplanes they used were of European manufacture. Most of the 250 tanks used by the AEF were provided by European allies, and, of the 18,000,000 tons of supplies and equipment used by the AEF in Europe, 10,000,000 tons were purchased or provided there. As for training, the device was hit upon of giving American recruits basic instruction in the United States and then more advanced training under European instructors in Europe. Junior officers were turned out *en masse* in as little as three months by officer candidate schools, and the Reserve Officer Training Corps (ROTC), established by the 1916 National Defense Act, helped college campuses to meet the need.

General John Pershing, commander of the AEF, had never commanded more than 16,000 men at one time, prior to 1917, but none of the other 5,175 regular army officers at the time was more qualified. Pershing had become famous in 1916, while commanding an expedition into Mexico in pursuit of Pancho Villa, the border-raider. But it was a long step from chasing Mexican bandit-revolutionaries to commanding a mass army. He and the other American commanders and staff officers had to work at a frantic pace in order to prepare themselves, as well as their forces, for the challenges of a war in Europe. While General Peyton C. March soon assumed the duties of army chief-of-staff and largely directed the mobilization of the land forces, Pershing and the AEF staff proceeded to

Europe to establish an American headquarters and to organize the arrival of American troops. Still, a year after the United States formally entered the war, the American presence in France consisted of only 320,000 troops and four combat-ready army divisions. Just eight months later, the AEF's strength had swelled to 2,000,000 men and forty-two divisions, and they had played a vital role in the final successful outcome of the war. The effectiveness of the American intervention in World War I was very much due to splendid American-European cooperation.

B. The Russian Collapse, the French Mutiny, and New German Methods of War in 1917. Before American strength could help bring about an Allied victory, the Allies came very close to losing the war in both 1917 and 1918. In February, 1917, the war-weary soldiers and workers in Petrograd (formerly St. Petersburg) turned on the monarchy and toppled it. Nicholas II and his family were placed under arrest, and political power was divided between the Petrograd Soviet (Council) of Workers and Soldiers and the Russian Duma or parliament. Alexander Kerensky, a moderate socialist, became head of the new republic. Still, by the summer of 1917, the Russian army was disintegrating before the advancing Germans, and, by fall, V. I. Lenin, leader of the Bolsheviks and recently returned from exile, had seized leadership of the Petrograd Soviet. In early November, Lenin led ten thousand armed followers in an overthrow of the Kerensky government. Peace negotiations with the Central Powers finally resulted in the Treaty of Brest-Litovsk in March, 1918, one that surrendered Poland and a large slice of western Russia, but which confirmed Lenin's grip on power.

Another favorable augury for the Germans was the Great Mutiny in the French army following the failure of Nivelle's offensive on the Aisne in April and May. In the wake of the loss of a further two hundred thousand men to no purpose, soldiers in fifty-four divisions—about half the army—followed the Russian example in setting up Soldiers' Councils and engaging in sit-down strikes. A frightened French government relieved Nivelle, and appointed Pétain—the hero of Verdun—to his place. Pétain's appointment had a calming effect on the French army. He acted quickly to bring about needed reforms in food, health, and recreation conditions, and in leave policies, while placing a temporary moratorium on French offensives. By summer the French army had recovered its discipline, but the Great Mutiny gave the Germans reason to hope that French morale was fragile.

A third reason for German optimism was a new system of infantry-artillery tactics worked out by officers under General Oskar von Hutier and tried out on the Eastern Front at Riga. The Hutier system called for intense, accurate, but brief preliminary bombardments, followed by the attack of specially trained *Sturmtruppen* (Storm Troops) armed with the new air-cooled machine-gun, the trench mortar, the hand-grenade, the flame-thrower (introduced at Verdun), as well as conventional weapons. The Storm Troops sought to penetrate weak places in the enemy front, finally linking up to create a gap which could be exploited by the regular German infantry. Meanwhile, German artillery hammered all approaches in order to prevent enemy reinforcements from reaching the front. The tactics had worked well in the East.

Before committing the German army entirely to the Hutier system, Hindenburg and Ludendorff gave it a final test on the Italian front in November, 1917. Six German and six Austro-Hungarian divisions used the new methods to shatter the Italian front at Caporetto in twenty-four hours. Many Italian troops were caught in local encirclements after the front had been penetrated, and others were so demoralized that they fled the battlefield. The offensive ground forward for fifty miles, finally inflicting 320,000 casualties on the Italians, before it halted at the river Piave. Logistical problems rather than Italian opposition, brought the episode to a close. The Italian army was so weakened and unnerved by Caporetto that it was a year before it had the capacity to attack. The Caporetto campaign erased any lingering doubts in the German high command that it had found an answer to the problem of breaking a continuous front, though the problem of logistics remained for the phase of exploitation. But time was running out on Germany because of the Allied blockade, and the new system offered the greatest hope for a victory in the West in 1918. Upon the success of that system, Hindenburg and Ludendorff were prepared to stake the fate of the Second Reich.

C. British Failures and Successes in 1917. The French failure on the Aisne, and the resultant mutiny already discussed, placed an even greater burden on the British in supporting the Western Front. Fortunately, the new conscript armies were joining Haig's BEF, but their general-in-chief continued to show little imagination or insight in his methods of assault. In April, 1917, the Canadians captured Vimy Ridge near Arras as part of an operation to draw German attention from the Aisne where Nivelle's offensive struck shortly after, but beginning in July the BEF was hurled into an offensive around Ypres that in many ways resembled the unfortunate Somme offensive of the year before. Again the bloody and muddy fighting achieved small gains even though it dragged on into November. The ultimate objective of Passchendale village fell on November 6, but it was just four air-line miles from the point where the BEF attack had jumped off in July. British casualties came to 240,000. Fortunately, Haig's reputation was somewhat restored by the successful tank attack at Cambrai in the same month that Passchendale fell, but even that success resulted in only local gains.

The greatest British successes on land in 1917 occurred in the Middle East. In 1916 the British forces in Egypt had managed to occupy the northern Sinai desert and to bring Palestine into striking range. General Sir Edmund Allenby then succeeded to the command of the Egyptian Expeditionary Force (EEF), and in the latter half of 1917 drove the Turkish army from Palestine and captured Jerusalem. Turkish rule in the Arabian desert also collapsed as the tribes there (under the direction of Major T. E. Lawrence) rebelled against their Turkish overlords. A British student of Middle Eastern archaeology before the war, Lawrence drifted into partisan warfare thanks to his knowledge of Arabic. The renewed British drive from the head of the Persian Gulf also made progress in 1917. In March, British troops under General Frederick S. Maude finally captured Baghdad and created the potential for a linkup with Allenby's forces, which in 1918 might sever Turkey from most of her Middle Eastern empire. But a final victory over Turkey would mean little if the Allies were defeated in Western Europe in 1918, and by that spring that possibility was by no means out of the question.

D. The Ludendorff Offensives, March–July, 1918. By March, 1918, the German High Command had concentrated 210 German divisions on the Western Front with a rifle strength of 1,559,000 men. Opposed to these forces were 164 Allied divisions with a rifle strength of 1,245,000 men. The Germans had decided to make their first great effort against the British line on the Somme, in hopes of severing contact between the British and French armies and then rolling the Anglo-Belgian armies into the sea. Ludendorff, who largely planned and directed the final German offensives of the war, massed sixty-seven divisions and three thousand guns for an attack on a British front held by twenty-six divisions and fewer than a thousand guns.

The first of the Ludendorff offensives began at dawn on March 21 with a tremendous artillery bombardment, followed by the advance of the Storm Troops. By afternoon the Germans had penetrated the front of the British Fifth Army in many places, and whole units had been surrounded or annihilated. As Haig's reserves withered away, the Germans advanced in the general direction of Amiens, a key rail junction and the last stop but one down the Somme Valley before reaching the sea. The situation became so critical for the Allies that on March 26 their highest political and military leaders met at Doullens to consider emergency measures. There Haig agreed at last to a French generalissimo in return for large-scale French reinforcements on the Somme. Chosen for the task was General Ferdinand Foch, then the French representative on the Allied War Council which had been formed in November, 1917, in the wake of the Caporetto disaster. Foch took up his duties as Allied generalissimo in April, 1918, just as sixteen French divisions

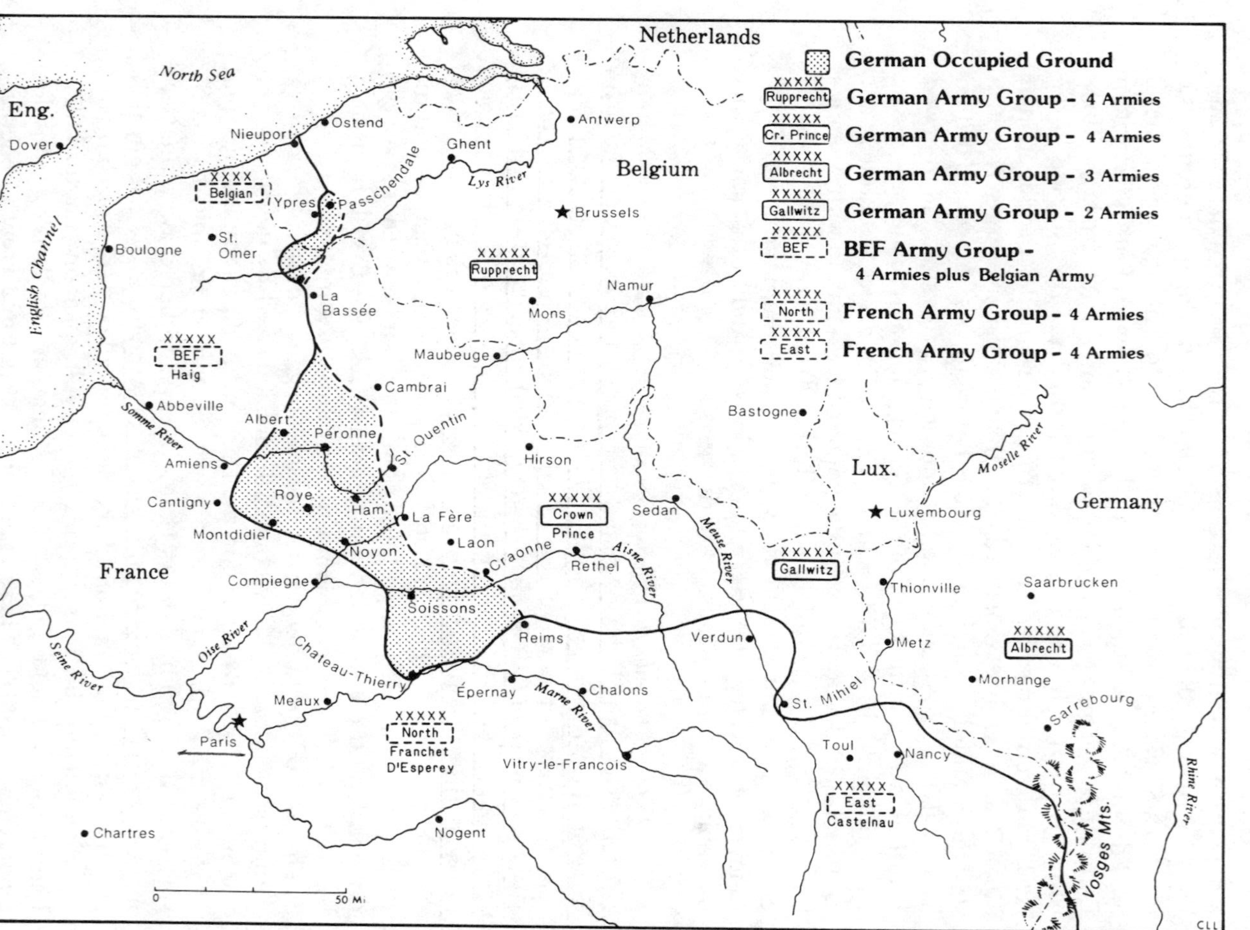

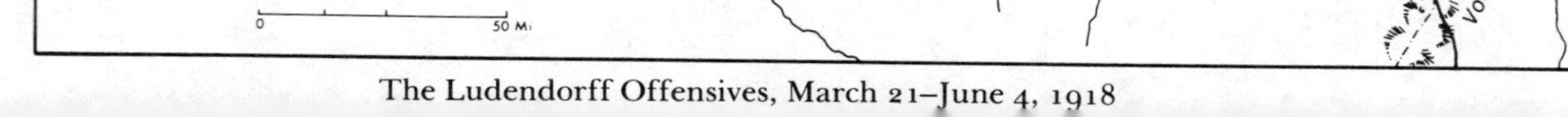
The Ludendorff Offensives, March 21–June 4, 1918

arrived on the Somme to aid in the defense against Ludendorff's offensive. German logistical problems, as well as stiffening Allied resistance, gradually brought the drive to a halt short of Amiens. Ludendorff shifted the weight of his offensive further north to the Lys, but by the end of April it was clear that the Allies had frustrated his efforts to reach the sea.

In the lull that followed, the Allies prepared their forces for a renewed German onslaught toward the Channel, but Ludendorff had decided on a complete shift of effort. During May he gradually and secretly concentrated forty German divisions opposite the Allied line on the Aisne, held by only eleven French and five battle-weary British divisions. Then suddenly on May 27 a new German offensive was unleashed that shattered the Allied line on the Aisne in less than a day. As the German forces surged toward the Marne, Foch rushed reinforcements to shore up the shoulders of the breakthrough, but by early June he lacked reserves, except for the uncommitted American troops, for sealing the bottom of the sack. Until then Pershing had followed a policy of not committing his troops to major fighting until enough men had arrived to form a complete American army. In the crisis, Foch appealed to Pershing to abandon his policy and send American divisions to the most threatened points along the Marne. Pershing quickly agreed and dispatched the Third Division to hold the crossing at Château-Thierry and the Second Division (with the U.S. Marine Corps Brigade attached) to hold adjacent ground to the west, including Belleau Wood. The German attack at Château-Thierry was soon repulsed, but a three-week battle took place for the ground to the west before the Germans abandoned their effort to reach the Marne. At the farthest point of the German advance, their troops were only thirty-seven miles from Paris. In early July, Ludendorff shifted his attacks to the flanks of the forty-mile salient his offensive had created in the Allied front, but the French troops held at Soissons and elsewhere. By mid-month the Germans had exhausted their reserves of men and materiel, and the crisis passed. Since mid-March, they had conquered ten times as much ground as all of the 1917 Allied offensives combined, and they had inflicted a loss of eight hundred thousand troops on the Allied armies. But they had failed to knock them out of the war, had taken a million casualties themselves (including many Storm Troopers), and were incapable of launching further offensives. In contrast, the Allied armies were on the rebound by mid-summer. American troops were arriving at French ports by July at the rate of two hundred thousand men a month, and Allied factories were rapidly making up for the material lost in the German spring and summer offensives. Foch sensed that at last the Allies might have the necessary forces for final victory on the Western Front.

E. Foch's Offensives to the End of the War, July–November, 1918. Until Foch's appointment as Allied generalissimo on the Western front in the spring of 1917, command arrangements between the French and British had been on a voluntary basis. Foch had more authority for centralized planning and execution of Allied operations as well as more forces by the midsummer of 1918. Though his method was to persuade, rather than to order, the commanders of the Allied armies at his disposal, to a large extent the final strategy which won the land war in Western Europe was Foch's alone. He proposed to use the ever-increasing Allied superiority in forces in a series of shifting attacks, each of which was aimed at a local goal and was well within the logistical capabilities of his armies. Much like Grant's offensives against the Confederacy in 1864–1865, he planned to wear down resistance until, at some point, there was a fatal crack in the enemy's defenses.

The first of Foch's offensives was aimed at eliminating the dangerous German salient to the Marne, a task carried out by mostly French troops from July 18 to August 3. By the end of the offensive, the Germans had withdrawn to their old positions on the Aisne. As a reward for this skillful operation which had not cost the French too many casualties, the French parliament voted Foch a marshal's baton on August 6. By then Ludendorff had concentrated his reserves behind the Aisne front in anticipation of further Allied attacks in that sector, but Foch was about to unleash his first surprise.

On August 8, General Haig launched an offensive in Flanders with eighteen Allied divisions (seven British, five Australian, four Canadian, and one American), led by an armored force of 414 tanks. The assault broke through the celebrated "Hindenburg Line" in this area, carefully constructed since 1917, and set off such a stampede of German troops to the rear that Ludendorff called August 8 the "Black Day" of the German army. For a time it seemed that Haig's drive could not be contained, and by September 3 it had recovered all ground lost to the Germans since March 21. When at last it came to a halt, the Germans had concentrated their forces heavily in the region.

By the time Haig's drive ended, the American First Army—a force of six oversized divisions—was ready for commitment. Once again Foch shifted his assault, this time to erase a small salient near Verdun at St. Mihiel, and to give Pershing and his staff much needed experience in conducting large offensive operations. To insure American success, Foch reinforced their attack with six French divisions, 3,000 guns, 2,200 airplanes, and 267 tanks. The drive, launched on September 12, wiped out the salient in four days, and again left the Germans wondering where the next blow would fall.

By late September, Foch was ready to carry out his most daring strategy of all. Instead of another single-front drive far from the point of the

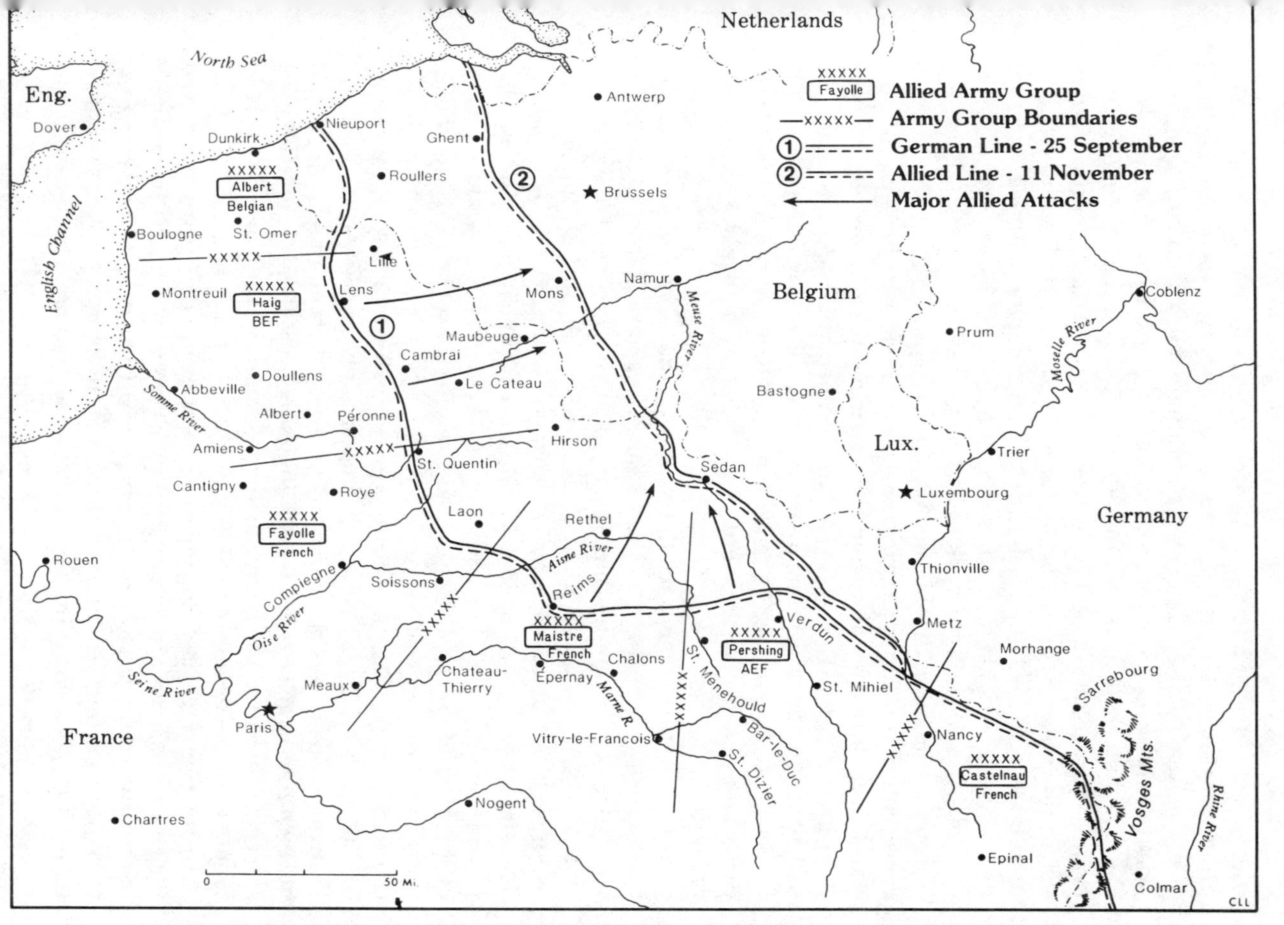

The Western Front, 1918: Final Allied Offensive, September 25–November 11

previous one, Foch had acquired enough forces to risk two simultaneous offensives. These drives were intended to put the Germans on the horns of a dilemma; if they concentrated enough reserves to stop one, they would probably lack the forces to stop the second. Foch's "victory offensive," as he called it, began on September 26, when 660,000 French troops and 220,000 American troops attacked north from the Verdun salient down the Meuse and into the Argonne Forest. The drive had as its ultimate goal the lateral railroad that ran along the southern fringe of the Ardennes, and without which Ludendorff would have great difficulty in shifting reserves. As Foch expected, the Germans gave top priority to holding the Meuse-Argonne region, and fought so ferociously there that, after the drive had been underway for a month, the Allies were only ten miles from their starting places. But German concentration on the Argonne tipped the balance in Flanders, where Haig had renewed his attack and the weaker German forces were steadily falling back. As early as September 29, Hindenburg confidentially told the Kaiser that prospects were grim if the Allies could keep up the pressure.

As the German armies on the Western Front slowly yielded ground before Foch's offensives, Germany's allies began to collapse. In the fall of 1918, Allenby's army in Palestine invaded Syria, captured Damascus, and advanced as far as Aleppo. The desperate Turkish government accepted Allied armistice terms on October 30 and Turkey left the war. The almost-forgotten Allied army in Greece launched a probe into the Balkans in late September, and, much to its surprise, it found the troops of the Central Powers in its path abandoning all resistance. The Italian army had its one great victory of World War I when its troops broke through enemy lines at Vitorio Veneto and eventually advanced to Trieste, the goal of its first attacks in 1915. The collapse of the Austro-Hungarian army was accompanied by internal revolution in the Hapsburg empire which brought down the monarchy. Vienna and Budapest severed relations, Austria capitulating to the Allies on November 3, and Hungary on November 6.

By the time Austria-Hungary left the war, Foch's offensives had driven the German armies almost entirely into Belgium. On Haig's front, about half of the country had been secured, and further east the Americans were approaching Sedan and the southern fringes of the Ardennes. Foch's armies consisted then of 220 divisions (106 French, 60 British and Dominion, 42 American, 12 Belgian, 2 Italian, and 2 Portuguese), while the German armies in the West had dwindled to the equivalent of 80 full-strength divisions. On the German homefront, people were afflicted by a severe shortage of food, and German factories were running out of raw materials from which to produce armaments. Internal German discipline began to break down when, on November 3, sailors of the High

Seas Fleet raised the standard of revolt when their ships were ordered to put to sea. Civilian disorders soon followed in Munich and then in Berlin itself. The Reichstag took control of foreign policy from the Kaiser, with whom the Allied governments refused to negotiate. Ludendorff had resigned his post on October 27, and General Wilhelm Groener had succeeded to the position as Hindenburg's chief deputy. The last stumbling block to an armistice was removed when, on November 9, the Kaiser abdicated the throne of Germany and fled to neutral Holland. Philip Scheidemann, head of the Socialist party—the largest in the Reichstag—proceeded to proclaim Germany a republic. A German delegation was received by Foch in his railway car at Compiègne, and the terms of an armistice were hammered out. All German troops were to be withdrawn behind their 1914 borders, Foch's armies were to occupy the German Rhineland, the German fleet was to be interned at Scapa Flow, and specific quantities of arms, railroad engines and rolling stock, and motor trucks were to be surrendered to the Allies. The Armistice went into effect at 11:00 A.M. on November 11, 1918, with German armies still standing on foreign soil, but there is little question that, had the war lasted longer, the Allied armies would have invaded Germany itself within a few weeks or months. Nevertheless, German ultranationalists after the war made much of the fact that the home front had collapsed rather than the army, and the new German republic bore the onus for both the armistice of 1918 and the signing of the Peace of Versailles in 1919.

By the time the Paris Peace Conference—the greatest diplomatic assemblage since the Congress of Vienna—had begun its deliberations in January, 1919, a host of new European states had emerged from the rubble of the former Hohenzollern, Romanov, and Hapsburg empires: Finland, Latvia, Estonia, Lithuania, Poland, Czechoslovakia, and Yugoslavia. Thus the Great War brought about an enormous change to the political order of Europe. In addition, the war's financial and human costs dwarfed those of any previous conflict. The direct financial costs have been put at $180,500,000,000, and the indirect costs at $151,612,500,000, but these sums would have to be multiplied many times to reach the equivalent in contemporary dollars. But most impressive are the casualty figures, which speak for themselves: 10,000,000 dead and 20,000,000 wounded or ill.

5

Between the World Wars, 1919–39

I. The Failure of the Treaty Approach to Prevent Rearmament and War

The years between the wars saw the greatest effort to that time to control armaments and to discourage war through treaty. The approach varied in form all the way from the dictated armament clauses in the Treaty of Versailles with Germany to the voluntary renunciations of war as an instrument of national policy under the Paris Peace Pact of 1925. The greatest practical progress in limiting armaments during the interwar years was made through naval treaties, but ultimately all efforts through treaty failed of their purpose. The reason was not the approach or the terms of the treaties themselves, but the unwillingness of Nazi Germany, Fascist Italy, and Imperial Japan to abide by the status quo. Their revisionist policies in the 1930s finally resulted in a second global war worse than the first.

In June, 1919, a German delegation was summoned to the Palace of Versailles outside Paris to sign, not to negotiate, a treaty of peace between Germany and her enemies of World War I. Though the Imperial German government which had waged the war had been replaced by the democratic Weimar republic, the peace terms were no less severe for that fact. They stripped Germany of its overseas empire and of a seventh of its territory in Europe. The loss of Alsace-Lorraine to France had been expected, and small territorial losses to Belgium and Denmark were tolerable, but the Germans deeply resented the large loss of territory to the new state of Poland. In addition, the Saarland was transferred to France for fifteen years (its return subject to local plebiscite), and Germany was saddled with a heavy reparations bill. The treaty made of the German Rhineland a demilitarized zone in which Germany was forbidden to station troops or to erect fortifications, but in which the Allies might station troops for up to fifteen years. Germany was also denied membership in the new League of Nations, founded at the Paris Peace Conference.

The Treaty of Versailles's limitations on the German armed forces are of special relevance to the study of the patterns of war. The postwar German army was reduced to the status of an *armée de métier* of one hundred thousand professional soldiers serving under long-term enlistments. All German military service had to be voluntary, and neither an army reserve nor paramilitary organizations were permitted. The army was denied tanks, poison gas, heavy artillery, and air forces, and technically it was not supposed to have any form of the traditional General Staff. The German navy was limited to fifteen thousand sailors, six old pre-dreadnought battleships, six light cruisers, twelve destroyers, and twelve torpedo-boats. The remainder of the High Seas Fleet, interned at Scapa Flow since the end of the war, was to be divided up among the Allies. (Much of it was scuttled by its crews when the terms of the peace treaty were learned.) The pre-dreadnought battleships could be replaced with ships displacing no more than ten thousand tons and carrying guns no larger than 11-inch. (The three built between the wars—the *Admiral Scheer,* the *Admiral Graf Spee,* and the *Deutschland*—were dubbed "pocket battleships" by the press.) An Inter-Allied Military Control Commission (IMCC) was to make periodic inspections in Germany, in order to insure German compliance with the armament provisions.

Ultimately, enforcement of the Treaty of Versailles depended upon cooperation among the United States, Britain, and France, but that cooperation proved lacking in the postwar period. The U.S. Senate rejected the treaty because it committed the United States to membership in the League. The state of war with Germany was ended by a joint resolution of both houses of Congress. In 1921, the American garrison in the Rhineland was withdrawn. Relations between Britain and France suffered after Germany defaulted on reparations payments in 1923 and French troops occupied the Ruhr in retaliation. By then Britain had come to realize that revitalized trade with Germany was worth more to her than reparations. The Ruhr Crisis ended in 1924, when American loans under the Dawes Plan allowed Germany to resume reparations payments to France. In 1925, the government of Gustav Stresemann in Germany signed the Locarno Pact, voluntarily recognizing Germany's new frontiers in the west and pledging not to change those in the east by force. The next year France sponsored Germany's entry to the League, and Britain withdrew her troops from the German Rhineland. The Young Plan in 1929 made it easier for Germany to pay reparations, and in 1930 the last French troops left the German Rhineland. That year too the IMCC made its final report on German armaments and was dissolved. The onset of the Great Depression caused Germany to default on reparations in 1932, and that summer a final settlement was made on the reparations issue. But in January, 1933, Adolf Hitler and the Nazi Party came to power in Germany, and the era of the Third Reich began. In

October, 1933, Hitler took Germany out of both the World Disarmament Conference and the League, and it was widely suspected that Nazi Germany was covertly rearming.

In 1921–1922, representatives of many powers met at Washington, DC, in order to seek a settlement in the Pacific and to head off the danger of a new naval race. From that conference emerged three treaties. The Nine-Power Treaty reaffirmed international support for the "Open Door" policy with China. The Four-Power Treaty obligated the United States, Britain, France, and Japan to respect each other's territory in the Pacific and the Far East, and limited fortification in the Pacific basin. Most important was the Five-Power or Washington Naval Treaty, which imposed limits on the world's leading navies.

The Washington Naval Treaty defined all warships larger than 10,000 tons displacement with larger than 8-inch guns as "capital ships." It decreed that, with specific exceptions, no capital ship could exceed 35,000 tons displacement or carry larger than 16-inch guns. A ceiling of 525,000 tons was placed on each of the capital fleets of the United States and Britain, and 310,000 tons on that of Japan (the so-called 5/5/3 ratio). In addition, France and Italy were each restricted to 178,000 tons in capital ships. A "battleship-building holiday" was put into effect for ten years, though some capital ships under construction could be completed. Except for specific exceptions, no aircraft carrier was to exceed 27,000 tons displacement, and the United States and Britain were allowed 135,000 tons in aircraft carriers, Japan was allowed 80,000 tons, and France and Italy were each allowed 60,000 tons. Although no agreement was reached on ratios for cruisers, it was agreed that "heavy" cruisers would carry 8-inch guns and "light" cruisers 6-inch guns. No agreement was reached on submarines, save that they would not be employed as weapons of *guerre de course* (France abstained from this pledge). Among the vessels exempted from the limits imposed by the treaty were the British battle cruiser *Hood,* which displaced over 40,000 tons and was the largest warship in the world for much of the interwar period; the American aircraft carriers *Lexington* and *Saratoga* (built on the hulls of ships originally intended to be finished as battle cruisers) which displaced 33,000 tons apiece when completed in 1927; and the Japanese carriers *Kaga* and *Akagi,* also converted ships, which, when completed, displaced 30,000 tons apiece.

At the London Naval Conference of 1930, the United States, Britain, and Japan agreed to a 10/10/7 ratio in cruisers, placed a limit of 57,200 tons on their respective submarine fleets, and extended the "battleship-building holiday" for another ten years. But Japanese militarists increasingly controlled Japan's policies after 1930, launching the invasion of Chinese Manchuria in 1931 and turning it into the puppet state of Manchukuo. When the League found Japan guilty of aggression, Japan left the League. In December, 1934, Japan served the required two-year notice of withdrawal from the limitations of the Washington and London naval treaties. Formally, all multilateral treaty limitations expired on December 31, 1936. Meanwhile, the Italian invasion of Ethiopia in 1935 had led to League condemnation and then to Benito Mussolini's withdrawal of Italy from the League. In March, 1935, Hitler disavowed the armament limitations of the Treaty of Versailles, and Britain resigned herself to German rearmament. However, Britain believed that she had headed off another Anglo-German naval race when, in June, 1935, Hitler signed an Anglo-German Naval Treaty which limited the German surface navy to a ceiling equal to 35 percent of the British fleet and conferred parity in submarines. Actually, Hitler gave away nothing by the treaty, since it would be years before the expanding German navy would reach its limits. In the meantime, the treaty helped to convince British leaders that they could do business with Hitler. In March, 1936, German troops entered the demilitarized zone of the German Rhineland in violation of the Treaty of Versailles, but Britain was unwilling to take action, and France was unwilling to act without British support. The Germans then began building the so-called West Wall—a line of fixed fortifications along Germany's western frontiers—the strongest segment of which was the Siegfried Line, opposite the French frontier. Though the Siegfried Line was not completely finished even by September, 1939, it served as a psychological, as well as a physical, barrier to French attack when Germany expanded to the east. Thus, one by one, all of the "bonds" of Versailles had been stripped away by 1937. Meanwhile, in 1936, Hitler and Mussolini had pledged, in the Axis Pact, that Nazi Germany and Fascist Italy would support each other's foreign policies.

In 1937, the Far East took the limelight when Japan launched an undeclared war on China, referred to as the "China Incident." Over the next three years, Japanese armies would occupy much of eastern China and imperil the interests of other powers in the Far East, in clear violations of the Nine-Power and Four-Power treaties made at Washington. In early 1938, Hitler's threats forced Austria—by then a landlocked country of only 6 million people—to accept union with Nazi Germany. Later in 1938, Hitler demanded cession of the Sudetenland, heavily peopled with Germans, from Czechoslovakia, and Prague called on its alliance with France. London and Paris were both appalled at the prospect of war over the Sudetenland issue and finally accepted proposals for a four-power meeting at Munich in September. The upshot of the Munich Conference was that Prime Minister Neville Chamberlain of Britain and French Premier Édouard Daladier of France agreed with Hitler and Mussolini that the Sudetenland would be transferred to Germany in return for Hitler's pledge that he would seek no more territorial changes in Europe. When Chamberlain returned to London, he thought he had brought with him "peace in our time." Actually, the Munich Pact only whetted Axis appetites and made Hitler and Mussolini contemptuous of Anglo-French leadership into the bargain.

Encouraged by the Anglo-French policy of appeasement, in March, 1939, Hitler cast aside his pledge at Munich and ordered German troops to occupy the rest of Czechoslovakia and the port of Memel in Lithuania. In April, Mussolini seized the opportunity to invade Albania on the Adriatic Sea. The Anglo-French governments were so enraged at Axis perfidy that Britain adopted peacetime conscription for the first time in her history, and both governments pledged aid to Poland, Rumania, and Greece against future Axis aggression. But in May, 1939, Hitler and Mussolini made the Pact of Steel—a full-fledged military alliance—and that summer Hitler began to make demands on Poland. Both Germany and the Anglo-French powers began to court Soviet Russia for a military alliance. On August 23, the Nazi-Soviet Pact was signed whereby, under its secret provisions, Hitler and Joseph Stalin agreed to attack and divide up Poland between them. Though Britain and France promptly made a military alliance with Poland in a last effort to deter Hitler, the peace of Europe was doomed. Treaties for peace had been replaced by pacts for aggression.

II. Armies

The principal topic of debate in the more advanced armies between 1919 and 1939 concerned the future of motorization and of armored warfare especially. Conservative soldiers held that the heavy tank was essentially an infantry-support weapon, while the light tank and armored car were properly assigned to cavalry for reconnaissance missions. Since conservatives held the upper hand in the British, French and American armies after World War I, armor in each army was divided between the infantry and cavalry branches. But whereas the French army shared with other mass continental European armies the problem that resources were too scarce to dispense totally with horse-drawn vehicles for supply beyond the rail-heads, the smaller Anglo-American armies were able to motorize their logistics almost entirely over the course of two decades, substituting motor trucks for horse-drawn vehicles in their supply columns. Since completely motorized supply columns were denied to them, the French and other continental armies had only the choices of mixing what motorization they possessed with horse-drawn equipment and spreading it through the whole force, or, alternatively, of concentrating it in a completely motorized *corps d'élite* within a traditional mass army. Down to 1939, the French army chose to motorize completely only a very few light mobile divisions and to distribute the rest of its motorization among the infantry divisions and their supply trains as far as it would go.

All three of the French generals-in-chief between the world wars were cautious in their attitude toward the organization of armor and motorization, and in general favored a strategic defensive for France in the event of another war with Germany. Henri Pétain had made his reputation with his unconquerable defense of Verdun in World War I, and he continued to believe in the power of the defensive during the interwar years. Not only was he relatively indifferent to developments in motorization and armor, he may have played a decisive role in the French decision in 1930 to build a powerful line of fixed fortifications across the hundred-mile-wide Lorraine Gap, the traditional gateway from Germany into France. Though the Maginot Line was named for André Maginot, the French minister of war when the credits were voted by the French parliament, it was really Pétain's monument.

General Maxime Weygand, Pétain's successor at the head of the French army, took relatively more interest in armor and motorization than Pétain, but under his administration French doctrine continued to stress that only traditional combinations of infantry and artillery could conquer and hold ground in a decisive fashion. Under Weygand, the French continued the practice of distributing heavy tank battalions piecemeal among the infantry divisions. Weygand did concentrate light tanks and armored cars in *Divisions Légère Méchanique* in anticipation that these divisions could carry out armed reconnaissance into Belgium in the event that France ever had to counter a second enactment of the German Schlieffen Plan, but once contact with the enemy was made and the battle developed, Weygand planned for the following French mass army to go on the defensive in the Belgian plains and to immolate German attacks on its firepower. General Maurice Gamelin, who succeeded Weygand as head of the French army, did not challenge the ideas of his predecessors down to 1939. The French war plan in 1939 called for the active army to serve as a *force de couverture* (covering force) for the mobilization of the reserve. Once mobilized, the mass army would remain on the defensive until its German opponent made some move, either through Belgium or against the defenses of the Maginot Line.

Among the critics of traditional thinking were the British general J. F. C. Fuller, Captain B. H. Liddell Hart, and Colonel Charles de Gaulle of the French army. Fuller, as chief-of-staff of the Royal Tank Corps in World War I, had extensive experience with armored operations, and he believed that a small, armored, and all-motorized army was preferable to maintaining the traditional branches. He visualized tanks of great speed and range penetrating the enemy's front and overrunning his centers of command, creating paralysis among his forces. Captain B. H. Liddell Hart visualized armored divisions composed of tanks and motorized infantry, which could make deep penetrations to sever communications and carry out strategic encirclements. De Gaulle, serving in a mass army, proposed the creation of armored divisions with as many as five hundred tanks apiece, manned by one hundred thousand long-service professional soldiers, which could not only act as weapons of offense, but could serve as a mobile reserve with which to counterattack enemy breakthroughs of the continuous front.

Soviet Russia was potentially a customer for the new ideas on armor and motorization after she survived a civil war and forced-draft industrialization under Joseph Stalin, Lenin's successor in power. Marshal Mikhail Tukhachevsky, the Red Army's commander-in-chief in the mid-1930s, carried out a number of experiments with armored motorized forces before his career, and innovation in the Red Army, was cut short by Stalin's great purges. The Russian generals who survived the purges became almost slavish adherents to Stalin's ideas on war, which relied on sheer quantities of armaments to offset their mediocre quality. Russian armored organization and tactics lagged well behind the German by 1939.

It seems ironical that Germany, denied armored fighting vehicles by the Treaty of Versailles and really without them until after 1933, should have developed the most advanced ideas on armored, motorized warfare of any army on the continent of Europe by 1939. Actually, the treaty stimulated Germany's interest in highly mobile forces by denying her fixed fortifications in the west and a traditional mass army. General Hans von Seeckt, Chief of the Army Command, encouraged experiments with trucked infantry and motor-towed artillery in the early 1920s. After his retirement in 1926, the Troop Office (the disguised Army General Staff of the period) set up a special section in 1928 to study the theoretical possibilities in armored warfare. Major Heinz Guderian, formerly an officer of light infantry, became familiar with the ideas of Fuller and Liddell Hart, both of whom had published books and articles in the 1920s, and in 1929 he hit upon his own conception of an armored or panzer division. Essentially, Guderian's panzer division was an armored-mechanized-motorized task force, one in which mobile infantry, artillery, engineers, and supply units were combined with a brigade of tanks in order to allow the tanks to fight with full effect. Guderian recognized that such armored-and-all-motorized divisions might serve to revive the tradition of the *Kesselschlacht*, or the battle of encirclement and annihilation, and thus lend decisiveness to ground warfare fo the future. Guderian's ideas were supported by Oswald Lutz, later the first general-in-chief of German armored forces, though he retired before World War II. Lutz and Guderian took the first opportunity to impress Hitler with exercises of motorized troops, and in 1935 the Army High Command (OKH) agreed to set up three panzer divisions on an experimental basis.

Despite the fact that these early formations were only equipped with the PzKw. I light tank, they looked so promising that by September, 1939, the number had been increased to six panzer divisions and a panzer brigade. By then the principal tanks in use (about 300 to a division) were the PzKw. I and the slightly better PzKw. II, but the excellent PzKw. III and PzKw. IV would soon replace them as Germany's principal types. The best of the German tanks were good compromises of speed, range, protection, fire-power, and versatility, as suited their roles and missions. They stood in contrast to the overly specialized Anglo-French designs.

In addition to the panzer divisions, the German army had two other types of all-motorized divisions by 1939. The four so-called light divisions combined regiments of motorized infantry with a light tank battalion in each division, and represented a compromise between the panzer division and the French DLM. Six motorized infantry divisions completed the *corps d'élite* of a mass army of slightly more than a hundred divisions on the eve of World War II. The German infantry divisions, which made up the vast majority of the army in 1939, were not greatly different in their organization and capacities from those of 1918. Still, with the close air support of the *Luftwaffe*, this combination of new and old style forces constituted the essence of the *Blitzkreig* ("Lightning War") which Hitler unloosed on Europe in 1939 and which soon laid more of Europe at Hitler's feet than at any man's since Napoleon.

No similar blitzkrieg vision inspired the American army between the world wars. Part of the problem was that the army was starved for funds. In addition, few army leaders until the late 1930s foresaw another major American commitment to Europe. A war in the Pacific with Japan would require different kinds of ground forces than would a continental war. Still another hindrance was the National Defense Act of 1920, which arbitrarily defined tanks as infantry weapons and armored cars as cavalry weapons. An Experimental Mechanized Force (EMF) in 1928, modeled on a similar British experiment in 1927, never came to much, in part because it was forced to use World War I equipment. Though General Douglas MacArthur, while army chief-of-staff in 1934, set up a mechanized cavalry brigade by transferring tanks from the infantry (he called them "combat cars" to get around the 1920 Act), the result was more like the French DLM than the German panzer division. Actually, the American army did not hit upon the right organization until the German panzers rolled over France in 1940. Within a few weeks after the French defeat, the Americans had cobbled together the First Armored Division. Fortunately, it was not too late to change tank designs, and mass production began on the M-4 Sherman, like the best of the German tanks, a good compromise on speed, range, protection, firepower, and versatility.

Neither Japanese armor nor armored organization was outstanding when, in 1938–1939, they encountered the Red Army in Manchurian border clashes. But the demonstrated inferiority of Japanese machines and organization came too late to result in major policy changes before the outbreak of the war in the Pacific. In that contest, amphibious mechanization was more important than armor for continental warfare, and Japan could not in the long run compete in resources with the United States.

III. Navies

Because of the treaty limitations already discussed, by the time serious naval rearmament got underway in the 1930s, many of the world's battleships and battle cruisers were aging. In addition to sheer age, most had been designed and built when airpower was in its infancy, and it was not always practical to reconstruct them against the new threats of aerial bombs and torpedoes. Accordingly, the new battleships that appeared in the late 1930s and in the early 1940s were, in fact, a quantum leap in dreadnought design over the so-called treaty battleships. Such were the USS *North Carolina* class with a speed of thirty knots, nine 16-inch guns, horizontal sloped armor to deflect aerial bombs, and numerous dual-purpose 5-inch and other antiaircraft guns. The most impressive of the World War II dreadnoughts were the Japanese *Yamato* and *Musashi,* at 70,000 tons displacement the largest such ships ever built. Each had a main battery of nine 18-inch guns capable of hurling 3,200-pound shells up to twenty miles. Besides antiaircraft guns, each was protected by an 8-inch-thick steel deck impervious to bombs weighing less than a ton and dropped from below 10,000 feet. Armor protection at belt-line was 19 inches thick. While both ships were to be sunk by air power, it took veritable fleets of aircraft to do it.

When the Second World War broke out in September, 1939, none of the new super-dreadnoughts was yet in service. The Germans possessed the *Scharnhorst* and the *Gneisenau,* displacing more than the three "pocket battleships" but armed with the same 11-inch guns. The five ships, taken together, were too few and too lightly armed to qualify as a battle line, and all of them were used in World War II as surface raiders. The *Bismarck,* a true dreadnought with 15-inch guns, was not launched until October, 1939, and not ready for service until the spring of 1941, when she too was employed as a surface raider. Her sister ship the *Tirpitz,* Germany's only other true dreadnought battleship in World War II, had to be used in the same way. In 1939, France had seven battleships, but the *Dunkerque* and the *Strasbourg* carried 13-inch guns and had been designed to counter the *guerre de course* sorties of the German "pocket battleships." Italy had four battleships and two under construction. Japan had ten battleships and battle cruisers, but the most recent had joined the fleet in 1921 and the two super-battleships were still being built. Britain had fifteen battleships and battle cruisers, the most recent having joined the fleet in 1925. The United States had fifteen battleships, the newest—the *West Virginia*—having joined the fleet in 1923. As late as December, 1941, the only new battleship in the American fleet was the *North Carolina.* All the battleships sunk or disabled at Pearl Harbor on December 7, 1941, were old.

Only France, among the European powers save Britain, launched an aircraft carrier between the world wars, the *Béarn* in 1927. The Germans laid down the carrier *Graf Zeppelin* in 1935, but after the *Luftwaffe* absorbed the German naval air arm the carrier was never finished. Five of Britain's six carriers in 1939 were modernized World War I vessels, but three new carriers were building. Part of the European indifference to aircraft carriers was based on the belief that carrier forces would be no match for land-based aircraft in Europe. Even Britain's carrier strength suffered from organizational and technical weaknesses. Until 1937, the Royal Navy owned the carriers and the Royal Air Force owned the planes and aircrews. By the time the Fleet Air Arm was wholly naval, it lagged behind the American and Japanese naval air services in both numbers of aircraft and in performance. Moreover, British carriers based only about half as many planes on the same tonnage as their American and Japanese counterparts. In December, 1941, nine British carriers based 450 aircraft when seven American carriers based 500 planes and nine Japanese carriers based 700 aircraft.

Cruiser design also varied among the world's three leading navies. The American and Japanese navies preferred a lesser number of heavy cruisers armed with 8-inch guns to a greater number of light cruisers with 6-inch guns. The British view was just the opposite. The difference was caused by Britain's need to protect the largest merchant marine in all parts of the world, and this could best be done with a greater number of more lightly armed vessels. In September, 1939, only fifteen of Britain's fifty-seven cruisers were heavy cruisers, and some of the others were classified as antiaircraft cruisers and armed with only 5-inch dual-purpose guns. Not even the British cruisers with 8-inch guns were a match for the five German ships armed with 11-inch guns in 1939, not to mention the battleships *Bismarck* and *Tirpitz* when they were ready for sea. The British had no choice after the outbreak of war but to escort all important convoys with battleships, battle cruisers, and aircraft carriers, as well as antisubmarine craft—a tremendous strain on British resources. Fortunately for the British, all of the large German ships were never available for commerce-raiding at one time. On the other hand, the German occupation of Norway and France in 1940 gave the Germans far better bases for a surface *guerre de course* than they enjoyed in

World War I. In addition to hunting down the raiders which got to sea, Britain found the solution to this problem to be air attack on the raider bases, a kind of resurrection of the old close blockade.

Destroyers developed in diverse directions before 1939. Large destroyers, displacing up to 3,500 tons and carrying 5-inch guns, were launched for service with the battle fleets. Smaller destroyer escorts, corvettes, and frigates served to protect merchant ships from submarines. Antisubmarine warfare got a tremendous boost from the development of "sonar" ("asdic" in the British navy), sound navigation and ranging. The device could detect and track underwater craft by bouncing sound waves off their hulls and measuring the "echoes." Combined with the traditional depth charge, sonar made the antisubmarine-craft a far greater threat to the submarine than even in World War I. On the other hand, the American and British navies, the first to possess sonar, became somewhat complacent that the device would largely negate the threat of submarine attack to merchant fleets. Actually, far more destroyers escorts and sonar sets were needed than were available at the outbreak of World War II. Also, new submarine tactics—such as the night surface attack—rendered sonar useless. Eventually, destroyerlike craft had to be equipped with both sonar and radar, and supplemented by land-based and sea-based aircraft, in order to deal adequately with the submarine.

Soviet Russia led the world in the number of submarines in service in September, 1939—perhaps 150—but most of them were small craft intended for coast defense. Italy ranked second with 104 submarines, but its underwater forces were designed for operations in the Mediterranean Sea and lacked great range. With a 100 submarines, the United States was third, but, in line with the traditional American opposition to submarine *guerre de course,* its underwater craft were intended for coast defense and operations with the battle fleet. However, the prospect of operations in the great distances of the Pacific led the United States to emphasize range in her submarines. France had 78 submarines, including the huge *Surcouf* (a 9,000-ton long-range submarine cruiser armed with two 8-inch guns and a catapult-launched seaplane), and Japan had 59 submarines (like the American, built for range but not *guerre de course*). Britain and Germany tied for sixth place with 57 submarines apiece in 1939, but only Germany's U-boat fleet had been designed with *guerre de course* in mind.

Between the world wars, German naval leaders had given much thought as to how to conduct a future *guerre de course,* even though after German rearmament commenced they hoped to create eventually a "balanced" fleet and one capable of commanding the sea. The relative paucity in submarines in September, 1939, was due to both the lateness of German rearmament and to Hitler's earlier assurances to Admiral

Erich Raeder, commander-in-chief of the navy from 1928 to 1943, that Germany would not be faced with war for many years. After 1933, Raeder had opted to give priority in shipbuilding to the larger vessels which took longer to complete, and when war came much sooner than expected Admiral Karl Dönitz's submarine fleet was excellent in many respects but small in numbers. Still, the U-boat command faced up to the task of waging *guerre de course,* even when Hitler was slow to place priority on building submarines. The German type of submarine called the IX-B sank more merchant tonnage than any other single type in the world. The IX-B displaced 1,200 tons submerged, had a surface speed of eighteen knots on diesel engines, and an underwater speed of seven knots on electric motors. It was armed with 21-inch torpedoes and a 4-inch deck gun, and later with an antiaircraft gun. But the problem of insufficient numbers was not overcome until 1942, by which time the Allied antisubmarine fleet was also swelling. A total of 1,178 submarines served Germany during World War II. Though they did tremendous damage to the Allied sea lanes, they finally failed of their purpose. On the other hand, some 300 American submarines, in a *guerre de course* strategy adopted after Pearl Harbor, finally decimated Japan's merchant marine. To be sure, the Japanese merchant fleet was far smaller than the Anglo-American counterpart which Germany's submarines attacked, and there were far fewer antisubmarine craft in the Japanese navy than in the Anglo-American.

Faced by the prospect of a war in the Pacific, both the United States and Japan took more interest in the problem of amphibious assault than did other countries. On the American side, the Joint Army-Navy Board sanctioned the efforts of the U.S. Marine Corps to find a satisfactory doctrine beginning in 1927. In the early 1930s, the Marine Corps both issued the *Tentative Manual for Landing Operations,* which became the "bible" of American amphibious assault doctrine in World War II, and created the Fleet Marine Force (FMF) to operate as an integral part of the fleet for the purposes of capturing advanced bases. The Marine doctrine covered all aspects of amphibious assault, including command relationships between land forces and the supporting fleet, ship-to-shore movement and communications, air and gunfire support, and amphibious logistics. No other country in the world had such an advanced doctrine by 1939, except Japan, which came up with similar solutions. The U.S. Army, which had neglected the problem to the eve of the Pacific War, adapted the Marine doctrine to its own purposes in 1941. And thanks to sound doctrine, most of the prototype equipment necessary for amphibious assault had been developed by the United States before the war. Thus, there was no great delay in deciding on the mass production of such designs as the bow-ramped Landing Craft Infantry (LCI), the Landing Ship Tank (LST), and the amphibious tank and personnel carrier.

Though the U.S. Marine Corps numbered only 18,000 troops in September, 1939, and no more than 50,000 by December 7, 1941, the Corps was prepared to serve as the cornerstone of the greatest amphibious assault force of the Pacific War. By 1945, at its peak strength, the Marine Corps numbered 485,000 men, six amphibious-assault divisions, and as many supporting air wings.

IV. Air Forces

Land-based air power was the focus of heated debate between the world wars. Air-power enthusiasts, such as General Giulio Douhet of Italy and General William ("Billy") Mitchell of the United States, believed that not only would air forces dominate future land and sea operations but that strategic air power might strike the vital centers of the enemy homeland and bring about the rapid collapse of the opposing society. More conservative military thinkers believed that air power would certainly be important in future wars, but that it would be exercised in the forms familiar from World War I.

In 1922, just after Benito Mussolini became Fascist dictator of Italy, Douhet became Italian minister for air. His book *Command of the Air* (1921) had brought him to the attention of a government interested in overhauling Italian military power. Douhet was instrumental in organizing a separate Italian air force—the *Regio Aeronautica*—but his plans for making it an offensive striking force at the expense of the army and navy aroused so much opposition from the traditional services that he finally resigned his post and returned to writing on air power. In the aftermath, the *Regio Aeronautica* developed into a mediocre air service of about fifteen hundred airplanes by 1939, equipped to support the other two services and to carry out high-level pattern bombing to close the central Mediterranean. It never met Douhet's requirement for an air force capable of long-range air strikes against the urban centers of other European countries.

Mitchell served as assistant chief of the Army Air Service for operations in France during World War I, where he came into contact with Hugh Trenchard and witnessed with approval the creation of the Royal Air Force in 1918. After the war, Mitchell returned to the United States convinced that his own country should have a separate air force as well. In 1921, he rigged the "battleship bombing tests" of that year in such a way that they were more useful for propaganda for air power than as tests to show how well dreadnoughts would stand up to aerial bombing under combat conditions. Still, the sinking of the old German battleship *Ostfriesland* greatly impressed the American public. Mitchell's intemperate criticisms of American military and naval leadership in 1925 led to his court-martial. Sentenced to five years' suspension from the service, he preferred to resign his commission altogether and to spend his final years until his death in 1936 writing and speaking on airpower issues as he understood them.

Under less abrasive leaders than Mitchell, the Army Air Service made slow but steady progress during the interwar years. It was retitled the Army Air Corps in 1926, a step toward autonomy, and in 1933 its mission was expanded to include coast defense. Its combat components were placed under a single headquarters for the first time in 1935, and in the same year the new four-engine B-17 Flying Fortress was test-flown. Originally developed as a weapon of long-range coast defense, the B-17 was easily adapted to the role of strategic bomber. The B-17, and the later B-24 Liberator, were equipped with the Norden bomb sight, the best high-level optical aiming device to appear in World War II. Still, the AAC remained relatively small down to even the fall of France in June, 1940. Then Congress untied the nation's purse strings, and Army air planners made preparations for an Air Corps of 400,000 men and 7,800 planes by June, 1942. Meanwhile, in June, 1941, the Army Air Corps was transformed into the Army Air Forces (AAF). General Henry H. Arnold served as both head of the AAF and as assistant chief-of-staff for air. By December 7, 1941, the AAF had a strength of 354,000 men and 2,864 aircraft. In the less than four years after Pearl Harbor, it had reached a strength of 2,400,000 men and 41,163 aircraft (13,930 of them four-engine, long-range bombers). In 1945, the AAF was the mightiest air force in the world.

Until 1933, Germany got around prohibitions in the Treaty of Versailles on air forces to a degree by exchanging technical knowledge on aircraft with the Russians in return for the use of an airfield near Lipetsk, where 180 German pilots had graduated by 1933. In some cases, German officers took up sport plane and glider flying. German aircraft companies inevitably learned much of military importance while building civilian aircraft of all kinds. Still, down to Hitler's accession to power, no real plans existed for a German air force in the future. Hitler gave responsibility for building the *Luftwaffe* to Hermann Göring, a pursuit pilot in World War I, and second only to Hitler in the Nazi Party by 1933.

Göring created the upper echelons of the *Luftwaffe* by transferring officers from the army and navy, and by commissioning civilian aviators. The *Luftwaffe* officially came into being in March, 1935, at which time Göring, until then minister for aviation, took on the added title of commander-in-chief of the air force. Göring himself was an empire-builder rather than an idea man, but General Walther Wever, the first chief of the *Luftwaffe* general staff, wanted an air force capable of launching independent air operations as well as serving to support the other two branches of the armed forces (naval aviation was subsumed under the *Luftwaffe* after 1935). He started work on a four-engine, long-range bomber similar to the B-17, but Wever's death in an aerial accident in 1936 removed his influence from the *Luftwaffe*'s higher circles. His successors as chief of the general staff were more interested in Ernst Udet's proposals for dive bombers for support of the army. Head of the *Luftwaffe*'s technical office, Udet was a former pursuit pilot and postwar stunt flyer. Work on the four-engine bomber was cancelled, and from the new interest evolved the famous Junkers 87 *Stuka*, the gull-wing, fixed-gear plane that almost symbolized the blitzkrieg for a generation. The excellent Messerschmidt Bf 109 fighter held the world's speed record before the war, but it had a combat radius of only 125 miles. The Dornier 17 and the Heinkel 111 were twin-engine bombers which, like the Ju-87 dive bomber, had a combat radius of about 500 miles. None of the German bombers were heavily armed or armored, but *Luftwaffe* doctrine emphasized surprise air attacks to destroy the enemy air force on the ground at the start of hostilities. Germany had about 3,000 combat aircraft in September, 1939, but was weak in reserves of pilots and aircraft.

The *Luftwaffe* was far superior in performance and capability to any other air force in Europe in 1939 except, perhaps, the British. The French *Armée de l'Air* had received its independence in 1933, but remained very much tied to the army's thinking and was less than half as numerous as the *Luftwaffe* by the showdown in 1940. Most of its aircraft did not compare with their German counterparts. The Soviet air force, organically part of the Red Army, was a great collection—ten thousand aircraft—of obsolescent machines. Newer planes were beginning to come off the production lines when the Germans attacked in June, 1941. The other air forces, save the British, hardly counted.

As early as 1936, the British Air Staff had selected four-engine bomber designs that later evolved into the Stirling, Halifax, and Lancaster bombers. These bombers could carry from six to nine tons of bombs as far as a thousand miles and return to base in England. Not many of the new bombers had been produced by the outbreak of the war or, indeed, until about 1941. In the meantime, the British relied on two-engine bombers of mediocre qualities. But fear of *Luftwaffe* attacks on the British Isles resulted, before the war, in priority being placed on the development of formidable fighter-interceptors such as the Hurricane and the Spitfire. Britain also made more progress than any other country in the world in the 1930s in developing an early warning system based on radio-detection-and-ranging or "radar." Twenty radar stations monitored the European approaches to England by September, 1939, and more were under construction. By the summer of 1940, British radar could detect and track aircraft as far away as seventy-five miles from the set, and Fighter Control using voice radio could vector the aircraft of Air Marshal Hugh Dowding's Fighter Command to intercept enemy planes short of their targets. In September, 1939, Britain had 2,000 combat aircraft, of which 750 were fighters.

Save for a few special naval air squadrons, Japan's land-based aviation was organically part of the army. As such, it developed only short-ranged aircraft and no strategic bombers. The Japanese Zero fighter was superior to the American P-40 Tomahawk in 1941, and Japanese twin-engine bombers were about as good as their American counterparts, the B-25 and the B-26, but Japan could never compete with the United States in either aircraft or pilot production in a long war. Moreover, whereas the United States introduced a variety of new aircraft after December 7, 1941, Japan was hard pressed to mass produce even existing types. Accordingly, performance fell off as the war went on. In 1939, Japan had about two thousand combat, land-based aircraft.

Experiments with airborne landings began soon after World War I in Italy, when General Allesandro Guidoni took a special interest in landing soldiers by parachute. By 1927, nine-man squads were jumping from Italian transports, but the program went into temporary eclipse in 1928 when Guidoni was killed in a parachute accident. In 1938, Air Marshal Italo Balboa founded a parachute-training school in the colony of Libya, but Italy carried out no significant airborne operations in World War II. The Soviet Union founded a parachute-training school in 1930, and in army maneuvers in 1935 a total of 1,500 troops were put into action from the air. In 1936, the number rose to 5,200 soldiers. In 1939, the Red Army claimed to have five airborne brigades and 50,000 trained parachute-soldiers.

German military observers at Russian maneuvers were the first to press on their army and the *Luftwaffe* arguments for airborne forces. In January, 1936, Göring ordered the formation of a *Luftwaffe* parachute battalion, and about the same time the German army created its own airborne unit. A struggle ensued as to whether airborne forces should be organically part of the army or the air force, one won by Göring in July, 1938, when all German parachute and glider troops were concentrated in the *Luftwaffe*'s Seventh Air Division under the command of General Kurt Student. The *Luftwaffe* also created the Twenty-Second Air-Landing Division, actually a force to be ferried to its objective and then landed in the aircraft. By September, 1939, Germany claimed twelve thousand troops trained for airborne assaults by parachute or glider.

Neither the U.S. Army nor the British army took much interest in airborne forces between world wars. The first simulated American airborne assault took place on maneuvers in 1932 and consisted of a single infantry company landed behind "enemy" lines. Little more was done with the idea down to the war. The British gave parachute training to a few soldiers before 1939, but nothing resembling airborne forces existed prior to the summer of 1940. Then, in the wake of the successful German airborne landings in Norway and the Low Countries, both the United States and Britain took an intense interest in airborne operations. Before the end of the war, Anglo-American airborne divisions—three American and three British—were serving in Europe, and composed an airborne army under the command of General Lewis Brereton. As many as three divisions were actually used at one time. The largest German airborne operation of the war—that against Crete in May, 1941—involved one division delivered by parachute and glider, and another division landed in airplane transports. The Russians never carried out an airborne operation with more than one division at a time, and the Japanese never employed more than one brigade delivered by parachute at a time.

The performance of air forces, of course, depended on the technical means at hand. By 1939, the airplane had come a long way from the primitive machine of World War I. The latest aircraft had fuselages of sheet metal, cantilever wings (struts and supporting wires located internally), enclosed cockpits with more sophisticated instruments and oxygen masks for high altitude flying, retractable landing-gear, and voice radio. Pursuit planes could fly in level flight at speeds up to about three hundred fifty mph, and bombers were fifty to a hundred mph slower. Two-engine air transports, such as the American C-47, could haul about three tons of supplies or thirty troops up to five hundred miles. The German DFS-320 glider carried up to fifteen soldiers. Navigation was by dead reckoning, corrected by ground observation and sometimes radio and celestial "fixes." Ground-attack aircraft were often provided with armor protection for the pilot and vital parts, as well as with self-sealing fuel tanks. By the outbreak of World War II, the last of the bi-planes were fast disappearing from the skies, and the mono-plane ruled the air in the second great conflict.

V. Electronic Warfare

Electronic warfare played a major role in World War II and in a variety of forms. Radar, originally used for early warning and fighter-control, could also direct the fire of ships at sea in darkness and in all kinds of weather. Airborne radar eventually aided the bombardier toward the end of the war. Another radar application was in the proximity or variable time (V-T) fuse. By constantly measuring the distance between the shell and the aircraft being fired at, the fuse determined the optimum moment for the shell's detonation. Since most shells brought down or damaged aircraft not by direct hits but from shell fragments, the V-T proved greatly superior to either chemical or mechanical fuses for antiaircraft artillery shells. In fact, the lethality of an antiaircraft gun was multiplied five times by using the proximity fuse. The V-T fuse was given much of the credit for the high percentage of German V-1 "buzz bombs" (pilotless cruise missiles) downed when Hitler's new weapons were launched against England in 1944. The V-T fuse played an equally important role in helping American ships in the Pacific to fend off Japanese *kamikaze* or suicide-plane attacks in 1944–1945. Anglo-American fears that Germany and Japan might learn the secrets of the V-T fuse from a dud caused a prohibition on V-T fused shells for surface-to-surface artillery until late in the war. Then V-T shells played a significant role in helping to repel the German Ardennes offensive in 1944, and in defeating Japanese forces on Luzon and Okinawa, where aerial bursts were especially effective.

An enormous increase in the use of the military radio took place between world wars. No other signal means had the radio's range, flexibility, and speed. But messages cast into the ether were easily intercepted by enemy radio monitoring and therefore depended upon encoding for their security. The most sophisticated encoding device between world wars was the German Enigma machine, a kind of complex electric typewriter which substituted other letters for the originals but never the same letter twice. Yet when an encoded message was received, it could be swiftly deciphered by typing it back into another machine with its rotors set in a prearranged fashion. German confidence in Enigma was such that all high commands used variations of the Enigma well before the war, and Japan even acquired still other variations for both its armed forces and its diplomatic service.

Polish intelligence made the first progress in breaking Enigma's secrets even before 1939, but not enough to save Poland from defeat. With the aid of the Poles who escaped to France and England with Enigma counterpart *Wicher* machines, still more penetration was made before the fall of France in 1940. Still, it was not until the summer of 1940 that the British Operation Ultra finally penetrated the secrets of the *Luftwaffe* Enigma. By 1944, the British could read messages from the Enigmas of any of the German armed forces and Hitler's headquarters. The American counterpart to Ultra was Magic, which concentrated on Japanese traffic. By December, 1941, the Japanese diplomatic code known as Purple had been penetrated by the Army Signal Intelligence Service, though nothing in the final messages between Tokyo and its embassy in Washington, D.C., indicated where the first blow would be struck in the Pacific. The Office of Naval Intelligence broke a Japanese naval code sufficiently in April, 1942, to allow U.S. commanders in the Pacific to anticipate correctly the Japanese drives into the Coral Sea and against Midway, and to a degree those American victories resulted from intelligence coups.

But radio intelligence successes were not always on the Allied side, and sometimes radio intelligence was ignored. A major German success was penetration of the American Black Code even before the United States formally entered the war but after American aid began to flow to Britain. Messages to Washington from the American military attaché in Cairo often contained information of value to the Germans about British forces in the Western Desert. Then, after the British deciphered the complete most-secret order from Hitler to his armed forces for the invasion of Russia in 1941, Stalin ignored their offering because he thought it was some kind of British trick to foment war between the Soviet Union and Nazi Germany. British agents captured in the Netherlands were used by the Germans to radio false and misleading information back to Britain. The list, of course, goes on and on. It suffices to say that the battle for information was continuous, sometimes favoring one side and sometimes the other, and only toward the end of the war clearly favoring the Allied powers. Still, Ultra and Magic, taken together, were perhaps the most important intelligence operations of the war, and highly influential to its outcome.

VI. The Wars between the World Wars

None of the wars between 1919 and 1939 gave much indication of the direction that World War II would take. They were either civil wars, in which the forces involved were not well equipped, or they were wars between states so unequal that no firm conclusions could be drawn. Certainly, none of them provided a thorough test of the new German conception of mass and mobility for decisive battle in the Napoleonic tradition, and none of them settled the debates over the proper role of air power and motorized-armored forces.

The Russian Civil War, which broke out just a few months after Russia left World War I, ended up involving foreign governments. It began in the summer of 1918 with rebellions against Lenin's government, led by former tsarist generals and admirals, and concentrated in the Baltic territories, in southern Russia, and in Siberia. Britain and France openly assisted the so-called White forces. The United States landed troops at Murmansk to keep supplies out of the hands of the Bolsheviks, and at Vladivostok in order to check the Japanese there. To combat the danger, Lenin's government founded the Red Army and appointed Leon Trotsky as commissar for war and as effective commander-in-chief of the forces in the field. Sometimes called the "Red Carnot," Trotsky put his considerable organizing talents into building an army of workers and peasants by propaganda and compulsion. He used former tsarist officers for technical positions when he found no better-qualified people at hand, and insured the army's political loyalty as a whole through a political commissar system similar to that of the deputies-on-mission of the French Revolution. Trotsky also founded schools for junior officers, which, by the end of 1919, had insured that four-fifths of all the Red Army's officers came from worker and peasant backgrounds. At its peak strength in the Civil War, the Red Army had a half million men.

The crest of the fortunes of the White forces was reached in 1919 and thereafter began to subside, but in 1920 Poland attacked Russia from the west and, aided by Ukranian nationalists, seized Russian territory as far east as Kiev. When a powerful Red Army counteroffensive drove the Poles back almost to the gates of Warsaw, French supplies and French general Maxime Weygand's advice made it possible for the Poles to counterattack and drive back the Red Army. Finally, in October, 1920, an armistice was reached, which, when confirmed by the Peace of Riga in March, 1921, left Poland with a large strip of territory which Soviet Russia still considered to be properly its own. By the end of the Russo-Polish war, the last of the White armies in the Crimea had been defeated and the Soviet regime was secure. Though some 9 million of the Tsar's subjects had been killed, wounded, or made ill in World War I, possibly more Russians, Poles, Balts, and Ukranians were victims of the Civil War. In any case, the Red Army emerged from the Civil War with a tradition of endurance in the face of adversity.

When the Chinese monarchy collapsed in 1911, an era of prolonged strife began in China that was to last nearly forty years. In 1921, Sun Yat-sen founded the Kuomintang (National Democratic) Party and a shaky central government, but much of China was really ruled by generals or "war lords." The Nationalist government established ties with the Soviet Russian government in order to get foreign aid, and Soviet military advisers helped to establish Whampoa military academy in 1924. Upon Sun's death in 1925, General Chiang Kai-shek, superintendent of Whampoa and a close associate of Sun, took up leadership of the Nationalist government. Under Chiang, the Nationalist government made a sharp turn to the right in its ideology and ruthlessly purged leftist elements in the party. A Marxist faction under Mao Tse-tung and Chu Teh retired to the hill country between Hankow and Canton, where they organized a peasant guerrilla war against Chiang's regime. In 1927 Chiang's armies defeated the independent war lords of the Yangtze valley, and in 1928 they seized Peking, the traditional Chinese capital. In the early 1930s they so heavily defeated Mao's forces in southern China that they were forced to make the "Long March" northward in 1935 to find security at Yenan in Shensi province.

Chiang's efforts to unite China under his leadership was complicated by Japanese intervention, first by the invasion of Manchuria in 1931, and then by an undeclared war on China in 1937. Chiang's armies were no match for the Japanese, which captured Peking, Shanghai, and much of the populated region of southern China. In December, 1937, the Japanese captured the Nationalist capital at Nanking, and in 1938 Chiang moved his capital to Chungking, the principal city in the remote province of Szechuan province bordering Tibet. The Japanese empire in China was populated by 170 million, or more than twice as many people as lived in Japan's home islands. Japan claimed that by 1940 its forces had suffered only fifty thousand casualties, while inflicting eight hundred thousand on the Chinese armies. Still, Japan had not terminated the "China Incident," and Chiang's government received material aid from Britain, the United States, and the Soviet Union. In northern China, Mao's Communist armies also continued to resist the Japanese. Complicating matters for the Japanese, in 1938 and 1939 there were serious border clashes with the Russians in Manchuria. The largest, at Khalkhin-Gol in the summer of 1939, ranged a Japanese army of 75,000 troops, 180 tanks, 500 guns and 450 aircraft against a Russian army, under General Georgi Zhukov, with 100,000 troops, 498 tanks, 750 guns and 580 aircraft. After that battle, in which the Japanese got the worst of it, Japan's militarists showed no interest in expanding Japanese territory at Russian expense.

The Italian invasion of Ethiopia in 1935 at first miscarried, but in March, 1936, a new Italian offensive with tanks, poison gas, and planes routed the primitive army of Haile Selassie, and the capital of Addis Ababa was occupied in May. But by far the most serious war involving European powers in the 1930s was the civil war in Spain. In July, 1936, elements of the Spanish regular army rose, under the leadership of General Francisco Franco and other Spanish generals, against the left-leaning Spanish republic founded in 1931. Franco's forces, who called themselves the Nationalists, quickly seized the most important provinces in northern Spain save Catalonia, but they failed to carry either the capital at Madrid or most of the provinces in the south. The Loyalist supporters of the Spanish government included a minority of the regular forces and the militia. When both sides discovered that they lacked the means to win the war without foreign aid, the Nationalists appealed to Fascist Italy and Nazi Germany, while the Loyalists appealed to Britain, France, and the United States.

The three major democracies ended up taking official positions of neutrality and nonintervention in the Spanish Civil War, though thousands of Communists, socialists, and liberals in those countries volunteered for service in "international brigades" on the side of the Loyalists. Soviet Russia sent minor contingents of armor and aircraft, as well as Soviet military advisers, to the Loyalist side, but not on a scale to compare with the aid rendered the Nationalists by Fascist Italy and Nazi Germany. Mussolini's government was the most responsive to Franco's plea, finally sending 50,000 troops, 750 warplanes, and many tanks and other war material. Hitler dispatched 16,000 troops and military technicians, a Condor Legion of 200 aircraft, and a few battalions of tanks. While the Germans got some practical experience of war in Spain and tested out some of their weapons there, the conditions were not conducive to any real test of the blitzkrieg doctrine.

Even with foreign aid to both sides, the Spanish Civil War became a long, drawn-out struggle of attrition. The mountainous nature of much of the country favored defense, and, despite repeated Nationalist attacks, Madrid did not fall until March 28, 1939. Among the more modern aspects of the war were the Condor Legion's indiscriminate bombing of the Basque town of Guernica on April 26, 1937, an attack that may have killed 5,000 people, and the airplane-tank spearheads in the Nationalist drive down the Ebro valley in 1938. At peak strength, the Nationalist army may have numbered 700,000 men, the Loyalist army about 600,000. The Loyalists were increasingly short on arms and equipment toward the end of the war, while the Nationalists steadily improved in this regard. By the end of the war in the spring of 1939, perhaps 600,000 people had died from its effects, half of them on the battlefield and at least 100,000 as victims of atrocities. The balance perished from famine and disease.

6

The Second World War, 1939–45

I. Hitler's War, 1939–41

A. The German Armed Forces to the Eve of War. From the time he took power, Adolf Hitler was determined to carry out a German expansion over central and eastern Europe (including western Russia) that would establish the dominion of the *Herrenvolk* ("master-race"), as Hitler conceived people of Germanic origin to be. The Greater Reich of which Hitler dreamed would be independent of overseas resources and based on the enslavement of the Slavic peoples, the union of all ethnic Germans, and the annihilation of inferior "races," especially the Jews. With the resources and *Lebensraum* ("living-space") afforded by the central-eastern European empire, Hitler believed that the Greater Reich could last a thousand years. He recognized, of course, that the realization of his dream would require the ruthless use of force and especially a powerful army for continental expansion.

The achievement of Hitler's dream also required armed forces responsible to his will. Accordingly, in 1938 he dismissed Field-Marshal Werner von Blomberg, the minister of war, and General Werner von Fritsch, the commander-in-chief of the army, on trumped-up issues because they were opposed to his policies. Hitler replaced the ministry of war with the *Oberkommando der Wehrmacht* (OKW or High Command of the Armed Forces), with himself as *Oberbefehlshaber* (commander-in-chief). The high commands of the army (OKH), the navy (OKM), and the air force (OKL) were made subordinate to the OKW, with General Wilhelm Keitel serving as Hitler's deputy. Hitler appointed General Walther von Brauchitsch as the new commander-in-chief of the army, a talented soldier but one not likely to stand up to Hitler in a difference of opinion. In August, General Franz Halder succeeded General Ludwig Beck as chief of the OKH General Staff. Though Halder involved himself in the so-called Green Plot to remove Hitler at the height of the Sudetenland

Crisis, the plot was quickly abandoned after Hitler's triumph at the Munich Conference. Willingly or unwillingly, most German soldiers went along with Hitler's leadership until nearly the end of the war.

Between 1933 and March, 1935, the German army had expanded by taking volunteers, and by the latter date had reached a strength of five hundred thousand men and twenty-one divisions. Its return to a *Nation-in-Arms* began with the March proclamation of compulsory military service in both the active army and in the reserve. Its further expansion was very rapid. On the eve of war in 1939, it had reached a strength of fifty-eight active divisions, fifty-one reserve divisions, and a total mobilizable strength of 2 million men. But the speed of German expansion had been achieved at a price. Only eighteen of the army's reserve divisions had passed through two years' active service, and the men in the rest of the reserve divisions had been trained on weekends and in summer camps. In addition, German industry had produced only enough motorization to fully equip sixteen of the active divisions and none of the reserve divisions. The sixteen motorized divisions (six panzer, four so-called light divisions, and six motorized infantry divisions) composed a *corps d'élite* of an army which otherwise relied on the railroad, what motorization was left over from the all-motorized units, horse-drawn supply, and its legs. Since so much of the army was composed of unmotorized or semimotorized divisions, like the army of 1914, its successful invasion of enemy territory was contingent on capturing enemy rail facilities and resources as it advanced, and defeating the enemy decisively not too far from its bases of supply. What differentiated the army of 1939 from that of 1914 was that the former had a powerful armored-motorized spearhead with a range of about two hundred fifty miles and a strong supporting tactical air force. With those advantages, it proved capable of reviving the dormant *Kesselschlacht* doctrine.

Heinrich Himmler's *Schutzstaffel* (SS), the "Defense Corps" of the Nazi Party, was not oriented to a combat role in September, 1939, and in the Polish campaign of that month furnished a single motorized regiment to the *Wehrmacht.* Since 1933, the SS had been preoccupied with internal security matters. The *Waffen* SS (Combat SS) was not founded until 1940, and in the May–June campaign of that year against France and the Low Countries it provided three divisions. The *Waffen* SS continued to expand, however, as the war went on, until in 1944 it reached a strength of five hundred thousand troops. From start to finish, it furnished a total of thirty-eight divisions. By way of comparison, the German army reached a peak-strength of 7 million troops in World War II and mobilized over three hundred divisions. Though the *Waffen* SS gave Hitler an elite, fanatical body of troops, whose political loyalty could be absolutely relied upon, German victory finally hinged on the performance of the German army and its supporting air force in the continental struggle.

B. The War from Poland to the Channel, September 1939–June 1940. The bloodless conquests of Austria and Czechoslovakia in 1938–1939 gave the OKH an opportunity to detect weaknesses and correct deficiencies in the German army. By 1939 it had confidence in its active divisions and in the best of the reserve divisions, but it had doubts about the readiness of the reserve divisions with little training. When it became clear in the summer of 1939 that a two-front war with the Anglo-French powers and Poland was likely, Brauchitsch and Halder decided upon a mobilization unusual in form. The *Wellen* ("waves") system that they adopted called for the active divisions and the best of the reserve divisions to be mobilized separately and on a more accelerated schedule than the other divisions. Most of the divisions mobilized on the accelerated schedule would be concentrated to attack Poland. The rest of the reserve divisions would be mobilized on the traditional two-week schedule, and, stiffened by a few of the active divisions, would be deployed in the defenses of the West Wall, particularly in those of the Siegfried Line facing the Franco-German frontier. If both the Polish and Anglo-French mobilizations also took the usual fourteen days, Poland might be struck down before the Anglo-French armies were ready to attack Germany's western frontiers. In that event, London and Paris might accept the *fait accompli* and make peace with Germany. The only remaining danger would be intervention on behalf of Poland by Soviet Russia.

The danger of Soviet intervention was removed by the signing of the Nazi-Soviet Pact on August 23, 1939, a measure by which Hitler not only removed a potential enemy, but gained a temporary ally. When Hitler ordered general mobilization on August 26, the OKH put the *Wellen* system into effect. The subsequent mobilization of the best divisions in the army went forward both smoothly and swiftly. By the night of August 31, a total of 1,512,000 German troops and sixty-two divisions had concentrated on the Polish frontiers, while Poland, which had begun general mobilization on August 29, had only two-thirds of its 600,000 troops and thirty-five divisions in position. The Anglo-French mobilizations did not get underway until after the German attack on Poland had begun.

The first *Blitzkrieg* ("Lightning War") of World War II got underway about dawn on September 1, 1939. A German air assault on Polish airfields was only partially carried out because of fog, but within three days of the start of operations some two thousand German warplanes had destroyed most of the Polish air force of a thousand planes either on the ground or in the air. Only 240 of the Polish planes were modern by German standards. Meanwhile, the German armored-motorized forces broke through the weak Polish frontier defenses at many points, spearheading the drives of Army Group North (Fedor von Bock) con-

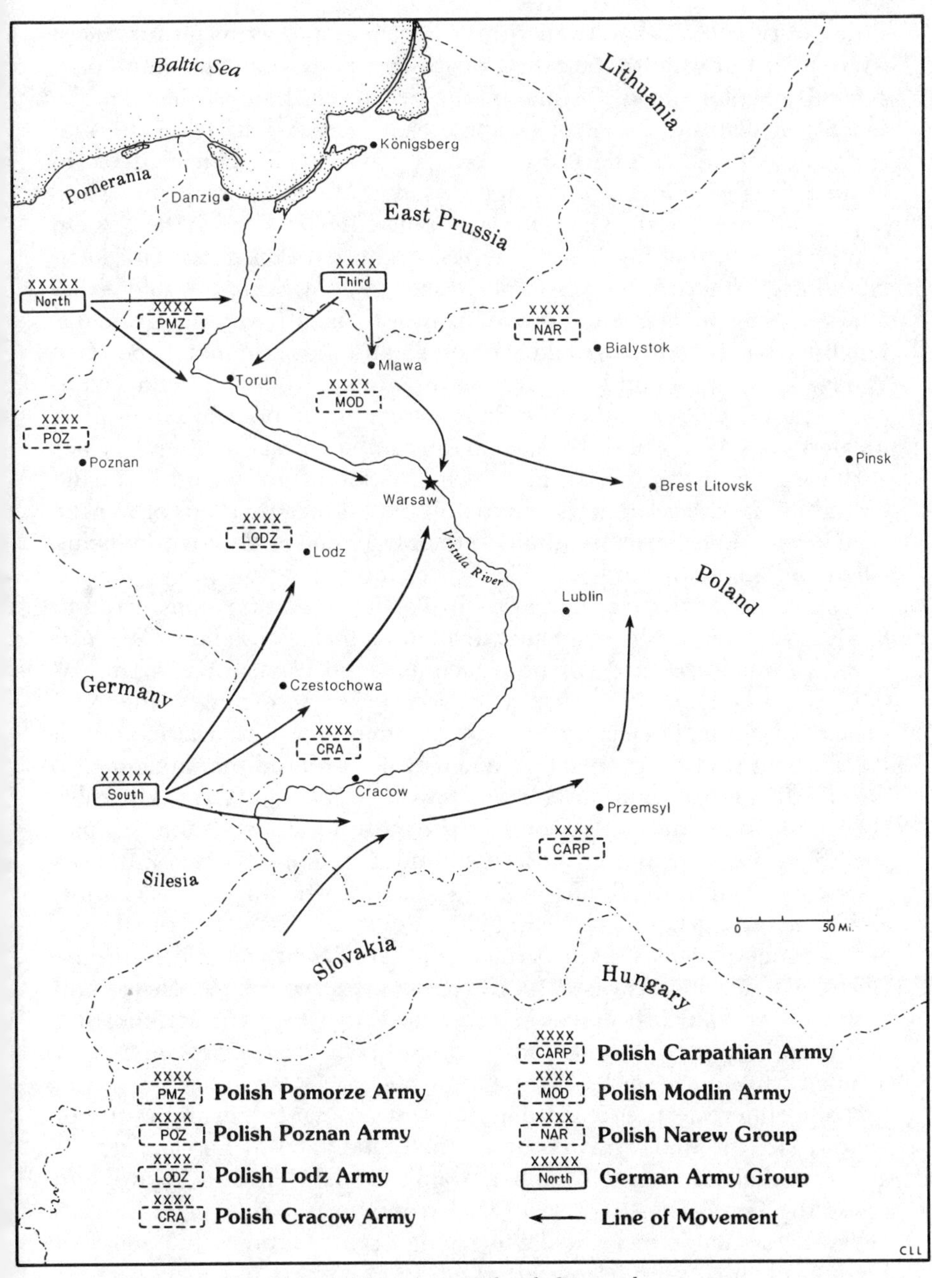

The German Attack on Poland, September 1939

sisting of two armies and twenty-three divisions, and Army Group South (Gerd von Rundstedt) composed of three armies and thirty-nine divisions. By September 9, German motorized forces had reached the defenses of Warsaw, the Polish capital, and *Kesselschlachten* (battles of encirclement and annihilation) were eliminating the Polish forces in western Poland. The large Polish garrison at Warsaw put up such stubborn resistance that the Germans were obliged to lay siege to the city. On September 17, the day before the last organized Polish resistance collapsed everywhere in western Poland except at Warsaw, the Red Army attacked eastern Poland and drove forward to link up with the Germans. Finally, after the *Luftwaffe* had repeatedly and indiscriminately bombed Warsaw for days on end, its garrison of 120,000 troops surrendered to the Germans on September 27. Except for some minor mopping-up of isolated pockets of Polish resistance, the campaign was at an end. It was at this time that the speed with which a nation of 30 million had been brought to its knees led newsmen to dub the German methods of war the "blitzkrieg." The Germans admitted to only 10,000 of their troops being killed and 40,000 wounded.

While most of the German army in Poland was being transferred to the West, Hitler and Joseph Stalin divided up their Polish booty between them. German-occupied Poland, which included Warsaw, had a population of 22 million, including 3 million Jews. Accordingly, the Nazi policies of ethnic persecution and, finally, genocide were carried out in Poland with particular savagery. When Hitler ordered the implementation of the "Final Solution" for the Jewish problem in 1941, Himmler chose Poland as the site for some of the most notorious of the German "death camps," including Auschwitz and Treblinka. The Polish Jews constituted half of the 6 million Jews in Europe who died at Nazi hands, easily the largest national group. The fate of the 8 million Poles in the Soviet zone was only slightly better than that of their compatriots in the German zone. Stalin caused some 10,000 captured Polish officers and noncommissioned officers to be taken to Katyn forest near Smolensk and there executed. The Germans discovered their graves when they invaded Russia in 1941.

While Hitler was preoccupied in the West during the fall and winter of 1939–1940, the Red Army occupied the Baltic states of Latvia, Estonia, and Lithuania, and in November, 1939, attacked Finland in order to revise the Finno-Soviet frontier. That frontier on the Kerelian isthmus between the Baltic Sea and Lake Ladoga came within a few miles of Leningrad (formerly Petrograd). The Finnish army put up a surprisingly effective defense behind the Mannerheim Line on the Kerelian isthmus, and also outmaneuvered Russian invasions north of Lake Ladoga in the winter snow. The Russians did not crack Finnish resistance until Stalin had committed 500,000 troops, 1,000 tanks, and 800 planes against a Finnish army that never exceeded 175,000 men and nine divisions. The "Winter War" ended on Stalin's terms in March, 1940, but the Red Army emerged from the episode with a diminished reputation. Still, in June, 1940, Stalin extorted the province of Bessarabia from Rumania, thereby placing the Red Army uncomfortably close to the oil fields around Ploesti, Germany's chief supply of European oil. On the other hand, Stalin fulfilled his pledges under the Nazi-Soviet Pact to deliver Russian oil and grain to the Third Reich and thus to help offset the effects of the British naval blockade.

Britain and France had gone to war with Germany on September 3, 1939, in fulfillment of their alliance with Poland. Despite the Pact of Steel, Mussolini had promptly declared Italy's neutrality. He told Hitler that his country was not sufficiently supplied with raw materials. Accordingly, the Anglo-French armies experienced no interference with their mobilizations and deployments, but by the time they completed them on September 15 the fate of Poland was a foregone conclusion. Aside from a few armed probes against the German frontier defenses, the Allies did nothing more in September. Then, after the Germans completed the transfer of forces to the Western Front in October, a long lull settled over the war referred to by newsmen as the "Phoney War" or the "Sitzkrieg." Actually, Hitler was eager to launch an offensive in the West in 1939, but bad weather and the pessimism of his generals finally persuaded him to postpone an attack until the spring of 1940, when the German forces would be expanded and strengthened.

At the outbreak of war, the British Home Fleet had taken up its war station at Scapa Flow, and once again the North Sea became a war zone. Thanks to the raw resources Nazi Germany could draw from eastern Europe and Russia, the British economic blockade was not as effective as that in the First World War. Still, Hitler worried about the security of iron-ore shipments from northern Sweden, so vital to German steel production. In warm weather, they were shipped across the Baltic, a sea controlled by Germany. When the northern Baltic was closed by ice in the winter, however, shipments went by rail to Narvik in Norway, then by water down the western coast of Norway to Germany. After the outbreak of war, iron-ore carriers avoided British interference by staying in the neutral coastal waters of Norway until they reached German protection, but Hitler feared that sooner or later the British would violate Norway's neutrality to stop the iron-ore traffic. In addition, Admiral Raeder was pressing for bases beyond the North Sea for his surface raiders, and Norwegian fjords would be ideal. But when indeed British destroyers did violate Norway's waters in February, 1940, it was not to interfere with ore-carriers but to liberate some three hundred British prisoners on the supply ship *Altmark,* returning to Germany after the *Admiral Graf Spee* was trapped and forced to scuttle at Montevideo on the South American coast in December. But the *Altmark* affair served as the catalyst in Hitler's decision to carry out an invasion of both Denmark and Norway before launching an offensive in the West.

The "Phoney War" ended suddenly on April 9, 1940, when the Germans launched Operation Exercise Weser, the invasion of Denmark and Norway, the former a stepping stone. The sudden thrust of a German motorized brigade into Jutland resulted in the occupation of the Danish peninsula within five hours, a strange contrast to the extended Danish resistance there to the Austro-Prussian armies in 1864. The German airborne capture of bridges leading from Jutland to the Danish islands made resistance on them hopeless as well, and Copenhagen announced a general Danish surrender on the first day of the campaign. Simultaneous with the invasion of Denmark, German destroyers landed troops along the Norwegian coasts as far north as Narvik. German airborne forces also descended on Norwegian airfields inland. In these operations, the Germans were aided by a knowledge of Norwegian defenses provided by Major Vidkun Quisling, a traitor whose name became infamous in Allied countries during World War II. Except in the far north of Norway, where the remnants of the small Norwegian army held out in hopes of Anglo-French aid, resistance in Norway collapsed quickly.

After Britain recovered from her surprise, the British Home Fleet struck back at the German invasion forces with great vigor. After the recapture of Narvik from the Germans, a British expeditionary force of sixty thousand troops was landed in the far north of Norway on April 17. Still, with their command of the seas between Jutland and Norway, the Germans were able to funnel six infantry divisions into southern Norway, and to fly in Luftwaffe squadrons to operate from captured Norwegian airfields. The British Home Fleet soon learned of the perils of operating in coastal waters in the face of strong land-based aviation, but at the same time the German navy took heavy losses at British hands. The British were finally compelled to withdraw their expeditionary force in early June, and by the end of the campaign they had lost an aircraft carrier, two cruisers, nine destroyers and six submarines. The German navy lost three out of eight cruisers (the *Königsberg* having the dubious distinction of being the first large warship ever sunk by carrier-based planes), twelve out of twenty destroyers, and four submarines. In addition, the battle cruisers *Scharnhorst* and *Gneisenau,* and the "pocket battleship" *Lützow* (formerly the *Deutschland*) had been damaged. Temporarily, the German navy was reduced to one operational warship larger than a cruiser. Still, Hitler's main goals in the campaign had been achieved. The iron-ore supply from Sweden was secure, and Raeder's surface fleet had bases beyond the North Sea. In addition, the Chamberlain government had resigned even before the campaign was over, and a new British government under Winston Churchill had taken its place.

(Edouard Daladier had given up the premiership of France to Paul Reynaud in March.) As it happened, Churchill took up his duties of prime minister on May 10, the day that Hitler launched the long-awaited German offensive in the West.

By May 10, 1940, the Germans had massed 136 army divisions in the West (including 10 panzer divisions and 6 motorized infantry divisions), 2,600 tanks and 3,700 aircraft. The ground forces were divided among three army groups and an OKH reserve. From north-to-south, the army groups consisted of Army Group B (Bock), composed of two armies and twenty-nine army divisions (including three panzer divisions and two motorized infantry divisions), supported by the *Luftwaffe*'s airborne division and its air-landing division; Army Group A (Rundstedt), composed of five armies and forty-five divisions (including seven panzer divisions and three motorized infantry divisions); and Army Group C (Wilhelm von Leeb), composed of two armies and twenty infantry divisions, serving in the Siegfried Line. Rundstedt's armored and motorized divisions were divided between a panzer group under General Ewald von Kleist (Panzer Group Kleist) and a separate panzer corps. Heinz Guderian, the pioneer of the panzer divisions's organization and, by 1940, a general, commanded one of the panzer corps in Panzer Group Kleist. The balance of the German divisions in the West were kept in the large OKH reserve.

Opposed to the Germans on May 10, 1940, were 108 French divisions in northern France (including 3 DLMs or light mechanized divisions, 10 motorized infantry divisions, and 3 *Divisions Cuirasée*) and a British Expeditionary Force (BEF), composed of 10 motorized infantry divisions and a tank brigade. The *Divisions Cuirasée* (DC) were intended by General Maurice Gamelin, the French general-in-chief, to be counterparts to the panzer divisions, but, in fact, they were inferior to the panzer divisions in organization, equipment, and doctrine. A fourth DC was organizing under General Charles de Gaulle, but only 800 of 3,000 French tanks were in units larger than battalion-size on May 10. The single British armored division was still in England, and after May 10 was committed to the Battle of France in a piecemeal fashion. The German advantage extended to the air where the 1,400 French planes and the 400 British planes based in France were technically inferior to the German aircraft for the most part, as well as being heavily outnumbered by them. Most of the British Spitfire and Hurricane fighters were behind radar safety in England. If the German offensive included the Netherlands and Belgium, the Dutch could mobilize five divisions, and the Belgians ten divisions, but the Dutch and Belgian air and armored forces were inconsequential.

The German offensive on May 10 was led off by massive German air attacks on airfields in Holland, Belgium, and eastern France. Most of the

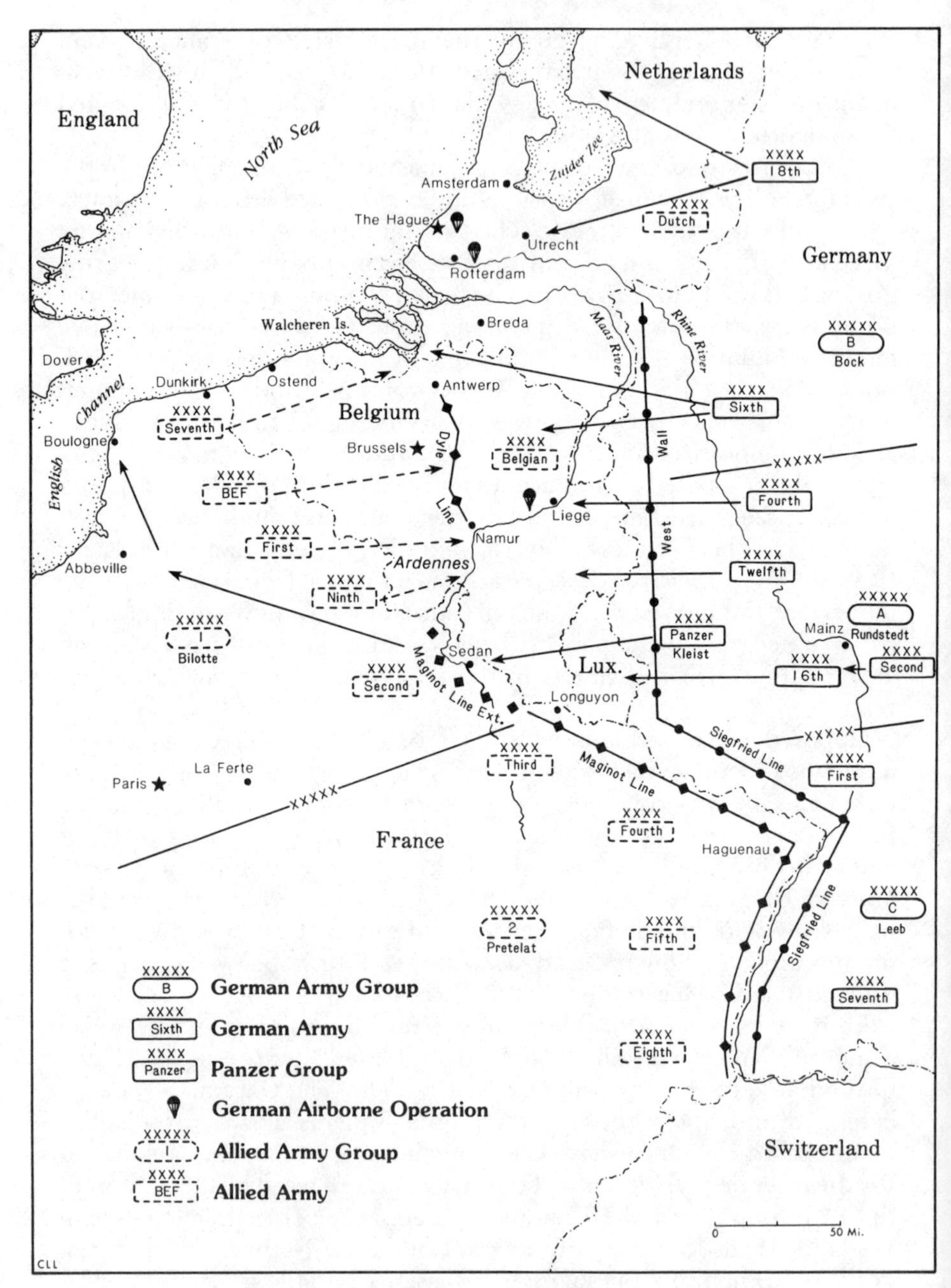

The German Offensive in the West, May 1940

General Heinz Guderian

SOURCE: Matthew Cooper, *The German Army, 1933–1945: Its Political and Military Failure* (New York: Stein and Day, 1978).

planes caught on the ground were destroyed within a day. German airborne troops seized strategic points on the Dutch and Belgian frontiers, including the fortress of Eben Emael at the Liège Gap, ahead of Army Group B's advancing ground forces. The overwhelmed Dutch army surrendered after five days, and the Belgian army made a hasty retreat to the Dyle River where it awaited help from the Anglo-French armies. Gamelin promptly ordered Allied Army Group One—consisting of three French armies and the BEF, and nearly all of the Allied motorized forces—to implement Plan D (advance to the Dyle) in the belief that the Germans were executing a broader version of the 1914 Schlieffen Plan. But the Allied wheel into Belgium left a weak pivot at the Ardennes, opposed to which was Runstedt's powerful Army Group A.

Spearheaded by Panzer Group Kleist and a separate panzer corps, Army Group A had begun its advance through the Ardennes on the first day of the offensive. This advance was, in fact, the master-stroke of the German operation called Case Yellow. Yellow had used Bock's forces to lure the Allied left wing into making a hasty advance into Belgium, the BEF and two French armies advancing to the west of the Meuse and one French army entering the northern Ardennes. The form of the Allied advance had left a weak link between the French Ninth Army in the northern Ardennes and the static French Second Army manning the so-called Maginot Line Extension, a line of weak fixed defenses just west of the Meuse facing the southern Ardennes. The German plan had been approved personally by Hitler after long debate and after Guderian's expressed confidence that armored-motorized forces could cross the southern Ardennes swiftly and quickly penetrate the French defenses along the Meuse. The plan aimed at positioning Rundstedt's forces so that they could drive westward across the communications of Allied Army Group One while it was engaged in a frontal battle with Bock's forces in Belgium.

In the event, German armored-motorized forces crossed the Ardennes so swiftly that Guderian's corps reached the Meuse at Sedan about noon on May 12. The Maginot Line Extension at that point, manned by inferior reserve divisions, was penetrated on May 13, and on May 14 Rundstedt's forces began to drive west with Panzer Group Kleist in the lead. The armored-motorized spearhead encountered hardly any opposition except for a weak Allied counterattack at Arras, before reaching Abbeville near the sea on May 20. Behind the spearhead, German infantry divisions were marching west, operating on the intact French rail system, and laying down a carpet of forces across the rear of Army Group One in Belgium. The Allied Army Group Two, forty static French divisions in the Maginot Line, were helpless to take action. After capturing Abbeville, the German spearheads moved north, capturing one port after another until it became clear that it was only a matter of

German PzKpfw III, one of the best tank designs of World War II.

SOURCE: Kenneth Macksey and John H. Batchelor, *Tank: A History of the Armoured Fighting Vehicle* (New York: Charles Scribner's Sons, 1970).

time before Army Group One and the Belgian army would be completely encircled and destroyed. Fortunately for the BEF and some of the other Allied troops, a German delay in seizing Dunkirk allowed General John, Lord Gort, the BEF commander, to order it occupied in force, and subsequently a British evacuation by sea (Operation Dynamo) saved 338,000 Allied troops, though nearly all their arms and equipment were lost. Elsewhere, however, the Flanders *Kesselschlacht* disposed of perhaps 500,000 troops and about forty divisions.

General Maxime Weygand had relieved Gamelin of command on May 18, and while the Germans were preoccupied in Belgium, he had used forty divisions to form a new line across northern France facing the threat from the north. But this "Weygand Line" was almost denuded of supporting air power and armor, and its divisions were no match for the combined forces of Rundstedt's and Bock's army groups when they started southward on June 5. The "Weygand Line" crumbled within a week. On June 10, Mussolini abandoned neutrality, and Italy entered the war against France and Britain. Ten French divisions on the Italian frontier beat back all Italian attacks; but meanwhile Reynaud's government had moved to Tours, and on June 13 it declared Paris an "open city" in order to save it from destruction. On June 14, for the second time in seventy years, Paris felt the tread of German boots. As the German drive continued south, Reynaud's government fled to Bordeaux, where on June 16 it resigned to make way for a new government under old Marshal Henri Pétain. Pétain requested armistice negotiations, and his emissaries were received at Compiègne in the same railroad car in which Foch had humbled the German representatives in November, 1918. Agreement was reached and on June 22 a general armistice went into effect between French and German forces. Fighting between the French and Italians ceased two days later. In just six weeks, the German army and air force had defeated one of Europe's mightiest armies and extended Hitler's control over most of Western Europe. His empire then extended from the Channel to central Poland, and well into Scandanavia.

C. From the Armistice of Compiègne to the Battle of Moscow, June 1940–December 1941. The Armistice of Compiègne in June, 1940, divided France into a German-occupied zone in northern France, which included Paris and a strip of territory along the Bay of Biscay to the neutral Spanish frontier, and an unoccupied zone in southeastern France, under Pétain's government, with a capital at Vichy. Hitler had allowed a measure of French sovereignty to survive, lest the French fleet and overseas territories rally to Britain and remain in the war. Churchill's fear that Hitler would somehow get control of the French fleet—interned in North African ports—caused him in July, 1940, to order naval attacks on major French naval units at Mers-El-Kebir (near Oran) as a preventive measure. Surviving French vessels fled to Toulon. French soldiers who got away to Britain before the armistice rallied around Charles de Gaulle in the Free French Movement, but most of France's forces overseas recognized the Pétain government and obeyed its orders. Vichy France maintained a precarious official neutrality in the war until November, 1942, when Anglo-American forces invaded Morocco and Algeria. Hitler then ordered all of France occupied, though his attempt to seize the French fleet at Toulon was foiled when its crews scuttled their vessels. Pétain's attempt at collaboration with Nazi Germany from 1940 to 1942 would earn him imprisonment for the rest of his life.

After the armistice with France, Hitler hoped, for a time during the summer of 1940, that Churchill's government would also come to terms with him. All he demanded, he told his generals, was a free hand on the continent. He was, in fact, so eager to get on with German eastward expansion that on July 21 he gave his first instructions for preparations of an invasion of Russia in 1941. But when Churchill made clear that his government intended to fight until the defeat of the Axis powers, Hitler ordered preparations for Operation Sea Lion, an invasion of England, in the summer of 1940. When German studies showed that such an invasion would be impossible unless the *Luftwaffe* could guarantee no interference from the British fleet and the Royal Air Force, even the attempt at an invasion began to hinge on the *Luftwaffe*'s ability to eliminate the RAF. As head of the *Luftwaffe,* Hermann Göring pledged that the RAF Fighter Command, the main hindrance, would be crushed within two weeks of the beginning of unlimited air operations against the British Isles. Operation Eagle Attack, the German air offensive, would employ three thousand aircraft, a third of them fighters.

The Battle of Britain, the collective term for the series of aerial engagements over England from August 12 to September 27, began with the Germans being opposed by a thousand Spitfire and Hurricane fighters and a pool of almost 1,500 fighter pilots. Aided by Fighter Control, radar, and Ultra (the secret code-breaking operation), the RAF Fighter Command proved almost impossible to surprise on the ground, and in the air the excellent British fighters exploited the weaknesses of the German aircraft. The Messerschmidt Bf 109, the only German fighter in a class with the Spitfire and Hurricane, lacked sufficient range to escort the German bombers to all targets in England, and unescorted bombers proved too weak in armor and defensive guns to withstand the fierce British air attacks. Accordingly, over the six weeks of the Battle of Britain, the *Luftwaffe* lost 1,400 aircraft (including 668 fighters) and about 2,000 aircrewmen. The RAF lost about 700 fighters and 618 pilots. British factories turned out new fighters about as quickly as they were lost, hence the real strain on the RAF was in pilot replacement. But the Germans could not keep up with either aircraft or crew losses, and after September 27 Göring terminated Operation Eagle Attack. Hitler postponed Operation Sea Lion until 1941, but he eventually discarded the idea of invading England altogether.

In the fall of 1940, Göring turned to a protracted program of nighttime bombing of British cities, the so-called Blitz. Night raiding was less costly in planes and crews, though bombing accuracy was poor. But by indiscriminate attacks on Britain's cities, especially London, Göring hoped to weaken British moral and damage the economy. The raids continued until the spring of 1941, when German air units were transferred to more pressing theaters of war elsewhere. A typical raid involved up to 200 bombers and the delivery of 600 tons of high-explosive bombs and incendiaries. The single most destructive of these raids occurred on the night of November 14, 1940, when 450 German bombers dropped 500 tons of incendiaries and bombs on the city of Coventry. Hundreds of Britons perished in the bomb blasts and flames, and the center of the city was destroyed. But the favorite German target was London, a target so huge that it was easy to find. About half of the 50,000 Britons killed and the 60,000 wounded during the "Blitz" lived in the greater London area. The British tried, and with some success, to confound the German efforts to improve bombing accuracy through radio navigation beams by developing electronic counter-measures (ECM). Antiaircraft artillery and eventually night fighters were pressed into service. Though the night bombing was an ordeal, the British people endured and the British economy never faltered for that reason. Moreover, RAF Bomber Command hit back at targets in Germany during the "Blitz."

Less spectacular than the "Blitz," but more menacing to Britain's survival over the long run, was the German *guerre de course* at sea. Between October, 1940, and May, 1941, Admiral Raeder sent a battleship, two battle cruisers, and two "pocket battleships," as well as a heavy cruiser and six converted merchantmen-raiders, into the North Atlantic by way of the Arctic Ocean and the Denmark Strait between Greenland and Iceland. All of these ships operated from the new bases in Norway. The British detailed battleships and battle cruisers to escort their most important convoys. But the day of the German surface-raider was relatively brief in the Atlantic. Ships which put back into French ports such as Cherbourg and Le Havre ran the risk of being damaged by British air attack while in port, while the British gradually became more efficient in tracking down raiders at sea. Though the new battleship *Bismarck* sank the battle cruiser *Hood* just south of the Denmark Strait in May, 1941, within days she herself was destroyed by torpedoes and the fire from battleships seven hundred miles from the safety of the port of Brest. The loss of the great ship on her maiden voyage led Hitler to forbid the sending of any more large warships into the Atlantic. Raeder confined the sorties of his other large ships to the waters off Norway and against convoys bound for the Russian arctic ports after June, 1941. Admiral Dönitz's U-boat command proved to be more of a long-term threat in the Atlantic. Between September, 1939, and June, 1941, the Germans built ninety-six new submarines and lost forty-one. Over the same period, U-boats sank 4 million tons and surface-raiders sank a million tons of British shipping, or about a fourth of Britain's pre-war total. As the British built or acquired 2.2 million tons of new merchant ships in this period, they were left with a net loss of 1.8 million tons, or not quite a seventh of their prewar tonnage. Still worse was to come for the British merchant marine.

Meanwhile, the war was spreading, and not entirely due to Hitler's intiatives. As early as the summer of 1940, Mussolini ordered his forces in Libya to invade British Egypt. But the September invasion by the Italian Tenth Army and 135,000 troops was soon stopped by the 30,000 troops of General Richard O'Connor's Western Desert Force, a part of General Archibald Wavell's Middle East Command. The frustrated Mussolini then ordered his forces in Albania to invade Greece in October, only to see them defeated and driven back into Albania. In mid-November, Admiral Sir Andrew Cunningham's fleet based on Alexandria, Egypt, made a daring raid into the central Mediterranean in order to launch aircraft-carrier strikes at the Italian fleet anchored in the Bay of Taranto. Three out of four of the Italian battleships were sunk or disabled. The crowning blow for the Italians in 1940 came on December 9, when the Western Desert Force defeated the Italian Tenth Army in Egypt and drove it back pell-mell into Libya. The British victory at Sidi Barrani was followed by another at Beda Fomm on Libyan soil in February, 1941, after which the Tenth Army hardly existed. At the price of 500 Britons killed and 1,400 wounded, O'Connor's force had destroyed ten Italian divisions and killed or captured 150,000 Italian troops.

Had O'Connor's Western Desert Force been permitted to drive on after Beda Fomm to capture the major port of Tripoli, the war in North Africa might have been over in a few more weeks. But Ultra had warned Churchill that Hitler was preparing a Balkan blitzkrieg and Greece would need all the help it could get. Accordingly, the Western Desert Force was ordered stripped of its veteran soldiers and its best equipment, which were sent back to Egypt to help form an expedition to Greece. Two inexperienced British divisions with old equipment under General Philip Neame occupied Cyrenaica (eastern Libya) as a secure flank for Egypt. The British did not expect any further trouble from the Axis forces in Libya. They might have thought again had they known that in February, 1941, General Erwin Rommel had arrived in Libya and that a *Deutsches Afrika Korps* (German Africa Corps), composed of a German panzer division and a "light" division, was on its way to North Africa.

Hitler's decision to send help to the Italians in North Africa and to launch a blitzkrieg in the Balkans was largely motivated by his desire to secure the German southern flank before beginning the invasion of Russia in June, 1941. He also feared that, from British bases in Greece, the RAF could launch air strikes at the oil fields at Ploesti in Romania. Only Greece and Yugoslavia refused his invitation to join the Axis alliance in the spring of 1941, and neither their forces nor the British expeditionary force sent from Egypt were any match for the two powerful German armies assembled to execute operations Twenty-Five (Yugoslavia) and Marita (Greece). Accordingly, when the German blow fell in April, Allied resistance speedily collapsed. The most populated parts of Yugoslavia were overrun by the Germans in five days, and the Anglo-Greek defense of upper Greece lasted only a little longer. By early May, the Germans had captured Athens and the British expeditionary force was evacuating through the port of Piraeus in the Peloponnesus. But hardly had the British withdrawn to the island of Crete than, later in May, the Germans launched their biggest airborne operation of the war (Mercury). The airborne invasion of Crete was successful, but the two German divisions involved were so damaged and so many planes were lost that the German airborne capacity was almost nil for months after Operation Mercury.

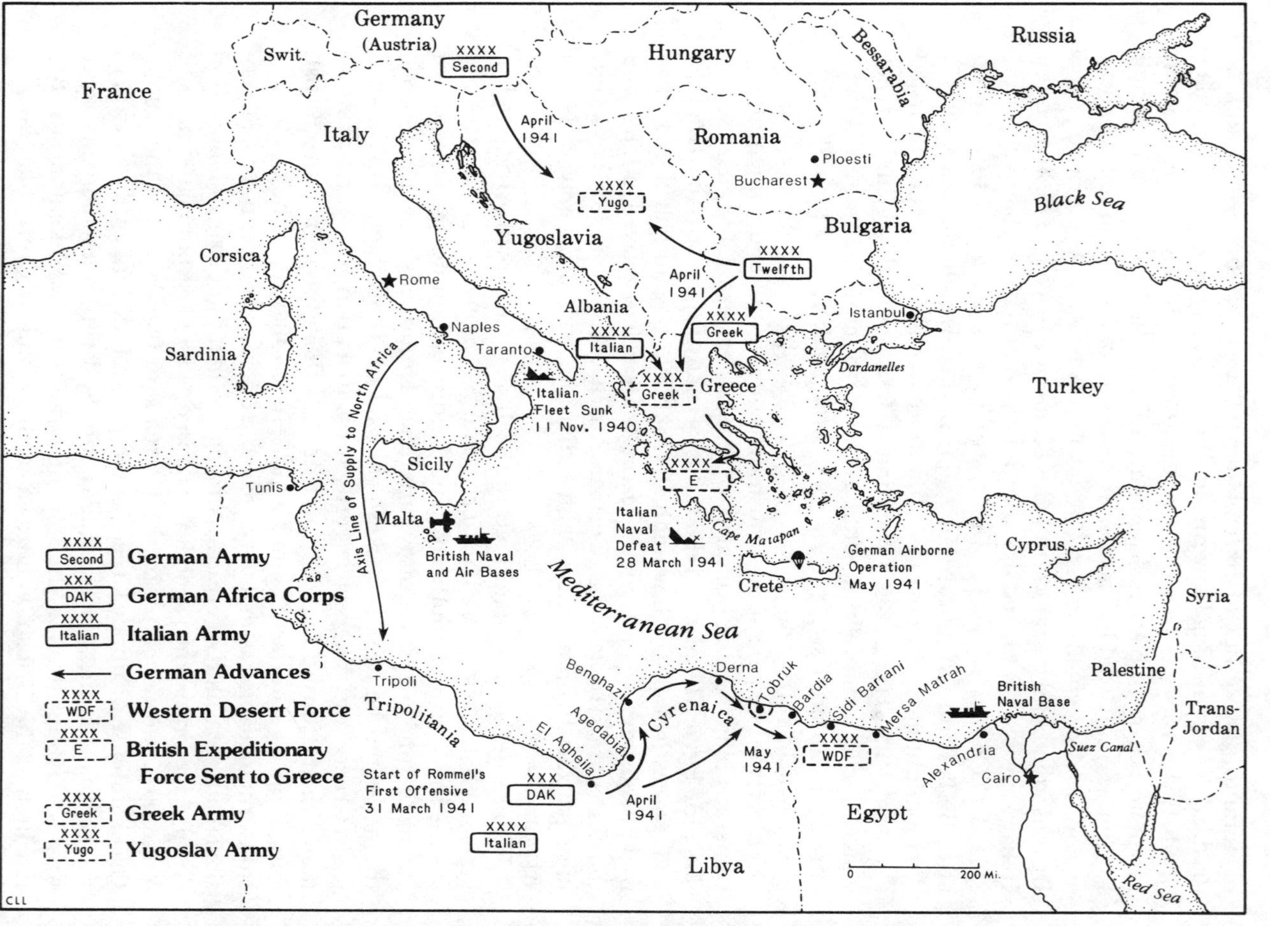

Axis Offensive in the Balkans and the Middle East, April–May 1941

Meanwhile, at the end of March, Rommel had joined a German "light" division—the first of the DAK to arrive—to the Italian forces in Tripolitania (western Libya) and launched an offensive against the British in Cyrenaica on his own authority. The unexpected Axis attack routed Neame's Western Desert Force from El Agheila eastwards, and, except for four brigades that took shelter in the bypassed port of Tobruk, the British fled behind the Egyptian frontier in April. O'Connor, who had rushed from Egypt in order to help restore order in the early phase of the offensive, was captured along with Neame during the British retreat. Only lagging Axis logistics, and the threat to his rear from Tobruk, kept Rommel from invading Egypt. After Rommel's offensive finally ground to a halt, Churchill gave top priority to rebuilding the Western Desert Force.

The arrival of a special convoy of two hundred tanks at Alexandria in June gave General Archibald Wavell the means to launch an offensive in order to relieve Tobruk. Fortunately for Rommel, the DAK's panzer division had arrived by the time Wavell launched Operation Battle-Axe, and he was able to parry Wavell's thrust. Churchill relieved Wavell in July, transferring him to India, and replaced him with General Sir Claude Auchinleck. Auchinleck convinced Churchill that he needed time to convert the Western Desert Force into a more powerful Eighth Army, and no major fighting, except around Tobruk, occurred again until November. Rommel used the interval to improve his logistics, add another panzer division to the DAK, and in August to combine the German-Italian forces into Panzer Army Africa. But British air and submarine attacks on Axis shipping from Italy to Tripoli, Rommel's major port of supply, continued to be a source of German anxiety.

The high point of the European war in 1941 was, however, Hitler's invasion of Russia. That spring, a total of 3.3 million German troops and 142 divisions assembled in eastern Europe for Operation Barbarossa. The forces included 19 panzer divisions, 14 motorized infantry divisions (including 3½ Waffen SS divisions), 4 "light" divisions, 2 mountain divisions, a cavalry division, and 102 infantry divisions. Also assembled were 3,350 tanks, 7,000 pieces of artillery, 600,000 motor vehicles besides the tanks, 625,000 horses, and over 100,000 horse-drawn wagons. But the diversion of *Luftwaffe* planes to the Mediterranean and the losses in the Battle of Britain resulted in only 2,250 German aircraft being available for the invasion of Russia. The Germans estimated that the Red Army had 178 divisions, 10,000 tanks, and 7,000 aircraft in western Russia, but they thought the quality of their forces would more than offset Russian numbers, given the element of surprise. Hitler predicted that the only hard fighting would be over within a month.

The greatest land war ever fought began at 3:30 A.M. on June 22, 1941, with a tremendous German pre-dawn barrage laid down on Rus-

Operation Barbarossa: The German Plan of the Invasion of Russia, June 1941

sian frontier positions. At first light, the *Luftwaffe* delivered massive air attacks on Soviet airfields within range. Within twenty-four hours, an estimated two thousand Russian planes were destroyed on the ground. Russian air losses mounted so rapidly over the next several weeks that the *Luftwaffe* enjoyed complete command of the air. On the ground, Army Group North (Leeb), composed of two armies, a panzer group, and twenty-six divisions, swept into the former Baltic states and headed for Leningrad. Army Group Center (Bock), composed of two armies, two panzer groups, and thirty-two divisions invaded Russian Poland and White Russia in the direction of Moscow. Army Group South (Rundstedt), consisting of three armies, one panzer group, and thirty-five divisions, struck into the Ukraine and advanced toward the Dnieper. The balance of the German divisions in the East were sent forward as reinforcements, as logistics permitted. Romania, desirous of regaining Bessarabia, entered the war with twelve divisions, while Finland attacked with sixteen divisions in order to recover territories lost to Russia in the "Winter War" of 1939–1940.

The greatest of the early German successes were on Bock's front, where, by the end of the encirclement battles of Minsk-Smolensk in August, a total of 475,000 Soviet troops, 4,530 tanks, and 3,400 pieces of artillery had been destroyed or captured. But forty-seven days of incessant marching and fighting had taken their toll, and the German infantry divisions were showing exhaustion. The OKH ordered Army Group Center to halt, rest its infantry, and repair its logistics before attempting to move toward Moscow. The panzer groups with Army Group Center were to conserve their resources for a final great battle at the Russian capital. But Hitler had other ideas. He proposed that while Bock's group rested, its two armored groups—under Hermann Hoth and Heinz Guderian—would be temporarily detached, Hoth's group to assist Army Group North, encountering stubborn resistance before Leningrad, and Guderian's group to aid Army Group South, also meeting tough resistance in the Ukraine. Brauchitsch and Halder opposed the proposal because it would add wear-and-tear on the armored-motorized groups even before the drive on Moscow began, and because it would delay the start of Bock's drive beyond the time his group needed to recuperate. Hitler had his way, however, and the two groups were detached. Hoth's panzers aided Army Group North in sealing in the defenders of Leningrad, and Guderian's armor aided Army Group South to achieve the greatest *Kesselschlacht* ever when 665,000 Russian troops were killed or captured at the Battle of Kiev. But most of the troops killed or captured turned out to be ordinary infantry of the sort most easily replaced by the *Stafka* (Soviet High Command). The better Soviet armored and motorized forces in the south had escaped the trap. Though Rundstedt moved on to capture Rostov, the Soviet forces in his front remained formidable.

Soviet T-34 tank, perhaps the best medium tank of World War II.

SOURCE: Kenneth Macksey and John H. Batchelor, *Tank: A History of the Armoured Fighting Vehicle* (New York: Charles Scribner's Sons, 1970).

As Brauchitsch and Halder had feared, Hoth's and Guderian's troops and machines were worn by the time they rejoined Army Group Center for Operation Typhoon, the drive on Moscow, in late September. Bock's advance began with a 40 percent shortage in tanks and a 30 percent shortage in trucks. Still, the *Luftwaffe* ruled the skies, the weather was fair, and a faulty Russian deployment in the Vyazma-Briansk position permitted another German *Kesselschlacht* in October. A total of 663,000 Russians, 1,000 tanks, and 5,000 pieces of artillery were destroyed or taken. Hitler was so elated over the news that he announced that the decisive battle of the Eastern campaign had been fought. But to his surprise, the Red Army was still not broken, and Vyazma-Briansk turned out to be the last German encirclement victory of the war.

After Vyazma-Briansk, the fall rains began, turning the unpaved Russian roads into quagmires. As wheeled vehicles mired down, Army Group Center's advance came to a halt. The grip of the mud was not broken until a freeze on November 7, but the dash of cold weather was a portent of the approach of winter. While the Germans were temporarily immobilized, Stalin and his generals completed the defenses of Moscow, five fortified lines collectively fifty miles deep, and containing 1,428 artillery emplacements, seventy-five miles of barbed wire, and vast numbers of tank-traps and mine fields. General Georgi Zhukov, the former chief of the General Staff, personally assumed command of the group of Russian armies assembled to defend the capital, including eighteen fresh divisions just arrived from the Far East.

The Battle of Moscow began on November 16, when Bock's army group first encountered the outer line of Moscow's defenses. Though

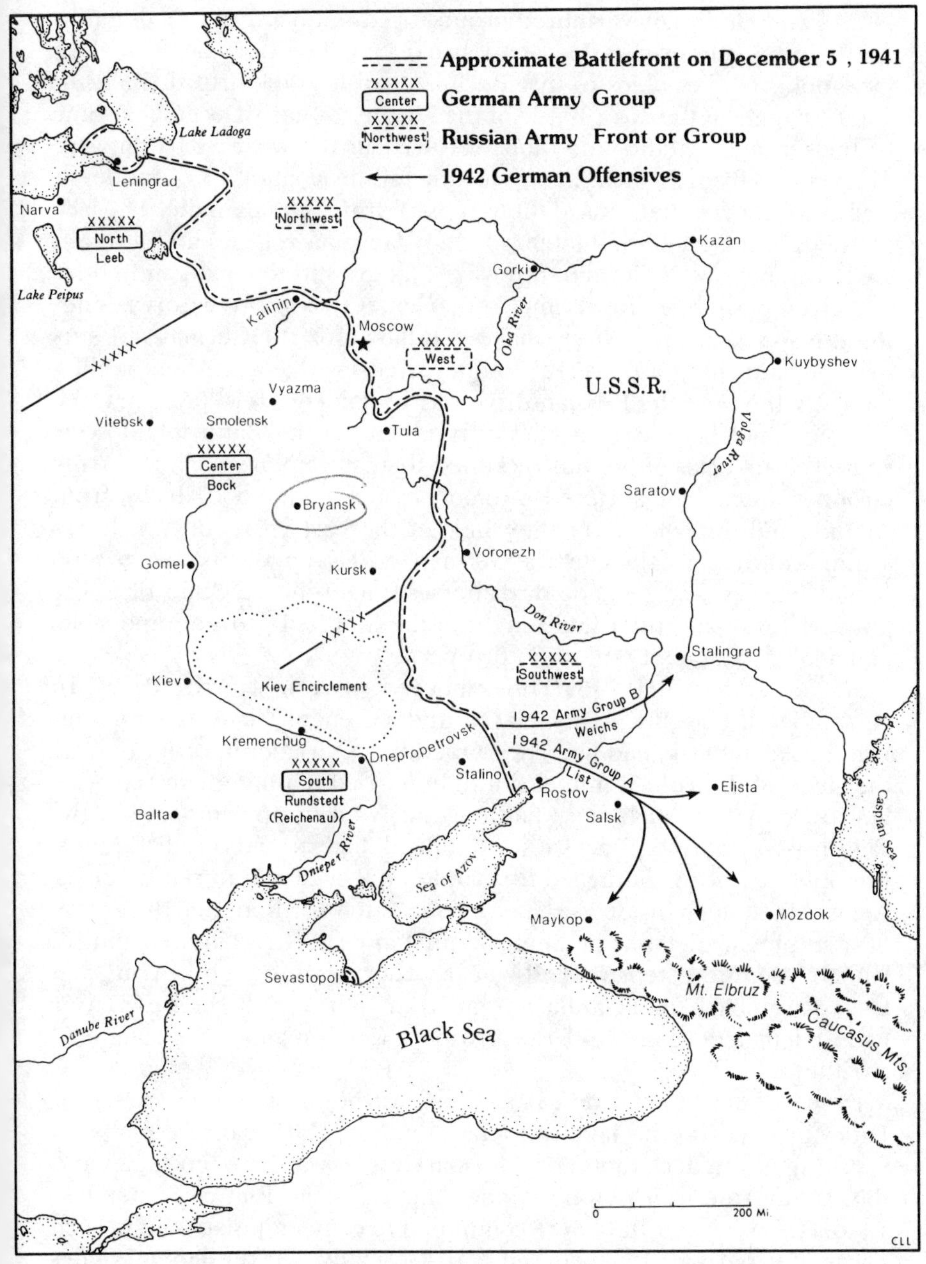

Eastern Front: Maximum Line of German Advance, 1941

Hoth's and Guderian's armored groups tried to turn the city's defenses north and south, every approach was blocked. The German frontal attack took such heavy losses that Bock likened it to the brutish chest-to-chest struggle in the 1914 Battle of the Marne. By early December, some of the German infantry divisions involved in the wearing battle were ninety miles from the nearest supporting rail-head, and lack of fodder as well as winter weather caused thousands of draft animals to die. The lack of enough anti-freeze immobilized many German vehicles and aircraft. By December 5, the German offensive had ground to a halt, and Hitler had given permission for Army Group Center to regroup before resuming the attack. But, on December 6, Zhukov took the Germans by surprise by launching a powerful counteroffensive that sent them reeling back. By the time the Russian drive was contained a few days later, the Germans had been driven back fifty miles. As the Battle of Moscow sputtered to a close, the OKH reckoned that, since November 16, Army Group Center had suffered 250,000 casualties (55,000 dead) from wounds and the cold. Over the whole of the Eastern Front, which was settling down to a stalemate, the Germans had lost 750,000 men, 75,000 motor vehicles, and 180,000 draft horses since June 22. Still worse, the quick victory that Hitler had sought in the East had proved impossible, and a long struggle there was in prospect.

Still other bad news for Hitler poured in from North Africa. In November, the Eighth Army, placed under General Sir Alan Cunningham by Auchinleck, had launched Operation Crusader in order to raise the siege of Tobruk. Rommel skillfully parried Cunningham's attacks, but in December Auchinleck had personally taken up command of the Eighth Army and its attacks toward Tobruk had turned out differently. Rommel had been compelled to abandon his siege and to retire Panzer Army Africa deep inside Cyrenaica. Fortunately for Rommel, the arrival of a shipment of tanks at Benghazi in January, 1942, allowed him to launch a counteroffensive, and by early February the Eighth Army had been driven back to El Gazala, not far from Tobruk. Still, the Desert War had stalemated again, and the prospect was for another struggle of attrition.

Even so, next to the defeat at Moscow, the most serious event for Hitler in 1941 was the Japanese attack on Pearl Harbor on December 7, resulting in the declaration of a formal state of war between Japan and the Anglo-American powers. Under the Tripartite Pact of September, 1940, Germany and Italy were committed to come to Japan's aid in such a war. But perhaps war between Nazi Germany and the United States would have come about in any case. The United States was a massive supplier of war material to Britain, and by the fall of 1941 the U.S. Navy was even escorting British ships part way across the Atlantic in an undeclared naval war with the German U-boats. Before December, 1941, was out, the Axis powers (now including Japan) were at war with Britain and the United States. Japan and Russia remained formally at peace until 1945, but World War II had become a series of interlocking conflicts on a global scale.

II. The European War, 1942–45

A. From Moscow to Sicily, January 1942–July 1943. In the immediate aftermath of the German reverse at Moscow in December, 1941, Brauchitsch submitted his resignation as commander-in-chief of the army and Hitler appointed himself to that position. He also decreed that the OKH would henceforth have total responsibility for the Eastern Front, while the OKW would assume responsibility for any others. Hitler, of course, was effectively supreme commander at both headquarters, which were located near one another in East Prussia as the war went on.

Winter weather forced a suspension of major operations on the Eastern Front until the spring of 1942, by which time the effects of climate and battle had raised the total of German casualties on the front to over a million men. Still, Hitler did not despair of a final victory over Stalin. The OKH-planned Operation Blue aimed at overrunning Soviet oil fields in the Caucasus and undermining both the Red Army and Soviet industry. After preliminary operations, Blue was launched on June 28 and immediately created a great gap in the Russian front in the south. Of the reorganized German forces carrying out the offensive, Army Group A advanced three hundred miles before a combination of fierce Soviet resistance and logistical problems finally brought it to a halt almost in sight of the Russian oil fields. Then Army Group B, protecting Army Group A's northern flank by advancing toward the Volga, found its Sixth Army engaged in a street-by-street battle for Stalingrad in the late summer. Halder urged Hitler to allow General Friedrich von Paulus, commander of the Sixth Army, to break off the battle and withdraw from the dangerously exposed Stalingrad salient, but Halder was only dismissed as chief of the OKH General Staff on September 24 for his pains. Kurt Zeitzler, Halder's successor, was of the same opinion as Halder, but Hitler stubbornly insisted on continuing the deadlocked battle in Stalingrad until late in November, when a powerful Russian offensive severed the Sixth Army's communications and trapped it inside the city. Though Hitler promoted Paulus to the rank of field marshal in order to encourage his determination to resist, all German attempts to relieve Stalingrad or to supply the garrison by air were failures. On January 31, 1943, Paulus and his remaining ninety-one thousand troops surrendered. His army was the first German army to surrender in the field since the Napoleonic Wars. Hitler's battle for Stalingrad had cost his forces some three hundred thousand men.

The Battle of Stalingrad turned out to be the point-of-return for the Red Army. Except for the abortive German offensive at Kursk (Operation Citadel) in July, 1943, the Red Army had the initiative on the Eastern Front for the rest of the war. Kursk was also the largest armored battle of World War II, with perhaps as many as six thousand tanks and armored self-propelled guns involved. As the Russian offensives slowly drove the Germans westward in 1943 and in the first half of 1944, the only realistic German hope lay in stalling the Soviet advance at some point, as the front narrowed and German lines-of-communication shortened. But even for this strategy to work, the Germans would also have to beat off any Anglo-American attack on Hitler's empire in Western Europe. In practice, the combined Allied strength would be too much for that of the Axis powers, and Hitler's dream of European domination would reap only total defeat for the Third Reich.

The year 1942 was also the turning point of the war in North Africa. That spring, Field Marshal Albert Kesselring, German Commander-in-Chief, South, managed to bring enough air power to bear on Malta that British air and submarine attacks from the island were temporarily suspended. In addition, from November, 1941, to February, 1942, the British navy suffered heavy losses both in the Mediterranean and in the Far East, especially in capital ships and aircraft carriers. Kesselring had concentrated two German and two Italian airborne divisions on the island of Sicily for a descent on Malta (Operation Hercules), but Hitler hesitated to give the crucial order for fear that the Italian navy would not carry out its part of the operation. The impatient Rommel refused to wait upon the outcome. On May 26, he launched a new offensive with Panzer Army Africa against the British position at El Gazala (Operation Theseus), defeated their forces, and then drove on to capture Tobruk on June 21. With supplies captured at Tobruk, his army then pressed into Egypt. Hitler was pleased and decided that the airborne invasion of Malta could be cancelled. He also ordered Kesselring to send much of his air force to the Eastern Front in order to support Operation Blue.

By July, Auchinleck had withdrawn the Eighth Army to a good defensive position at El Alamein, the terminus of the desert railroad from Alexandria, eighty miles to the east. Between July 3 and July 21, the Eighth Army beat off a series of German attacks on the El Alamein position. Rommel suspended his efforts until Panzer Army Africa could repair its tanks and stockpile supplies. During the lull, which lasted until late August, Churchill relieved Auchinleck, abolished the Middle East Command, and created a new Near East Command in its place. He appointed General Sir Harold Alexander to head the Near East Command, of which the Eighth Army was a part; and General Bernard L. Montgomery took up the command of the Eighth Army. Rommel made a final effort to get by the El Alamein position at the Battle of Alam El

Halfa Ridge (Second El Alamein), but the Eighth Army fought Panzer Army Africa to a draw in late August and early September. By then it was clear to Rommel that a tremendous build-up of forces was going on behind the lines of the Eighth Army. His own forces, far from their main base at Tripoli, were dwindling in strength. In addition, the British Tenth Submarine Flotilla had returned to its bases on Malta and, joined by 250 British aircraft flown into the island, had resumed its attacks on Axis shipping between Italy and Tripoli. Under the circumstances, Rommel saw no alternative but to request permission to withdraw his forces behind the Libyan frontier and to stake out a defensive position in Cyrenaica. Hitler refused the request.

By the last half of October, the Eighth Army had reached a strength of 200,000 troops, 750 aircraft, 1,000 tanks, and as many pieces of artillery. The troops were well supplied with food, water, fuel, and spare ammunition. In contrast, Panzer Army Africa had 100,000 troops (ill-supplied with rations, water, or fuel), 675 planes (275 German), 500 tanks (211 German), and 500 guns. Many of the men were ill or exhausted from a long time in the desert. It was, therefore, with great confidence that Montgomery launched Operation Lightfoot on October 23 in the third and last Battle of El Alamein. For thirteen days, the Eighth Army systematically hammered Panzer Army Africa to fragments until, on November 3, Rommel ordered what remained of his forces to begin a withdrawal to Libya. When his army crossed the frontier on November 8, only half of his original force of German troops and a fifth of his Italian troops were still with him. His armored component was down to thirty tanks. The triumphant Montgomery and the Eighth Army followed Rommel's forces in leisurely pursuit.

On November 8, too, Hitler received other bad news from North Africa. About a hundred thousand Anglo-American troops had invaded the Vichy French territories of Morocco and Algeria (Operation Torch). After largely token resistance, the Vichy French forces in both provinces surrendered, on the orders of Admiral Jean-François Darlan. Hitler retaliated by ordering German occupation of both Vichy France and its remaining North African territory of Tunisia. The relatively short distance between Italy and Tunisia made it a potential safe haven for the retreating Panzer Army Africa, while the province could be occupied ahead of the Anglo-Americans by General Jürgen von Arnim's Fifth Panzer Army. After Panzer Army Africa's withdrawal to southern Tunisia was complete at the end of January, 1943, it was reorganized as the Italian First Army (including the DAK) under Rommel's command. The Italian First Army manned the Mareth Line—old French fortifications facing Libya—while the Fifth Panzer Army defended northern Tunisia. Meanwhile, U.S. General Dwight D. Eisenhower, Allied commander-in-chief of Operation Torch, had made contact with

Montgomery's Eighth Army, and Alexander assumed command of the new Eighteenth Army Group, composed of the British First and Eighth armies, the U.S. II Corps, and a French corps.

In mid-February, 1943, Rommel and Arnim launched a spoiling offensive, Rommel directing an armored raid toward Kasserine Pass which mauled elements of the inexperienced U.S. II Corps. The commander of the II Corps was relieved, and General George S. Patton, Jr., substituted in his place. Just after the raid, on February 23 Rommel was made commander-in-chief of all Axis forces in Tunisia, then titled as Army Group Africa. But Rommel's offensive against the Eighth Army on March 6 went badly at Medenine, and later that month he turned over command in Tunisia to Arnim and flew back to Germany for health treatment. He never returned to North Africa. Arnim's forces, fifteen divisions (eleven German, four of them panzer divisions), were confronted by twenty Allied divisions (most of them British), with command of the air and the sea. Gradually, Allied attacks compressed the Axis Tunisian foothold. Tunis, the major port, fell on May 7, and the last organized resistance ceased on May 13. In all, the Allied forces had inflicted Axis casualties during the campaign and suffered 75,000 casualties in the process. The Italian navy, fearful of Anglo-American sea and air power, made no effort to evacuate Axis forces before surrender.

After a respite of two months following the Axis surrender in Tunisia, the Allies forces in the Mediterranean launched an invasion of Sicily (Operation Husky). The invasion was carried out by the Fifteenth Army Group (Alexander), composed of Montgomery's Eighth Army and the new U.S. Seventh Army under Patton. Each side initially committed nine divisions to the battle, but the Allied forces were supported by 3,350 aircraft (against 1,400 Axis planes, half of them German) and possessed command of the sea. The stubborn German defense of the so-called Messina Corner delayed Montgomery's straightforward advance across the island toward the narrows between Sicily and Italy, but it was partially overcome by a daring motorized end-run by Patton's forces by way of Palermo. Still, the Germans were able to withdraw three of their four divisions to Italy before Axis resistance on Sicily collapsed on August 17. The Battle of Sicily involved 475,000 Allied soldiers, sailors, and airmen, of whom 22,000 became casualties. The Axis powers lost 275,000 men on Sicily, all but 25,000 of them Italian.

Even while the Sicilian campaign was underway, on July 24 the Fascist Grand Council in Rome stripped Mussolini of his powers, and later that day King Victor-Emmanuel III ordered him placed under arrest. A new Italian government under Marshal Pietro Bodoglio opened secret negotiations with Eisenhower's headquarters in Algiers in order to remove Italy from the war before it became a battleground between German and Allied forces. As explained below, the Anglo-American high command actually had no plans to follow up the conquest of Sicily with an invasion of Italy, but the opportunity was too great to be missed. The invasion of Italy in September, 1943, even as the Italian government surrendered, had great consequences for the further Allied prosecution of the war.

B. The U-Boat War, the Allied Strategic Air Offensive, and Hitler's V Weapons. In 1942, the German U-boat campaign established a record for the war by sinking 1,279,000 tons of Allied shipping in the North Atlantic and 5,605,000 tons world-wide. In addition, Admiral Dönitz added 190 submarines to his U-boat fleet, while losing only 92. But in 1943, German fortunes at sea began to decline. Though U-boats sank 1,147,000 tons in the North Atlantic, the world-wide figure dropped to 2,649,000 tons. And while Dönitz added 225 submarines, he lost 234 in 1943. The advent of the *Schnorkel* in 1944, a pipe with a float-valve that allowed submarines to recharge batteries underwater, reduced the time submarines had to remain on the surface, but in all of 1944 the U-boats sank only 169,000 tons in the North Atlantic and 694,000 tons world-wide. A total of 175 U-boats were added, but 235 were lost. In the remaining five months of the European war in 1945, U-boats sank 271,000 tons of Allied shipping in the North Atlantic and 404,000 tons world-wide, but 165 submarines were lost and only 70 were added. For World War II as a whole, German U-boats sank 6,846,000 tons of Allied shipping in the North Atlantic and 14,316,000 tons worldwide. This record was accomplished by 1,170 German submarines, all but 57 of which were built after the outbreak of war. In the process of the war, a total of 784 U-boats and 49,000 submariners were lost.

The failure of the German submarine *guerre de course* is explained by several factors, including the lateness of major expansion of the U-boat fleet. But the Anglo-American navies gave top priority to building a huge antisubmarine fleet, including long-range patrol planes, and one well equipped with sonar and radar. By 1943, the threat of land-based planes from the American Atlantic and Gulf coasts had forced Dönitz to order his submarines to operate deeper inside the Atlantic and away from some of the most vulnerable sea lanes. The "jeep carrier," actually a small aircraft carrier that could accompany merchant convoys, was an economical threat to submarines beyond the range of land-based planes. Finally, Anglo-American ship-building added 35,300,000 tons of merchant shipping from 1939 to 1945, while 33,600,000 tons were lost to all causes.

The U.S. Eighth Air Force joined RAF Bomber Command in England in the summer of 1942, but at first the Americans had only a handful of B-17s. In contrast, as early as May, 1942, Bomber Command carried out the first of the "Thousand Bomber Raids" against Germany, the first target being the German Rhineland city of Cologne. British attacks were made at night to hold down aircraft losses, but the resulting bombing accuracy left much to be desired. Professor Frederick Lindemann (later Lord Cherwell), Churchill's scientific advisor, rationalized mass-area bombings on the grounds that they would help to destroy civilian morale. His view was endorsed by Air Marshal Sir Arthur Harris, Chief of Bomber Command toward the end of the war. But though the policy, put into effect, razed parts of German cities that had nothing to do directly with the German war effort, German morale did not break, and industrial production actually continued to rise until September, 1944, when it finally declined under intense Anglo-American bombing. Still, 80 percent of all the bomb tonnage delivered against Germany fell in the last ten months of the war. In addition, only gradually did the Allied air planners come to see that results were obtained not purely from the tonnages delivered, but from a proper selection of targets. In fairness it must be said that mass strategic bombing was still in an experimental stage in World War II.

The American air doctrine in 1942 differed considerably from the British. It assumed that heavy bombers could make daylight raids without fighter escorts, and that precision bombing could be carried out against sensitive industries directly related to the enemy's war production. Both the B-17 and the B-24 bombers were equipped with the sophisticated Norden bomb-sight for visual high-level attacks. But the Americans underrated the difficulties in putting their doctrine into practice. Extensive cloud-cover over northern Europe interfered with the optics of the Norden bomb-sight, while unescorted bombers proved much more vulnerable to enemy fighters than expected. These weaknesses did not fully reveal themselves, however, until 1943, when the American bombers began to invade the air space of the Reich proper, and the *Luftwaffe* Fighter Command felt compelled to make a major effort against them. American losses on raids from both England and bases in North Africa mounted inexorably from August to October. On August 1, 177 four-engined bombers based in North Africa tried a low-level attack on the German-controlled oil refineries at Ploesti,

British long-range bombers of the World War II era: Halifax, Manchester, and Stirling.

SOURCE: John Batchelor et al., *Air Power: A Modern Illustrated Military History* (New York: Exeter Books, 1979, in association with Phoebus Company/BPC Publishing, London).

Evolution of the U.S. B-17 bomber: series D, E, and G, World War II.

SOURCE: John Batchelor et al., *Air Power: A Modern Illustrated Military History* (New York: Exeter Books, 1979, in association with Phoebus Company/BPC Publishing, London).

HALIFAX Mk II SERIES I

This sub-variant of the Mk II Halifax mounted a two-gun Boulton Paul dorsal turret amidships but dispensed with the manually-operated beam guns, giving it a total of 6 × ·303 machine-guns

AVRO MANCHESTER

Gross weight: 50,000 lb **Span**: 90 ft 1 in **Length**: 70 ft **Engine**: 2 × 1,760 hp Rolls Royce Vulture **Armament**: 8 × ·303 machine-guns **Crew**: 7 **Speed**: 264 mph at 17,000 ft **Ceiling**: 19,200 ft **Range**: 1,630 miles **Bomb load**: 10,350 lb

Developed just before the war as a medium bomber, but marred by the unorthodox Vulture engine which led to its withdrawal in 1942, less than two years after it entered service

SHORT STIRLING Mk III

Gross weight: 70,000 lb **Span**: 99 ft 1 in **Length**: 87 ft 3 in **Engine**: 4 × 1,650 hp Bristol Hercules XVI **Armament**: 8 × ·303 Browning machine-guns **Crew**: 8 **Speed**: 270 mph at 14,500 ft **Ceiling**: 17,000 ft **Range**: 2,300 miles **Bomb load**: 14,000 lb

B-17D 'FLYING FORTRESS'

Gross weight: 50,000 lb **Span**: 103 ft 9 in **Length**: 67 ft 11 in **Engine**: 4 × Wright Cyclone R-1820 **Armament**: 6 × ·50, 1 × ·30 machine-guns **Crew**: 9 **Speed**: 323 mph at 25,000 ft **Ceiling**: 37,000 ft **Range**: 2,100 miles **Bomb load**: 10,500 lb

Spearhead of the USAAF's daylight raids on Occupied Europe. The D model carried less armament than later versions, one of which – the B-40 fighter – carried up to 30 machine-guns and cannon in an unsuccessful attempt to provide an escort for B-17 formations

B-17E 'FLYING FORTRESS'

Gross weight: 53,000 lb **Span**: 103 ft 9 in **Length**: 73 ft 10 in **Engine**: 4 × Wright R-1920-65 **Armament**: 15 machine-guns **Crew**: 9 **Speed**: 317 mph at 25,000 ft **Ceiling**: 36,600 ft **Range**: 3,300 miles **Bomb load**: 4,000 lb

This version of the famous B-17 was the first to live up to the name 'Flying Fortress', with the addition of tail, ventral and front upper gun turrets, the last power-operated

B-17G 'FLYING FORTRESS'

Gross weight: 65,500 lb **Span**: 103 ft 9 in **Length**: 74 ft 4 in **Engine**: 4 × Wright Cyclone R-1820 **Armament**: 11 machine-guns **Crew**: 10 **Speed**: 287 mph at 25,000 ft **Ceiling**: 35,600 ft **Range**: 2,000 miles **Bomb load**: 6,000 lb

Among other modifications, the G model of the B-17 introduced a two-gun 'chin' turret to help repel attacking fighters

Rumania—an area defended as zealously as the Reich itself—only to lose 54 aircraft and 532 aircrewmen. On August 17, the Eighth Air Force in England launched 516 B-17 bombers against the Messerschmidt works at Regensberg and the ball-bearing industry at Schweinfurt, and lost 60 bombers and 540 aircrewmen. The heavy losses in daylight raids over Germany continued to mount until the so-called Black Week of the Eighth Air Force in October. On the last day of the Black Week, of 219 B-17s attacking the ball-bearing plants at Schweinfurt, 60 were shot down and 138 returned to base seriously damaged. The week as a whole had cost the Eighth Air Force a quarter of its aircrewmen in England.

After the Black Week, the Americans effectively suspended daylight raids over the Reich until February, 1944. In the meantime, they produced large numbers of the new P-51 Mustang fighter, equipped with dropable fuel tanks so that they could escort bombers all the way to the target. General James Doolittle replaced General Ira Eaker as commander of the Eighth Air Force (Eaker was transferred to the command of the new Fifteenth Air Force in Italy), while General Carl Spaatz was appointed as overall commander of American strategic air forces in the European Theater of Operations. Beginning in February, 1944, the American air offensive against Germany was aimed primarily at gaining command of the air. In the so-called Big Week of February 22–25, some 3,800 daylight sorties were flown over the Reich by U.S. air forces, and 2,351 sorties were flown by Bomber Command. Though 226 U.S. and 157 RAF bombers were lost in these raids, German fighter losses were very heavy. As the round-the-clock pounding of Germany continued into March, the Americans especially aimed at petroleum facilities, aircraft-production factories, and enemy airfields. By the end of the month, the strength of the German Fighter Command had been reduced by 800 aircraft and many pilots. Shortages of high-octane aviation gasoline became so severe that by June 6, 1944, only 125 German fighters in western France were operational.

Despite the tremendous Allied air effort, the best year of the war for German armament production was 1944, though shortages of fuel and damage to German transportation systems made it impossible to deliver or use all the armament produced. Still, of the 113,514 aircraft built by Germany in World War II, 40,593 were constructed in 1944. Of the 39,225 tanks and other armored fighting vehicles produced, 19,050 were turned out in 1944. In addition, and despite the heavy bombing of the German aircraft industry, hundreds of new jet-propelled fighters were turned out in 1944, planes which might have turned the tide of the air war over Germany had not fuel shortages kept most of them on the ground. In retrospect, German production would have been even higher without the strategic bombing, but the air attack on German transportation and fuel seems to have had a more immediate effect than the attacks on other targets.

Thanks to earlier mistakes in the development of the *Luftwaffe,* Hitler had no strategic air force with which to retaliate for the Anglo-American bombing of Germany, but he placed much hope in the new *Vergeltungswaffen* (the "weapons of retaliation"), the V-1 and the V-2. The V-1 was a cruise missile powered by a jet engine, and about twenty-five feet in length. Carrying a ton of high explosive, it flew as fast as 450 mph and as far as about 200 miles. When its engine ran out of fuel, it simply went down wherever it happened to be, killing and destroying indiscriminately. The Germans launched the first V-1 missiles at England about two weeks after the invasion of Normandy in June, 1944, and until Allied ground advances put the V-1 out of range, 7,400 of them were launched from France and 800 from Holland. Most of them were destroyed by British fighters and antiaircraft guns, but the ones which arrived killed or injured 24,165 Britons. Another 7,800 V-1 missiles launched at Allied-occupied cities on the continent, above all Antwerp, inflicted 10,000 casualties.

The V-2 was a liquid-fuel, rocket-engine ballistic missile, also capable of delivering a ton of high explosive up to about two hundred miles. Designed by Dr. Werner von Braun, the V-2 was fifty feet in length, five feet in diameter at its broadest point, and weighed twenty-four tons when ready for launch. Of the total weight, nine tons was taken up in fuel which was totally consumed in the sixty seconds in which the V-2 rose as high as sixty miles above the earth. It plummeted toward its target as fast as 3,500 mph. Like the V-1, the V-2 had poor accuracy, but it was even more feared than the V-1 because there was no defense against it once launched. A total of 1,500 V-2s were hurled across the English Channel before their bases were either captured or bombed out of commission. They killed or injured 9,235 Britons. Another 1,500 V-2s were lobbed at continental cities, again Antwerp was the chief target, and inflicted 10,000 casualties.

Though the V weapons were introduced too late in the war to affect its outcome, next to the atomic bomb they were the most terrifying weapons to appear in World War II. Had the war come five years later, and had the Germans been able to match the V weapons with atomic warheads, the course and probably the outcome of World War II would have been different. The Allied destruction of the Third Reich came none too soon as it was. The V weapons also heralded today's cruise and ballistic missiles, easily the most destructive delivery systems invented to date. Thus, by introducing the V weapons in the closing stages in World War II, the Germans opened a new era of warfare.

C. From Sicily to the Elbe, August 1943–May 1945. The rearmament of the United States had effectively begun after the fall of France in the spring of 1940 and the adoption of the first peacetime conscription act in American history in September. But the production of armaments was partially diverted to the aid of Britain, especially after the passage of the Lend-Lease Act in March, 1941. Under the act, the President could "lend" U.S. arms and equipment to foreign powers whenever in his judgment it served the national interest. But Lend-Lease also provided the excuse for American naval operations in the fall of 1941 against German U-boats in a "Neutrality Zone" that Franklin D. Roosevelt finally extended more than halfway across the Atlantic. Meanwhile, American troops had occupied Iceland. By December 7, 1941, the strength of the Army of the United States had grown from 270,000 to 1,462,000 troops, but many of the new divisions being formed were still untrained and without a full complement of arms and equipment.

Under those circumstances, it is somewhat remarkable that after the Joint Army-Navy Board was replaced by the wartime improvisation of the Joint Chiefs of Staff, General George C. Marshall, the Army Chief-of-Staff, believed that a cross-Channel invasion of France and a direct drive into Germany was possible in 1942. The Anglo-American allies had formed a Combined Chiefs-of-Staff organization in early 1942 to facilitate joint planning, hence Marshall's plan (Operation Sledgehammer) had to have the approval and support of the British. But Dwight Eisenhower, Marshall's representative to the British Combined Chiefs of Staff Committee in London, soon discovered that there was no British enthusiasm for Operation Sledgehammer. The British chiefs believed that a proper use of Anglo-American limited resources would be an invasion of Vichy French North Africa (Operation Torch) in order to threaten the rear of the Axis forces based in Libya. Reluctantly, first Eisenhower and then Marshall came around to the British way of thinking in July, 1942.

Early in 1943, while the Tunisian campaign was underway, Roosevelt, Churchill, and their military advisers met at Casablanca to plan further moves. There Marshall accepted British arguments against a cross-Channel invasion in 1943 (Operation Roundup), but he was afraid that after operations in Tunisia were concluded another major Anglo-American effort in the Mediterranean would so tie up their forces that a cross-Channel invasion in 1944 would be either weakened or abandoned altogether. Churchill favored an attack on the "soft underbelly" of Europe, perhaps through the Balkans, and linking up with the Russians on the Eastern Front. In order to insure that there would be no such diversion from the cross-Channel operation, Marshall insisted that any operation in the Mediterranean after Tunisia must be limited in scope. A compromise with the British brought about the selection of Sicily (Operation Husky) an operation which, if successful, would deal a heavy blow to Italian prestige and open the central Mediterranean to Allied shipping. Marshall did not intend that Sicily would also be a stepping-stone to Italy.

Unfortunately for Marshall, Operation Husky proved to be too successful. Even before its conclusion, Mussolini had fallen from power and a new Italian government under Marshal Badoglio had offered to negotiate a surrender. Even Marshall had to agree with General Sir Alan Brooke, chief of the Imperial General Staff, that a chance to take Italy out of the war and to occupy the Italian peninsula quickly, could not be ignored. From northern Italy, Allied land forces could threaten southern France, Austria, and the Balkans, while Allied air forces in Italy would be much closer to southern Germany. Accordingly, Alexander was ordered by Eisenhower to form a new Fifteenth Army Group—composed of General Mark W. Clark's U.S. Fifth Army and Montgomery's Eighth Army—as soon as practicable for an invasion of the Italian mainland. Unfortunately for the Allies, the Italian surrender negotiations—undertaken in secret—dragged on so long that Hitler found time to send reinforcements to Kesselring, Commander-in-Chief, South, and to get General Heinrich von Vietinghoff's Tenth Army moved into southern Italy. On September 2, a day before Badoglio's government finally agreed to Allied terms, Montgomery's Eighth Army invaded both the "toe" and "heel" of the Italian "boot," and on September 9 Clark's Fifth Army began landing at Salerno south of Naples. But on the day of the Salerno landing, the Italian king, prime minister, and army chief-of-staff fled to British lines at Brindisi, as the Germans moved to occupy Rome. On September 12, a daring German airborne raid freed Mussolini from captivity in his mountain-top prison and spirited him to northern Italy, where he would play out the rest of the war in Europe as head of a rump Fascist state totally dependent on German good will.

Any Allied hope for the quick conquest of Italy went glimmering. In its place dawned the reality of a harsh and unrewarding campaign. The Allied armies slogged their way slowly forward against determined German resistance, Clark's army west of the Appenines and Montgomery's army east of the mountains. Naples did not fall to the Fifth Army until October, and by winter the Allied forces were completely stalled before the German "Gustav Line." When the Teheran Conference convened in November, Churchill urged postponement of the cross-Channel invasion, tentatively scheduled for the spring of 1944, in order to provide reinforcements for the stalled Italian front. Marshall, his worst fears realized, found an unexpected ally in Joseph Stalin, who had been urging a major "Second Front" on the Western allies since 1942. Finally, a compromise was reached whereby it was agreed that more strength would be diverted to Italy, but in 1944 the extra forces would be used to invade the southern coasts of France in conjunction with the cross-Channel invasion. The invasion of the French Mediterranean coast was to be called Operation Dragoon (originally Operation Anvil, but the name was changed after Churchill claimed that he had been "dragooned" into accepting it rather than a plan to invade the Balkans). Also at Teheran, President Roosevelt announced that Eisenhower had

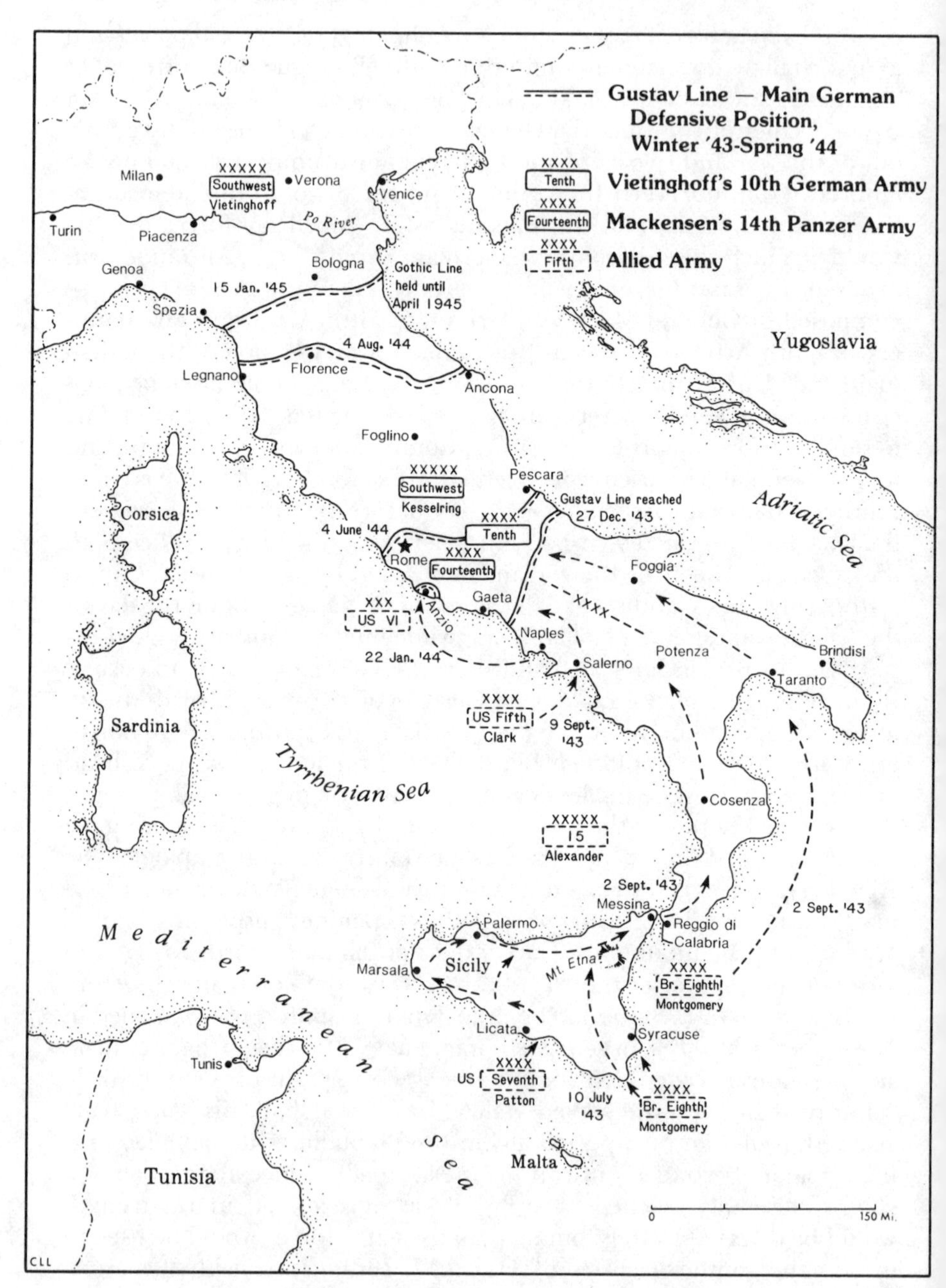

The Italian Campaign, July 1943–January 1945

been chosen to command the cross-Channel invasion (finally called Operation Overlord). At the turn of the year, Eisenhower gave over his post as Allied Mediterranean commander-in-chief to British General Sir Henry M. Wilson. Montgomery, who was to serve as Eisenhower's deputy in Operation Overlord, handed over command of the Eighth Army to General Oliver Leese and also left for London and the Supreme Headquarters, Allied Expeditionary Force (SHAEF).

In January, 1944, the Fifth Army tried to break the "Gustav Line" in the Monte Cassino sector with the attack of a National Guard division. The attack was bloodily repulsed on the banks of the river Rapido, in a smaller American version of the British World War I disaster at the Somme. An amphibious attack by the U.S. VI Corps at Anzio, just south of Rome, also in January, ended badly. The VI Corps failed to take advantage of its temporary surprise, and barely survived the counterattacks of the German Fourteenth Panzer Army (General Eberhard von Mackensen). Even with reinforcements, it was unable to break out of its beachhead, despite strong air and naval support. Not until May, 1944, did the attacks of other Allied troops down the Liri valley finally bring about a link-up with troops at Anzio. The U.S. Fifth Army entered Rome on June 4, 1944, just two days before the beginning of Operation Overlord, and too late for Allied troops in the Mediterranean to invade southern France in conjunction with the invasion of Normandy. Operation Dragoon was postponed until August.

After D-Day in Normandy, the Italian theater became one of secondary importance. Alexander was transferred to Washington to replace Field Marshal Sir John Dill as British representative on the Combined Chiefs of Staff, and Clark succeeded to the command of the Fifteenth Army Group. (Lucian Truscott replaced Clark in command of the Fifth Army.) Kesselring was injured in a car accident in October, 1944, and was replaced by Vietinghoff as Commander-in-Chief, South. With twenty understrength divisions, the Germans defended northern Italy with such tenacity that the Fifteenth Army Group had only reached the valley of the Po river by April, 1945, when Eisenhower's and Zhukov's armies were overrunning Germany. On April 29, 1945, Vietinghoff agreed to surrender his command to Clark within three days; the day before Italian partisans shot Mussolini and his mistress out-of-hand, and the day after Hitler committed suicide in his Berlin bunker.

By June, 1944, the war in Europe was approaching its climax. The Red Army had reached a strength of 400 divisions (of the 503 it mobilized in World War II) and 6,500,000 men on the Eastern Front, then located approximately on the prewar Russian frontiers in the west. Opposed to the Russians were 4,300,000 Axis troops in 198 divisions. They were not only outnumbered by the Russians, but were inferior in arms and equipment. In 1944, Soviet industry produced 29,000 ar-

Cut-away of U.S. M-3 Sherman Tank, World War II.

SOURCE: Kenneth Macksey and John H. Batchelor, *Tank: A History of the Armoured Fighting Vehicle* (New York: Charles Scribner's Sons, 1970).

mored fighting vehicles, 56,000 pieces of artillery and antitank guns, and 32,300 aircraft. In all but one major category of armament production, the Soviets had outstripped the Germans. In addition, the Anglo-American Allies had sent the Russians a total of 400,000 trucks, 22,000 aircraft, and 12,000 tanks. And, whereas German production was divided over several fronts, the Russian production was concentrated on the Eastern Front.

In contrast to the Soviet and Axis behemoths on the Eastern Front, heavily labor-intensive and dependent on railroad and horse-drawn supply, the forces assembled in England for Operation Overlord were much smaller in number, but much more machine-intensive. On June 6, 1944, Eisenhower commanded thirty-eight divisions (twenty U.S., fourteen British, three Canadian, and one Free French), most of them effectively motorized and many of them armored. His troops numbered about 2,000,000 of whom 1,627,000 were American. They were supported by the mightiest air armada and fleet ever assembled for a single operation:

12,000 aircraft and 5,300 ships (including 1,000 warships). Behind the force in Britain were thirty-six American divisions in the United States earmarked for the ETO. The "Mighty Endeavor," as President Roosevelt called the cross-Channel invasion in 1944, amounted to a powerful air-land-sea fist of men and machines aimed at northern France and ultimately at Germany's solar plexis. Success would depend on an early lodgement on the coast, to be followed by a rapid build-up of forces for a break-out from the beachhead. The spearhead of the attack amounted to twenty thousand airborne troops and seventy thousand troops to be landed over the beaches, in all just eight divisions upon whose performance everything else depended.

The German forces in Western Europe awaiting invasion in June, 1944, hardly compared with those forces which had so handily defeated the Anglo-French armies four years earlier. Field Marshal Rundstedt, Supreme Commander in the West (OB West), had fifty-eight divisions (including ten panzer divisions), and 1,500,000 troops in France and the Low Countries, but only a small proportion of the German divisions were completely mobile. Thanks to Allied air operations and shortages of oil, only 125 German aircraft in northern France were operational by the day the invasion began. Rommel, who commanded Army Group B (composed of the Seventh and Fifteenth armies), was responsible for defense of the coast between the Pas de Calais and Cherbourg. As it happened, the invasion would fall on the front of his Seventh Army. Given the Allied command of the air, Rommel placed his faith in a German defense near the beaches and retention of vital ports without which, the Germans assumed, a sustained invasion would be impossible. Unknown to the Germans, the Allies had constructed, in great secrecy, artificial harbors ("Mulberries") which, once an initial lodgement was made on the French coast, would be towed from England and anchored off the invasion beaches. Protected by artificial breakwaters, these harbors would enable large ships to unload in deep water; their cargoes would be moved to shore by either pontoon causeways or landing craft. Probably no other technological invention involved in the invasion surprised the Germans more, or did more to undermine their basic strategy.

The invasion, launched early on June 6, 1944—the most important D-Day in World War II—was led off by three airborne divisions (two American and one British) and five amphibious divisions on a forty-mile front between Caen and the base of the Normandy (or Cotentin) peninsula. Including supply troops, the initial force came to 174,320 troops and 20,081 vehicles. The fiercest German resistance was offered to American troops who landed on Omaha Beach, but lodgements were secured there as well as on Utah (American), Juno, Sword, and Gold (Anglo-Canadian). About 10,000 Allied casualties were suffered in the

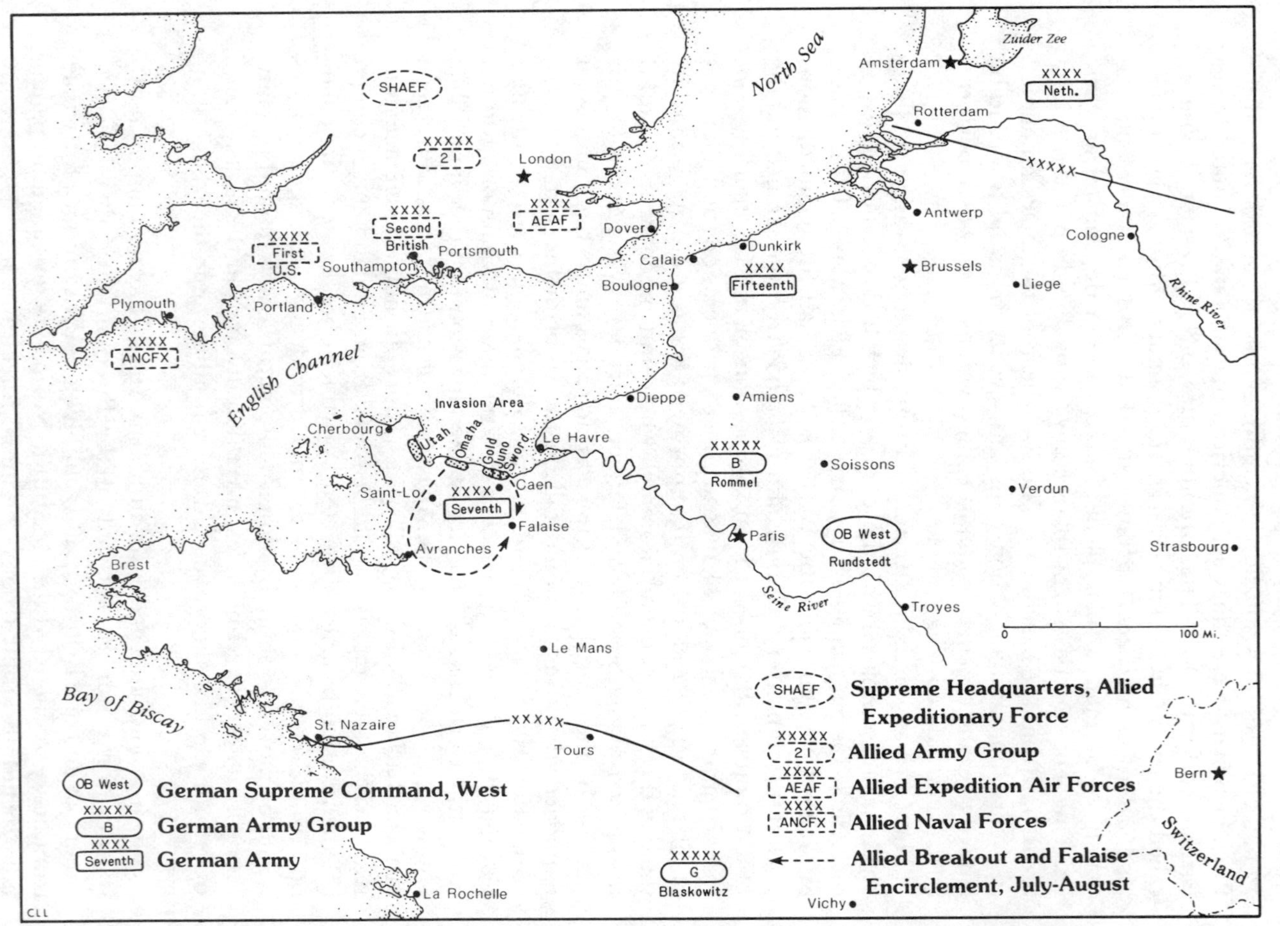

Allied and German Deployment in the West on Eve of June 6, 1944 and the Normandy Invasion

first twenty-four hours of Operation Overlord. The period of Allied build-up and expansion of the beachhead continued until late in July. By July 1, a million men and 150,000 vehicles were within the beachhead, and by then both the "Mulberries" and the Allied air attacks on German reserves streaming to the beachhead had confounded the earlier German hope of throwing the invasion back into the sea. When Rundstedt recommended to Hitler that the battle in western France be broken off and the German armies withdrawn to Germany's old West Wall defenses, he was replaced as OB West by Field Marshal Gunther von Kluge on July 3.

As July wore on, a series of disasters overtook the Germans. On July 17, Rommel's staff car overturned after being strafed by a British fighter, and the field marshal was badly injured. Kluge had to add the command of Army Group B to his other duties as OB West. Then on July 20 occurred the Bomb Plot against Hitler in his East Prussian headquarters. The bomb, left by Major Klaus von Staufenberg in a brief case in a conference room, was nearly successful, but Hitler survived the explosion with minor injuries. He then ordered a savage retaliation against German officers involved in the plot. While mass arrests by the Gestapo and SS were underway, the Allies inside the Normandy beachhead with a strength of twenty-five divisions, launched break-out efforts on July 25. In the western end of the beachhead, Patton's Third Army led the way for General Omar Bradley's Twelfth Army Group; and Montgomery's Twenty-First Army Group attacked from the eastern end of the beachhead. When Kluge foresaw that both efforts would succeed and that the rest of his forces on the perimeter of the beach-head would be threatened with encirclement, he urged Hitler to allow him to order a retreat before it was too late. Instead, Hitler insisted on making an armored counterattack. Warned by Ultra of Hitler's strategy, Bradley's army group had time to deploy properly to meet the threat. The last German assaults were beaten back by the night of August 7, but Hitler refused to allow a general retreat until General Jacob Dever's Sixth Army Group, consisting of the U.S. Seventh Army and the French First Army, launched Operation Dragoon against the French Mediterranean coast. Kluge relayed the withdrawal order just before his relief as OB West by General Walther Model. The order came too late to save all the German forces in western France. On August 18, Patton's Third Army captured the town of Falaise, severing the last line of German withdrawal, and in the subsequent Falaise *Kesselschlacht* some three hundred thousand German troops were killed or captured.

As the battered and decimated German army withdrew toward the Franco-German border and into the Low Countries, a Free French division led the Allied armies into Paris on August 25. By then the city was already partially liberated by the French Forces of the Interior (FFI), an umbrella organization of Resistance groups totaling perhaps two hundred thousand men and women throughout France. After Paris was liberated, General de Gaulle organized a provisional government and set about mobilizing more French forces to join the Allied war effort. Though in early September, Hitler reinstated Rundstedt as OB West, the situation looked desperate for the German cause. But Hitler gave priority to the West in the allocation of his reserves and new armaments, the old frontier defenses of the West Wall could be refurbished, and he had good reason to believe that the "Mulberries" at the original point of invasion had about reached their limits. By-passed German garrisons at the Channel ports either fought on or, as had been the case with Cherbourg in June, surrendered only after destroying docking facilities in a way that would take months to repair. Montgomery's army group managed to capture the inland port of Antwerp largely intact as it advanced into Belgium in September, but German troops still controlled the banks and islands of the river Schelde connecting Antwerp to the sea. Thus, just as German resistance began to stiffen again, Eisenhower's armies were plagued with supply problems and especially shortages in fuel.

In late August, Montgomery convinced Eisenhower that his army group should receive a temporary priority in fuel allocations so that it might complete the conquest of Belgium and the Netherlands, opening the possibility of an Allied thrust across the Lower Rhine and thence into the north German plain. In mid-September, Montgomery launched Operation Market-Garden. Operation Market was an Anglo-American–Free Polish airborne effort to seize key bridges ahead of the British XXX Corps pushing overland across the eastern Netherlands (Operation Garden). The British airborne effort at Arnhem miscarried with the loss of most of an airborne division; and, with the failure, the advance of the XXX Corps was held up indefinitely. In the wake of the failure, Eisenhower rejected Montgomery's renewed proposal for a crossing of the Lower Rhine and a "pencil-like thrust" across the north German plain to Berlin. He could not afford to restrict the fuel supplies of his other army groups for what, at best, was a "long shot." Instead, he ordered Montgomery's group to concentrate on protecting the northern flank of the Allied Expeditionary Force and on opening the Schelde to the sea. By then Antwerp clearly held the answer to the Allied supply problem. Montgomery's forces finally cleared the Schelde, but the first merchant ship bearing supplies for the Allied armies did not reach Antwerp until November 28. Even then, the city was the frequent target of V-1 and V-2 attacks, and the flow of supplies only gradually increased.

The main burden of attacking the German frontier in October and November fell to the American Sixth and Twelfth army groups. Bradley's Twelfth Army Group, consisting of the Ninth, First, and Third

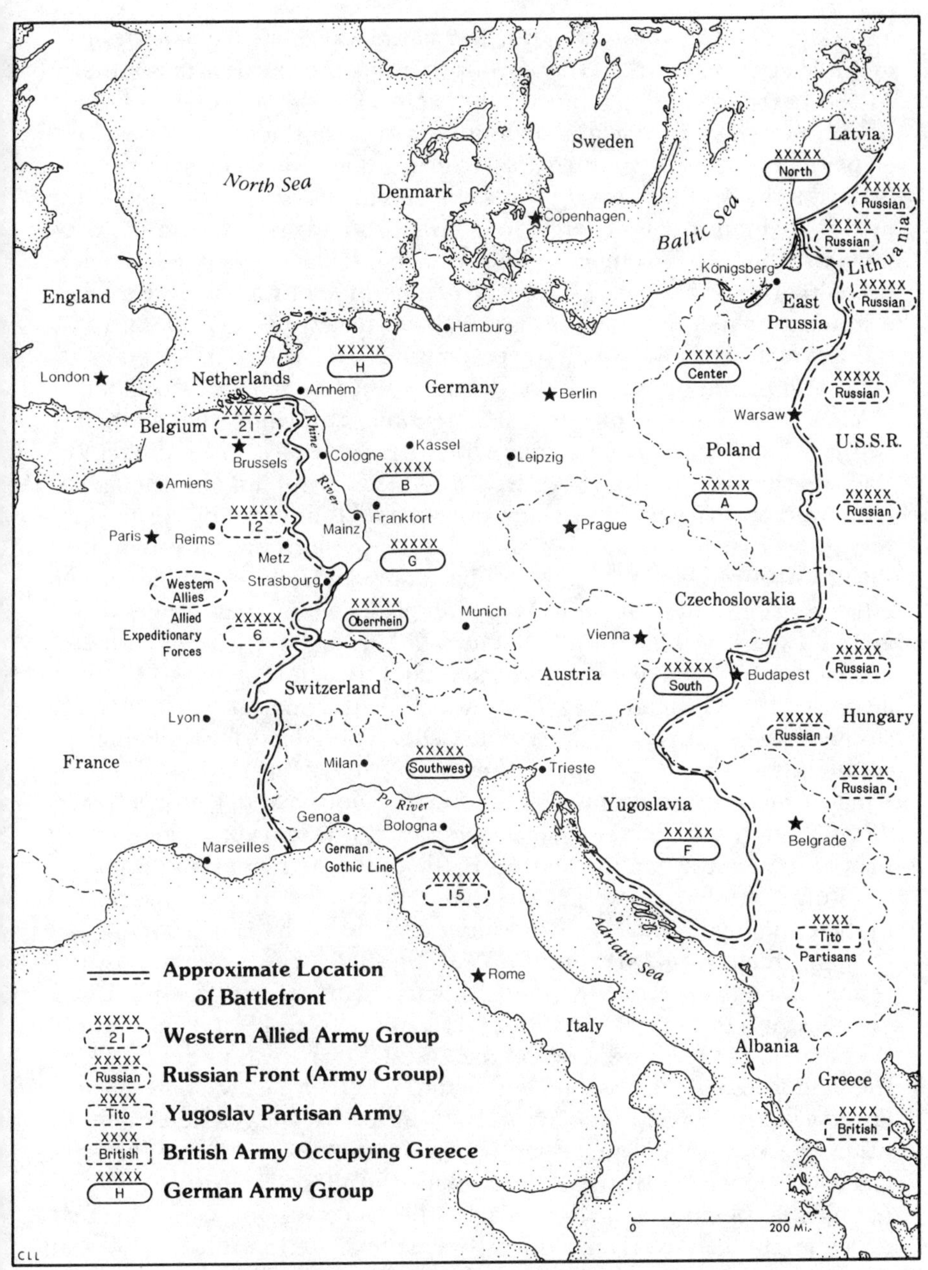

The European Battlefronts, December 15, 1944

armies from north to south, stretched all the way from Aachen to south of Metz. Dever's Sixth Army Group carried the burden in southern Alsace-Lorraine and as far as the neutral Swiss frontier. Though Eisenhower had forty-eight divisions on the continent by November, eight of them were stranded in western France for lack of transport. Accordingly, Bradley's group was stretched thin, particularly in its lines in the Ardennes, where only four American divisions covered forty miles of front. By December, 1944, German intelligence had not failed to detect that weak place in the Allied front, and Hitler was eager to exploit it in what turned out to be his last major offensive of the war. Secretly, the Germans massed twenty-three divisions and their last reserves of tanks and planes opposite the Ardennes in the first half of December.

Ultra gave no hint of German intentions regarding the Ardennes before Rundstedt launched a powerful offensive there on December 16. Bad weather practically grounded the Allied air forces, and the attack destroyed or drove back the four American divisions caught by surprise. Eisenhower rushed two American airborne divisions by truck to occupy the key road centers at St. Vith and Bastogne; and, joined by elements of other divisions, these divisions kept both places out of enemy hands even after Bastogne was surrounded. The weather improved enough on December 23 for the Allied air forces to go into action. After a fifty-mile advance, the German spearhead which had gone the furthest was stopped just short of the Meuse at Celle. The Allied forces launched counterattacks on the flanks of the "bulge" or salient in their lines, an Anglo-American effort attacking from the north, and Patton's Third Army from the south. This pincer operation finally trapped many German troops, and when the Second Battle of the Ardennes (or "Battle of the Bulge") ended in late January, 1945, Hitler had lost 300,000 troops in the struggle. Eisenhower's casualties came to perhaps 100,000.

Meanwhile, since D-Day in the West, the Red Army's operations had removed Finland, Rumania, and Bulgaria from its list of undefeated enemies, and by early in 1945 its forces had occupied Poland and were at the borders of the Third Reich in the East. Hungary was under attack by the time Roosevelt, Churchill, and Stalin held their last wartime conference in early February, 1945, at Yalta in the Crimea. The Ardennes offensive, and stubborn German resistance after its conclusion, had delayed the approach of the Western Allied armies to the Rhine. If this formidable barrier could be held by the Germans for long, the Red Army might well overrun most of Germany as well as most of Eastern Europe. But at Yalta, Stalin agreed to a Western military presence in Berlin after the surrender and to a Four-Power government (Britain, France, the United States, and the Soviet Union) over Germany after the war. The unexpected American capture of the Ludendorff bridge intact at Remagen in early March compromised the German plan for an ex-

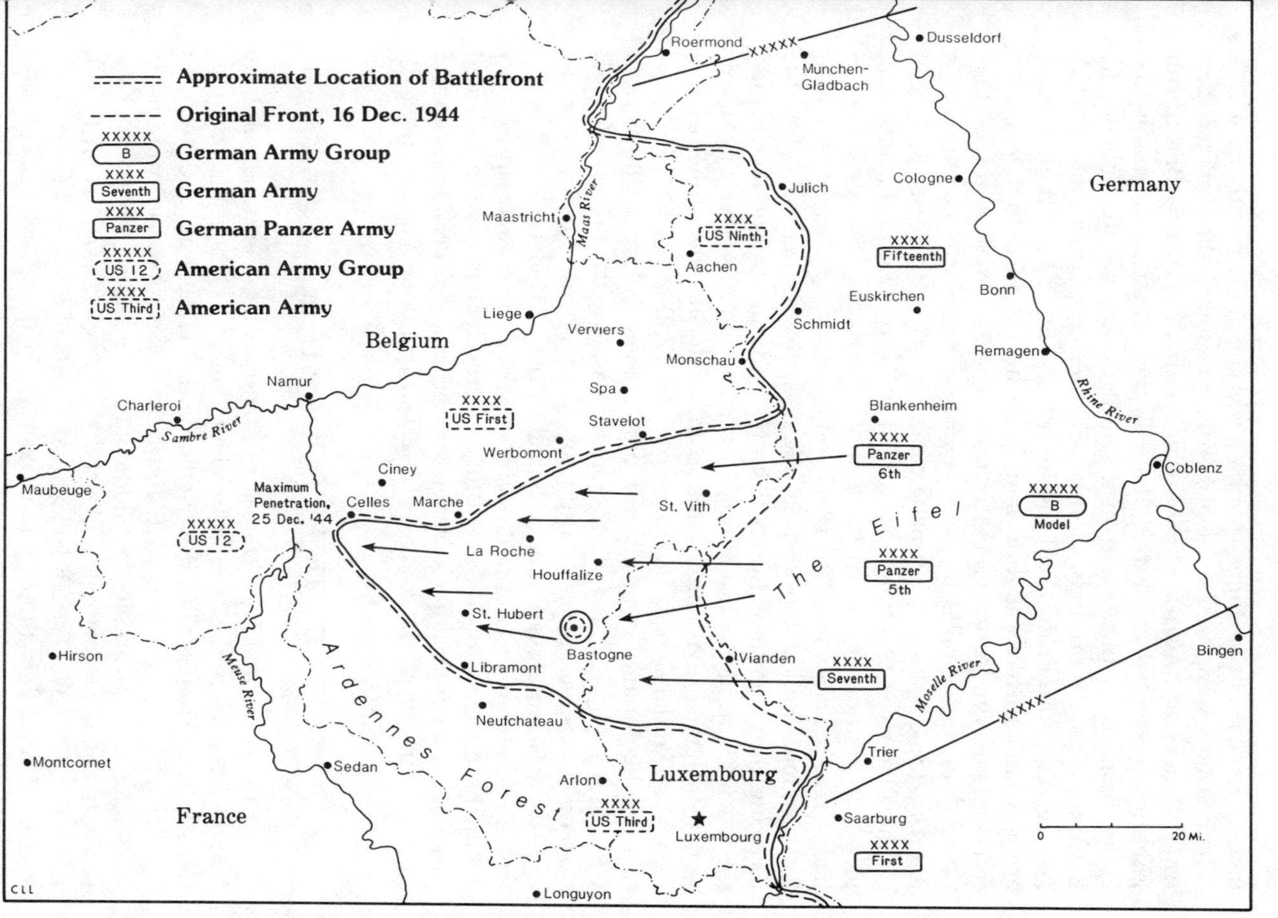

The German Ardennes Offensive: Situation on December 25, 1944

tended defense of the Rhine, though it was late in the month before the Allied armies were well across. A bare possibility then existed that Anglo-American forces might share in the final capture of Berlin. But Eisenhower was less concerned about Berlin than about a rumor that Hitler intended a final stand in a so-called National Redoubt in the Bavarian Alps. Accordingly, Eisenhower directed the Sixth and Twelfth army groups into central and southern Germany, while Montgomery's army group occupied the Ruhr and then wheeled north to pin German forces against the North Sea. As a consequence, no Western forces came closer than ninety miles to Berlin before the German surrender. On April 25, the U.S. First Army made contact with the Red Army at Torgau on the Elbe river, severing Germany in half. By then Berlin was completely surrounded by Soviet forces and under siege. The Soviet troops had to take the city street-by-street in bitter fighting. Hitler had no plans for a National Redoubt in Bavaria, and he spent the final days of his life directing the defense of Berlin from his underground bunker behind the Reich Chancellery until his suicide on April 30. His powers as Führer were transferred to Admiral Dönitz, commander-in-chief of the German navy since January, 1943. Dönitz exercised his authority from headquarters on the Jutland Peninsula for only a week before he dispatched General Alfred Jodl, chief of OKW Operations, to make an unconditional surrender at Eisenhower's headquarters at Rheims. Eisenhower accepted the German surrender on behalf of all the Allies on May 8. A day later, Field Marshal Keitel ratified the surrender terms in occupied Berlin in the presence of Marshal Zhukov. President Roosevelt had died suddenly of a cerebral hemorrhage on April 12, and President Harry S Truman announced the coming of V-E Day from the White House.

III. The Pacific War, 1941–45

A. The Road to Pearl Harbor. Tensions between Japan and the United States over the "China Incident" began to reach crisis proportions when France and the Netherlands fell before the German blitzkrieg in the spring of 1940 and Britain was forced to concentrate her forces at home and in the Middle East. The United States was left as the only major power that might check Japanese ambitions on British Burma and Malaya, French Indochina (Vietnam, Laos, and Cambodia), and the Dutch East Indies (Sumatra, Borneo, Java, and western New Guinea). This "Southern Resources Area," as the Japanese termed it, was rich in rice, rubber, tin, bauxite, and oil, and in Japan's possession could make her almost self-sufficient in raw resources.

As early as May, 1940, President Roosevelt ordered the United States Fleet (soon retitled the U.S. Pacific Fleet), then on maneuvers in

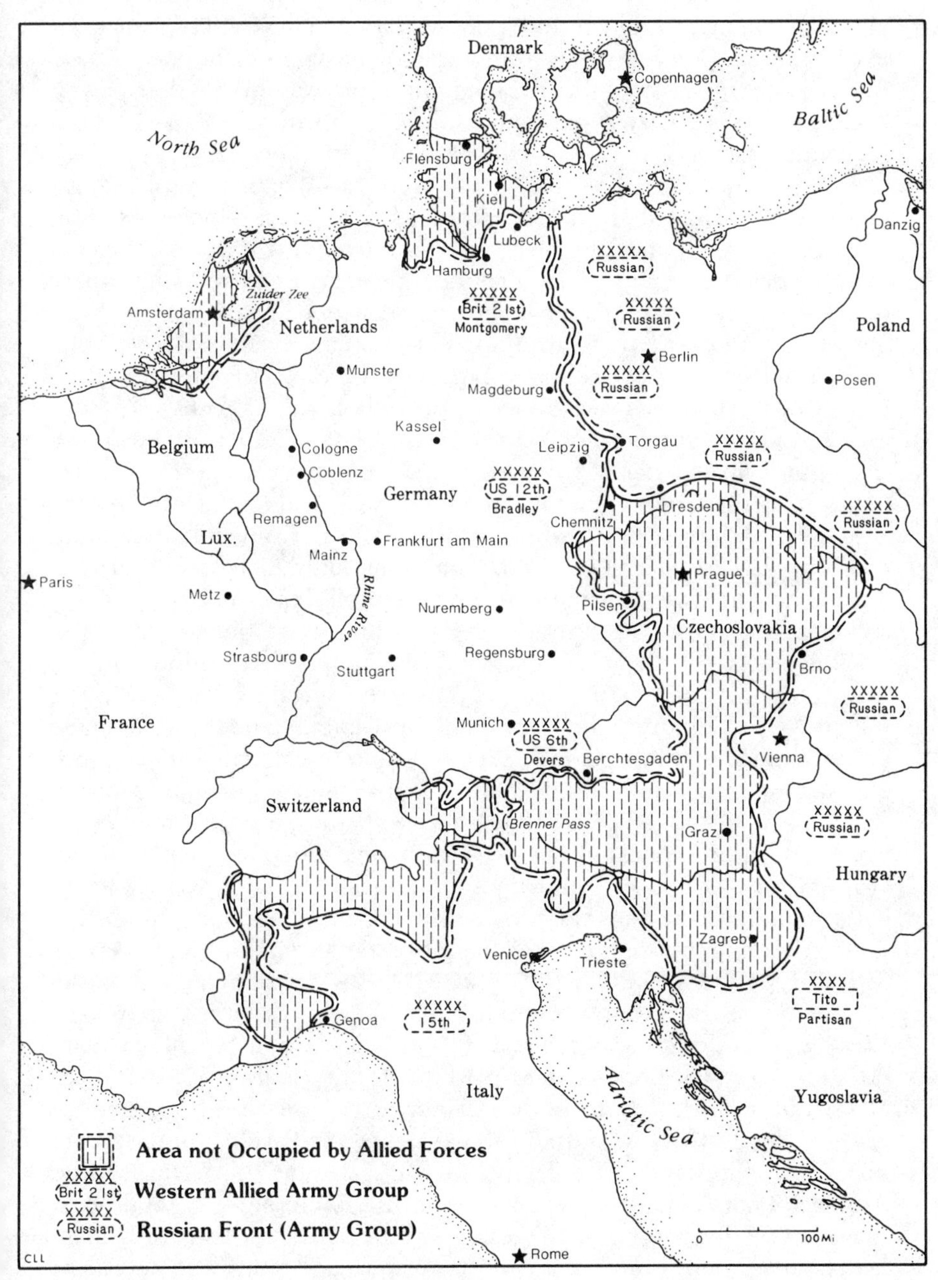

The European Battlefronts, May 7, 1945

Hawaiian waters, to remain indefinitely at its Pacific war station at Pearl Harbor instead of returning to its permanent base on the West Coast. But, despite the warning that the fleet's presence was intended to convey, in the summer of 1940 Japan sent troops into northern Vietnam and in September signed the Tripartite Treaty with Germany and Italy. Roosevelt retaliated by adding scrap iron and aviation gasoline to a growing list of forbidden trade with Japan, a measure which seemed to work when the Japanese made no further moves into Southeast Asia for the time being. Actually, Japan's councils were divided over what course to take. But in April, 1941, Japan signed a nonaggression pact with Soviet Russia in order to secure Japan's rear in the event of war with the United States; and that summer Japanese forces occupied south Vietnam. Roosevelt then severed nearly all trade relations with Japan and imposed a total embargo on oil shipments. The oil embargo was especially damaging to Japan, for she normally imported 90 percent of her needs from the United States. When the British Middle Eastern and the Dutch Far Eastern oil companies honored the American embargo, Japan was left with an oil reserve which could last only eighteen months at most. The American price for resumption of oil shipments to Japan was stiff; total Japanese withdrawal from Indochina and China.

While Japanese representatives in Washington tried to find a diplomatic compromise for the crisis in Japanese-American relations in the fall of 1941, Japan's cabinet headed by General Hideki Tojo made preparations for war. In a struggle that would hinge primarily on naval and air power, Japan would have the initial advantage. Admiral Isoroku Yamamoto's Combined Fleet numbered 10 battleships and battle cruisers, 6 large and 4 small aircraft carriers (basing a total of 750 planes), 36 cruisers, 113 destroyers, and 63 submarines. The U.S. Navy had 17 battleships and 6 aircraft carriers as its major units, and it was undergoing further expansion; but about half of its battleships and carriers were with the Atlantic Fleet. The U.S. Pacific Fleet was assigned 9 old battleships and 3 carriers, but of these a battleship and a carrier were on the West Coast undergoing overhauls. The only other non-Japanese dreadnoughts in the Pacific were the British battleship *Prince of Wales* and the old battle cruiser *Repulse,* both at Singapore. The U.S. Navy had 24 cruisers, 80 destroyers, and 56 submarines in the Pacific, but they were divided by thousands of miles between the fleet at Pearl Harbor and Admiral Thomas Hart's Asiatic Fleet in the Philippines. A total of 11 cruisers, 20 destroyers, and 13 submarines of the British-Australian-Dutch navies were scattered about the Western and Southwestern Pacific areas.

The Naval Section of Imperial Headquarters originally planned to seize the Southern Resources Area, the American Philippines, Guam, and Wake Island, using lesser naval forces. The Combined Fleet was to be held in reserve to deal with the U.S. Pacific Fleet if it steamed into the Western Pacific in order to launch a counterattack. But when it became clear that the U.S. Pacific Fleet had been semi-permanently based at Pearl Harbor after May, 1940, Admiral Yamamoto pressed for a change of contingency plans. He proposed to begin the Pacific War with a surprise carrier-strike at the Pacific Fleet at its base in Pearl Harbor. If the attack were successful and the fleet were destroyed or paralyzed for a long period, Japanese forces would have little difficulty in overrunning the Western Pacific. When Yamamoto finally convinced the Naval Section that the attack on Pearl Harbor was both feasible and wise, Admiral Chuichi Nagumo's special carrier striking force, composed of six large carriers, two battleships, and several cruisers, destroyers and tankers, secretly assembled at Tankan Bay in the Kuriles and awaited orders to execute its mission.

On November 2, 1941, Tojo's cabinet received Emperor Hirohito's assent to war with the United States if the negotiations at Washington had not turned out successfully by the end of that month. Though the imperial decision was not made known through the radio cables sent between Tokyo and its embassy in Washington, the tenor of those communications—read through the code-breaking operation Magic—suggested that Japan might take military action against the United States before the end of the year. On November 24, General Marshall and Admiral King sent their respective commands in the Pacific a war warning. Admiral Husband E. Kimmel, commander of the Pacific Fleet at Pearl Harbor, and General Walter Short, commander of U.S. Army forces in the Hawaiian islands, believed that the initial Japanese attack was likely to fall on the Philippines, Guam, and Wake Island. Their measures of defense on Oahu, where Pearl Harbor is located, were restricted to preventing sabotage by the large Japanese resident population. When the Pacific Fleet returned from exercises at sea to Pearl Harbor on the first weekend of December, its battleships anchored together as usual in "Battleship Row" off Ford Island, without the benefit of protective torpedo nets, and many sailors were granted shore-leave. Air and sea patrols were carried out in the direction of the Japanese Marshalls and Carolines, but little attention was paid to the northern approaches of Oahu. The island's limited radar coverage was restricted to nighttime hours.

Meanwhile, Nagumo's carrier force departed Tankan Bay on November 26 under strict radio silence and set a course for Oahu by the unfrequented waters of the North Pacific. Nagumo did not acknowledge the cryptic order from Tokyo on December 2 to proceed with the attack without further communication. A little before dawn on December 7, 1941, and after a voyage of four thousand miles, Nagumo's force arrived at a point two hundred miles north of Oahu, still undetected by the

Americans. At first light, the Japanese carriers—the *Akagi, Kaga, Soryu, Hiryu, Shokaku,* and *Zuikaku*—began launching the first of 360 planes in three waves. The first wave of planes arrived over Pearl Harbor about 8:00 A.M., and the last wave had completed its work and retired from the scene by 10:00 A.M. They left behind them five American battleships sunk, beached, or capsized, and three more battleships badly damaged. The attack had also sunk or damaged three cruisers, three destroyers, and lesser craft. Ashore, about two-thirds of the three hundred Army and Navy planes on Oahu had been destroyed. A total of three thousand American casualties had been suffered, two-thirds of them fatalities. Nagumo's losses came to twenty-nine planes and fifty airmen. In addition, the Japanese lost a fleet submarine and five midget submarines sent on a separate sortie against Pearl Harbor.

As Yamamoto had hoped, the U.S. Pacific Fleet was so severly damaged by the Pearl Harbor raid that it was unable to interfere seriously with the initiial Japanese operations to seize the Southern Resources Area and the outlying Pacific territories necessary for Japanese defense of the Area. On the other hand, the Americans had been fortunate that none of the three carriers assigned to the Pacific Fleet had been in port on December 7. The *Lexington* and *Enterprise* were returning from ferrying planes to Midway and Wake islands, and the *Saratoga* was still on the West Coast. Indeed, Nagumo's uncertainty as to the whereabouts of the carriers, once their absence at Pearl Harbor was reported on the morning of December 7, had caused him to cancel plans for additional strikes at the fuel storage tanks and repair facilities at Pearl Harbor. Had the tanks and repair facilities been destroyed too on December 7, the remains of the Pacific Fleet would have been withdrawn over two thousand miles further east to bases on the West Coast, and American communications to Australia and New Zealand might have been severed. Instead, the fleet remained based at Pearl Harbor, the base was repaired, and even the sunken battleships—save the *Arizona*—were eventually raised and repaired.

B. From Pearl Harbor to Midway, December 1941–June 1942. Pearl Harbor was not the only naval disaster to befall Japan's enemies in the first week of the Pacific War. On December 10, Japanese land-based naval aircraft operating from airfields around Saigon in southern Indochina, spotted the British battleship *Prince of Wales* and the battle cruiser *Repulse* proceeding without air cover or escorts up the coast of Malaya in order to break up reported Japanese landings. In a short span of time, the heavy Japanese air attacks sent both vessels to the bottom. Thus, in less than a week's time, Japanese air power had sunk or disabled more dreadnoughts in combat than had been lost to enemy action in the entire time since the dreadnought type first appeared in 1906.

The Imperial Navy also dealt swiftly with the remaining Allied naval power in the Far East. What little was left by February, 1942, was destroyed in the Battle of the Java Sea. In the same month, the Japanese captured Singapore—the most important Allied naval base west of Pearl Harbor. Though the Imperial Army committed only ten out of its fifty divisions to Pacific and Southeast Asian drives, before the end of April they had seized the oil of the Dutch East Indies, held Indochina and Malaya, and were driving the British from Burma to the eastern frontier of India. The great subcontinent of India was so seething with unrest due to these developments that the British government hastily promised it postwar independence in order to gain Indian support against the Japanese.

Of the American possessions in the Far East and western Pacific, Guam fell almost at once without a struggle, the gallant Marine defense of Wake Island collapsed two days before Christmas, 1941, and only in the Philippines did the Japanese encounter prolonged resistance. General Douglas MacArthur had been trying to create an "Asiatic Switzerland" out of the Philippines since his retirement from the U.S. Army in 1935 and his appointment as Military Advisor to the Philippine Commonwealth in preparation for independence in 1944. But in December, 1941, his forces consisted of only 30,000 U.S. Army regulars and an Army of the Philippines composed of 100,000 half-trained and poorly armed troops. U.S. air strength in the Philippines came to 35 modern bombers and 107 fighters on December 7, 1941, and half the bombers, caught on the ground, were destroyed on the first day of the war. After Japanese troops began to land on Luzon, the most northern and most important of the islands in the Philippines, MacArthur's forces on the island began a fighting withdrawal to the peninsula of Bataan on the west side of Manila Bay. While they were holding out there, President Roosevelt ordered MacArthur to turn over command in the Philippines to General Jonathan Wainwright and to proceed to Australia, where he would assume direction of a new Allied Southwest Pacific Command. MacArthur left the Philippines in March, and subsequently the remains of Wainwright's command retreated to the island of Corregidor at the mouth of Manila Bay for a final stand. Wainwright surrendered his forces on May 7, 1942, exactly six months after Pearl Harbor. The American stand in the Philippines was the only prolonged resistance that the Japanese encountered in the first months of the war.

Despite final Japanese victory in the Philippines, Imperial Headquarters had reason for concern about the course of the war. In April, 1942, the American carriers *Enterprise* and *Hornet* had made a daring sortie to a point only eight hundred miles from the home islands. At that point, the *Hornet* launched sixteen U.S. Army B-25 bombers under the command of General James Doolittle. The bombers had proceeded to raid Tokyo and other Japanese cities. Though little damage was inflicted, the incident led Admiral Yamamoto to order preparations for an operation by the Combined Fleet to complete the destruction of the U.S. Pacific Fleet in June. In early May, before that operation got underway, a Japanese task force entered the Coral Sea, intent on the seizure of Port Moresby on the "tail" of the New Guinea "bird." Unexpectedly, it encountered the U.S. carriers *Yorktown* and *Lexington.* In the first purely aerial naval battle in history, on May 7–8, American air strikes sank the small Japanese carrier *Shoho* and so damaged the *Shokaku* and shot down so many planes from the *Zuikaku* that both large Japanese carriers were put out of action for months. The Japanese attacks sank the *Lexington* and damaged the *Yorktown,* but the Japanese task force retired from the Coral Sea. The *Yorktown* limped back to Pearl Harbor for hasty repairs.

The Battle of the Coral Sea confirmed Yamamoto in his belief that a decisive naval battle must be forced on the U.S. Pacific Fleet as soon as possible. His plan was to carry out a surprise occupation of the island of Midway, then ambush the U.S. Pacific Fleet when it rushed from Pearl Harbor to launch a counterattack. The plan was sound, but, unknown to Yamamoto, the same American code-breaking that had allowed Admiral Chester W. Nimitz, Kimmel's successor, to anticipate the Japanese sortie into the Coral Sea, also forewarned him of the planned Japanese descent on Midway in early June. Accordingly, Nimitz ordered Admiral Raymond Spruance to form a Task Force 16 around the carriers *Yorktown, Hornet,* and *Enterprise* and to locate it about three hundred miles north of Midway where it might serve to ambush the approaching Japanese forces.

On June 4, Admiral Nagumo's carrier group, reduced to the carriers *Akagi, Kaga, Soryu,* and *Hiryu,* launched an air strike against Midway's defenses. While the recovered aircraft were being refueled and rearmed for another attack on Midway, a Japanese scout plane located Task Force 16. But before the Japanese could rearm their planes with torpedoes and armor-piercing bombs, American planes swept down on the Japanese carriers. Japanese Zero fighters shot down Torpedo Squadron 8 to the last plane (only an ensign out of the whole squadron survived), but American dive bombers soon turned the *Akagi, Kaga,* and *Soryu* into flaming wrecks. An aerial strike from the *Hiryu* severely damaged the already weakened *Yorktown,* and she was finished off the next day by a Japanese submarine. But more American air strikes sent the *Hiryu* to the bottom. When Spruance withdrew his force to the east to keep out of gun range of Yamamoto's battleships that night, essentially the Battle of Midway was over. On June 5, the Combined Fleet commenced a withdrawal to the Western Pacific, and Spruance subsequently returned his force to Pearl Harbor. The Battle of Midway had cost the Japanese four large carriers, a cruiser, 322 planes, and 3,500 sailors and airmen. The

Americans at sea had lost a carrier, a destroyer, 150 planes, and 307 sailors and airmen. A few hundred American casualties had been suffered on Midway from bombing.

After Coral Sea and Midway, the Japanese Combined Fleet did not risk another major fleet action for two years, in the meantime committing only detachments in support of the Japanese defense of key islands. Effectively, the Japanese went on the defensive in the Central Pacific. In the South Pacific, they still had hopes of capturing all of New Guinea and the Solomon islands north of it, and thereby to put themselves in a position to isolate Australia and New Zealand from American reinforcements. Accordingly, the safety of the British dominions became the dominating factor in Allied strategy until 1943.

C. The Campaigns for Guadalcanal and Papua, August 1942–February 1943. After the reverse at Coral Sea, Japanese troops tried to cross the Owen Stanley Mountains and capture Port Moresby. Other Japanese forces moved to seize bases in the southern Solomons, with special attention given to building an airfield on Guadalcanal. But Anglo-American commanders in the South Pacific were taking their own measures. Admiral Robert L. Ghormley, then heading up a South Pacific Command to protect New Zealand, assembled General Alexander A. Vandegrift's First Marine Division in the New Hebrides and prepared to "cork up" the Solomons "bottle" by an offensive into the islands. MacArthur, whose forces south of the Owen Stanley Mountains were preparing to hold their position in Papua at all costs and thus to protect northern Australia, were also preparing for a deadly struggle. MacArthur wanted to add the South Pacific Command to his Southwest Pacific Command, but on July 2, 1942, the Joint Chiefs in Washington decided that Ghormley and the command would remain subordinate to Admiral Chester W. Nimitz, Commander-in-Chief, Pacific Fleet, and also commander of the Pacific Ocean Area. Nimitz's headquarters remained at Pearl Harbor.

Operation Watchtower, the first American island-offensive of the war, began on August 7, 1942, when twenty thousand U.S. Marines landed on Guadalcanal and the smaller island of Tulagi nearby. Besides construction workers, only two thousand armed Japanese were on the island, and they faded into the jungle. U.S. Naval Construction Battalions ("Seabees") set to work on the air strip, bringing it to completion on August 20. Basing five Marine air squadrons, it was named Henderson Field in honor of a Marine aviator who had died at Midway. Admiral Fletcher had covered the landings of the carriers *Saratoga, Wasp,* and *Enterprise,* but he soon left the scene to a force of American and Australian cruisers. On the night of August 9, a force of Japanese cruisers and destroyers from Rabaul—a base in the northern Solomons six hundred miles from Guadalcanal—arrived under Admiral Gunichi Mikawa. Mikawa's force

IJN *Yamoto,* 1941, the final development of the "super-dreadnought."
SOURCE: Peter Padfield, *The Battleship Era* (New York: David McKay, 1972).

USS *New Jersey,* 1943, firing broadside in World War II.
SOURCE: Peter Padfield, *The Battleship Era* (New York: David McKay, 1972).

surprised the American-Australian naval forces, and in the Battle of Savo Island the Japanese sank five Allied cruisers and damaged the sixth. Mikawa's force might then have wrecked the Allied transports off Lunga Point, but it used the remaining hours of darkness to get out of range of American planes and returned to Rabaul.

Mikawa's sortie from Rabaul down the "Slot"—the watery corridor between the parallel strings of islands which formed the Solomons—was only the first of many to come in the protracted Battle of Guadalcanal. The sorties aimed at damaging both Allied forces and landing reinforcements for the slowly growing Japanese garrison on the island. They came with such nighttime regularity for a few months that Marines referred to them collectively as the "Tokyo Express." As the naval fighting around the island intensified, Admiral William "Bull" Halsey relieved the exhausted Ghormley of the South Pacific Command. The Battle of Guadalcanal reached its climax in the October–November period both ashore and afloat. On October 26, twenty-nine thousand Japanese troops launched an all-out effort to drive the Marines into the sea, and were defeated with difficulty over four terrible days of fighting. During November, the Marines were reinforced by fifty thousand Army troops under General Alexander Patch. At sea, Admiral Nobutake Kondo led the largest concentration of Japanese warships seen since Midway into the southern Solomons, but in a series of naval battles his force was compelled to retire to Rabaul at the end of November. By then the Naval Section of Imperial Headquarters was ready to abandon Guadalcanal, but the Army Section—which had assembled sixty thousand fresh troops at Rabaul—insisted that the effort go on. For another month, Japanese convoys continued to land troops on Guadalcanal at great cost. Finally, on January 4, 1943, Imperial Headquarters ordered the command at Rabaul to begin evacuating the forces left on the island. The last Japanese detachment left under cover of night on February 7, seven months to the day after U.S. Marines first landed at Lunga Point.

The Battle for Guadalcanal cost both sides dearly. The Japanese army lost 23,000 of the 37,000 troops it committed to the campaign, while American troops suffered 5,800 casualties. The Japanese navy lost the small carrier *Ryujo,* the battleships *Hiei* and *Kirishima,* and numerous cruisers and destroyers. Both the small carrier *Zuiho* and the large carrier *Shokaku* were damaged. At sea, the Allies lost the American carriers *Wasp* and *Hornet,* while the *Saratoga* and *Enterprise* were damaged. The new battleship *South Dakota* was damaged in one of the first battleship duels of the Pacific War, and the new battleship *North Carolina* was damaged by a torpedo from a Japanese submarine. For a time, the new battleship *Washington* remained the only Allied operational dreadnought in the South Pacific. But Operation Watchtower had, indeed, "corked up the bottle" in the Solomons against further Japanese expansion on that axis, while, as it turned out, giving the Allies the initiative in the islands. In addition, while the battle was going on, American ship-building and aircrew replacement was continuing at a rate that the Japanese could not equal; and by 1943 the balance of power in the South Pacific was shifting in favor of the Americans.

MacArthur's campaign for Papua in New Guinea was about as long and as gruelling as the American campaign for Guadalcanal. First, American and Australian troops beat back the Japanese drive over the Owen Stanley Mountains, then seized the initiative to press the Japanese troops back on their base at Buna. Perhaps in a fit of overeagerness to finish off the enemy there, MacArthur ordered General Robert L. Eichelberger to use his thirty thousand troops and three divisions in a frontal attack against twelve thousand Japanese soldiers in prepared positions. The Japanese fended off the attack while inflicting heavy losses, and also managed to evacuate all but three thousand of their men by sea when the position at Buna became hopeless. Twice as many Allied troops died in the Papuan campaign as in the campaign for Guadalcanal, and the Buna episode perhaps taught MacArthur the importance of bypassing enemy opposition wherever possible. In any case, both he and other Allied commanders in the Pacific were eventually to raise the "island-hopping" technique to a fine art.

D. The Twin-Axis Strategy and the Drive to the Philippines to June 1944. Once the initiative in the South Pacific had passed to the Allies in early 1943, MacArthur proposed to exploit it by a concentration of forces in his Southwest Pacific Command for a drive up the coast of northern New Guinea and then a jump into the Philippines from the south. If the Philippines could be seized, Japan's lines of communication to the Southern Resources Area could be severed by sea and air action, and Japan's economy—deprived of vital raw materials—would eventually collapse. But while admirals King and Nimitz favored a strategy of severing Japan from her Southern Resources Area, they proposed to do so by a Central Pacific drive either to the Philippines or to Taiwan. MacArthur's plan would rely more heavily on Army troops and land-based aviation; the King-Nimitz plan would emphasize naval and Marine operations.

When the Joint Chiefs could not agree on which of the two proposals to adopt, they passed the matter on to President Roosevelt. Roosevelt finally decided that the United States could support both strategies simultaneously. His decision was made more on political than strategic considerations, but it turned out to be the right one. The "Twin-Axis Strategy," as it came to be called, was one that kept the Japanese guessing as to where the next American blow would fall and served to confuse

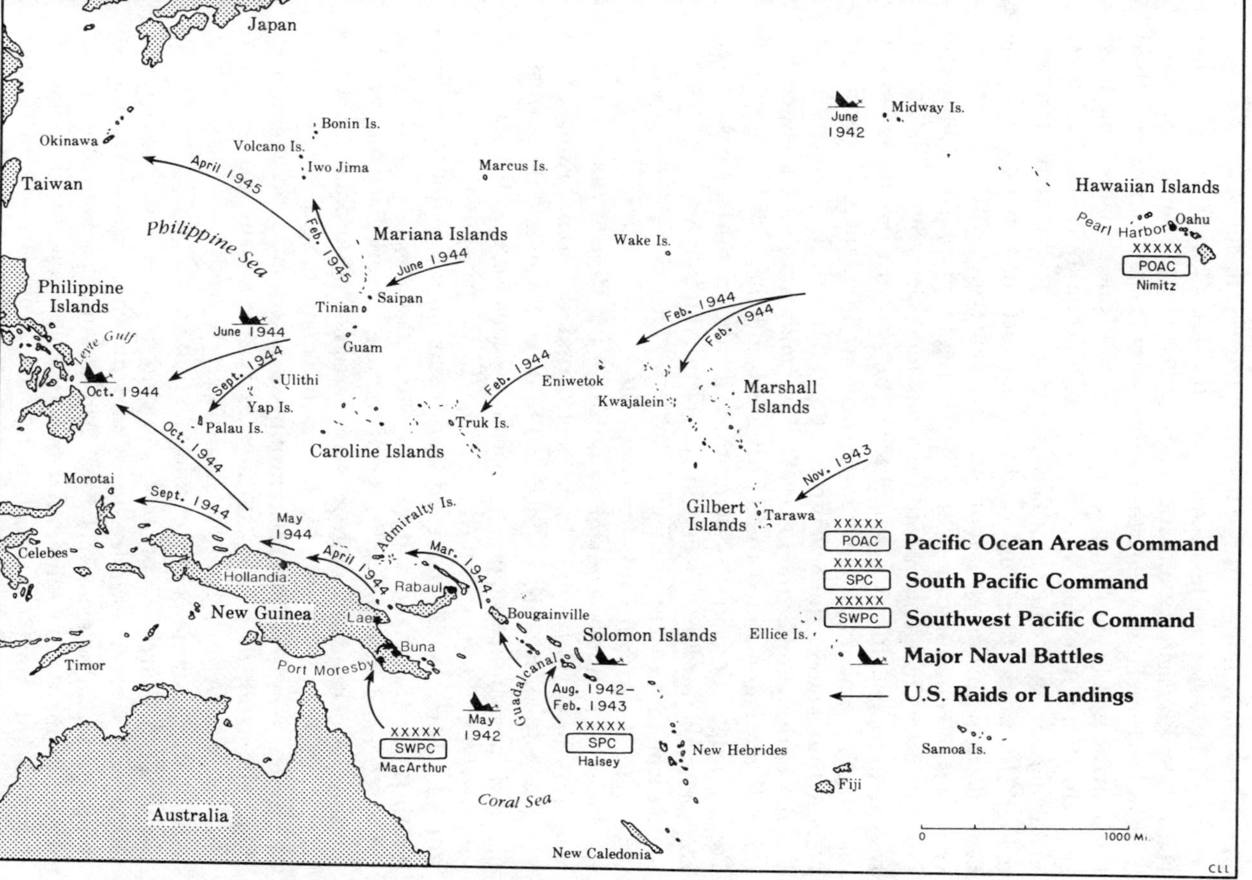

The Pacific Theater of War: Twin-Axis Strategy and Conversion on the Philippines

and divide their forces. But MacArthur was not mollified by the decision, and he was even less happy with the Joint Chiefs' decision that Halsey's South Pacific Command, set for a drive up the Solomons, would be kept separate from MacArthur's Southwest Pacific Command, poised for a drive up the northern coast of New Guinea. Halsey remained subordinate to Admiral Nimitz at Pearl Harbor. In addition, Nimitz made it clear that when conflicts in timing and allocation of means existed, he would give due weight to the fact that operations in the Central Pacific promised a more rapid advance toward Japan and her vital lines of communication, and they were also more likely to precipitate a decisive engagement with the Combined Fleet. Since Nimitz controlled the naval forces in the Pacific, he was in a good position to allocate naval and amphibious forces or to withhold them. Accordingly, "MacArthur's navy," the Seventh Fleet and Seventh Amphibious Force, was not entirely under the general's command. Admiral Halsey, on the other hand, commanded the Third Fleet and the Third Amphibious Force for operations in the Solomons, and Admiral Spruance was given command of the Fifth Fleet and the Fifth Amphibious Force for the drive through the Central Pacific.

Despite MacArthur's problems with the Navy, by the spring of 1943 his forces were much stronger than during the Papuan campaign. Besides the support of the Seventh Fleet (Admiral Thomas Kinkaid), his Southwest Pacific Command included four American and three Australian divisions, and two more American divisions were on the way. General George C. Kenney's Allied Air Force (formed around the U.S. Army Fifth Air Force) had a thousand land-based aircraft. Admiral Halsey's South Pacific Command had an initial strength of two Marine divisions, a New Zealand division, and several hundred Army-Navy aircraft. In addition, American carrier groups were assigned periodically to support the South Pacific Command. In practice, and despite the fact that MacArthur's and Halsey's relationship was based on cooperation rather than command, their joint advance to isolate Rabaul was well coordinated. The Army's land-based airpower proved its worth when in March, 1943, Kenney's far-reaching aircraft surprised a Japanese convoy in the Bismarck Sea on its way to land troops at Lae, New Guinea. His planes sank the whole convoy and drowned an estimated seven thousand Japanese troops. Halsey's Air Command Solomons (Air-Sols) proved its mettle too when, after the American code-breakers learned that Admiral Yamamoto was about to make an inspection tour of Japanese defenses on Bougainville, two Army P-38 long-range fighters intercepted his plane over the island in April, 1943, and shot it down while it was in the process of landing. Admiral Mineichi Koga succeeded Yamamoto as commander of the Combined Fleet.

By the time Halsey's forces had "island-hopped" through the Solomons to reach Bougainville in November, 1943, MacArthur's forces had parried a Japanese counteroffensive on New Guinea at Wau, captured Salamaue, outflanked Lae and Finschhafen, and finally placed themselves where they might invade New Britain, the location of Rabaul. Other landings by MacArthur's and Halsey's forces on Green, St. Matthias, and the Admiralty islands in late 1943 and early in 1944 completely surrounded Rabaul. Admiral Koga decided to abandon the base without a fight. The losing Japanese battle for the Solomons had cost them three thousand aircraft, while the battle on New Guinea had cost them a thousand more. The Japanese army's aviation was becoming as decimated as that of the Japanese navy.

The drive across the Central Pacific was delayed in its start by the insistence of the Joint Chiefs that Attu and Kiska in the Aleutians, the chain of islands extending southwest from Alaska, be recaptured from the Japanese, who had seized them in June, 1942, as a diversion for the Midway operation. Thus the Fifth Fleet's advance into the Central Pacific did not begin until November, 1943, with an invasion of the Gilbert islands. Spruance's force boasted six large aircraft carriers, five light carriers, eight so-called escort carriers, five new and seven old battleships, seventeen cruisers, fifty-six destroyers, twenty-nine troop transports, and hundreds of landing craft. The Fifth Amphibious Force supported the Fifth Marine Amphibious Corps, under command of General Julian C. Smith. The Fleet Train, an innovation of the U.S. Navy, not only accompanied the Fifth Fleet to serve as a mobile source of fuel, ammunition, and supply, it had repair facilities which it could set up at advanced bases, so that only the most seriously injured ships had to return to Pearl Harbor or the West Coast.

Spruance's forces easily captured lightly defended Makin and Abemama islands, but the story was different when the Second Marine Division assaulted tiny Betio Island in the Tarawa Atoll. Some three thousand Imperial Japanese marines manned positions well protected by concrete, log, and sand fortifications. The supporting sea and air bombardments before five thousand U.S. Marines tried to land on November 20 were imperfect, and the Marine landing craft became stuck on a coral reef a thousand yards from the beaches. When the Marines had to advance the rest of the way on foot through shallow water, hundreds were killed and wounded by scathing Japanese fire. Two more bitter days of fighting were required to wipe out Japanese resistance. All but a handful of the defenders either fought until they were killed or committed suicide. The U.S. Marines suffered 991 dead and 2,311 wounded.

Though General Smith called Tarawa a costly mistake, the lessons learned from that experience were usefully applied to the invasion of Kwajalein in the Marshall islands on February 1, 1944. There the supporting fire was carefully directed and the beaches were assaulted according to plan by 40,000 troops. In the outcome, American casualties ashore came to only 372 killed and a few hundred men wounded. In contrast, the Japanese casualties came to 7,870 out of 8,675 Japanese defenders, and the Japanese casualties were nearly all fatalities. The Fifth Fleet was hardly touched by a weak Japanese aerial response. The American operation at Kwajalein was rightly called "an almost perfect" amphibious assault, and demonstrated that proper doctrine and training could save lives as well as win battles.

In his movements through the Gilberts and Marshalls, Spruance hoped to provoke a decisive battle with the Combined Fleet. When in February, 1944, the Fleet was reported at Truk in the Carolines, Admiral Marc A. Mitscher's fast-carrier task force (Task Force 58) was dispatched in a raid toward Truk in hopes of dealing a damaging blow to an enemy caught at anchor. Instead, American pilots found that the Combined Fleet had retreated still further into the Western Pacific, and Mitscher had to be content with the sinking of two hundred thousand tons of Japanese merchant shipping and two enemy destroyers, and the destruction of 275 Japanese planes. But the Japanese retreat from Truk opened the way for the Americans to occupy Eniwetok, another stepping stone toward the Marianas and the Philippines beyond.

With the Japanese abandonments of Rabaul and Truk, a new strategy debate insued over the final approach to the Philippines. After much discussion, President Roosevelt again settled the matter by approving a proposal by the Joint Chiefs that called for MacArthur's forces to continue up the northern coast of New Guinea, while Halsey's Third Fleet and amphibious forces would be shifted to the Central Pacific drive. Henceforth, the Third and Fifth fleet headquarters would alternate in the planning and execution of operations with the same forces. The immediate goal of the Central Pacific drive was occupation of key islands in the Marianas group, beginning with Saipan.

When Spruance's Fifth Fleet moved against Saipan in mid-June, 1944, it constituted the largest naval-amphibious force yet seen in the Pacific War: seven large carriers, eight light carriers, seven new battleships and seven old battleships, twenty-nine cruisers, and sixty-nine destroyers. A total of 956 aircraft were based on the carriers. The entire force came to 535 ships of all kinds, the transports bearing 127,000 Marine and Army troops. Saipan, an island fourteen miles long and ten miles wide, was defended by 32,000 Japanese troops in well dug-in positions in mountainous terrain. In addition, Admiral Soemu Toyoda, who succeeded Koga as commander-in-chief of the Combined Fleet after the latter was lost at sea in March, 1944, had adopted the A-Go plan that provided for a novel use of Admiral Jisaburo Ozawa's Mobile Fleet (three large carriers, six light carriers, and five battleships). Ozawa would launch his 460 planes far out in the Philippine Sea, too far for American planes to reach his carriers and return. The Japanese planes were to make their attacks on Spruance's force, land on Saipan or Tinian for refueling, then return to their carriers. But Ozawa's flyers had only half as many flying hours on the average as their American counterparts, and the Zero was inferior as a fighter compared to the new U.S. Navy F6F Hellcat. In addition, the American fleet boasted a fantastic array of antiaircraft batteries, the shells of the larger guns equipped with proximity or variable-time (V-T) fuses. Those Japanese planes which penetrated the American fighter screen would face a veritable "wall" of flak.

The Battle of the Philippine Sea (June 19–20, 1944) commenced with a series of Japanese air attacks on Spruance's fleet off Saipan, but the Japanese naval strategy backfired. In the so-called Great Marianas Turkey Shoot, 315 Japanese planes were downed over an eight-hour span. By the end of the battle on June 20, the Japanese toll had risen to 426 carrier planes and 445 airmen, while another 50 land-based aircraft on Saipan were also lost. Still worse, on June 19, Ozawa's carriers had blundered into a group of American submarines who promptly torpedoed and sank the new carrier *Taiho* and the veteran carrier *Shokaku*. On June 20, Spruance risked a long-range strike which resulted in the sinking of the carrier *Haiyo*, though 130 American planes had to ditch for lack of enough fuel to return to their carriers. Seventy-six of the pilots were rescued from the sea. Ozawa broke off action after the engagement on June 20 and retired his force from further fighting around Saipan. Though his Mobile Fleet still had carriers, they were almost denuded of planes or pilots. In effect, the Battle of the Philippine Sea had about finished off Japan's naval aviation.

The battle for the island of Saipan was predictably bitter, the last Japanese resistance not being extinguished until July 10. Nearby Tinian and Guam, defended respectively by nine thousand and eighteen thousand Japanese troops, held out until nearly the end of July. Because of the large Japanese civilian population on Saipan, the final Japanese death toll reached sixty thousand. Many of the civilians, no less than the soldiers, preferred death to capture and committed suicide. The Japanese behavior reinforced the American belief that Japan would never come to terms until the home islands were either invaded or starved into submission. Actually, the outcomes of the Battle of the Philippine Sea and the fighting on Saipan finished Tojo as a war leader. His cabinet resigned on July 18, and the emperor appointed Admiral Mitsumasa Yonai as the new premier. Yonai received the doleful news that aside from naval and military defeats, U.S. submarines were sinking Japanese merchant ships at such a rate that the supply of food and raw materials from overseas was dwindling. (Altogether, U.S. submarines sank 4 million tons of Japanese shipping during the war.) But the Allied policy of "unconditional surrender" deterred Yonai from a direct approach to the American government. No cabinet could entertain a peace that would threaten the safety of the semidivine emperor.

E. The Philippines, Iwo Jima, and Okinawa, October 1944–June 1945. As the fighting for the Marianas was coming to a close in July, 1944, admirals King and Nimitz proposed that the American forces completely by-pass the Philippines, where there were very large Japanese forces, and seek to capture Taiwan instead. From Taiwan, American land, sea, and air forces could as easily sever Japanese communications to the Southern Resources Area, and a Taiwan strategy would spare the Filipino people the ordeal of a long and bloody campaign of liberation. MacArthur fiercely opposed the proposal, arguing that he had made a personal pledge that American forces would return to the Philippines as soon as possible, that American prisoners-of-war (POW's) would be liberated sooner, and that only in the Philippines would the Americans find large indigenous support. When the Joint Chiefs referred the matter to Roosevelt, he decided in favor of MacArthur's arguments, and the Philippines once more became the focal point of the Pacific offensives.

In order to get forces into position for an invasion of the southern Philippines, in September, 1944, MacArthur's command seized Morotai, an island just north of the "head" of the New Guinea "bird," while Nimitz's forces invaded the Palaus and occupied Peleliu. While the seizure of Morotai was relatively easy, the resistance of ten thousand Japanese troops on Peleliu was ferocious. A total of two thousand Americans were killed and ten thousand were wounded, nearly 40 percent of the attacking force and the highest combat casualty rate of any amphibious assault in American history. But the unopposed capture of nearby Ulithi provided the U.S. Navy an excellent anchorage, and every subsequent operation of the Central Pacific forces was launched, at least in part, from the base of Ulithi.

Meanwhile, air strikes into the southern Philippines revealed that the southern islands were nearly empty of Japanese planes. MacArthur suggested, therefore, that his forces and those of the Central Pacific should join in a daring landing on the island of Leyte in the east-central Philippines, making it a stepping stone to the crucial island of Luzon. When the Joint Chiefs both accepted the idea and advanced the date of the Philippine invasion by two months to October 20, 1944, the scene was set for the biggest amphibious assault of the Pacific War and, as it turned out, the greatest naval battle in history.

The scale of the American operation against Leyte set new standards in the Pacific War. General Walter Krueger's Sixth Army numbered nearly 200,000 troops, and 60,000 were put ashore on the first day of operations. They were supported by Admiral Kinkaid's Seventh Fleet, consisting of six old battleships under Admiral Jesse Oldendorff, and numerous light carriers, escort carriers, cruisers, destroyers, and patrol-torpedo (PT) boats. Admiral Halsey's Third Fleet had responsibility for maintaining general command of the air and sea should the Japanese Combined Fleet make an appearance. The most powerful component of the Third Fleet was Admiral Mitscher's Task Force 38 (TF-38), composed of eight large carriers, eight light carriers, seven new battleships, twelve cruisers, and fifty-four destroyers, and over a thousand aircraft.

Within an hour of the news of the American landing on Leyte, Imperial Headquarters proceeded to execute the Sho-1 plan. Ozawa's Mobile Fleet (four carriers and ninety planes) was to serve as a decoy off the northern Philippines in order to lure Halsey's forces away from the vicinity of Leyte. Admiral Takeo Kurita's First Striking Force (the super battleships *Yamato* and *Musashi,* three other battleships, twelve cruisers, and fifteen destroyers) was to steam from Brunei Bay, Borneo, through the San Bernardino Strait in the Philippines, and finally to descend on the landing beaches from the north. Admiral Shoji Nishimura's Second Striking Force (two battleships, a cruiser, and four destroyers) would leave Brunei Bay and head for Surigao Strait in the Philippines, finally approaching the landing site from the south. A third force of three cruisers and four destroyers under Admiral Kiyohide Shima in the Pescadores near Taiwan, would follow the Second Striking Force through Surigao Strait.

The series of widely scattered naval actions between October 23 and October 26, 1944, have been collectively called the Battle of Leyte Gulf or the Second Battle of the Philippine Sea. On October 23, American submarines spotted Kurita's force in the South China Sea, sank two Japanese cruisers, and so damaged a third that two destroyers were detailed to escort it back to Brunei Bay. Kurita and the rest of his force continued toward San Bernardino Strait. On October 24, Ozawa's Mobile Fleet was spotted north of the Philippines, while Nishimura's force was detected heading for Surigao Strait. Halsey's TF-38 maneuvered to launch air attacks on Kurita's force while it was passing through San Bernardino Strait on the afternoon of October 24, sinking the *Musashi* with nineteen torpedo hits and many bombs. Kurita's force reversed course, and Halsey promptly set a nighttime course to intercept Ozawa's carriers the next morning. He was unaware that Kurita's force had turned around again and was making a nighttime passage through San Bernardino Strait. Meanwhile, Kinkaid had sent Oldendorff's battleships and nearly all the rest of his heavy fighting units to intercept the Nishimura-Shima force at the Surigao Strait.

October 25 proved to be the decisive day of the campaign. Early that morning, Oldendorff's forces crossed the T of the Japanese force in Surigao Strait, and the fire from battleships and waves of torpedoes from American destroyers and PT boats nearly tore the Japanese column apart. Of Nishimura's original force, only a destroyer survived. After a brush with the Americans, Shima's force turned back. But later that morning to the far north, Kurita's force had passed through San Bernardino Strait and was rapidly approaching the landing site at Leyte, led by the super battleship *Yamato.* As the huge collection of American shipping in Leyte Gulf frantically sought safety in flight, the escort carriers launched planes and the destroyers and destroyer-escorts there sought to cover their retreat. But while Kurita's force was still off the coast of Samar and twenty-eight miles from the landing site at 9:00 A.M., it inexplicably reversed course and began a withdrawal toward San Bernardino Strait, which it subsequently negotiated successfully. On October 26, Halsey's TF-38 launched planes that sank two of Kurita's cruisers as his column crossed the Sibuyan Sea, but the climax of the battle had already passed. Ozawa's four carriers had been sunk the day before.

The so-called Battle of Leyte Gulf is the largest naval action in history, involving even more ships and tonnage than Jutland. The Japanese navy lost three battleships, four carriers, ten cruisers, and nine destroyers (306,000 tons and 5,000 men). Numerous other vessels had been damaged. American naval losses came to one light carrier, two escort carriers, two destroyers, and a destroyer-escort (37,000 tons and 500 Americans). A number of other vessels were damaged. The outcome effectively finished the career of the Combined Fleet in World War II. Even before the naval battle was over, however, the Japanese were resorting to new and unprecedented measures. The first *Kamikaze* attacks of the war fell on vessels in Leyte Gulf on October 24, and by the end of the day of October 25 additional raids had accounted for an escort carrier and damage to three additional escort carriers. The *Kamikaze* ("Divine Wind") or Special Attack Corps was organized by Admiral Takijiro Onishi, commander of the First Air Fleet in the Philippines. The Corps sought volunteers willing to fly bomb-laden aircraft directly into American ships in order to assure hits. The *Kamikaze* craze soon spread to other Japanese commands, and became a standard air measure as the war went on.

Meanwhile, General Tomoyuki Yamashita managed to get 70,000 troops into Leyte, and the island was not declared secure until Christmas Day, 1944. The Japanese death count came to 68,000 men, and another 10,000 troops had died by drowning when their convoys trying to get to Leyte were bombed by American planes. The American casualties on Leyte, ashore and afloat, came to 15,500 men.

Krueger's Sixth Army invaded Luzon in January, 1945. While supporting the invasion, the Seventh Fleet was hit by waves of *Kamikazes.* Numerous American ships, most of them small, were sunk or damaged. On the night of January 9, Halsey's Third Fleet passed through Luzon Strait in order to ravage Japanese shipping on the South China Sea, and over subsequent days its carrier planes ranged as far south as Camranh Bay in French Indochina. Combined with U.S. submarine operations in the area, Halsey's foray completed the severing of the Japanese sea lanes between the home islands and the Southern Resources Area. In late January, Halsey's fleet returned to the anchorage at Ulithi in the Palaus, Halsey turned over command to Admiral Spruance, and the Third Fleet became the Fifth Fleet again.

On Luzon, the battle spread to Manila which was nearly demolished in a street-by-street battle until Japanese resistance collapsed in March. Yamashita and his remaining troops retired to the hills and mountains of northern Luzon, where they continued to resist until Japan surrendered in August, 1945. Only then did Yamashita order his remaining 40,000 men, out of the 170,000 troops he had originally commanded, to lay down their arms. By July 1, when the Sixth Army handed over to Eichelberger's Eighth Army for the final mopping-up on Luzon, it had suffered 8,140 men killed and nearly 30,000 wounded or missing. Many thousands of Filipinos had died in the fighting on Luzon.

While the battle for the Philippines was still in its early stages, work was completed on a giant air base on Tinian in the Marianas, and still another base was being built on Saipan. From these bases the Army Air Forces (AAF) planned to launch a strategic bombing offensive against the Japanese home islands with the B-29 Superfortress, the largest four-engine bomber of World War II built in large numbers. The B-29's great range would enable it to reach Japan, about 1,700 miles from the Marianas, and return to base. The B-29s were concentrated in the Twenty-First Bomber Command (later the Twenty-First Air Force) under General Curtis LeMay. The first of the B-29 raids on the Japanese home islands occurred on November 24, 1944, when LeMay led 111 of the aircraft from Tinian. By February, 1945, LeMay's command boasted over three hundred B-29s, each capable of carrying eight tons of bombs or incendiaries as far as southern Japan. On March 9, 1945, 279 B-29s took off from airfields on Tinian and Saipan, and, in a low-level, incendiary attack, set off a firestorm in Tokyo that destroyed sixteen square miles of the city and 267,000 buildings. An estimated 185,000 Japanese died in this attack, the most destructive air raid in World War II. Other attacks in the spring of 1945 devastated Osaka, Kobe, and Nagoya. By summer, 8 million Japanese had fled the cities, and oil, aircraft, and shipbuilding production had plummeted.

But the strategic bombing of Japan was at a price. Many damaged B-29s were failing to make the long return flight to the Marianas by early in 1945, and the Joint Chiefs ordered a suitable island seized in the Volcano-Bonin group for an emergency landing strip. The choice fell on Iwo Jima. The U.S. Fifth Fleet and three Marine divisions set out for their objective in February, and, after the island had been bombarded, the Marines landed on February 19. Instead of the quick five-day operation planned, the seizure of Iwo required nearly a month, as 60,000 U.S. Marines battled 21,000 entrenched Japanese troops. In addition to bitter resistance on the island, the forces involved on the American side had to endure waves of *Kamikaze* attacks from the Japanese home islands. When the battle finally ended, only 200 Japanese soldiers had been taken alive. Ashore and afloat, the Americans had suffered 24,891 casualties, 6,821 of them fatal. The second *Saratoga* was so badly damaged that it had to be withdrawn for the duration of the war. Still, the air strip on Iwo eventually saved the lives of many airmen and numerous B-29s too damaged over Japan to make the flight back to Tinian or Saipan.

American planners expected that a full-fledged invasion of Japan would be necessary to end the war, and they chose the large island of Okinawa in the Ryukyus (sixty miles long and averaging eighteen miles in width) to serve as a major staging base for that invasion, once it was seized. The island was defended by 97,000 Japanese troops under General Mitsuro Ushijima, and was within range of 2,000 Japanese planes in Japan and on Taiwan. The mission of capturing Okinawa was given to General Simon Buckner's Tenth Army, composed of four Army and three Marine divisions, and totaling 285,000 troops. But in the softening-up attack by the Fifth Fleet between March 18 and March 21, 1945, Admiral Mitscher's TF-38 suffered heavy damage to the second *Wasp,* the second *Yorktown,* and to the carrier *Franklin.* Fortunately, the British Pacific Fleet (two battleships, four carriers, six cruisers, and fifteen destroyers) under Admiral Sir Bruce Fraser had arrived in time to take part. The main landings began on April 1, but resistance intensified inland beginning on April 4. Between April 6 and April 7, seven hundred Japanese aircraft raided the Allied fleet off Okinawa, half of them *Kamikazes.* Thirty-four Allied naval craft were sunk, though none larger than a destroyer, and 368 other vessels were damaged. Among the more severely injured ships were four American and three British large aircraft carriers, ten battleships, thirteen light and escort carriers, five cruisers, and sixty-seven destroyers. On April 7, 280 of Mitscher's planes sank the giant battleship *Yamato* when it sortied from Japan in order to help repel the invasion of Okinawa. Ashore, the battle for the island dragged on for three months. At its close, only 7,400 of Ushijima's soldiers had been taken alive, and at least 10,000 Japanese civilians on the island had died. The Allies suffered 49,000 casualties (12,500 deaths).

F. The Atomic Bomb, Russian Intervention, and the End of the Pacific War, August–September 1945. As the battle for Okinawa was ending, American staff planners working on Operation Olympic (the invasion of the Japanese home islands) were coming to some grim conclusions. Assuming the invasion could be launched in the late summer or fall of

1945, they believed the last Japanese resistance would not be snuffed out before 1947. The battle might cost a million American casualties. Alternatively, the United States might try to starve Japan into submission, but, in fulfillment of his pledges made at Yalta, Stalin would enter the war before fall 1945; and the Red Army was sure to overrun Manchuria and Korea, whose fates would then be left to Soviet disposal. Either way, the Anglo-American powers might be cheated out of much say in the final disposal of Japan's empire on the mainland of northern Asia.

Unknown to the staffs planning Operation Olympic, the highly secret Manhattan Project, launched in early 1942, was about to reach fruition, and thereby to remove the necessity of either an invasion or a blockade of the Japanese home islands. On July 16, 1945, a nuclear test-device (Trinity) was successfully exploded in the desert near Alamogordo, New Mexico. The news was flashed to President Truman, then attending the Potsdam Conference in Germany with Stalin and Churchill. While American scientists prepared two atomic bombs for use against Japan, on July 26 the Potsdam Declaration demanded again that Japan surrender unconditionally. Though the Japanese cabinet had changed premiers several times since Tojo's fall, no Japanese government could submit to such terms and survive. As Japan made no direct response to the Potsdam Declaration, Truman believed that he had no choice but to use the atomic bombs in hopes of ending the war quickly and saving the lives of thousands of American servicemen. He was unaware that the Japanese government did not understand that the unconditional surrender formula applied only to the Japanese armed forces.

The components for the two atomic bombs were shipped to Tinian aboard the cruiser *Indianapolis* (sunk by a Japanese submarine on its return voyage, with a great loss of life), and placed at the disposal of a specially trained squadron of B-29s commanded by Colonel Paul W. Tibbets, Jr. The city of Hiroshima was chosen as the first target because it was both a military headquarters and an industrial center. Tibbets himself piloted the B-29 "Enola Gay" when it took off from Tinian on August 6, 1945, and headed for Japan. The bomb was dropped at 8:15 A.M., detonating two thousand feet above the city's center. The resulting blast—equal to that from 20,000 tons of TNT—and heat immediately killed an estimated seventy thousand Japanese and destroyed five square miles of the city. Injuries from flying debris, burns, and deadly radiation killed at least as many more Japanese over the next few weeks and months. Large numbers of other survivors would have shortened lifespans. On August 8, Soviet Russia declared war on Japan, and Red Army troops began invading Manchuria, Korea, and southern Sakhalin island. On August 9, a second atomic bomb was dropped on Nagasaki, killing at least forty-five thousand people outright. Stunned by the mass slaughter from the air and by Soviet intervention, the Japanese cabinet received the emperor's assent to a request for an armistice on almost any terms. The Japanese government was relieved to learn not only that the emperor's personal safety was assured but that he might remain on his throne as a figurehead monarch. General MacArthur would head up the Supreme Command, Allied Powers (SCAP) in occupation of Japan. A general armistice in the Pacific was declared on August 14 (V-J Day), and a formal Japanese surrender to Allied delegations was conducted by General MacArthur in Tokyo Bay on September 2 on the decks of the U.S. battleship *Missouri.* Meanwhile, Washington and Moscow had agreed that Korea would be temporarily divided into Soviet and American occupation zones at the 38th parallel. Chiang Kai-shek's armies returned to northern China, but the fate of Soviet-occupied Manchuria remained in doubt. Mao Tse-tung's Communist armies found there a new base for their war against Chiang.

The Pacific War cost the lives of 750,000 Japanese servicemen, to which must be added 500,000 more who died on the Asian mainland after December, 1941. Perhaps 750,000 Japanese civilians died in the home islands and on islands in the Pacific. Approximately 350,000 American servicemen were casualties of the Pacific War, 89,000 of them U.S. Marines. (American casualties in the European Theater of Operations came to about 500,000.) Many thousands of non-Japanese Asians died in the Pacific War and in the East Asian War, the latter fought in China and Southeast Asia between 1941 and 1945. (See next section.) By any standard, it had been an ordeal as terrible as the one in Europe.

G. The China-Burma-India Theater and the Close of the War for East Asia. The China-Burma-India (CBI) theater was more closely connected with the Sino-Japanese War in East Asia than with the Pacific War. Still, American policy-makers placed a high priority on assisting the British to hold India and in keeping Nationalist China in the war against Japan. In the spring of 1942, the Japanese invasion of Burma cut the Burma Road by which the British had sent supplies to the land-locked Nationalist government at Chungking, and until Burma could be recovered the Americans undertook to fly the "Hump" of the Himalayas to keep the Chinese armies supplied. Chiang Kai-shek accepted U.S. General Joseph ("Vinegar Joe") Stilwell, an old "China Hand," as his chief-of-staff, and General Claire Chennault's American Volunteer Group (the "Flying Tigers") was expanded eventually into the Fourteenth Air Force.

Nationalist China proved to be a weak reed, primarily because of corruption in Chiang's bureaucracy. Stilwell, tactless as he was honest, refused to turn a blind eye. Under Wavell, the British in India were more interested in recovering their former colonies of Burma and Malaya than in assisting Chiang. Often working at cross-purposes, the Allies in the CBI achieved little until the fall of 1943 except to train some Chinese and Indian divisions, and to carry out raids into Burma with Ord Wingate's Chindits (Long-Range Penetration Groups).

Matters began to improve in the CBI in November, 1943, when the Anglo-American Southeast Asia Command (SEAC) was formed under Admiral Louis Mountbatten, with Stilwell serving as his deputy. In India, the U.S. Tenth Air Force and RAF wings were combined into the Eastern Air Command under General George E. Stratemeyer. Plans were laid to establish a Twentieth Bomber Command in China composed of B-29s, which were to begin a strategic bombing campaign against Japan. In early 1944, Stilwell's Chinese armies and Mountbatten's Anglo-Indian armies began separate but coordinated offensives into Burma. The Chinese performance was disappointing, but under the command of General Sir William Slim, the Anglo-Indian armies inflicted heavy losses on the Japanese Fifteenth Army and recovered northwest Burma as far as Imphal. The major American achievement of the year in the CBI was a strike at Myitkyina by General Frank D. Merrill's 5307th Composite Unit ("Merrill's Marauders"). Once a pipeline was built from Ledo to Myitkyina, the air ferry into China could avoid the formidable "Hump." In China, however, the Japanese offensives in April–May, 1944, took the airfields in the Hankow-Canton area, and American interest in B-29 raids from China withered. Friction between Stilwell and Chiang reached the point in October, 1944, that Roosevelt replaced Stilwell with General Albert C. Wedemeyer. The old CBI theater was divided and thereafter Mountbatten's SEAC concentrated on the theater in Burma.

Burma turned out to be the principal area of Allied success in Southeast Asia in 1945. Much of the credit belongs to Slim, a great if uncelebrated commander in World War II. His Fourteenth Army out-fought and outmaneuvered a tenacious Japanese enemy in some of the most difficult jungle terrain in the world, often depending solely on air supply. After neutralizing the enemy forces at Mandalay, Slim's forces entered Rangoon on May 3, effectively ending the campaign for southern Burma. In northern Burma, mixed American, British, and Chinese forces finally opened the Ledo Road to China, and the first truck convoy reached Kunming in February, 1945. Mountbatten's plans for invading Malaya in the late summer of 1945 were cancelled after Japan's surrender in August.

IV. World War II: Summary and Conclusions

The patterns of war in such a global conflict as World War II were necessarily diverse, but the importance of machine warfare, mass production, and scientific development and application are so self-evident that they hardly need further comment. Perhaps less obvious but of great importance to the patterns of war was the emergence of combined operations. As the war went on, the traditional dividing lines between land, sea, and air forces faded, and among the Anglo-American forces especially interservice doctrine and leadership became crucial to success. Combined operations also implied close cooperation among Allied forces as well as among the forces of a single country. The Anglo-American example of the Combined Chiefs of Staff was really without precedent, yet the forthright debate within its councils over strategy and methods not only pointed the way to final victory, it managed to do so with a remarkable economy of force, considering the scale of the challenge.

Soviet Russia put an estimated 20,000,000 people into uniform at one time or another during the war, and as many as 12,500,000 at one time near its end. Perhaps as many as 11,000,000 of these were in the Soviet ground forces. The United States mobilized about 16,000,000 men and women, with 12,100,000 being the peak strength. Of this number, 6,100,000 were serving with the Army Ground Forces, 2,400,000 with the Army Air Forces, 3,000,000 with the Navy, and 600,000 with the Marine Corps. The British Empire mobilized 8,700,000, France 3,000,000, Germany 11,000,000, Japan 6,100,000, and Italy 3,000,000. The Soviet Union was the hardest hit of the great powers in casualties, an estimated 22,000,000 dead, of which 7,500,000 were in the Soviet armed forces. Next hardest hit was China with 13,500,000 military-civilian deaths. Britain suffered 485,000 military deaths and 100,000 civilian deaths. France incurred 250,000 military fatalities and 360,000 civilian dead. The United States sustained 850,000 casualties, 400,000 of them fatal, or about three times the number of casualties it had suffered in World War I. But there were relatively few civilian deaths. Among the Axis powers, Germany led the list in casualties with 3,500,000 military deaths and 3,810,000 civilian deaths. Japan suffered over a million military dead and 750,000 civilian deaths, while Italy had 330,000 military fatalities and 85,000 civilian dead. When the dead of other countries are added, perhaps 55,000,000 people perished during World War II.

Finally, the outcome of World War II completely disrupted the traditional balances of power not only in Europe, long the focal point of world power, but all over the globe. While German, Japanese, and Italian power had been wholly eliminated, neither Britain nor France could recover their former importance. Soviet Russia emerged as the great European-Asian power, only offset by the power of the United States. The European empires in Asia and ultimately in Africa had been dealt a mortal blow from which they would never recover, as nationalism became rampant in their former colonies. The advent of nuclear weapons cast an ominous shadow over the peace achieved in 1945. Even then it was clear that the future world order would depend upon the relationship between the United States and Soviet Russia, allies in World War II only by circumstance and with fundamentally different ideological and foreign policy goals.

7

The Patterns of War since 1945

The patterns of war since 1945 have emerged against a background of several historic developments. The first has been the continuing technological revolution of the twentieth century, especially as regards nuclear explosives, their carriers, and the increasing importance of nuclear and nonnuclear missiles. The second is the continuing Cold War between the United States of America and the Union of Soviet Socialist Republics, super-powers in a class by themselves after World War II, and the tendency of many countries to form behind one or the other of them in opposing blocs. The third has been the decline of traditional Western imperialism and the breakup of the overseas empires in Asia and Africa. The myriad successor states of those defunct empires have oriented themselves to the West, or to the Communist bloc, or to the so-called Third World of non-aligned countries. And finally, the United Nations Organization, beset with Cold War rivalries and an explosion of national sovereignties across the globe, has met with only limited success in its peace-keeping mission. Regrettable as it is to say, war has become all too common in the turbulent world since 1945.

I. The Early Cold War, 1945–50

The Cold War in Europe began with quarrels between Soviet Russia and its former Western allies over a peace treaty with Germany and the Soviet imposition of Communist governments in countries overrun by the Red Army during the course of World War II. Britain, France, and the United States protested Joseph Stalin's arbitrary changes of the frontiers in Eastern Europe to Soviet advantage and without reference to the West, and they were especially angry over Soviet treatment of Poland, for whose independence Britain and France had gone to war in 1939. Tensions were further heightened by the outbreak of a Communist-inspired civil war in Greece even before the end of World War II, followed by the overthrow of the democratic government in Czechoslovakia in March, 1948. When Stalin then imposed a land blockade of the Western sectors of occupied Berlin beginning in May, correctly or not the governments of Western Europe and North America concluded that Stalin was capable of launching a military drive to the English Channel for the complete domination of Europe. The Red Army retained 175 mobilizable divisions after World War II, quite the largest modern military force in both Europe and in the world at the time, and one feared by the West as a possible tool of Soviet aggression. The Cold War had begun in earnest.

While an Anglo-American Berlin Airlift supplied the garrisons and people of West Berlin for a year, and the Marshall Plan (announced in 1947) aided Western Europe's economic recovery, the West European and North American governments began to take measures for their common defense. In April, 1949, the representatives of twelve nations—the United States, Canada, Britain, France, Italy, Portugal, Belgium, the Netherlands, Luxembourg, Denmark, Norway, and Iceland—met in Washington, D.C., in order to sign the North Atlantic Treaty. The treaty created the North Atlantic Treaty Organization (NATO), a NATO Council and a NATO Defense Committee. The members of the pact pledged to treat an attack on any of their number as an attack upon all, and in time of peace to take common measures of defense. Then, after Stalin lifted his Berlin Blockade in May, 1949, the United States, Britain, and France formed their German occupation zones into the Federal Republic of (West) Germany with a capital at Bonn in the Rhineland, and placed West Germany under NATO protection. By the end of 1949, the Soviet occupation zone had been converted to the German Democratic Republic (GDR) with a capital in East Berlin. West Berlin was left an enclave of West Germany, 110 miles inside the territory of the GDR and, as such, a point of recurring friction between East and West for decades to come.

The Western empires and mandates in the Middle East, such as remained after World War II, were for the most part quickly liquidated, but the decision of the United Nations to partition Palestine between Arabs and Jews in 1948 soon led to local war and an extension of the Cold War to the Middle East. The Jewish community in Palestine proclaimed their territory to be the state of Israel in May, 1948, and the Palestinian Arabs, who had opposed partition, took up arms against Israel. The Palestinian Arabs were supported by the governments of Egypt, Jordan, Lebanon, Syria, and Iraq. The Israeli Defense Forces (IDF) were improvised from earlier Jewish military institutions, the *Hagannah* (militia) and the *Palmach* (striking companies), created before and during World War II for defense against Arab attacks. Before the outbreak of war in 1948, both arms and European Jews had been smuggled into Palestine, and the IDF was led by officers many of whom had learned the craft of war while serving with the Allied forces. Still, the world was surprised when the IDF threw back all Arab invasions in 1948 and went on to occupy all of Palestine except the Arab quarter of Jerusalem and the Gaza Strip adjacent to the Sinai desert. The War of Liberation was finally ended with a truce arranged by the United Nations in January, 1949. By then, some eight hundred thousand Palestinian Arabs had fled to other Arab countries, especially to the Kingdom of Jordan. From their ranks, in time, were drawn recruits from various anti-Zionist movements, including the Palestinian Liberation Organization (PLO), eventually to be the most important. In addition, after the 1948 war the more militant of the Arab governments discovered that the Soviet Union was willing to supply Arab armies with arms and advisors. The more conservative Arab governments, such as the oil-rich Kingdom of Saudi Arabia, were caught between their suspicions of the USSR and their hatred of Israel.

The Far East also became an unstable region after World War II. Soviet forces withdrew from Manchuria in 1946, but not before turning over arms to Mao Tse-tung's armies, then on the point of resuming civil war with Chiang Kai-shek's government. Mao's forces finally drove forward to victory over Chiang's forces on the mainland of China in the fall of 1949. While Mao signed a mutual-aid pact with Stalin, the United States continued to recognize Chiang's government, confined to the island of Taiwan. Soviet forces withdrew from Korea in 1948, but left behind a People's Republic under Communist Kim Il Sung. By the time American troops withdrew from southern Korea in 1949, President Syngman Rhee had established a Republic of Korea below the 38th parallel. Rhee's government at Seoul, and Kim's government at Pyongyang, each claimed to be the only legitimate government in Korea, and the possibility of war between them was quite real by 1950.

Elsewhere in the Far East, the United States granted independence to the Philippines in 1946, but retained naval and air bases in the islands. In December, 1946, after France refused to confer independence on its colony of Indochina (composed of Vietnam, Laos, and Cambodia), Communist Ho Chi Minh of the Vietminh (the League for the Independence of Vietnam) launched a rebellion against French rule. Native opposition to the Dutch in the East Indies led to the creation of the Republic of Indonesia in 1949. Britain granted independence to India in 1947, and Muslim Pakistan promptly broke away from India to form a separate state. Britain granted independence to Burma in 1948, but in the same year a Communist rebellion broke out in Malaya. The British deferred their departure there until they could hand over to a non-Communist government. Unexpectedly, the "Malayan Emergency" (also known as the "War of the Running Dogs") lasted twelve years before the Republic of Malaysia was secure. Thailand (Siam), never colonized by the West, retained its traditional independence.

In the turbulent postwar world, the United States gradually cobbled together a defense policy that, it hoped, would meet the needs of its own defense and that of allied states. The National Security Act of 1947 created the basic structure of postwar national defense by designating the armed forces as the National Military Establishment (NME) and dividing the NME into the departments of the Army, the Navy, and the Air Force. A civilian secretary presided over each department and was responsible to a Secretary of Defense. Statutory recognition was given to the Joint Chiefs of Staff, designated as the chiefs-of-staff of the Army and Air Force and the Chief of Naval Operations. The Joint Chiefs were to be assisted by a Joint Staff. The Joint Chiefs directed the interservice commands overseas and certain special branches such as the Strategic Air Command (SAC). The 1947 Act also created the Central Intelligence Agency (CIA) and the National Security Council. In 1949, the Act was amended to transform the NME into the Department of Defense, to broaden the powers of the Secretary of Defense, and to create the post of Chairman of the Joint Chiefs. (General Omar Bradley was first to hold the post.) In 1951, after the outbreak of the Korean War, the Commandant of the Marine Corps was added to the roster of the Joint Chiefs.

The administration of President Harry S Truman was first to make air-atomic power the cornerstone of American defense. Even before the Army Air Forces became the United States Air Force, the Strategic Air Command was created in 1946 for the long-range delivery of nuclear weapons. After the creation of a separate Air Force in September, 1947, SAC remained the most important of its commands. This heavy reliance on air-atomic power reflected not only the great power of the atomic bomb, but also the unwillingness of the public to make either the personal or financial sacrifices necessary for the recreation of large conventional forces so soon after World War II. In addition, American monopoly on the atomic bomb was expected to last for many years, and during World War II the land-based American air forces had created a tradition of strategic bombing. Besides air-atomic power, the so-called Truman Doctrine, announced in 1947, pledged arms and military advisors to any country threatened with indirect, as well as direct, "totalitarian aggression," in practice a promise to aid against internal insurgencies such as that going on in Greece by 1947. Greece became the first recipient of military aid under the rubric of the Truman Doctrine, and subsequently the royal Greek army was able to crush the Communist rebellion. Through both air-atomic deterrence and aid under the Truman Doctrine, President Truman hoped to prevent Communist aggression without involving Americans in combat.

In the early Cold War, SAC's principal bomber types were the B-29, the B-50 (an improved version of the B-29), and the B-36 Peacemaker. The B-29 and B-50 were conventional, four-engine, propeller-driven aircraft that required overseas bases in order to attack targets in the Soviet Union. The B-36 was the world's first intercontinental bomber, a huge machine eventually powered by six conventional gasoline engines and four jet engines. It could make round-trip flights between bases in the continental United States and Russian targets five thousand miles away with a five-ton bomb load equal to one Hiroshima-style nuclear fission bomb. Even after Russia began to produce large numbers of jet-engined interceptor-fighters, such as the Mig-15, General Curtis LeMay, the long-time head of SAC, believed that enough of his bombers could get through Russian air defenses to inflict fatal blows on Soviet population centers.

American confidence in the Truman defense policy was somewhat shaken in August, 1949, when Soviet Russia tested a nuclear fission bomb years ahead of prediction. Though the Soviet Tu-4 Bull (a NATO designation), the longest-ranged of the Soviet bombers at the time, could not deliver an atomic bomb to the United States, it could threaten cities in Europe and Asia. In addition, Soviet intercontinental bombers were under development. And most disconcerting, the CIA reported to the National Security Council that the USSR was working on a hydrogen fusion or thermonuclear bomb with many times the power of the nuclear fission bomb. In a policy-document called NSC-68, the National Security Council urged Truman to order the development of an American H-bomb as soon as possible, and to recommend to the Congress an expansion of American conventional forces. On January 30, 1950, Truman signed an executive order for the development of an H-bomb, but he did little to promote expansion of American conventional forces until the outbreak of the Korean War six months later.

II. The Korean War, 1950–53

On June 25, 1950, nine divisions and 135,000 troops of the North Korean People's Army (NKPA) crossed the 38th parallel in a general invasion of South Korea. When the resistance of the 100,000 troops of the Army of the Republic of Korea (ROK Army) proved of no avail, President Rhee's government in Seoul abandoned its capital and joined the retreat of the ROK Army deeper inside South Korea. North Korea's aggression challenged both the peace-keeping mission of the United Nations and the American policy of Communist "containment" in Europe and Asia.

Upon President Truman's motion, the U.N. Security Council convened on the matter of the Korean emergency within twenty-four hours after the report of the outbreak of fighting. Over subsequent days, the Council branded North Korea as the aggressor, called on member-states

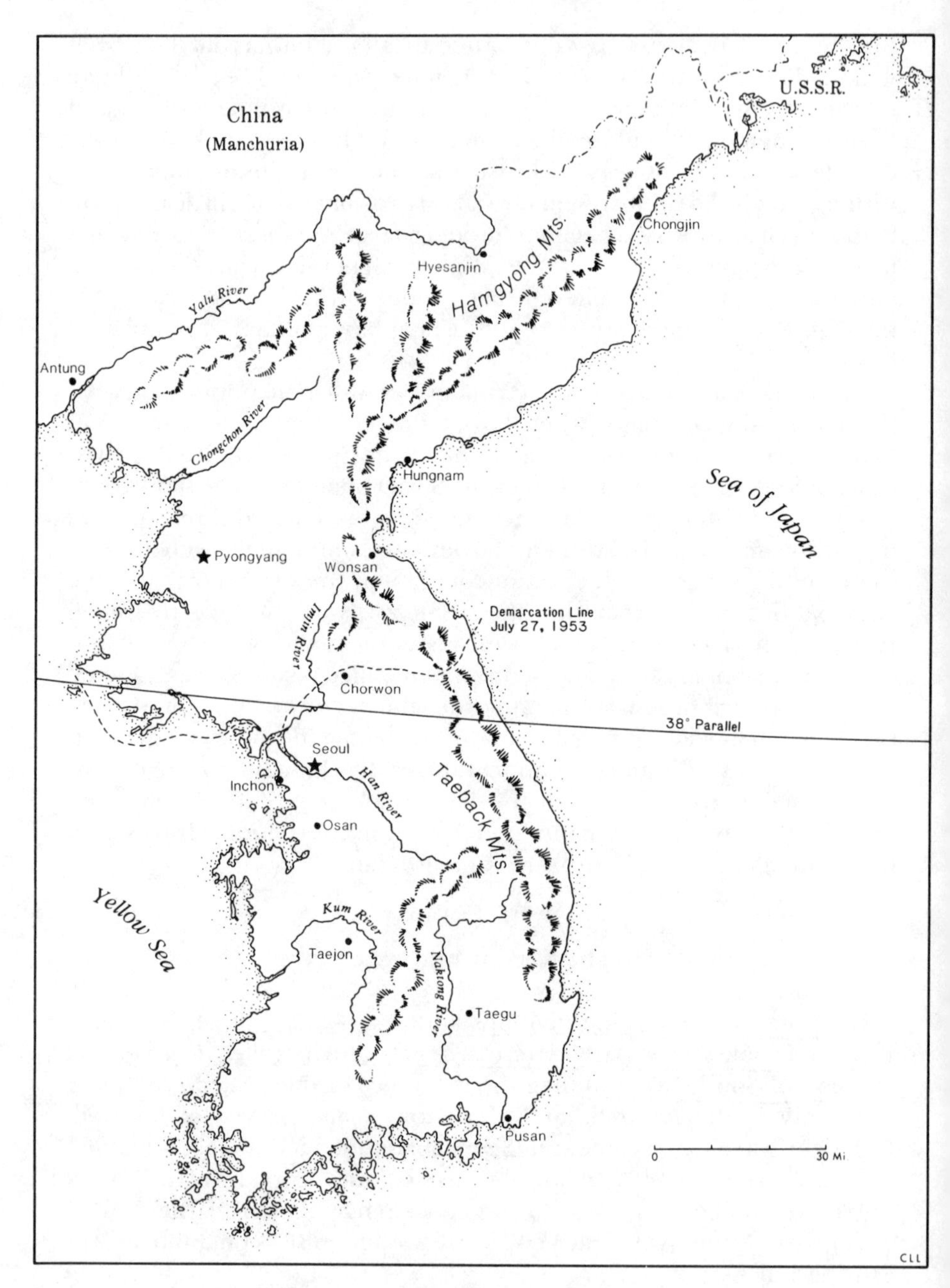

The Korean War Theater, 1950–1953

of the U.N. to contribute forces to a United Nations Command, and appointed the United States to serve as the executive agent for the U.N.'s intervention. The Council approved Truman's nomination of General Douglas MacArthur to serve as Commander-in-Chief, United Nations Command (CINCUNC), a duty he added to his existing posts of Supreme Commander, Allied Powers in Japan (SCAP), and Commander-in-Chief, U.S. Far East Command (CINCFE). All these measures were taken in the absence of the Soviet delegate to the Security Council, who otherwise might have vetoed the Council's actions. Fortunately for the Council, the USSR was then boycotting Council sessions over the U.N. failure to admit the People's Republic of China in place of Nationalist China.

Besides the ROK Army, only elements of four U.S. Army divisions in Japan, composing General Walton Walker's Eighth Army, were immediately available as ground forces for the U.N. Command. They were so short of men and equipment that three divisions had to "cannibalize" the fourth to have enough manpower and arms. Even then, their combat readiness left much to be desired. The U.S. Far Eastern Air Forces and the Seventh Fleet, based in the Philippines, were not ready for a Korean emergency; and the Seventh Fleet, in addition to supporting the Eighth Army's operations in Korea, was given the task of "neutralizing" the Formosa Strait between mainland China and Taiwan.

The first American casualties of the Korean War were taken on July 5 near Osan when a reinforced battalion tried unsuccessfully to delay a column of enemy tanks. The Americans soon joined the retreat of the ROK Army, the latter reduced to forty thousand men. MacArthur's strategy began to pivot on holding the port of Pusan in the extreme south of Korea. On July 19, Walker established his headquarters at Taejon, assumed operational control over the ROK Army, and began to direct a withdrawal of his forces to an arc of hastily improvised defenses known as the Pusan Perimeter. During August and into September, the NKPA made repeated efforts to break through the defenses; but, while the battle raged on, Walker's command was reinforced by an Army division and a Marine brigade from the United States, miscellaneous units from Pacific posts, and a British brigade from Hong Kong. With the arrival of these reinforcements, the strength of the U.N. forces inside the Pusan Perimeter rose to almost one hundred thousand troops by mid-September.

Meanwhile, the arrival of troops and supplies in Japan allowed the U.S. Army division left behind to be refitted for combat. A Marine division had also arrived from the United States. Instead of using these divisions to reinforce Walker's command in the Pusan Perimeter, MacArthur convinced the Joint Chiefs to allow him to form them into an amphibious X Corps under General Edward Almond. MacArthur proposed to land the X Corps at the harbor of Inchon (Operation Chromite), where it would be only a short distance from Seoul, the hub of road and rail communications in South Korea. If the operation worked, the enemy around Pusan would be deprived of supplies and reinforcements; and, in conjunction with an offensive by Walker's forces, it would set the stage for a Korean-style *Kesselschlacht* in which the NKPA south of the 38th parallel would be quickly destroyed. MacArthur was willing to risk the tricky tides at Inchon and a possible repulse on the coast in order to achieve that goal.

'50 On September 15, the X Corps went ashore at Inchon in the last major U.S. amphibious assault to date. Surprise was so complete that within two days the port was captured and the X Corps could press on toward Seoul. On September 20, Walker's forces broke through the enemy lines at Pusan, and within a week units of the Eighth Army had linked up with the X Corps. Caught in the middle, the NKPA disintegrated. Only thirty thousand of its troops managed to escape death or capture by fleeing through mountainous eastern Korea to the safety of the 38th parallel. On September 27, MacArthur flew from Tokyo to Korea in order to join President Rhee's triumphal return to his capital at Seoul.

In the meantime, the United States was lobbying the U.N. General Assembly for an expansion of war goals to include an unified Korea. The return of the Soviet delegate to the Security Council made further action through that body impossible. While debate in the General Assembly continued, MacArthur ordered ROK units of the U.N. Command to begin an invasion of North Korea on October 1. Other U.N. forces, including American, followed on October 5. On October 9, the U.N. General Assembly passed a vaguely worded resolution favoring "the restoration of peace and security throughout Korea," which the Truman administration interpreted as approval of the invasion of North Korea already underway. But the original goals of the U.N. intervention in Korea had been changed and, as it turned out, with grave consequences for both the U.N. and the United States.

Ten days after the U.N. resolution on Korea, American troops occupied Kim Il Sung's capital at Pyongyang, but the North Korean government had fled to Chinese protection at the Manchurian border. Meanwhile, the Indian government, which had diplomatic relations with Peking, passed along warnings that Mao Tse-tung would not tolerate U.N. troops at the Yalu, the river which divides Manchuria from North Korea over much of its length. On October 15, Truman met with MacArthur at Wake Island in a conference to discuss the danger of Chinese intervention. MacArthur discounted the danger and felt confident that he could deal with it should it occur. Nevertheless, Truman authorized him to halt the U.N. advance at any point south of the Yalu if he felt his command was in danger, and he ordered him not to use other than ROK troops as the U.N. Command approached the Yalu, in order to avoid needless provocation of Mao's government. But after returning to Tokyo, MacArthur ordered the advance to continue and ignored his instructions not to use non-ROK troops near the Yalu. In addition, he continued to direct the X Corps and associated ROK troops east of the Hamgyong mountains from his headquarters, while Walker had direct command over the Eighth Army and ROK troops west of the Hamgyong The line of ROK troops through the mountain chain was weak. Still, MacArthur seemed unconcerned about a possible mass intervention of Chinese forces when, on November 24, he ordered a final closing to the Yalu on both fronts and predicted that the war would be over by Christmas.

MacArthur's ill-placed confidence was swept away beginning on November 26 when three hundred thousand Chinese People's Volunteers (CPVS), actually veteran soldiers of the Chinese People's Liberation Army, launched a massive counteroffensive against the U.N. Command south of the Yalu. On November 28, MacArthur radioed Washington that he faced "an entirely new war," and requested permission to withdraw the X Corps and associated ROK troops through the ports of Hungnam and Wonsan and to regroup them in South Korea. The Eighth Army west of the Hamgyong mountains broke off action as best it could and began a retreat toward South Korea overland. The worst American defeat suffered since the early phases of the Battle of the Bulge in 1944 was followed by the longest uninterrupted retreat in the history of the U.S. Army. On December 23, as the Eighth Army was recrossing the 38th parallel, Walker was killed in a jeep accident. The Joint Chiefs immediately dispatched General Matthew Ridgway as his replacement. En route, Ridgway briefly conferred with MacArthur in Tokyo, insisting that all U.N. troops in future be placed under his Eighth Army headquarters. MacArthur agreed. On December 28, Ridgway took up his new duties at Taejon.

The retreat of the U.N. forces finally came to a halt early in January, 1951, when a line was formed across Korea which, at its nearest point, was about seventy miles south of Seoul. The Communist pressure on the U.N. Command had begun to slacken as Chinese and North Korean supply lines lengthened, and as fierce U.N. air attacks began to take their toll. But while the U.N. retreat was still underway in December, MacArthur had bombarded the Joint Chiefs with requests to take measures that would broaden the war, under the threat that the U.N. Command could not remain in Korea otherwise. Specifically, MacArthur wanted permission to order air attacks on enemy bases in Manchuria and on bridges spanning the Yalu, and to accept Chiang Kai-shek's offer of Nationalist troops to serve in Korea. MacArthur also urged that the Seventh Fleet be ordered to end its "neutralization" of the Formosa Strait so that Chiang's forces on Taiwan could attack Chinese coasts. Truman, the Joint Chiefs, and George C. Marshall, Secretary of Defense since September, were reluctant. On December 14, a new resolution of the U.N. General Assembly had called for a ceasefire and a negotiated peace in Korea, not an expansion of the war. In addition, General Omar Bradley, Chairman of the Joint Chiefs, feared that a Soviet attack on Western Europe might be in the offing, and he was anxious to strengthen American forces assigned to NATO. The other Joint Chiefs—General J. Lawton Collins, Army Chief-of-Staff, General Hoyt S. Vandenberg, Air Force Chief-of-Staff, and Admiral Forrest Sherman, Chief of Naval Operations—agreed with Bradley that the Korean War should be broadened only if there were no other way to allow the U.N. Command to save South Korea.

The matter was settled on January 15, 1951, when Ridgway briefed a delegation of the Joint Chiefs, led by Collins and Vandenburg, at his headquarters in Korea. Ridgway believed not only that the U.N. Command could beat off further Communist attacks on his current line, but also that, with arriving reinforcements, the U.N. Command could recover most of South Korea. Ridgway soon demonstrated the validity of his strategy. Though his command had only 365,000 troops to an estimated half million Communist troops, his late winter and spring offensives in 1951 steadily drove back the Chinese and North Korean forces, and Seoul was recaptured on March 14. Truman was about to propose an armistice on the basis of the *status quo ante bellum,* when MacArthur—perhaps chagrined by the rejection of his strategy—preempted the action by making a broadcast from Tokyo, boasting of the U.N. victories and implying more drastic military action if the Communist side did not seek peace at his hands. Truman was forced to cancel plans for a more conciliatory speech, and the United Nations was thrown into confusion over American policy and who was deciding it. Truman's patience with MacArthur finally collapsed when, on April 5, Joseph Martin, Republican leader in the House of Representatives, read a letter from MacArthur on the House floor in which the general agreed with Martin's critical views of Truman's conduct of the war. After consulting with Marshall and the Joint Chiefs, Truman relieved MacArthur of all his commands and transferred his name to the retired list on April 11. Ridgway succeeded MacArthur as CINCUNC, CINCFE, and SCAP, while General James Van Fleet replaced Ridgway as commander of the Eighth Army.

MacArthur's abrupt relief and retirement stirred up a wave of protest among his supporters in the United States, but it settled the question of limiting the war in Korea as long as the Truman administration was in power. Moreover, on June 23, Jacob Malik, Soviet representative to the U.N., announced that the Communist high command in Korea was willing to discuss an armistice. Talks began at Kaesong on July 8, and later that summer the site was moved to Panmunjom. But no quick agreement was reached, and both negotiations and the war dragged on for two more years before terms were reached.

During the final two years of the Korean War, the battlefront resembled the Western Front in World War I. The Korean peninsula was bisected by two opposing lines of trenches, barbed-wire entanglements, bunkers, and mine fields. Battles were fought, sometimes many times over, for commanding ground such as Pork Chop Hill and Heartbreak Ridge. The costly but indecisive fighting made the American electorate restless and the Democrats vulnerable to an election upset. In 1952, Dwight D. Eisenhower resigned his position as Supreme Allied Commander, Europe (SACEUR) in order to seek the Republican nomination for the presidential election of November. As the Republican nominee, he won a smashing victory over Adlai Stevenson, the Democratic nominee, in part by promising that if elected, "I will go to Korea." Ridgway replaced Eisenhower as SACEUR, and General Mark W. Clark succeeded Ridgway as CINCUNC and CINCFE. (The position of SCAP was abolished after the 1952 signing of a peace treaty and mutual-defense pact between Japan and the United States.) General Maxwell Taylor replaced Van Fleet in command of the Eighth Army in January, 1953.

Meanwhile, two lines of American nuclear research had reached fruition. In November, 1952, a thermonuclear device set off in the Pacific produced a blast equivalent to that from 10 million (10 megatons or 10 MT) tons of TNT, or five hundred times more powerful than the bomb which leveled Hiroshima. Then in January, 1953, the U.S. Army opened the age of tactical atomic weapons when one of its 280-mm (11.2-inch) cannon test-fired an atomic shell. The shell burst miles away with the force of two thousand tons (2 kilotons or 2KT) of TNT, or about a tenth of the force released by the Hiroshima bomb. Nuclear explosive could also be provided for small bombs and rockets. In the light of these developments, the Joint Chiefs recommended to Eisenhower on March 27 that the ban on nuclear weapons in Korea be reconsidered. Eisenhower rejected the use of tactical atomic weapons in Korea, but they were to play a big role in his defense policy after the Korean War.

One reason for Eisenhower's decision not to employ nuclear weapons in Korea was the death of Stalin on March 5, 1953, and a perceptible change in mood in the Kremlin under the new "collective leadership." In addition, at long last, progress was being made on the stalled prisoner-of-war issue. Eisenhower's patience finally paid off when on July 27 an armistice was signed at Panmunjom. It provided a Demilitarized Zone (DMZ), approximating the location of the battlefront, as the new frontier between North and South Korea. The DMZ zigzagged across the 38th parallel, but in general slightly increased South Korea's territory over that of June, 1950. But the price for this slight change of boundaries had come high. An estimated 1,600,000 Korean civilians and 850,000 Korean soldiers (550,000 NKPA and 300,000 ROK) had been killed, wounded, or were missing. The Chinese may have suffered 900,000 casualties. American casualties came to 147,000 men, 33,000 of them dead. A total of 4,460 Americans taken prisoner were returned, but 2,730 had died in

Communist prisoner-of-war camps. Though twenty-one "brain-washed" American POW's refused repatriation, 50,000 out of 120,000 NKPA troops taken prisoner, and 6,000 out of 20,000 Chinese taken prisoner, did not wish to be returned to their homelands. The U.N. Command charged the Communist side with brutality to POW's, while the Communist side charged the U.N. Command with "germ warfare." (Plagues did sweep Manchuria during the war, but they seem to have been the result of natural phenomena.)

The sixty NKPA-CPV divisions finally concentrated on the Korean battlefront, and the thirty more divisions guarding North Korean coasts from amphibious attack toward the end of the war, may have totaled 1.5 million men. For the most part, they were composed of hardy peasant-infantry armed with automatic small-arms and mortars, but were weak in armor, artillery, and air-support. Though the USSR furnished much of the arms and equipment used by the Chinese and North Koreans during the war, for the most part this aid came in the form of basic weapons. Nearly all the aircraft furnished by the Soviet Union, perhaps four thousand planes, were fighter-interceptors and used mostly to protect Communist supply lines from the front to the Yalu. The air space above the corridor between the Yalu and the Chongchon river about fifty miles further south, became famous as "Mig Alley." There, mostly F-86 Sabrejets tangled with Mig-15s, the Americans downing eight hundred fifty Migs to the loss of only fifty-eight of their own planes between 1951 and 1953. The Mig-15 was an excellent fighter, but Communist pilots were inexperienced and no match for American pilots, some of whom had been "aces" in World War II. Communist ground fire was the main source of U.N. air losses, and the fighter-bomber as a type was the most downed aircraft in the U.N. inventory. The United States lost thirty-five hundred aircraft in Korea to all causes.

The equivalent of about twenty U.N. divisions were at the front toward the end of the Korean War. The best equipped were the eight U.S. divisions and the British Commonwealth Division. Among American novelties was the 75-mm recoilless cannon, the plastic armored vest for torso protection, and the use of small helicopters and the mobile army surgical hospital (MASH) to get wounded men from the front line and into the hands of surgeons quickly. In the first year of the war, the Truman administration relied primarily on regular Army, Army Reserve, and National Guard units (two National Guard divisions were sent to Korea eventually) to form the basis of American mobilization, but toward the end of the war the majority of soldiers in Korea were wartime draftees. The 1951 Universal Military Training and Service Act envisioned the recreation of a *Nation-in-Arms.* A total of six Army divisions, two Guard divisions, and a Marine division (reinforced) served in Korea, and a second Marine division was kept in reserve in Japan.

The American armed forces grew almost exponentially during the

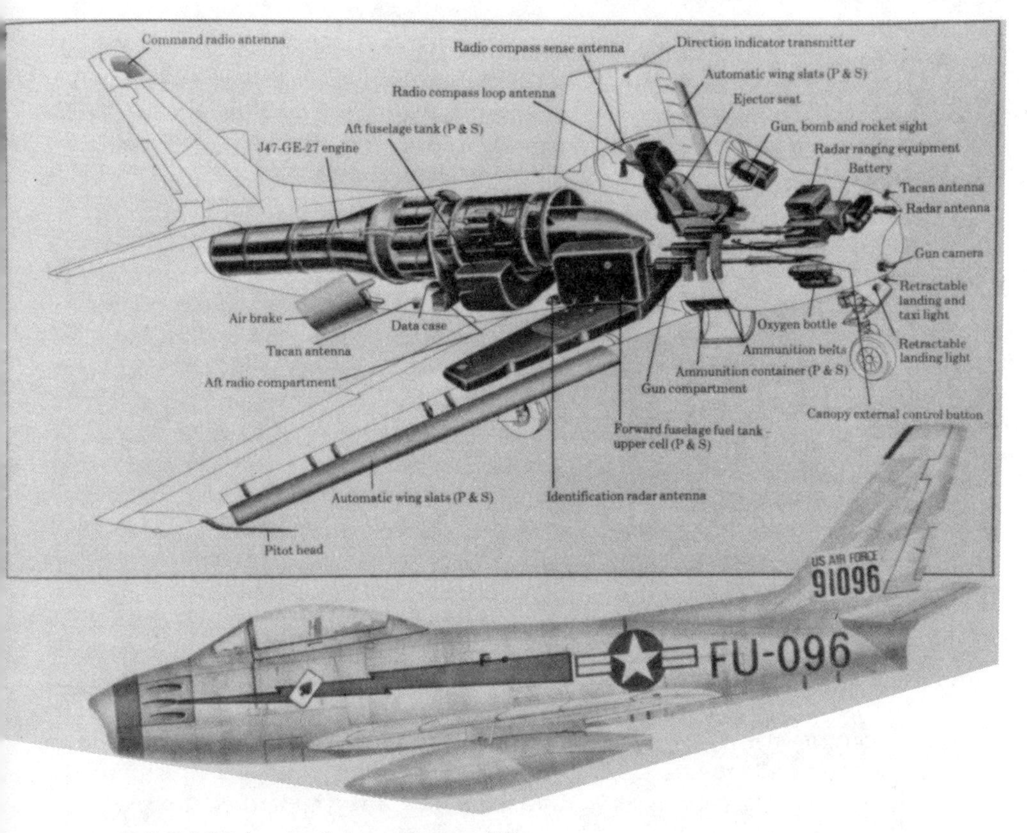

U.S. F-86 Sabre jet fighter, Korean War.

SOURCE: John Batchelor et al., *Air Power: A Modern Illustrated Military History* (New York: Exeter Books, 1979, in association with Phoebus Company/BPC Publishing, London).

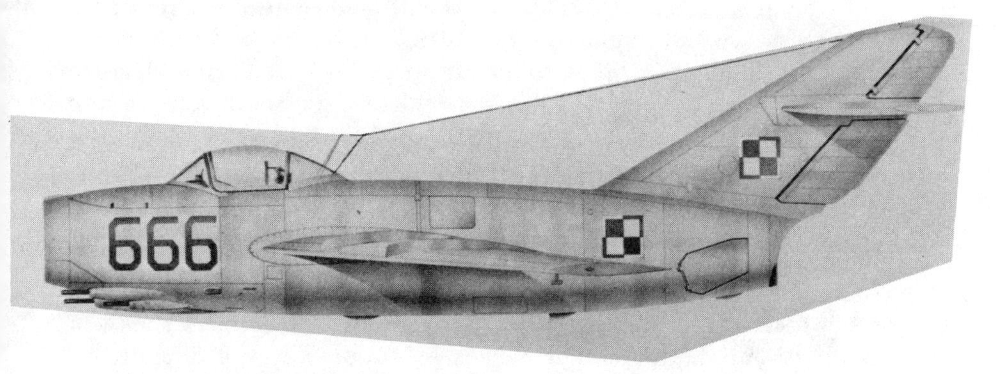

Soviet Mig-15 jet fighter, Korean War.

SOURCE: John Batchelor et al., *Air Power: A Modern Illustrated Military History* (New York: Exeter Books, 1979, in association with Phoebus Company/BPC Publishing, London).

Korean War. The Army increased from 591,000 men and ten understrength divisions to 1,533,000 men and twenty full-strength divisions. The Marine Corps grew from 75,000 men and two understrength divisions to 245,000 men and three full-strength divisions. The Navy increased from 377,000 sailors and 600 warships to 765,000 men and almost 1,200 warships. (Most of the additional warships were recommissioned World War II vessels drawn from the Fleet Reserve, but new construction included the 72,000-ton *Forrestal*, the first of the supercarriers.) The Air Force expanded from 400,000 men and 7,500 planes to 800,000 men and 14,000 planes. The Navy-Marine air forces grew from 4,500 planes to 7,500 planes.

The U.N. effort in Korea involved the contributions of a sizable number of countries. The British Commonwealth Division (which included contingents from Britain, Canada, Australia, New Zealand, and the Union of South Africa) was the largest ground unit offered, aside from the American and South Korean. Turkey sent an infantry brigade. The other countries which sent combat forces were Belgium, Colombia, Ethiopia, France, Greece, the Netherlands, the Philippines, Thailand, and Luxembourg. The typical contribution was a battalion of infantry, though some countries sent planes and ships in addition, and little Luxembourg sent an infantry company. Aside from American and South Korean troops, 44,000 U.N. troops served in Korea, of whom 17,260 were casualties by war's end. At peak strength, the U.N. Command in Korea had 793,000 soldiers, sailors, marines, and airmen, quite the largest force ever to serve under the flag of the United Nations.

III. The Eisenhower Years, 1953–60

In his first year as President of the United States, Eisenhower was preoccupied with bringing the Korean War to an end and with the early stages of demobilization of American forces in Korea (three, later two, Army divisions remained, but a main reliance for South Korea's future security was placed on the 550,000 troops of the ROK Army). Eisenhower first placed his own stamp on American defense policy when, in 1954, Charles Wilson, Eisenhower's first secretary of defense, announced the so-called New Look. In essence, the New Look substituted nuclear firepower for manpower in the American armed forces. By a programmed transition to a heavy reliance on an atomic armory ranging all the way from thermonuclear bombs to the smallest artillery shell which could be fitted with atomic explosive, supposedly the United States would have "more bang for the buck" (in Wilson's words) and could afford to reduce its numbers in uniform. In addition, John Foster Dulles, the new secretary of state announced in early 1954 that the United

States was prepared to "retaliate massively" for local aggression as well as large, implying a readiness to use tactical nuclear weapons against Korean-like attacks. U.S. forces defending Western Europe would also be equipped with tactical nuclear weapons, supposedly to offset superior numbers of Soviet conventional forces.

Over Eisenhower's two terms and eight years in office, the numbers of Americans in uniform declined in every service but the Air Force. By 1960 the U.S. Army had been reduced to 873,000 men and fourteen divisions, and the Pentomic division, with which the Army was experimenting, was hardly capable of fighting in anything but a nuclear environment. The Navy had been reduced to 650,000 men and a thousand combat ships, but more super-carriers had been launched and the USS *Nautilus* (commissioned in 1955) was both the world's first nuclear-powered ship and submarine. The Marine Corps had shrunk to 190,000 men and three understrength divisions. The Air Force, the most favored of the services under the Eisenhower administration, had increased to 975,000 men and 137 wings, 54 of the wings assigned to SAC. During the 1950s, the six jet-engined B-47 Stratojet had replaced the B-29 and B-50 bombers in overseas bases, while the B-52 Stratofortress (powered by eight jet engines) had replaced the B-36 as the nation's intercontinental bomber. Each type of plane was capable of in-flight refueling from tanker aircraft. The B-47 had a maximum speed of 600 mph. with a ten-ton bomb-load. The B-52 could carry a thirty-ton bomb-load as fast as 650 mph. At peak strength in manned aircraft in 1958, SAC boasted no fewer than two thousand B-47 and B-52 aircraft in its inventory.

But Soviet military development did not stand still in the 1950s. In August, 1953, Soviet Russia tested an H-bomb. During the rest of the decade and into the next, the United States and Russia carried out frequent nuclear tests, the largest number by the United States (245) and the largest in size by the Soviet Union. Perhaps a record was set in 1961 when a Soviet nuclear device produced 58 million tons (58 megatons or 58MT) of TNT equivalent in explosive effect. Meanwhile, in 1954, two types of Soviet intercontinental bombers—the Mya-4 Bison and the Tu-95 Bear—went into production. In July, 1955, Eisenhower offered the so-called Open Skies Plan (OSP) at a Summit Conference at Geneva with top Kremlin leaders. The OSP proposed an exchange of strategic information between the United States and Soviet Russia, the exchange to be followed by over-flights of each country in order to verify the data. Nikita S. Khrushchev, First Secretary of the Communist Party, USSR, and the dominant figure in the Kremlin, caused the OSP to be rejected on grounds that it was merely a blind for Western intelligence collecting. In 1956, Eisenhower authorized the beginning of an over-flight program aimed at Russia and using the new U-2 high altitude "spy plane" developed for the CIA. Until May, 1960, when a surface-to-air missile brought down an U-2 near Sverdlovsk, the Soviets were helpless to prevent the flights. Among other things, U-2 cameras revealed that the much-feared "Bomber Gap" favorable to the Soviet Union was nonexistent. No more than about three hundred of the Bison and Bear heavy bombers had been produced, or a bomber fleet about 15 percent as large as the American fleet of long-range bombers.

But for a time in the 1950s there seemed to be more substance for an American fear of a "Missile Gap" in favor of the USSR. After World War II, both the United States and the Soviet Union had pushed the development of long-range missiles, both cruise and ballistic, though the Soviets gave greater attention to the latter. As early as April, 1947, Joseph Stalin chaired the first session of Soviet rocket-scientists on ballistic missiles in order to dramatize the importance he attached to their development. Both the United States and Soviet Russia recruited scientists from the old German V-2 program, Werner von Braun working for the United States, and other leading German scientists for the Russians. By 1955, Soviet research vehicles had delivered test-warheads as far as a thousand miles, and that year the USSR went into mass production of the medium-range ballistic missile (MRBM) SS-3 Shyster. Late in the decade, Russia put into production the SS-4 Sandal, an intermediate-range ballistic missile (IRBM) dangerous to fifteen hundred miles. But by mid-1957, the United States had a counterpart to the Shyster in the Thor and a counterpart to the Sandal in the Jupiter IRBM. Accordingly, American leaders assumed that the Soviet Union was making no more rapid progress toward an intercontinental ballistic missile (ICBM) than the United States. Full-range tests of the American ICBMs Atlas and Titans were not scheduled until almost the end of the 1950s.

American complacency was shaken when in August, 1957, the USSR tested an ICBM—later identified as an SS-6 Sapwood—over a range of five thousand miles with a flight-time of half an hour. In theory, such a weapon could be matched with a thermonuclear warhead to pose an appalling threat both to American cities and to SAC's bombers on the ground. Still another blow was struck against American confidence when in October, 1956, the rocket-engine of the Sapwood was used to loft Sputnik, the earth's first artificial satellite, into orbit and thus open the Space Age. The Eisenhower administration responded to the military implications of these developments with a crash program. The Jupiter IRBMs, as soon as they were ready for deployment, were rushed to NATO bases in Europe where they would be within range of Soviet territory. Many of SAC's bombers were placed on "Airborne Alert," in the air, fully armed and ready to leave for their assigned targets in Russia upon proper signal from the ground. Work was accelerated on the ICBM programs, and in November, 1958, the first full-range test of an Atlas was carried out. For the longer run, research was pressed to replace the liquid-fuel ICBMS with the solid-fuel Minuteman, which could be safeguarded in concrete, underground silos, and with the solid-fuel Polaris IRBM, which could be launched from underwater from a new class of nuclear-powered ballistic missile submarines (SSBNS). The Minuteman had a 1MT warhead, as did the Polaris, but the latter had a range of only twenty-eight hundred miles. Still, from European and Asian waters, the SSNB could threaten many parts of the USSR. The United States planned to build a thousand Minuteman missiles and enough Polaris missiles for forty-one SSBNS, each carrying sixteen missiles. The USS *George Washington,* the first of the SSBNS, would be operational before the end of 1961.

As matters turned out, American fears of a "Missile Gap" even over the short run were as unfounded in fact as the earlier fears of a "Bomber Gap." The SS-6 turned out to be more of a test-bed than a practical ICBM, and the much more reliable SS-7 Saddler and SS-8 Sassin (each with a 5MT warhead and a seven-thousand-mile range) did not appear until the early 1960s. Even then, for several reasons, the accuracy of Soviet missiles was poor and production did not compare with American ICBM production. By October, 1962, the month of the Cuban Missile Crisis, SAC had eighty operational ICBMS to half as many for the USSR, while the Navy had nine SSBNS (with 144 Polaris missiles) to none in the Soviet fleet. Such diesel-powered missile submarines as the USSR possessed could not launch from underwater. Given SAC's edge in bombers, any gap in thermonuclear power was clearly against the USSR.

Eisenhower was less successful in maintaining superiority over the Soviets in tactical nuclear weapons. By the late 1950s, such weapons were appearing among Soviet troops in Eastern Europe in large numbers, while the Soviets continued to maintain their superiority in conventional forces. Critics of the New Look argued that an exchange of tactical weapons would kill millions of civilians on either side of the "Iron Curtain" and might ignite a thermonuclear war between the super-powers as well. John F. Kennedy, the Democratic Party's nominee in the presidential election of 1960, declared that the New Look had left the United States and its allies in Europe with the unpalatable choices of "holocaust or humiliation." When Kennedy took office in January, 1961, he was determined to bring about a fundamental change in many areas of American defense policy, especially in regard to the defense of Europe.

But the defense of Western Europe involved problems beyond the Soviet threat. At the Lisbon Conference of 1952, the NATO Council had approved plans for a West European conventionally armed army of ninety-two divisions (half in reserve), and in the same year welcomed Greece and Turkey to NATO's ranks. But also in 1952, Britain had tested an atomic bomb and then opted to have its own national nuclear-deterrent not controlled by the Supreme Headquarters, Allied Powers in Europe (SHAPE). In 1954, France rejected plans for a highly integrated

West European NATO army (the European Defense Community) in favor of a coalition of sovereign national forces. In 1955, France and other NATO countries laid down as conditions of West Germany's admission to NATO and the right to rearm that West Germany must produce no atomic weapons or secure them from other countries. France, however, went on to develop an atomic bomb by 1960 and, like Britain, to have a national nuclear deterrent force *(force frappe)* not controlled by SHAPE. Meanwhile, the original plan for a West European NATO army of ninety-two divisions had given way to one of twenty-seven divisions and about as many in reserve. Of the twenty-seven, five were American, and only they had any direct access to nuclear weapons. With such a variety of forces and obligations, the difficulty of coming up with a coherent plan for Western European defense becomes apparent.

West Germany's admission to NATO was the occasion for the Soviet organization of the Warsaw Pact the same year. Officially designated as a defensive alliance, the Warsaw Pact pledged a common defense against outside attack among the Soviet Union, East Germany, Poland, Czechoslovakia, Hungary, Romania, Bulgaria, and Albania. (Communist Yugoslavia, which, under Marshal Tito, had broken with Stalin in 1948, stood aloof.) In practice, the Warsaw Pact served Soviet interests more than it promoted the defense of Eastern Europe. A Soviet marshal assumed command of the Warsaw Pact forces, and it was quickly demonstrated that membership in the Pact was hardly voluntary. When a revolution in Hungary in 1956 threw up a Socialist government that wished to sever its ties with the East Bloc, Khrushchev promptly dispatched tanks to Budapest and crushed the new government. Again, in 1968, the other Warsaw Pact armies joined the Soviets in overthrowing the reforming Czech Communist government of Alexander Dubček when it strayed too far from the norm. At that time, Leonid Brezhnev, who had replaced Khrushchev in October, 1964, announced the so-called Brezhnev Doctrine, namely the duty and right of the "Socialist Camp" to discipline any of its members who might err in domestic or foreign policy. Since the other members of the "Socialist Camp" of Eastern Europe could hardly discipline the Soviet Union, in practice the doctrine served Soviet foreign policy.

Cold War problems extended far beyond Europe in the Eisenhower years. The rebellion of the Vietminh against French rule in Indochina reached its climax in the spring of 1954, when the best of Ho Chi Minh's generals—Vo Nguyen Giap—managed to trap sixteen thousand French Union forces in the fortress of Dienbienphu near the Lao border in northern Vietnam. By then the French colonial forces had suffered 150,000 casualties in eight years of fighting, and the French people were tired of the conflict. When the French high command appealed for help to the United States, already paying 80 percent of the costs of the war,

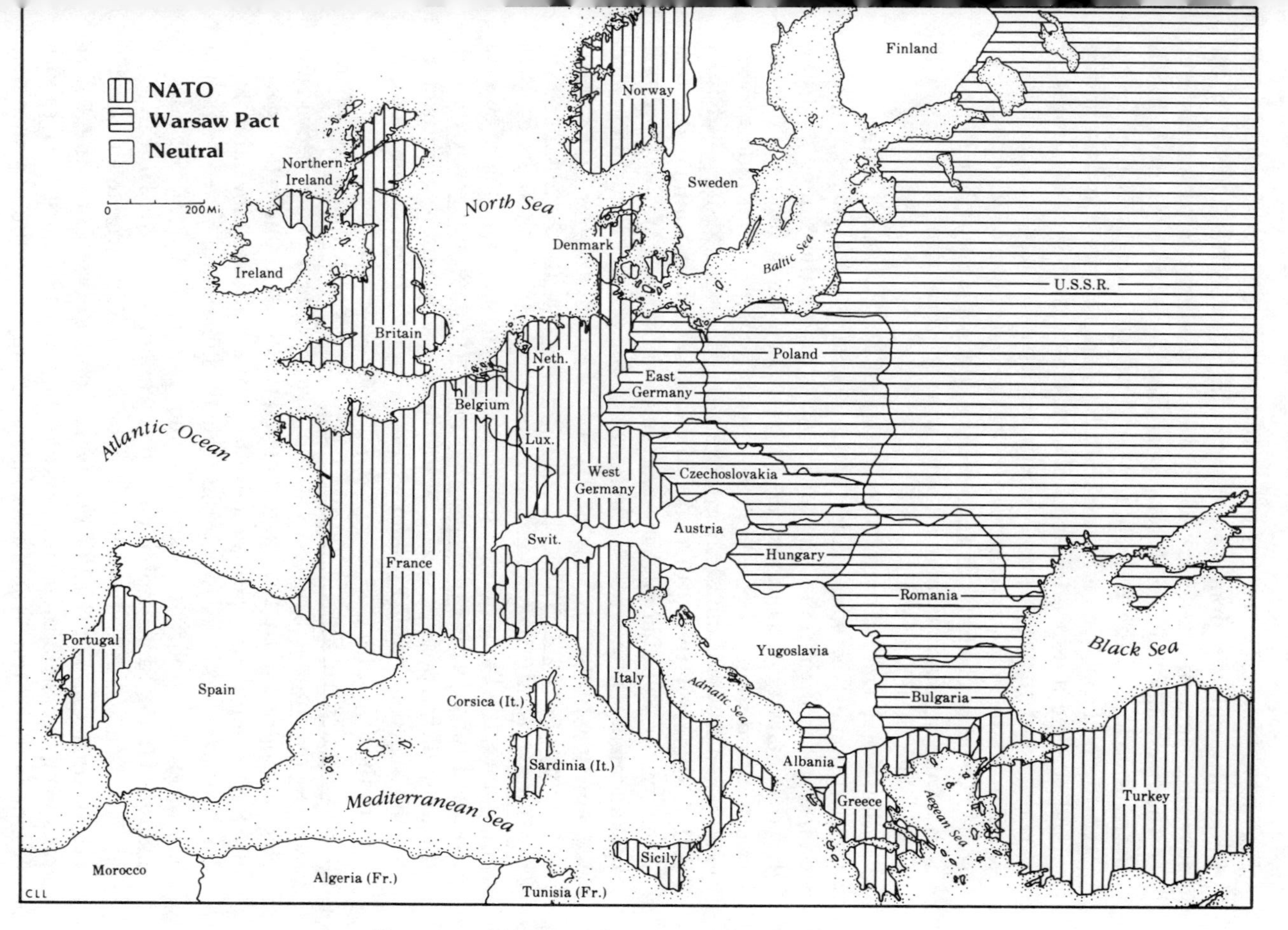

European NATO and Warsaw Pact Countries, 1955

Eisenhower and Dulles briefly considered armed intervention, but found little public support so soon after the Korean War. On May 7, the surviving eight thousand French and French-allied troops surrendered at Dienbienphu, and in July a peace conference at Geneva finally brought a close to the Indochina War. Under the terms of the Geneva Accords, the French would leave Indochina entirely, Laos and Cambodia would become independent and neutral states, and Vietnam would be partitioned at the 17th parallel between Ho's Democratic Republic of Vietnam to the north and the Emperor Bao Dai's State of Vietnam to the south. General elections in 1956 were to determine whether the partition would remain permanent and what government, if any, should finally rule all of Vietnam.

John Foster Dulles, the U.S. Secretary of State, was determined that the partition of Vietnam would remain permanent and that South Vietnam would remain non-Communist. Accordingly, the United States offered military and economic aid to Ngo Dien Diem, Bao Dai's prime minister, and soon to become President of the Republic of (South) Vietnam when it was established in 1955. An American Military Advisory and Assistance Group, Vietnam (MAAGV), set about training the new Army of the Republic of Vietnam (ARVN), and, with Washington's encouragement, Diem ignored the mandate for general Vietnamese elections in 1956 under the Geneva Accords. The Demilitarized Zone (DMZ) at the 17th parallel became a permanent political frontier between the two Vietnams. Meanwhile, in September, 1954, the United States, Britain, France, the Philippines, Thailand, Pakistan, Australia, and New Zealand had formed the Southeast Asia Treaty Organization (SEATO), with the avowed purpose of discouraging further Communist expansion in Southeast Asia. Under President Diem, South Vietnam became a signatory to the SEATO Pact.

In 1957 guerrilla warfare broke out in rural South Vietnam aimed at Diem's government, and ARVN and internal security police proved unable to suppress it. By 1960 an estimated twenty thousand rebels were in the field when their leaders met to form the National Liberation Front (NLF) and to entitle its forces the People's Liberation Army (PLA). The NLF received support and encouragement from Ho Chi Minh's government in Hanoi, some supplies and men coming down the Ho Chi Minh Trail through Laos and eastern Cambodia. Diem referred to all supporters of the NLF as *Viet Cong* (Vietnamese Communists). Later, the Americans would refer to them as the VC. In January, 1961, just after John F. Kennedy took office, Diem made a special appeal to the new president for aid against the rising insurgency. Kennedy's response to that appeal would set the United States on the road to its most unfortunate foreign military involvement since the founding of the American republic.

French colonial troubles did not end with the withdrawal from Indochina. In September, 1954, revolt against French rule broke out in Algeria and soon spread to neighboring Morocco and Tunisia. By 1956, France had abandoned Morocco and Tunisia, but Algeria was its oldest North African territory and technically a part of metropolitan France. The French colonial army and the *colons* threatened to revolt against any government in Paris that proposed peace negotiations with the Algerian rebels. Despite the commitment of four hundred thousand troops to Algeria, however, the war reached a crisis point in May, 1958, when the Fourth Republic abdicated its powers to General Charles de Gaulle. As President of the Fifth Republic, de Gaulle surprised the world by exercising a firm hand over the colonial army, gradually bringing its terrorist Secret Army Organization (OAS) under control, and finally negotiating Algerian independence in 1962. French military-civilian casualties in the war came to one hundred thousand, and perhaps twice as many Algerians were killed and wounded.

Still, the greatest crisis faced by the Eisenhower administration came in 1956 as the outcome of the Suez Crisis of that year. In 1952, a military coup toppled the monarchy of King Farouk in Egypt and brought to power a militant Egyptian republic soon led by Colonel Gamal Abdel Nasser. Nasser dreamed of uniting the Arab peoples against Israel, and tried to strengthen Egypt militarily by importing Soviet arms. The Suez Crisis began in July, 1956, when Nasser nationalized the Suez Canal and provoked the governments of Britain and France. As they began secret preparations for war, they found a natural ally in Israel, long barred from using the Canal and often plagued by the raids of Egyptian *fedayeen* from the Sinai desert. The Second Arab-Israeli War erupted on October 29, when the Israeli Defense Forces (IDF) struck without warning into the Sinai, routed Nasser's forces there, and then advanced toward the Suez Canal. Anglo-French planes then raided Egyptian bases in the Nile valley, and an Anglo-French expeditionary force began moving across the Mediterranean for a landing at the northern end of the Canal. With Egypt on the brink of total military defeat, Khrushchev threatened Soviet military intervention, even to the point of raining down Soviet rockets on London and Paris.

In order to defuse a situation that might have led to world war, the Eisenhower administration moved in the United Nations for a resolution calling for a ceasefire and the withdrawal of all foreign troops from Egyptian soil. Without American support, Britain and France could not face down Russia, and Israel could not carry on without at least tacit support from the West. In early November, the Anglo-French invasion was halted and Israeli forces began their withdrawal from the Sinai. U.N. peacekeeping forces temporarily occupied the Suez Canal and served as observers in the Sinai desert. The crippled Canal was placed back into operation in April, 1957, and the 1956 war seemed only to heighten

Nasser's popularity among Arabs and to increase Soviet influence in the Middle East. The outbreak of civil war between Christians and Moslems in Lebanon was only narrowly averted when Eisenhower sent U.S. Marines into the country briefly in 1958. By the time Eisenhower left office in January, 1961, the Middle East was still another problem-area without ready solutions.

The final problem of the Eisenhower years came close to home when on January 1, 1959, a long civil war in Cuba ended with the overthrow of the right-wing military dictatorship of General Fulgencio Batista and its replacement with a revolutionary government under Fidel Castro. Within a few months, thousands of Cubans had fled to Florida, and Castro was moving toward a Communist philosophy. After he appropriated American private property on the island (but left the American base at Guantanamo undisturbed), the Eisenhower administration was placed under great pressure to take action against the Castro regime. Eisenhower approved a CIA plan to train a Cuban exile brigade in Guatemala (where an American-inspired coup had overthrown a left-learning government in 1954), but he left to his successor the decision as to how and when to use the force. John F. Kennedy had pledged to take action in his 1960 campaign for the presidency, and the Cuban problem, like so many others, fell to his lot.

IV. The Vietnam War Era, 1961–73

After the Kennedy administration took office in January, 1961, Robert S. McNamara, the new secretary of defense, announced a new defense policy called Flexible Response. On the strategic level, the policy called for a Counter-Force doctrine which would direct American strategic nuclear weapons selectively against Soviet military targets, including airfields and missile-launching sites, as long as Soviet attacks spared American cities. The primary weapons of Counter-Force were to be the land-based ICBM Minuteman and the submarine-launched ballistic missile (SLBM) Polaris. McNamara foresaw no need for strategic bombers in the new policy over the long haul, hence he cancelled plans for the development of a B-70 bomber to replace the B-52.

After Kennedy's death in 1963 and Lyndon B. Johnson's accession to the presidency, another change in American strategic doctrine took place. By the late 1960s, the Polaris was proving to lack the precise accuracy needed to strike hardened Soviet missile sites, and the earlier American confidence that strategic nuclear war could be both controlled and limited was fading. By the time McNamara left office at the end of February, 1968, a new doctrine of Mutual Assured Destruction (MAD) had replaced Counter-Force. The MAD doctrine presupposed that the

U.S. Air Force B-52 bomber.
SOURCE: Ray Bonds, ed., *The U.S. War Machine: An Illustrated History of American Military Equipment and Strategy* (New York: Crown Publishers, 1978).

only value in American strategic nuclear weapons lay in their ability to deter a direct Soviet nuclear attack on the United States. It further presupposed that such an attack would never be considered by the Kremlin if it believed that no possible "first-strike" could destroy enough of the American strategic systems that a devastating American counter-strike could not be mounted. Thus, MAD implied that a finite number of strategic-weapons systems, suitably protected from a "first strike," would be sufficient and that any additional systems would be as unnecessary as they were costly. Since the USSR faced the same situation in regard to strategic nuclear weapons, it followed that the Soviet-American strategic arms-race was reaching the point of diminishing returns. In that case, the security interests of both countries would be best served by a bilateral agreement to cap the strategic arms-race. The MAD doctrine and its assumptions led directly to the American interest in strategic arms limitation talks near the end of the decade.

The Johnson administration completed the deployment of the strategic forces developed under the Eisenhower and Kennedy administrations. In 1968, the last of 41 Polaris-launching submarines was commissioned, bringing the total of sea-based Polaris missiles to 656. As many as 416 of the Polaris missiles could be at sea at all times. The Poseidon, which eventually replaced the Polaris, was the first sea-based missile-launcher equipped with multiple, independently targetable reentry vehicles (MIRVs), in effect "smart" warheads which separated in space to seek out widely separated targets. Each Poseidon could carry as many as fourteen MIRVs, each MIRV with an explosive force of 40KT. The Minuteman III was equipped with three MIRVs, each with a force of 170–350 KT. A total of five hundred fifty in the thousand-missile Minuteman force were Mark IIIs. In addition, the single-warhead Titan II, the last of the American liquid-fuel ballistic missiles, numbered fifty-four missiles and each carried a warhead of 9MT. In 1965, the last of the B-47 bombers was retired, and that year for the first time SAC's ICBMS outnumbered its bombers, but 650 B-52s remained in service. When Lyndon Johnson left office in January, 1969, the so-called Triad of American strategic forces—land-based ICBMS, SLBMS, and the remaining B-52 bombers—could deliver a total of forty-five hundred nuclear bombs and warheads with a combined explosive force of 5,100MT. In other words, the American strategic firepower was equal to perhaps millions of Hiroshima-sized atomic bombs. Such had been the development of American nuclear strategic forces in less than twenty-five years.

At the end of Johnson's term in office, the USSR was still lagging behind the United States in strategic nuclear forces. It possessed eight hundred fifty ICBMS, all liquid-fuel. The most powerful types were the SS-9 Scarp and the SS-11 Sego, introduced in 1965 and 1966 respectively. Thanks to enormous rocket-engines, each type could hurl a 25MT warhead, a reflection of the Soviet advantage in "throw-weight" as compared with American ICBMS, but also a compensation for the poorer accuracy of the Soviet missiles as compared with the American. The Soviet Union was still further behind the United States at sea, where by 1969 the Soviet navy had only a handful of nuclear-powered, ballistic-missile submarines. They mounted in total only forty SLBMS of a design inferior to either the American Polaris or the Poseidon. (The first test of a Soviet MIRVed ballistic-missile launcher—a land-based weapon—did not occur until December, 1974.) Only 155 of the old Soviet Bison-Bear bombers were still in service. The Soviet strategic forces, heavily weighted in favor of land-based ICBMS, were estimated to have 1,100 nuclear bombs and warheads with a combined nuclear explosive force of 2,300 MT. On the other hand, there was no indication that the Soviets intended to let up in their deployment of new systems unless some kind of agreement was reached with the United States.

The doctrine of Flexible Response also affected American preparations to meet local and regional aggression. John Kennedy had been impressed by the arguments presented in B. H. Liddell Hart's book *Deterrent or Defense* (1960). In that work, the British defense expert held that a suitably armed but relatively modest conventional force for the defense of Western Europe made more sense than a force armed with

U.S. Minuteman ICBM in its silo.

SOURCE: Ray Bonds, ed., *The U.S. War Machine: An Illustrated History of American Military Equipment and Strategy* (New York: Crown Publishers, 1978).

nuclear weapons that might destroy Western Europe in the process of defending it. Liddell Hart did not favor abandoning all tactical nuclear weapons, but he believed that they should be the last line, not the first line, of Western European defense. Their real value lay in deterring Warsaw Pact forces from resorting to their tactical nuclear weapons. In line with such thinking, Kennedy supported an expansion of American conventional ground forces. By the time of his death, the strength of the U.S. Army had reached 975,000 men and sixteen full-strength divisions, about a third of the divisions serving in the U.S. Seventh Army in West Germany, and backed by a sizable Army Reserve and National Guard.

But the U.S. Army changed in more ways than just size. It discontinued experiments with the Pentomic division in favor of a flexible organization for conventional warfare called ROAD (Reorganization Objectives, Army Division). The so-called ROAD division was "sculpted" to perform a variety of missions, according to circumstances, by assigning to its three brigades any combination of specialized battalions (originally, the types of battalions available were motorized, mechanized, armored, or airborne). In addition, the Army pioneered the Airmobile Division, one that could move tactically entirely by helicopter, and it also developed Special Forces (Green Berets) which, as the American involvement in the Vietnam War deepened, concentrated on the techniques of counterinsurgency. Of all the armed forces in the 1960s, the Army most perfectly conformed to the doctrine of Flexible Response, with its emphasis on nonnuclear action.

During his 1960 campaign for the presidency, Kennedy had pledged to take positive action against Castro's government in Cuba; and in April, 1961, the Cuban exile brigade trained by the CIA in Guatemala was landed on Cuba's western shore at the Bahía de Cochinos (Bay of Pigs). But no Cuban insurrection against Castro's government followed the landing, and Castro's militia effectively counterattacked to defeat the brigade. The Bay of Pigs fiasco diminished the prestige of the Kennedy administration. Then in August, 1961, the government of the German Democratic Republic solved the problem of skilled East German labor escaping to the West through West Berlin by erecting the Berlin Wall. Though Kennedy denounced the action by the GDR, it was obvious that his government could really do nothing about it except pledge never to abandon West Berlin.

But Kennedy's most serious challenge came in the fall of 1962 when U-2 spy planes revealed that launching sites for Soviet SS-4 and SS-5 missiles were being prepared in Castro Cuba. Once the missiles were installed, they would have been within range of two-thirds of the continental United States and would have about doubled the megatonnage that the Soviet strategic forces could have launched against the United States in a nuclear war. By the time Kennedy resolved to take action in mid-October, forty SS-4s were on the island (although not yet operational). Kennedy imposed a "quarantine" on Cuba and established a line in the Atlantic which Soviet missile-bearing ships crossed at their peril. He then pressed Moscow to order removal of the missiles in Cuba, the destruction of their launching sites, and also the removal of Soviet-made Il-28 jet bombers in Cuba. After two tension-filled weeks in which the world seemed on the edge of nuclear war, the Khrushchev government agreed on October 28 to withdraw both the missiles and the bombers in return for an American pledge never again to threaten Communist Cuba. Thus passed the greatest threat to world peace since the 1956 Suez Crisis.

The Cuban Missile Crisis turned out to be a watershed in Soviet-American rivalry. The near-brush with nuclear war sobered both Washington and Moscow, and made them more prone to seek accommodation in some areas. In 1963, the so-called Washington-Moscow Hot Line was established, a direct teletype link for better "crisis management" in future. Also in 1963, the United States, the Soviet Union, and Great Britain signed a Partial Nuclear Test-Ban Treaty which obligated them not to conduct atomic explosions in the atmosphere or underwater. (France and the People's Republic of China, a nuclear power after 1963, refused to cosign the document.) In addition, as a product of a "gentlemen's agreement" between the USSR and the United States, the United States withdrew its Jupiter missiles from Western Europe.

Besides the Russians, Kennedy and then Johnson had trouble with America's Western European NATO allies. Given the fact that Britain and France had independent nuclear-deterrent forces, and the only nuclear weapons pledged to NATO control were American, some NATO states urged the creation of some means for a more equal control of nuclear weapons within NATO. The problem was made more complicated by the prohibition on West Germany's possessing, as well as making, nuclear weapons. Kennedy's solution was the so-called Multi-Lateral Force (MLF), one version of which was U.S.-supplied IRBMS manned by mixed NATO crews and answerable only to the NATO Council. But command and control problems hampered implementation of the MLF in any form, and neither France nor Britain showed any inclination to participate. After Johnson succeeded Kennedy, he continued to offer the solution until 1967, when Soviet Russia pointed out that an MLF would complicate any strategic arms limitation talks. The idea became wholly irrelevant in 1968, when the Nuclear Non-Proliferation Treaty committed all members of NATO and the Warsaw Pact not already nuclear-armed to forego both the manufacture and the possession of nuclear weapons. Meanwhile, in 1966, de Gaulle had withdrawn French forces from the NATO force-structure, and required the removal of the NATO political and military headquarters from France to Belgium. (France continued to pledge to come to the defense of Western Europe if it were threatened.) In 1968, the NATO Council approved negotiations with the Warsaw Pact for mutual and balanced force reductions, though nothing came of the idea until the 1970s.

But the most fateful events for the United States in the 1960s took place far away from Europe. The twelve-year American involvement in Vietnam began in the month that Kennedy took office and agreed to send President Diem of South Vietnam more military aid to combat the rising strength of the VC insurgency. In February, 1962, the U.S. Military Assistance and Advisory Group, Vietnam (MAAGV), which had existed since 1954, was converted to the Military Assistance Command, Vietnam

(MACV). Over its eleven-year history, MACV was variously commanded by generals Paul Harkins (1962–1964), William Westmoreland (1964–1968), Creighton Abrams (1968–1972), and Fred Weyand (1972–1973). Fewer than a thousand officers and men served at a time in the old MAAGV, but the growth of MACV was to be prodigious.

By 1963, MACV had 11,300 advisory and technical personnel in South Vietnam, but the war was going no better against the VC. The Army of the Republic of Vietnam (ARVN), created on the model of the U.S. Army, was well armed by Asian standards, but its methods seemed ineffectual against the enemy it faced. Still worse, Diem's policies had alienated many non-Communists in South Vietnam, including the powerful Buddhist hierarchy and officers in South Vietnam's Joint General Staff. On November 1, 1963, a military coup in Saigon overturned Diem's government and led to his execution out-of-hand a few hours later. President Kennedy had scarcely begun to deal with the military junta which replaced Diem's government when he too fell victim to an assassin's bullets on November 22. The problem of Vietnam passed on to Lyndon Johnson.

Johnson believed that Ho Chi Minh's government in Hanoi controlled the insurgency in South Vietnam, and he sought means with which to strike at it directly. In 1964, he sanctioned a covert war against North Vietnam under the Pentagon's Operations Plan 34A. The covert war, run by the CIA, mostly amounted to American assistance to South Vietnamese raids into North Vietnam, acts of sabotage north of the 17th parallel, and secret operations against the Ho Chi Minh Trail in Laos. But Johnson also moved U.S. naval forces into the Gulf of Tonkin and near North Vietnamese coasts. After clashes between North Vietnamese patrol-torpedo (PT) boats and two American destroyers in the Gulf on August 2 and 4, 1964, Johnson ordered nearby aircraft carriers to launch a retaliatory raid on the PT-boat base at Vinh on August 5, the first American overt act of war against North Vietnam. At the President's request, on August 7 Congress passed the so-called Gulf of Tonkin Resolution, one that empowered the President to take whatever military measures he saw fit in order to protect American servicemen in Southeast Asia and to protect South Vietnam. Though few congressmen realized it at the time, they had in effect declared a state of war with North Vietnam. Even fewer knew of the covert war Johnson had waged in 1964, or that South Vietnamese coastal raids preceded the attacks on the American destroyers nearby.

In November, 1964, Johnson handily defeated Republican challenger Barry Goldwater for the presidency, and, with another four years in office assured, he stepped up the war against North Vietnam. Using the machinery of the Southeast Asia Treaty Organization (SEATO), Johnson shifted squadrons of fighter-bombers to bases in Thailand and increased

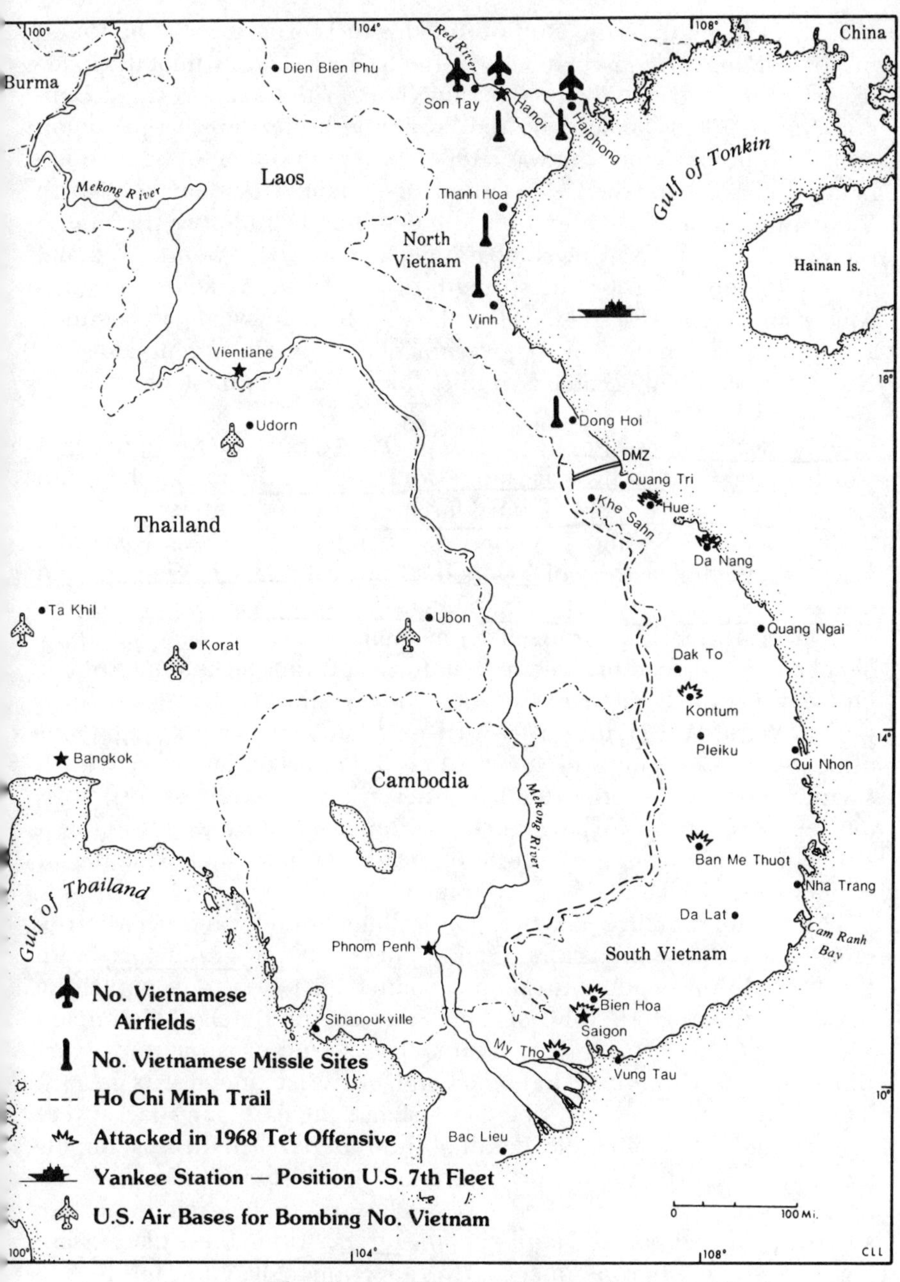

The Vietnam War: Southeast Asia

U.S. naval strength in the Gulf of Tonkin. In February, 1965, he found his formal *casus belli* in VC attacks on the barracks of U.S. military advisory personnel at both Pleiku and Qui Nhon. With the approval of General Nguyen Van Thieu, who took over the leadership of the Saigon junta in February (and who was later elected as President of South Vietnam), Johnson launched a program of sustained bombing of North Vietnam on March 2 (Operation Rolling Thunder). Before the month was out, Army and Marine combat units had arrived in South Vietnam, and by the end of 1965 the strength of MACV had swelled to 185,000 American troops, with still more on the way. By then, what had begun as a civil war between the Saigon government and local insurgents aided by North Vietnam had become a conflict chiefly between the United States and North Vietnam.

Operation Rolling Thunder had as its avowed purpose the injuring of North Vietnam so badly that Hanoi would call off the war in the south rather than endure more. From March 2, 1965, to October 31, 1968, when Operation Rolling Thunder was abandoned, U.S. Air Force and Navy planes flew a total of 350,000 sorties over North Vietnam and delivered 3 million tons of ordnance against North Vietnamese targets. The targets themselves ranged from military training camps, supply depots, rail and road bridges, and all forms of transportation, to public utilities and North Vietnam's small factory system. Over a similar timespan in World War II, the Army Air Forces had dropped 1,554,463 tons of bombs on Germany and 502,781 tons of bombs on Japan. Yet North Vietnam, a nation of only 16 million, never lost its morale or the means to keep its economy working. Such phenomenal endurance raises interesting questions about the patterns of the air war in Vietnam, and the air weapons with which that war was waged.

The eventual failure of Operation Rolling Thunder has been attributed to a number of factors. One of these was the gradualness with which the Johnson administration permitted air power to be applied to North Vietnam. Both Johnson and Secretary of Defense McNamara apparently thought of Rolling Thunder as a kind of aerial tourniquet which should be gradually tightened on North Vietnam until its government gave in to American demands. Hence the early air attacks were restricted to the "panhandle" south of the 19th parallel, the least important part of North Vietnam economically. Even after attacks were extended as far north as the Red River Delta, and to the capital at Hanoi and the principal port of Haiphong, the targets within these places were highly restricted. In consequence, Ho's government had time in which to prepare its people physically and psychologically for their ordeal from the air, and to import much economic and military aid from both China and the USSR. The Johnson air strategy conflicted with the lesson of past experience that air power is most effective when applied with great intensity over the shortest possible time, and against the greatest weaknesses in the enemy's socioeconomic system. Ultimately, the Johnson strategy of attrition—of wearing down Hanoi's will and material resources—proved a two-edged sword.

Another weakness of Operation Rolling Thunder was the F-105 Thunderchief, the Air Force plane which carried out most of the land-based air missions over North Vietnam. The F-105, an aircraft developed during the Eisenhower era with its penchant for tactical nuclear weapons, was never intended to fly at very low altitudes or to be repeatedly exposed to conventional antiaircraft fire. Accordingly, it was not provided with armor protection for the pilot or vital parts, nor with redundant hydraulic systems or self-sealing fuel tanks. When the F-105 squadrons based in Thailand were required to make repeated low-level raids in the Red River Delta against a formidable array of antiaircraft weapons, their losses were sometimes appalling. By 1968 no fewer than eight thousand antiaircraft guns ranging from 20-mm to 100-mm in caliber (the larger ones radar-controlled and with proximity-fused shells) made North Vietnamese skies the most flak-filled since World War II. In addition, batteries of Soviet-supplied, SA-2 Guideline surface-to-air missiles were such a threat to high-flying aircraft that the United States did not risk B-52 raids very far into North Vietnam until nearly the end of the war. Of the total of 915 U.S. aircraft shot down over North Vietnam to October 31, 1968, antiaircraft guns accounted for 750, surface-to-air missiles (SAMS) for 117, and Soviet-made Mig-17 and Mig-23 fighters for 48. Another 1,400 American aircraft were damaged over North Vietnam in this period. There were few air-to-air combats over North Vietnam, but American fighters (mostly F-4 Phantoms) destroyed 111 Migs. In the off-again-on-again American air attacks on North Vietnam between 1969 and 1973, an additional 475 planes were lost.

The Americans assumed primary responsibility for the ground war in South Vietnam about the time that numerous regiments of the North Vietnamese Army (NVA) began coming down the Ho Chi Minh Trail. In the fall of 1965, MACV forces thwarted an NVA effort to cut South Vietnam in half across its narrow waist between the western highlands and the coastal city of Hue. By 1966, both NVA and PLA forces had returned to guerrilla operations. General Westmoreland switched MACV tactics to "Search and Destroy," in order to uncover enemy bases and to drive enemy forces back on Laos and Cambodia. But a quick victory over an enemy practiced in the arts of "protracted warfare" was impossible, and the war dragged on through 1967 as the strength of MACV mounted toward 480,000 troops. Meanwhile, the helicopter—both as a troop-carrier and as a "gun-ship"—proved invaluable against a fast-moving and elusive enemy.

While American numbers grew in Vietnam, so did the casualties. Between January, 1961, and March, 1965, only 400 American servicemen had lost their lives serving in Southeast Asia. The toll had risen to about 30,000 by March, 1968. By the time Johnson left office in January, 1969, the total of dead had reached 40,000 and the total of wounded had grown to 250,000 men. The fact that NVA-PLA casualties were far higher than the American and South Vietnamese was cold comfort to the American public, many of whom found measuring progress in the war in terms of "body count" repulsive. Matters were made worse by Johnson's decision not to carry out a general mobilization of the Reserve and the National Guard, but to rely on a stepped-up draft in order to provide extra manpower for the war. Thousands of young men found themselves drafted to fight in a war the purpose of which they hardly understood when thousands of citizen-soldiers were allowed to remain home. By the late 1960s, opposition to the draft had combined with opposition to the war in general. In order to escape conscription, many young men fled to Canada, some overseas, and some simply became fugitives in their own country. By 1973, there were 570,000 apparent draft offenders. Of those men who did enter uniform, 563,000 were discharged under less-than-honorable conditions, about a third of them among the 2,100,000 individuals who served in Vietnam at one time or another between 1961 and 1973.

The final blow to Johnson's war policy came early in 1968, when attention was focused on an attempted Communist siege of five thousand U.S. Marines in a fire-base (fortified artillery camp) near Khe Sanh in far northern South Vietnam. On January 30, and coinciding with the beginning of Tet or the Vietnamese lunar New Year holiday, the VC launched a massive offensive throughout South Vietnam. The offensive eventually affected 36 out of 44 provincial capitals, 5 out of 6 autonomous cities, 64 out of 242 district capitals, and 50 of the so-called strategic hamlets or new-life villages of the South Vietnamese rural pacification program. By the time the fighting associated with Tet began to subside in late March, Westmoreland estimated that 50,000 of the VC had been killed, while 15,000 ARVN and fewer than 5,000 MACV personnel had been killed or injured. But the Communist losses may have paid for themselves in the tremendous psychological effect that the offensive had on the American public, already war-weary and doubtful about the wisdom of the intervention in Vietnam to begin with. Such a wave of hostility to the war swept over the United States that, on March 31, Johnson went on national television to announce that his administration was prepared to discuss an armistice with North Vietnam, that it was suspending air attacks on North Vietnam above the 20th parallel as a token of its earnestness, and that Johnson himself would not be a candidate for reelection in the fall of 1968. Effectively, the American aim of total victory in Vietnam had been abandoned.

Peace talks between the United States and North Vietnam opened in

May, 1968, but neither the NLF, which in 1969 had restyled itself as the Provisional Revolutionary Government (PRG), nor the Saigon government sent separate delegations to the peace talks until 1971. Ultimately, the Vietnamese peace negotiations lasted more than twice as long as those that ended the Korean War. Nor were they much affected by Ho Chi Minh's death in September, 1969. Premier Pham Van Dong adhered to his policies. Meanwhile, a Republican administration under Richard Nixon entered the White House with the slogan "Peace with Honor." Melvin Laird, the new secretary of defense, called the Nixon strategy "Vietnamization," or the programmed expansion and strengthening of ARVN while American combat forces were gradually withdrawn from South Vietnam. Before "Vietnamization" went into effect, the American build-up in South Vietnam reached its peak in March, 1969, with 543,000 men, eight Army divisions, and two Marine divisions. While the four-year withdrawal was underway, another 20,000 Americans died and 115,000 were wounded.

Congress increasingly limited the President's latitude in waging the war after 1969, partly out of fear that Nixon was getting the United States even deeper into the Southeast Asian "quagmire." In March, 1970, General Lon Nol led a military coup which toppled the "neutralist" government of Norodom Sihanouk in Cambodia. Lon Nol's government then gave tacit approval to ARVN and MACV forces crossing the eastern borders of Cambodia in order to seek out VC-NVA bases. But the "Cambodian Incursion" that began in April sparked angry protests on American college campuses, and on May 4 National Guardsmen fired on protestors in Ohio ("the Kent State Massacre"). Public reaction was so hostile to both the "Incursion" and the Kent State incident that Nixon announced that the American participation in the Cambodian invasion would be ended on July 1. But Lon Nol's coup had provoked civil war with Pol Pot's *Khmer Rouge,* the Cambodian Communist movement; and, in order to render Lon Nol's government assistance, Nixon approved secret air strikes into both Cambodia and Laos in violation of Congressional strictures which limited American military action to Vietnam. Another ill omen for the future was an ARVN offensive into Laos in early 1971, an effort to cut the Ho Chi Minh Trail that ended disastrously for the South Vietnamese and threw doubt on the effects of the "Vietnamization" program.

In June, 1971, Daniel Ellsberg, a former official in the Defense Department who had become disillusioned with the war, "leaked" to the *New York Times* a classified Pentagon history of American involvement in Vietnam to the end of Lyndon Johnson's administration. When the so-called Pentagon Papers were published, for the first time the public and most members of Congress learned how Johnson had manipulated American intervention in 1964–1965. Nixon, worried that "leaks" about his illegal bombings in Laos and Cambodia might reach the public, ordered the creation of a White House Special Investigations Unit (nicknamed the "Plumbers") to prevent embarrassing revelations from his staff. The "Plumbers" went on from their original assignment to a forced entry of the office of Ellsberg's psychiatrist and finally to the famous break-in of the Democratic Party's headquarters in the Watergate Office Complex in June, 1972. The apprehension of the intruders would eventually lead to the Watergate Scandal and Nixon's resignation in August, 1974, though by that time the war in Vietnam was over for the Americans.

At Nixon's behest, in 1970 Congress had overhauled the Selective Service System in order to make it more equitable and to reduce it as a factor in antiwar agitation. The revised draft system reduced the period of vulnerability from age eighteen-to-twenty-six to just one year, and then men were selected by lottery instead of according to the whims of local draft boards. Those who passed safely through the year of vulnerability could go about their lives with no further fears of compulsory military service. The new system was tolerated by the majority of young male Americans, but the Vietnam War had struck a fatal blow to the principle of compulsory military service in the United States. As the war was ending, the draft law expired, and there was no effort by the President or the Congress to revive peacetime conscription. Military service in the United States remains voluntary to this writing.

At the beginning of 1972, only seventy thousand American troops remained in South Vietnam, and Nixon's goal was to get them all out by the time of the November presidential elections. But in March, an NVA invasion of South Vietnam across the DMZ at the 17th parallel brought on a new crisis. The attack by fourteen NVA divisions sent the ARVN forces reeling back. Nixon pulled out all stops in an air offensive against North Vietnam in order to hamstring the NVA drive, including the aerial mining of North Vietnamese coasts. Though the Communist drive occupied most of Quang Tri province, it was finally contained in July. Attention then shifted to the Paris peace negotiations, where Henry Kissinger, Special Assistant to the President for National Security Affairs, was orchestrating proposals on the American side. In late October, Kissinger announced, "Peace is at hand." In early November, Nixon won a landslide victory over his Democratic challenger George McGovern, but soon after, the peace talks collapsed. In December, Nixon ordered a ten-day bombing campaign by B-52s against Hanoi and Haiphong, one that reportedly killed or injured five thousand people (1,300 dead), and cost the United States fifteen of its B-52 bombers, plus eleven other aircraft. Premier Pham Van Dong then agreed to resume negotiations in January if the attacks were stopped. Finally, on January 23, 1973, the Paris Peace

Accords were signed, effectively bringing to an end the longest war in American history.

The Paris Peace Accords provided for the complete withdrawal of American armed forces from South Vietnam, the return of all Americans held as prisoners-of-war, and a prohibition on reinforcements for the 150,000 NVA troops in South Vietnam. Under a general armistice, a Council of National Reconciliation was to work out the final fate of South Vietnam by peaceful means. Between January 23 and March 29, when the last American troops left South Vietnam, a total of 595 Americans held as prisoners-of-war were returned to American custody, most of them airmen who had been shot down over the north. The fate of approximately 2,500 other Americans officially listed as missing-in-action (MIA) remains unknown to this writing. In addition, the war had cost the United States almost 60,000 dead and over 300,000 wounded. Material losses included 3,700 fixed-wing aircraft and over 4,000 helicopters. Enormous quantities of arms and equipment had been used up on the ground. The direct costs of the war to the United States in 1973 dollars has been placed at $109 billion. Nor had the United States received much support from its SEATO allies during the war. Token forces were sent by Australia, New Zealand, the Philippines, and Thailand; but the only really significant "Third Country" contribution were two army divisions from South Korea.

Worst of all, the American sacrifices were in vain. The peace in South Vietnam soon collapsed, and the Communist offensives in Laos, Cambodia, and South Vietnam, in the spring of 1975, rolled forward to victory. In the wake of Saigon's surrender on April 30, the name of the city was changed to Ho Chi Minh City, the final American humiliation in a long and unhappy ordeal.

Even as the Vietnam War was entering its final throes in 1972, relations between the United States, on the one hand, and Soviet Russia and the People's Republic of China, on the other, underwent the most drastic change since World War II. Part of the change resulted from tensions between Moscow and Peking, as the result of conflicts over ideology and territorial boundaries. In 1969, Soviet and PRC troops actually fought each other along the Manchurian border. Accordingly, both Moscow and Peking began to seek better relations with the United States. Early in 1972, Nixon flew to Peking to confer *de facto* diplomatic recognition of Mao Tse-tung's government and to join Mao in a declaration opposing Soviet hegemony in the Far East. Then in May, 1972, Nixon joined Brezhnev in the Kremlin to sign the long-sought Strategic Arms Limitation Treaty (SALT I), the most significant arms-control measure to that time since the Washington Naval Treaty of 1922. A five-year Interim Agreement under SALT I imposed an upper limit of 1,618 ICBMS and 950

SLBMS on the USSR and 1,054 ICBMS and 710 SLBMS on the United States. (The larger number allowed the USSR reflected the American advantage in MIRVed missiles.) Parity was granted in the new class of Anti-Ballistic Missiles (ABMS), each side being allowed two hundred ABM launchers with single warheads and restricted to two launch-sites. The ABM Agreement was of indefinite duration, though either party could withdraw from its limitations by serving six-months' notice. Provision was made for the negotiation of a second Interim Agreement on offensive weapons before the first expired in 1977. The signing of SALT I was widely hailed as the beginning of a new era of *détente* between the United States and the Soviet Union.

Perhaps the final event of the Vietnam War Era of importance to the patterns of war was the so-called Six-Day War between Israelis and Arabs in 1967. By that year the Israeli Defense Forces (IDF) had perfected their *Nation-in-Arms,* one of the most thorough-going in history. On the eve of the Six-Day War, 75,000 troops were on active duty (only 3,000 of them professional soldiers), and the rest of the 250,000-man army was in reserve. In a nation of only 2 million Jews, both mobilization and the conduct of the war had to be carried out with great speed in order not to place too great a strain on the economy and national morale. The Israelis possessed 800 tanks, 350 modern jet fighters and ground-attack aircraft, and 31 mobilizable brigades. In contrast, Nasser's Egypt, Israel's primary enemy, had an army of 275,000 troops, 900 tanks, and 385 jet aricraft, the arms and equipment supplied by Soviet Russia. Syria, then linked with Egypt through the United Arab Republic, had an army of 65,000 troops, 350 tanks, and 76 jet aircraft. The Kingdom of Jordan, linked with Egypt by a military alliance signed just before the war, had 55,000 troops, 300 tanks, and 21 jet aircraft. Accordingly, Israel seemed to face long odds in these combined forces.

Under the circumstances, if war were inevitable, Israel's best chance lay in mobilizing rapidly for a sudden strike at her most powerful enemy—Egypt—then dealing with Syria and Jordan as circumstances developed. Moshe Dyan, Minister of War, and formerly IDF chief-of-staff in the 1956 War, ordered mobilization on June 2, and by the night of June 4 the Israeli forces were ready for action. Early on June 5, Israeli planes circumvented Egyptian radar by flying out over the Mediterranean and then approaching the coast from an unexpected direction. Most of Nasser's planes had been destroyed on the ground by noon. The morning air blitz was accompanied by a rapid drive of Israeli forces into the Sinai desert and the adjacent Gaza Strip. Only two out of seven Egyptian army divisions were deployed for battle, and all of them were rapidly beaten. A total of 50,000 Egyptian troops were killed or captured, and the IDF destroyed or captured 300 tanks, 500 pieces of artillery, and 10,000 trucks. Within six days, the IDF had occupied the whole

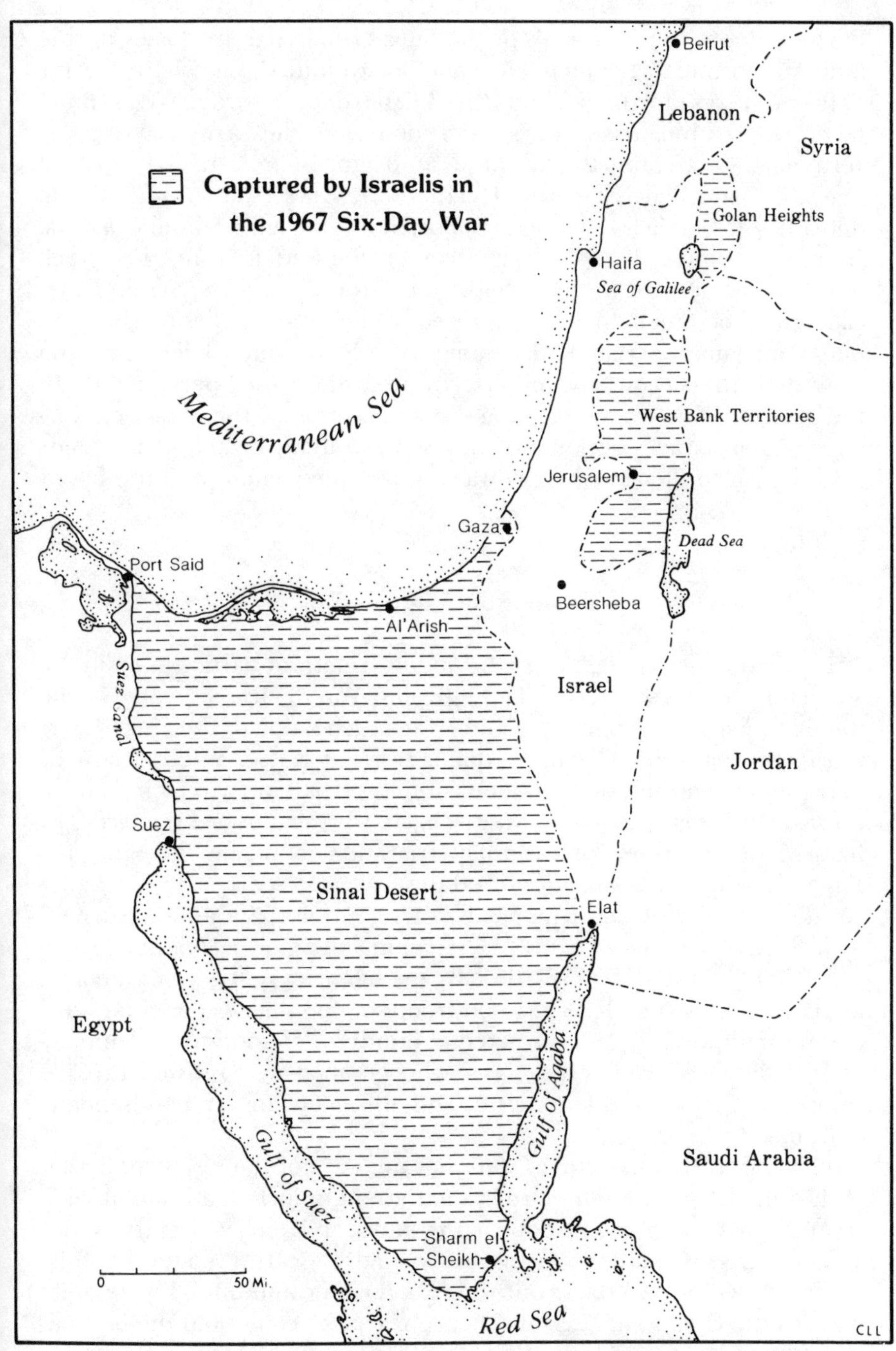

The Arab-Israeli Theater of War, 1948–1973

of the Sinai to the east bank of the Suez Canal. The IDF losses on the Sinai front came to 275 men killed and 800 wounded. Elsewhere, the IDF defeated 55,000 Jordanian and Palestinian troops in Jordan's West Bank territories within three days, and occupied the Arab quarter of Jerusalem. On the fourth day of the campaign, 20,000 Israeli troops and 250 tanks stormed the Golan Heights on Syria's frontier with Israel, defeating 40,000 Syrian troops, supported by 300 tanks, within two days. Its forces being halfway to Damascus on the Syrian front, the Israeli government decided to heed the U.N. call for a cease-fire. Syrian losses came to 10,000 men killed or captured, while IDF casualties on the combined Jordanian-Syrian fronts came to only 200 men killed and 400 wounded. In its economy and effectiveness, the Israeli performance in the Six-Day War was almost a perfect application of the blitzkrieg doctrine of war. Israel's opponents were so thoroughly beaten that a major Arab threat to the Jewish state was not mounted again until the fall of 1973.

V. Since the Vietnam Era

The first major conflict after the end of American participation in the Vietnam War was the so-called Yom Kippur War of October, 1973. In the wake of Egypt's defeat in 1967 and Israeli occupation of the Sinai desert to the east bank of the Suez Canal, President Nasser waged a war of harassment against Israeli positions until his death in 1970 from natural causes. He was succeeded by Anwar Sadat, who abandoned the tactics of harassment for those of careful preparation to regain the Sinai for Egypt. Though he actually reduced the Soviet presence in Egypt, Sadat readily accepted Soviet armaments for his project. Syria also rearmed with Soviet weapons in hopes of regaining the Golan Heights, lost to Israel in the Six-Day War of 1967. By the fall of 1973, Egypt's army had increased to a strength of 285,000 troops, 2,000 tanks, 500 jet aircraft, and most importantly as it turned out, hundreds of antitank and antiaircraft weapons of the latest designs. The Syrian army possessed 125,000 troops, 800 tanks, 300 jet aircraft, and also many antitank and antiaircraft missiles.

The Israeli Defense Forces were not unaware of the Egyptian-Syrian build-up, and by the fall of 1973 their strength included a mobilizable ground force of 270,000 troops, 1,175 tanks, and 400 jet aircraft. About 100,000 troops were on active duty, and the army could be fully mobilized within two days. But whereas Jewish communities were quite close to the Golan Heights, and hence reservists could join the occupation forces there quickly, the Israeli front along the Suez Canal was two hundred fifty miles from the nearest Jewish community, and it would take at least two days for large numbers of reservists to join the Israeli forces there. The Israelis had built the so-called Bar Lev Line of fortified outposts along the eastern bank of the Canal and manned it with a brigade of infantry. An Israeli armored brigade further inside the Sinai served as a back-up force, but these brigades alone could not stop a major Egyptian attack. The Israeli General Staff counted on sufficient warning of such an impending attack to have time in which to reinforce the Bar Lev Line adequately.

The first of Sadat's accomplishments was to design a joint attack by Egypt and Syria on Israel without the Israeli intelligence picking up clues in time to give the IDF General Staff warning. Not only was the build-up of Egyptian forces opposite the Suez Canal and Syrian forces facing the Golan Heights carried out with great secrecy, the attacks were planned to take place simultaneously on October 6, Yom Kippur, or the Jewish religious Day of Atonement, when the Israelis would be presumably at a low level of readiness. The second of Sadat's accomplishments was to have a ready strategy for Israel's response to Egyptian penetration of the Bar Lev Line, one that hinged on the new antitank and antiaircraft weapons. Thus, both the timing and manner of the Egyptian attack on the afternoon of October 6 caught the Israelis by surprise.

The Yom Kippur War began at the unusual hour of 2 P.M., when Egyptian planes suddenly descended on Israeli artillery positions behind the Bar Lev Line and quickly knocked them out of action. Then special assault troops began crossing the Canal at numerous points using pneumatic boats and penetrating the Bar Lev Line at many places. The scattered Israeli brigade defending the line was too overextended to offer effective resistance. Once behind the line, Egyptian antitank weapons were deployed, which made short work of the Israeli armored brigade that tried to counterattack. Another surprise for the Israelis was the complex of antiaircraft weapons just west of the Suez Canal, which defeated Israeli aerial efforts to knock out the pontoon bridges being quickly built so that more Egyptian forces could be poured into the Sinai desert. While the Egyptian attack was underway, Syrian infantry and armor assaulted the Israeli fortified positions on the Golan Heights.

The Israeli General Staff ordered a hurried general mobilization in the first hours of the Yom Kippur War, and decided to give priority to the defense of the Golan Heights, where a Syrian breakthrough would immediately threaten Jewish communities. In fierce fighting that lasted three days, the quick arrival of reservists and the tenacious defense of the forces in place managed to retain most of the Israeli positions. There was to be no general Syrian breakthrough into Israel, nor a reconquest of the Golan Heights. But in the Sinai desert, Israeli forces arriving piecemeal had been unwisely thrown into ill-prepared counterattacks against the Egyptian positions in a zone about ten miles deep into the Sinai, and all had been rebuffed with the added loss of two more Israeli armored brigades. Israeli air losses were also very heavy as the result of repeated attacks on bridges across the Suez Canal, in the face of both conventional antiaircraft artillery and surface-to-air missiles. At the end of these failed Israeli attacks, the IDF General Staff ordered its Southern Command to suspend offensive operations for the time being and concentrate on defense and a review of its tactics. The battle in the south began to lull.

The Israeli General Staff decided to launch its first counterattacks against the Syrians in order to recover all positions on the Golan Heights and to drive their forces toward Damascus. As the momentum of the Israeli attacks in the north picked up from October 9 on, first Iraqi and then Jordanian reinforcements arrived to join the Syrian troops, but to no avail. All the lost Israeli positions on the Golan Heights were regained and IDF forces pressed beyond the ceasefire line of 1967 toward Damascus. Not until the Syrians had been driven back to Sasa on October 14 was the IDF offensive in the north brought to a close. Syrian calls for help to Egypt finally provoked an Egyptian offensive against Israeli positions in the Sinai on October 14, but the attack was repelled with heavy loss. At its conclusion, the Israeli Southern Command was at last ready to assume the offensive.

On October 15, IDF forces, amounting to three divisions, silenced Egyptian antitank weapons with well-directed artillery fire, then used armor and infantry in mutual support to penetrate the front between the Egyptian Second and Third Army corps all the way to the Suez Canal. After establishing a bridgehead across the Canal, Israeli forces then wheeled north and south. Those going north attacked and destroyed the network of antiaircraft batteries which had protected bridges across the Canal earlier. The forces going south cut the communications of the Third Egyptian Army Corps on the far side of the Canal and prepared the ground for a *Kesselschlacht.* Israeli strength, greatly reduced in tanks and planes in the first days of the war, was increased again by emergency deliveries of tanks and planes from the United States. When Israeli troops reached the city of Suez, at the southern terminus of the Canal, it became clear that the Egyptian army was on the edge of catastrophe, despite its earlier successes.

But the battle never came to its natural conclusion. Repeated efforts by the United Nations to bring the fighting to a halt finally succeeded on October 25, when both Israel and its enemies agreed to an armistice. Under subsequent arrangements, Israeli forces were withdrawn into the Sinai, and the Egyptians were left with a strip of territory, about ten miles deep, east of the Canal, The Israelis retained their former positions in the Golan Heights. Thus, the immediate outcome of the war was only a very modest change in boundaries and an opportunity for Egypt to revive the use of the Suez Canal, moribund since the 1967 war. But for the patterns of war, the Yom Kippur War was mostly significant for the important role of antitank and antiaircraft weapons, and the heavy expenditure of war material by both sides. The Israelis had lost a quarter of their prewar armor and a fifth of their prewar air force, and their 3,000 killed and wounded exceeded the combined losses of the 1956 and 1967 wars. Egyptian losses were estimated at 15,000 killed and wounded; 8,301 were taken prisoner, and there were heavy losses in armor and planes. Syrian losses were placed at about 10,000 men, and also large losses of tanks and planes. Counting the armored fighting vehicles contributed by Iraq and Jordan, perhaps more tanks and self-propelled guns took part in the Yom Kippur War than at the Battle of Kursk, the largest armored action of World War II. The startling loss of so much of the armor and airpower committed in a war that lasted well under a month gave professional soldiers the world over something to ponder.

In the aftermath of the Yom Kippur War, a basic shift took place in the Middle East. Saudi Arabia sought to make the United States follow a more even-handed course in its Middle East policies by imposing a limited oil embargo on shipments to America. Anwar Sadat recognized Israel's right to exist in return for a staged Israeli withdrawal from the Sinai desert and some resolution of the Palestinian problem. Though Sadat himself was assassinated by Muslim fanatics on the anniversary of his attack on Yom Kippur in 1981, the Egyptian government continued to follow his policy of accomodation with Israel. In 1982, Israel returned the last of the Sinai to Egypt. After 1973, Israel's defense problem was focused on her northern borders, where Syria remained no less hostile than before and where beginning in 1975 Lebanon was torn by civil war between Christian and Muslim. After Palestinian guerrillas occupied southern Lebanon in great strength, Israel launched a "Lebanese Incursion" in 1982 that went all the way to Beirut. At this writing, Israeli forces have retired to positions in southern Lebanon, an international peace force has failed to bring about a cease-fire in the war between Christians and Muslims, and Syrian forces remain in eastern Lebanon. The Palestinian Arab problem remains unresolved, and Israel's survival still depends heavily on her armed forces.

The *détente* between the United States and Soviet Russia that began with the signing of SALT I fell on hard times in the decade which followed. At first, the prospect was more promising. In October, 1973, the long-deferred Mutual and Balanced Force Reduction (MBFR) talks between NATO and the Warsaw Pact began at Vienna, and in July, 1974, Nixon and Brezhnev met at Moscow to sign a codicil to SALT I that reduced the number of ABM launchers allowed each side to one hundred, and the number of ABM launch-sites to one. But after Nixon's resignation in August, 1974, and Gerald Ford's assumption of the presidency, the latter found it harder to get along with the Russians. Progress on a new Interim Agreement on offensive strategic arms (so-called SALT II) was very slow, with important differences separating the two countries. Some progress was made in reducing those differences by the Vladivostok Accords in November, 1974, but Ford left office in January, 1977, without an agreement. Jimmy Carter, his successor in office, agreed with Brezhnev that the old Interim Agreement would be kept informally in effect after its expiration in October, 1977, if a SALT II had not been negotiated by that time. In addition, the MBFR Talks had been subsumed under the Conference on Security and Cooperation in Europe, which concluded with the Helsinki Accords in 1975. Though no military agreements were made except for the exchange of Warsaw Pact and NATO observers at maneuvers, the Western powers finally recognized the new frontiers in Eastern Europe, while both Communist and non-Communist governments pledged to increase trade and cultural exchanges, and to better protect human rights. Still, tensions between the United States and Russia especially were slowly braking *détente* to a complete halt.

The rise of Soviet-American tensions began with the Yom Kippur War and what the United States considered to be the unwarranted Soviet meddling in the Middle East and in Africa. The United States objected to Soviet use of Cuban surrogate troops to influence the outcome of civil war in the African country of Angola, and their use in another African war between Ethiopia and Somolia. It also objected to Soviet influence in South Yemen in the Arabian peninsula. Events also redounded to Soviet advantage when a fundamentalist Muslim revolution in Iran toppled the pro-American Shah of Iran in January, 1979, and a very anti-American government under the Ayatollah Khomeini came to power. Still, in June, 1979, Carter and Brezhnev finally signed a second Interim Agreement on strategic arms, in what turned out to be the last gesture of *détente* in the decade.

The SALT II agreement allowed each side a maximum of 2,400 offensive strategic weapon-systems, to be reduced to 2,250 systems by January, 1981, with subcategory of limitations on land-based ICBMS, SLBMS, cruise missiles, and strategic aircraft. But by the signing of SALT II, the Soviet strategic forces had come a long way since the signing of SALT I seven years earlier. The USSR had 1,400 ICBM launchers, a new giant SS-18 ICBM under deployment, 880 SLBMS, and 140 Bison-Bear bombers. These forces were capable of delivering 5,600 nuclear bombs and warheads, worth 5,500MT of nuclear explosive. In June, 1979, the United States possessed 1,054 land-based ICBMS, 656 SLBMS, and 385 B-52 bombers, but it no longer had a monopoly on MIRVS. The 9,800 American strategic nuclear bombs and warheads could deliver a combined yield of 4,000MT, or slightly less than in 1972.

Factions in the U.S. Senate strongly opposed SALT II, but in November the Senate Foreign Relations Committee reported the treaty favorably to the Senate floor. Earlier in the month, however, militant Iranian students had seized the grounds and staff of the American embassy in Teheran, and staff members were being held hostage for the return of the former Shah, then being treated for health problems in the United States. The events in Teheran caused a wave of xenophobia to sweep over the United States, unfavorable to the ratification of SALT II. The final blow to the treaty came on December 24, when Soviet forces intervened in the civil war in Afghanistan on the side of the Communist government in Kabul, an action which was viewed as aggressive by the American people and government. In January, 1980, Carter withdrew SALT II from further consideration by the Senate and vowed not to resubmit it until Soviet forces were withdrawn from Afghanistan (an executive agreement implementing the terms of SALT II remained in effect).

In the final months of the Carter presidency, an important change of direction in defense policy took place. Carter approved the development of both a new heavy MX ICBM and a new Trident II SLBM for deployment in the mid- and late-1980s. (He rejected a B-1 bomber to replace the B-52, hoping to use airborne cruise missiles to extend its useful life.) In July, 1980, he approved Presidential Directive 59 (PD-59) which authorized the Pentagon to plan for limited nuclear war on a scale not considered since the adoption of the MAD doctrine of the 1960s. The so-called Nuclear Utilization Target Selection (NUTS) doctrine envisioned a controlled nuclear response to Soviet aggression. Carter also approved a NATO recommendation for the deployment of a so-called Two-Track System of Pershing II ballistic missiles and Tomahawk cruise missiles in Western Europe, beginning in December, 1983. The Two-Track System was in response to Soviet deployment of MIRVed SS-20 ballistic missiles aimed at Western Europe. Brezhnev threatened that if the Two-Track Missile deployment began, the Soviet Union would take appropriate measures of retaliation.

Despite his belated "hard line" on defense policy, and perhaps because of several unrelated factors, Carter went down to a heavy defeat at the polls at the hands of Republican Ronald Reagan in November, 1980. Reagan was a long-time critic of both the SALT process and *détente* with the Soviet Union. With a Republican-dominated Senate to support him, Reagan effectively abandoned SALT II and called for the spending of $1.6 billion on national defense over the next five years after taking office in January, 1981. He reapproved the Carter decisions on the MX and the Trident II, and resurrected the B-1 bomber project. His program also included expansion of conventional forces, though he agreed that military service should be voluntary in time of peace. (Draft registration, but not the draft, had been revived by the Carter administration.) In addition, he approved the Two-Track Missile deployment in

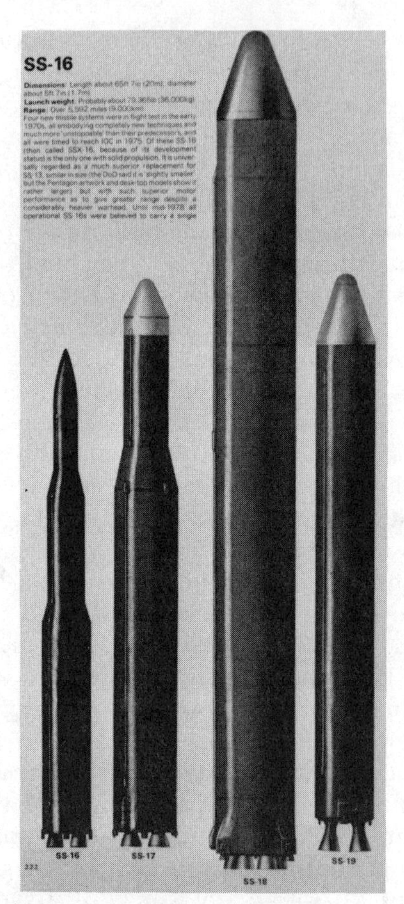

Soviet ICBMS: SS-16, SS-17, SS-18, and SS-19.

SOURCE: Ray Bonds, ed., *The Illustrated Encyclopedia of the Strategy, Tactics and Weapons of Russian Military Power* (New York: Bonanza, 1982).

Western Europe, scheduled to begin in December, 1983. His actions, combined with fierce verbal denunciations of the Soviet Union, brought on a renewed freeze in the Cold War.

Still, the return to the atmosphere of the Cold War did not go unresisted. In the early 1980s occurred the largest anti-war movements in the United States since the height of American involvement in the Vietnam War. This activity was accompanied by widespread opposition to the Two-Track system in Europe. Perhaps as a result of these pressures, Reagan agreed to negotiations on Intermediate Nuclear Forces (INF) in Europe beginning in the fall of 1981, and also to negotiations toward a Strategic Arms Reduction Treaty (START) beginning in June, 1982. But little progress was made in either set of negotiations—both of which were conducted in Geneva—down to November, 1983. At that time, and

Soviet SAM-2 Guideline, surface-to-air missile.

SOURCE: Ray Bonds, ed., *The Illustrated Encyclopedia of the Strategy, Tactics and Weapons of Russian Military Power* (New York: Bonanza, 1982).

actually ahead of schedule, Reagan ordered the first batteries of the Pershing II ballistic missile to West Germany and the first of the Tomahawk cruise missiles to Britain. The government of Yuri Andropov, which had succeeded to power upon the death of Brezhnev in November, 1982, promptly broke off the INF talks and suspended the START negotiations indefinitely. Even the Mutual and Balanced Force Reduction negotiations in Vienna on conventional forces were suspended. For the first time in over fourteen years, no nuclear-arms negotiations were underway between the United States and the Soviet Union. The absence of sustained negotiation on nuclear weapons continued down to the death of Yuri Andropov on February 9, 1984, and the rise of a new

Soviet leadership. The situation at this writing does not suggest any rapid improvement in nuclear-arms control or in relations between the United States and the Soviet Union.

About forty wars took place in the decade after 1973, some of them continuing down to this writing. The bloodiest of these is the on-going Iranian-Iraqi War, in its fourth year by 1984, and which so far has claimed an estimated 250,000 lives. But from the "high tech" point of view, the most interesting of the wars between 1973 and 1983 was the Anglo-Argentinian war over the Falklands and the dependency of South Georgia, a war primarily decided by conventional but sophisticated air-naval weapons.

After diplomacy failed to settle the conflicting claims of Britain and Argentina to the British-held islands off the tip of South America in the spring of 1982, without warning Argentine forces occupied the Falklands and South Georgia on April 2–3. Britain responded to the Argentine invasion by dispatching to the South Atlantic the largest task force sent out from the home islands since World War II. The object of the task force was to recover uninhabited South Georgia and to rescue the two thousand British subjects in the Falklands, most of them on East Falkland. The British task force, commanded by Admiral John Woodward, was eventually composed of two aircraft carriers (basing thirty-six Harrier "jump jets," vertical take-off and landing or VERTOL aircraft), twenty-three modern destroyers and frigates, four nuclear-powered attack submarines, eight large amphibious warfare vessels, and some thirty transports, tankers, and auxiliary vessels. It also transported some nine thousand army and marine troops, together with their weapons and equipment.

In late April, the British drew first blood when a naval helicopter disabled an Argentine submarine with air-to-surface rockets during the reoccupation of South Georgia against minimal Argentine resistance. On May 2, as the task force entered the waters around the Falklands, a British submarine torpedoed and sank the old Argentine cruiser *General Belgrano* with the loss of 370 Argentine lives. Thereafter, the obsolescent Argentine navy remained near its continental coasts. Perforce, the fight was carried to the British fleet off the Falklands by 250 jet aircraft of the Argentine air force based on the mainland. On May 4, an Argentine aircraft launched a French-made Exocet air-to-surface missile against the British destroyer *Sheffield* at a range of almost twenty miles and fatally damaged the ship. (Later in May, another Exocet sank the large cargo vessel *Atlantic Conveyor.*) The air attacks on Woodward's fleet reached their peak after British landing operations commenced against East Falkland on May 21. Within a few days, aerial attacks sank an assault ship, two frigates, and a destroyer, while damaging ten other British warships. The Harriers (nine of which were lost to all causes), surface-to-

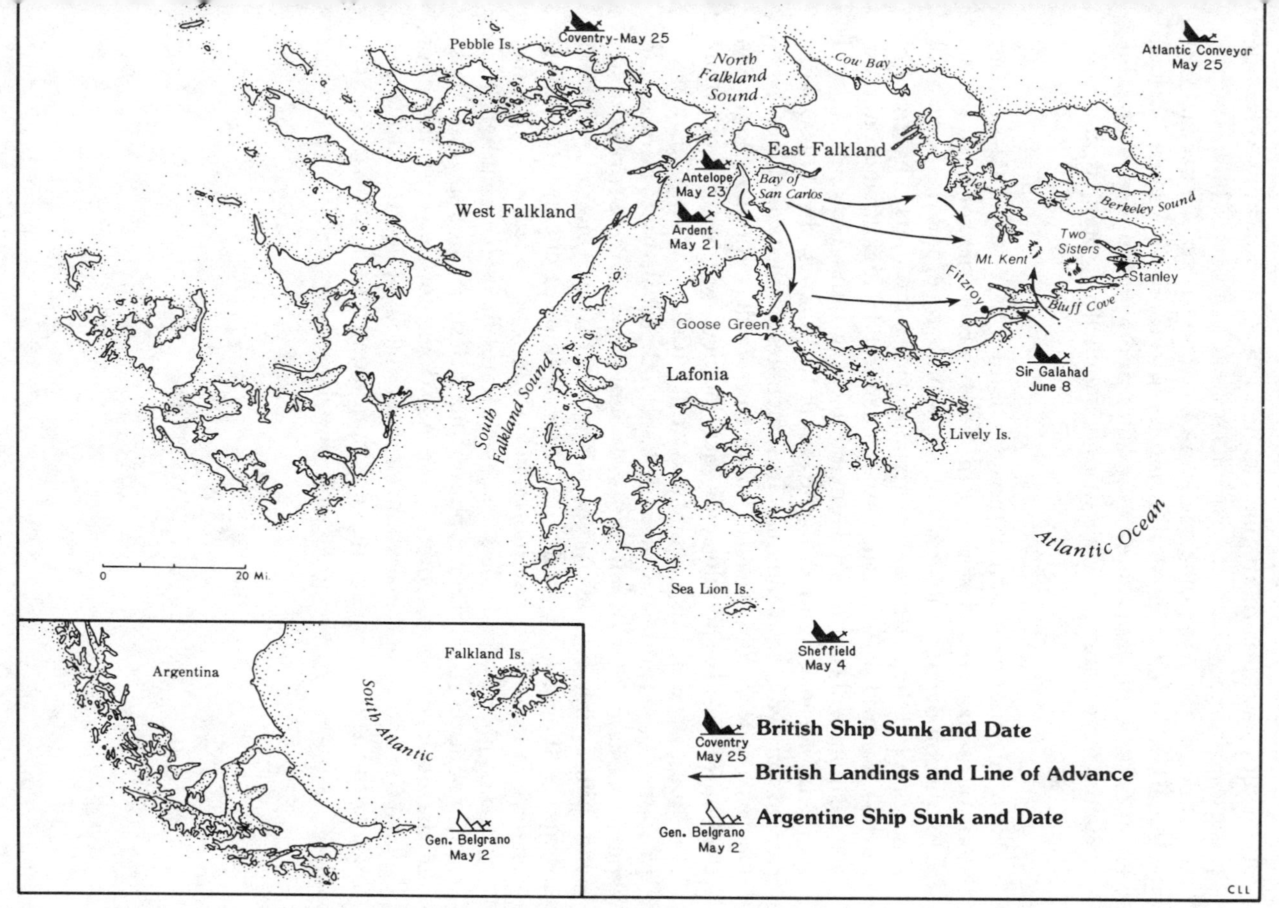

The Anglo-Argentine War in the Falklands: Operations May 21–June 8, 1982

air missiles, and antiaircraft guns claimed 109 of the attacking Argentine planes. Fighting ashore on East Falkland ended in early June with the surrender of the Argentine garrison of 13,000 troops. An exchange of prisoners followed a general armistice in the South Atlantic. British losses in the campaign came to 255 killed and 777 wounded. Argentine casualties were estimated at about 1,500 men killed, wounded, and missing.

With this brief recitation of the facts in the war for the Falklands, our study of the patterns of war over the last two centuries comes to a close. A prediction of future patterns of war would go beyond the purview of this work, but the patterns since 1945 provide a few hints. The threat of nuclear war and of ever more exotic chemical, biological, and radiological weapons will continue to loom in the background. However, short of a world holocaust, fighting, to the end of the century, should be mainly carried on with conventional, if sometimes sophisticated, weapons. Guerrilla warfare and the tactics of terrorism will continue to flourish in the Third World especially, and such methods will bring about more attention to counterinsurgency and antiterrorism warfare. "Star War" weapons of the future may include laser and particle-beam devices, and radar-resistant "Stealth" aircraft. Self-liquidating, aerosol-spread toxins and binary nerve gases pose impressive threats, but, like nuclear weapons, they can be safely used only against an enemy who cannot retaliate in kind. They are more likely to be used by technically sophisticated countries against less advanced states than against other "high tech" countries. Still, the weapons of mass destruction, especially those of the nuclear variety, pose an ongoing threat to the very survival of global civilization, and mankind would do well to put more energy into a search for new designs for peace than into one for new patterns of war.

Selected Bibliography

Addington, Larry H. *The Blitzkrieg Era and the German General Staff, 1865–1941.* New Brunswick: Rutgers University Press, 1971.

Albion, R. G. *Forests and Sea Power: The Timber Problem of the Royal Navy, 1652–1862.*Hamden, Conn.: Archon Press, 1965.

Alden, John Richard. *The American Revolution, 1775–1783.* New York: Harper and Row, 1954.

Ambler, John S. *The French Army in Politics, 1945–1962.* Columbus: Ohio State University Press, 1966.

Ambrose, Stephen E. *Eisenhower and Berlin, 1945: The Decision to Halt at the Elbe.* New York: W. W. Norton and Company, 1967.

———. *The Supreme Commander: The War Years of General Dwight D. Eisenhower.* Garden City, N.Y.: Doubleday and Company, 1969.

Amrine, Michael. *The Great Decision: The Secret History of the Atomic Bomb.* New York: Charles Putnam's Sons, 1959.

Anderson, Bern. *By Sea and By River: The Naval History of the Civil War.* New York: Alfred A. Knopf, 1963.

Anderson, Romola and R. C. *The Sailing Ship.* New York: W. W. Norton and Company, 1963.

Andreski, Stanislav. *Military Organization and Society.* Rev. ed. Berkeley: University of California Press, 1968.

Asprey, Robert B. *The First Battle of the Marne.* Philadelphia and New York: J. B. Lippincott Company, 1962.

———. *War in the Shadows: The Guerrilla in History.* 2 vols. Garden City, N.Y.: Doubleday and Co., 1975.

Ballard, Colin R. *The Military Genius of Abraham Lincoln.* Cleveland and New York: The World Publishing Company, 1952.

Barber, Noël. *A Sinister Twilight: The Fall of Singapore, 1942.* Boston: Houghton Mifflin Company, 1968.

———. *The War of the Running Dogs: The Malayan Emergency, 1948–1960.* New York: Weybright and Talley, 1971.

Barker, Arthur J. *Arab-Israeli Wars.* New York: Hippocrene Books, 1980.

Barnett, Correlli. *Britain and Her Army, 1509–1970: A Military, Political and Social Survey.* New York: William Morrow and Company, 1970.

———. *The Desert Generals: New Edition.* Bloomington: Indiana University Press, 1983.

———. *The Sword-Bearers: Supreme Command in the First World War.* Bloomington: Indiana University Press, 1975.

Barrett, John G. *Sherman's March Through the Carolinas.* Chapel Hill, N.C.: University of North Carolina Press, 1956.

Bartlett, C. J. *Great Britain and Sea Power, 1815–1853.* Oxford: The Clarendon Press, 1963.

Baskir, Lawrence M., and Strauss, William A. *Chance and Circumstance: The Draft, The War and the Vietnam Generation.* New York: Alfred A. Knopf, 1978.
Bauer, K. Jack. *The Mexican War, 1846–1848.* New York and London: The Macmillan Company, 1974.
Baxter, J. P. *The Introduction of the Ironclad Warship.* Hamden, Conn.: The Shoe String Press, 1968.
Beatie, R. H. *Road to Manassas: The Growth of Union Command in the Eastern Theater from the Fall of Fort Sumter to the First Battle of Bull Run.* New York: Cooper Square Publishers, 1964.
Bekker, C. D. *Defeat at Sea: The Struggle and Eventual Destruction of the German Navy, 1933–1945.* New York: Henry Holt and Company, 1955.
Bennett, Geoffrey. *Nelson the Commander.* New York: Charles Scribner's Sons, 1972.
Benoist-Méchin, Jacques. *Sixty Days That Shook the West: The Fall of France, 1940.* Translated by Peter Wiles. New York: Charles Putnam's Sons, 1963.
Berger, Carl. *The Korea Knot: A Military-Political History.* Rev. ed. Philadelphia: University of Pennsylvania Press, 1964.
Berghahn, V. R. *Germany and the Approach of War in 1914.* New York: St. Martin's Press, 1973.
Berman, Larry. *Planning a Tragedy: The Americanization of the War in Vietnam.* New York and London: W. W. Norton & Company, 1982.
Bernardo, C. J., and Bacon, Eugene H. *American Military Policy: Its Development since 1775.* Harrisburg, Pa.: The Stackpole Company, 1961 [1955].
Billias, George A., ed. *George Washington's Generals.* New York: William Morrow and Company, 1964.
———. *George Washington's Opponents: British Generals and Admirals in the American Revolution.* New York: William Morrow and Company, 1969.
Black, Robert C. *The Railroads of the Confederacy.* Chapel Hill: University of North Carolina Press, 1952.
Blair, Clay, Jr. *MacArthur.* Garden City, N.Y.: Doubleday, and Company, 1977.
———. *Silent Victory: The U.S. Submarine War Against Japan.* New York: J. B. Lippincott Company, 1975.
Blumenson, Martin and Stokesbury, James L. *Masters of the Art of Command.* Boston: Houghton Mifflin Company, 1975.
Bonds, Ray, ed. *The Illustrated Encyclopedia of the Strategy, Tactics and Weapons of Russian Military Power.* New York: Bonanza Books, Inc., 1982.
———. *The U.S. War Machine: An Illustrated Encyclopedia of American Military Equipment and Strategy.* New York: Crown Publishers, Inc., 1978.
Brodie, Bernard. *A Guide to Naval Strategy.* Rev. ed. New York, Washington and London: Frederick A. Praeger, 1965.
———. *Strategic Air Power in World War II.* Santa Monica, Cal.: Rand Corporation, 1957.
———. *Strategy in the Missile Age.* Princeton: Princeton University Press, 1959.
Brodie, Bernard and Fawn. *From Crossbow to H-Bomb.* Rev. ed. Bloomington: Indiana University Press, 1973.
Browne, Courtney. *Tojo: The Last Banzai.* New York, Chicago and San Francisco: Holt, Rinehart and Winston, 1967.
Bryant, Arthur. *The Turn of the Tide: A History of the War Years Based on the Diaries of Field Marshal Lord Alanbrooke . . .* Garden City, N.Y.: Doubleday and Company, 1957.
Caidin, Martin. *The Tigers are Burning.* New York: Hawthorne Books, 1974.

Callahan, Raymond. *The Worst Disaster: The Fall of Singapore.* London and Newark: Association of University Presses and the University of Delaware Press, 1977.

Calvocoressi, Peter, and Guy Wint. *Total War: Causes and Courses of the Second World War.* London: Penguin Books, 1979.

Carver, Michael, ed. *The War Lords: Military Commanders of the Twentieth Century.* Boston and Toronto: Little, Brown and Company, 1976.

Catton, Bruce. *Glory Road: The Bloody Route from Fredericksburg to Gettysburg.* Garden City, N. Y.: Doubleday and Company, 1956.

———. *This Hallowed Ground: The Story of the Union Side of the Civil War.* Garden City, N.Y.: Doubleday and Company, 1956.

Challenger, Richard D. *The French Theory of the Nation in Arms, 1866–1939.* New York: Russell Press, 1955.

Chandler, David G. *Atlas of Military Strategy.* New York: Free Press, 1980.

———. *The Campaigns of Napoleon.* New York: Macmillan and Company, 1966.

———. *Dictionary of the Napoleonic Wars.* New York: Macmillan and Company, 1979.

Chapman, Guy. *Why France Fell: The Defeat of the French Army in 1940.* New York, Chicago and San Francisco,: Holt, Rinehart and Winston, 1968.

Chuikov, Vasili I. *The Battle for Stalingrad.* Translated by MacGibbon and Kee, Ltd. New York, Chicago and San Francisco: Holt, Rinehart and Winston, 1964.

———. *The Fall of Berlin.* New York, Chicago and San Francisco: Holt, Rinehart and Winston, 1968.

Clark, Alan. *Barbarossa: The Russian-German Conflict, 1941–1945.* New York: William Morrow and Company, 1965.

———. *The Donkeys.* New York: William Morrow and Company, 1961.

Clausewitz, Carl von. *On War.* Translated and edited by Michael Howard and Peter Paret. Princeton: Princeton University Press, 1976.

Coffman, Edward M. *The War to End all Wars: The American Experience in World War I.* New York: Oxford University Press, 1969.

Coggins, Jack. *Arms and Equipment of the Civil War.* Garden City, N.Y.: Doubleday and Company, 1962.

———. *The Campaign for North Africa.* Garden City, N.Y.: Doubleday and Company, 1980.

Cohen, Stephen P. *The Indian Army: Its Contribution to the Development of a Nation.* Berkeley: University of California Press, 1971.

———. *Vietnam: Anthology and Guide to a Television History.* New York: Alfred A. Knopf, 1983.

Coles, Harry L. *The War of 1812.* Chicago and London: University of Chicago Press, 1965.

Collier, Basil. *A History of Air Power.* New York: Macmillan and Company, 1974.

———. *The Lion and the Eagle: British and Anglo-American Strategy, 1900–1950.* New York: Capricorn Books, 1982.

Cook, Chris, and Stevenson, John. *The Atlas of Modern Warfare.* New York: G. P. Putnam's Sons, 1978.

Cooper, Matthew. *The German Army, 1933–1945: Its Political and Military Failure.* New York: Stein and Day, 1978.

Corvisier, André. *Armies and Societies in Europe, 1494–1789.* Bloomington and London: Indiana University Press, 1979.

Craig, Gordon. *The Battle of Königgrätz: Prussia's Victory over Austria, 1866.* Philadelphia and New York: J. B. Lippincott Company, 1964.

———. *The Politics of the Prussian Army, 1640–1945.* New York: Oxford University Press, 1964.
Cunliffe, Marcus. *Soldiers and Civilians: The Martial Spirit in America, 1775–1865.* Boston: Little, Brown and Company, 1968.
Curtiss, John S. *The Russian Army under Nicholas I, 1825–1855.* Durham, N.C.: Duke University Press, 1965.
Dallin, Alexander. *German Rule in Russia, 1941–1945: A Study of Occupation Policies.* New York: St. Martin's Press, 1957.
Davis, Burke. *The Campaign that Won America: The Story of Yorktown.* New York: The Dial Press, 1970.
———. *Gray Fox: Robert E. Lee and the Civil War.* New York and Toronto: Holt, Rinehart and Winston, 1956.
Davis, William C. *Battle At Bull Run: A History of the First Major Campaign of The Civil War.* Garden City, N.Y.: Doubleday and Company, 1977.
Dawidowicz, Lucy. *The War Against the Jews, 1933–1945.* New York: Holt, Rinehart and Winston, 1975.
Deichmann, Paul. *German Air Force Operations in Support of the Army.* New York: Arno Press, 1962.
Demeter, Karl. *The German Officer Corps in Society and State, 1650–1945.* Translated by Angus Malcolm. New York and Washington: Frederick A. Praeger, 1965.
Dew, Charles B. *Joseph R. Anderson: Ironmaker to the Confederacy.* New Haven and London: Yale University Press, 1966.
Divine, Robert A., ed. *The Cuban Missile Crisis.* Chicago: Quadrangle Books, 1971.
Downey, Fairfax. *The Guns at Gettysburg.* New York: Collier Books, 1962.
Doyle, Edward, and Lipsman, Samuel. *The Vietnam Experience.* 3 vols. to date. Boston: Boston Publishing Co., 1981.
Duffy, Christopher. *The Army of Frederick the Great.* New York: Hippocrene Books, 1974.
———. *Fire and Stone: The Science of Fortress Warfare, 1668–1860.* London and Vancouver: David and Charles, 1975.
Dunlop, J. K. *The Development of the British Army, 1899–1940.* London: Methuen, 1968.
Dunnigan, James F. *How to Make War: A Comprehensive Guide to Modern Warfare.* New York: William Morrow and Company, 1982.
Dupuy, R. Ernest and Trevor N. *Encyclopedia of Military History from 3500 B.C. to the Present.* New York: Harper and Row, 1970.
Dupuy, T. N. *A Genius for War: The German Army and General Staff, 1807–1945.* London: Macdonald and Jane's, 1977.
———. *The Evolution of Weapons and Warfare.* Indianapolis and New York: The Bobbs-Merrill Company, 1980.
Earle, Edward Meade, ed. *Makers of Modern Strategy: Military Thought from Machiavelli to Hitler.* Princeton: Princeton University Press, 1943.
Eisenhower, John D. D. *The Bitter Woods: Hitler's Surprise Ardennes Offensive.* New York: G. P. Putnam's Sons, 1969.
Ellis, John. *The Social History of the Machine Gun.* New York: Pantheon Books, 1975.
Emme, Eugene M., ed. *The Impact of Air Power: National Security and World Politics.* Princeton: D. Van Nostrand Company, Inc., 1959.
Erickson, John. *The Soviet High Command.* New York: St. Martin's Press, 1962.
Esposito, Vincent J., ed. *The West Point Atlas of American Wars, 1689–1953.* 2 vols. New York: Frederick A. Praeger, 1959.

Esposito, Vincent J., and Elting, John Robert. *A Military History and Atlas of the Napoleonic Wars.* New York: Frederick A. Praeger, 1964.
Falk, Richard A., Kolko, Gabriel, and Lifton, Robert Jay. *Crimes of War: A Legal, Political-Documentary and Psychological Inquiry into . . . Criminal Acts in Wars.* New York: Vintage Books, 1971.
Fall, Bernard B. *Hell in a Very Small Place: The Siege of Dien Bien Phu.* New York: Vintage Books, 1968.
———. *The Two Viet-Nams: A Political and Military Analysis.* Rev. ed. New York and London: Frederick A. Praeger, 1964.
Falls, Cyril. *The Art of War from the Age of Napoleon to the Present Day.* New York: Oxford University Press, 1961.
———. *The Great War, 1914–1918.* New York: Capricorn Books, 1959.
———. *A Hundred Years of War, 1850–1950.* New York: Collier Books, 1953.
Farrar, L. L., Jr. *The Short-War Illusion: German Policy, Strategy and Domestic Affairs, August–December 1914.* Santa Barbara and Oxford: ABC Clio, 1973.
Farwell, Byron. *Queen Victoria's Little Wars.* New York, Evanston, San Franciso and London: Harper and Row, 1972.
Fay, Sidney. *The Origins of the World War.* 2 vols. London and New York: Free Press, 1966 [1928–1930].
Fehrenbach, T. R. *This Kind of War: A Study in Unpreparedness.* New York: Macmillan and Company, 1963.
Feis, Herbert. *Japan Subdued: The Atomic Bomb and the End of the War in the Pacific.* Princeton: Princeton University Press, 1961.
Ferro, Marc. *The Great War, 1914–1918.* Translated by N. Stone. London: Routledge and Kegan Paul, 1973.
Fitzgerald, Frances. *Fire in the Lake: The Vietnamese and the Americans in Vietnam.* New York: Vintage Books, 1973.
Fredette, R. H. *The Sky on Fire: The First Battle of Britain, 1917–1918, and the Birth of the Royal Air Force.* New York: Holt, Rinehart and Winston, 1966.
Fuller, J. F. C. *A Military History of the Western World.* 3 vols. New York: Funk and Wagnalls Company, 1954–1956.
———. *The Conduct of War, 1789–1961.* New Brunswick: Rutgers University Press, 1961.
Fussell, Paul. *The Great War and Modern Memory.* New York: Oxford University Press, 1975.
Gallagher, Matthew P. *The Soviet History of World War II: Myth, Memories and Realities.* New York and London: Frederick A. Praeger, 1963.
Galland, Adolf. *The First and the Last: The Rise and Fall of the German Fighter Forces, 1938–1945.* Translated by Mervyn Savill. New York: Henry Holt and Company, 1954.
Garthoff, R. L. *Soviet Military Doctrine.* Glencoe, Ill.: Free Press, 1953.
———. *Soviet Strategy in the Nuclear Age.* New York: Frederick A. Praeger, 1958.
Gates, John M. *Schoolbooks and Krags: The United States Army in the Philippines, 1898–1902.* Westport, Conn., and London: Greenwood Press, Inc., 1973.
Glover, Michael. *Wellington as Military Commander.* London and Princeton: B. T. Batsford, Ltd., and D. Van Nostrand Company, Inc., 1968.
Goldberg, Alfred, ed. *A History of the United States Air Force, 1907–1957.* Princeton, New York, Toronto and London: D. Van Nostrand Company, Inc., 1957.
Goodspeed, D. J. *The German Wars, 1914–1945.* Boston: Houghton Mifflin Company, 1977.
———. *Ludendorff: Genius of World War I.* Toronto: Macmillan and Company, 1966.

Gordon, Harold J. *The Reichswehr and the German Republic, 1919–1926*. Princeton: Princeton University Press, 1957.
Gorlitz, Walter. *History of the German General Staff, 1657–1945*. Translated by Brian Battershaw. New York and London: Frederick A. Praeger, 1953.
Gosnell, H. Allen. *Guns on the Western Waters: The Story of River Gunboats in the Civil War*. Baton Rouge: Louisiana State University Press, 1949.
Goulden, Joseph C. *Korea: The Untold Story of the War*. New York: Times Books, 1982.
Goutard, A. *The Battle of France, 1940*. Translated by A. R. P. Burgess. New York: Ives Washburn, 1959.
Graham, Gerald S. *The Politics of Naval Supremacy: Studies in British Maritime Ascendancy*. New York: Cambridge University Press, 1965.
Gray, Edwyn A. *The Killing Time: The German U-boat War, 1914–1918*. New York: Charles Scribner's Sons, 1972.
Greenfield, Kent R., ed. *Command Decisions*. New York: Harcourt, Brace and Company, 1959.
Gregory, Barry, and Batchelor, John. *Airborne Warfare, 1918–1945*. New York: Exeter Books, 1979.
Grenfel, Russell. *The Bismarck Episode*. New York: Macmillan and Company, 1962.
Hackett, John Winthrop. *The Profession of Arms*. New York: Macmillan and Company, 1983.
Hassler, Warren B., Jr. *General George B. McClellan: Shield of the Union*. Baton Rouge: Louisiana State University Press, 1957.
Hastings, Max, and Jenkins, Simon. *The Battle for the Falklands*. New York and London: W. W. Norton & Company, 1983.
Heckman, Wolf. *Rommel's War in Africa*. Translated by Stephen Seago. Garden City, N.Y.: Doubleday and Company, 1981.
Herold, J. Christopher. *Bonaparte in Egypt*. New York, Evanston and London: Harper and Row, 1962.
Hersh, Seymour, M. *My-Lai: A Report on the Massacre and its Aftermath*. New York: Vintage Books, 1970.
Herwig, Holger H. *The German Naval Officer Corps: A Social and Political History, 1890–1918*. Oxford: The Clarendon Press, 1973.
Hezlet, Arthur. *Aircraft and Sea Power*. New York: Stein and Day, 1970.
Hibbert, Christopher. *The Great Mutiny: India, 1857*. New York: The Viking Press, 1878.
———. *Waterloo: Napoleon's Last Campaign*. New York, Toronto and London: New American Library, 1967.
Higginbotham, Don R. *The War of American Independence: Military Attitudes, Policies and Practice, 1763–1789*. New York: Macmillan and Company, 1971.
Higgins, Trumbull. *Soft Underbelly: The Anglo-American Controversy over the Italian Campaign 1939–1945*. New York and London: The Macmillan Company and Collier-Macmillan, Ltd, 1968.
Highham, Robin. *Air Power: A Concise History*. New York: St. Martin's Press, 1972.
———. *Armed Forces in Peacetime: Britain, 1918–1940*. London: Foulis, 1963.
———. *The Military Intellectuals in Britain, 1918–1939*. New Brunswick: Rutgers University Press, 1966.
Hilton, Richard. *The Indian Mutiny: A Centenary History*. London: Hollis and Carter, 1957.
Hittle, James D. *The Military Staff: Its History and Development*. Westport, Conn.: Greenwood Press, Inc., 1975 (1961).

Hogg, Ian V. *Artillery.* New York: Ballantine Books, 1972.

———. *Fortress: A History of Military Defense.* New York: St. Martin's Press, 1975.

Holley, I. B., Jr. *General John M. Palmer, Citizen Soldiers, and the Army of a Democracy.* Westport, Conn. and London: Greenwood Press, 1982.

———. *Ideas and Weapons: Exploitation of the Aerial Weapon by the United States during World War I.* New Haven: Yale University Press, 1953.

Holloway, David. *The Soviet Union and the Arms Race.* New Haven and London: Yale University Press, 1983.

Horne, Alistair. *The Fall of Paris: The Siege and the Commune, 1870–1871.* New York: St. Martin's Press, 1965.

———. *The Price of Glory: Verdun, 1916.* New York: St. Martin's Press, 1963.

———. *A Savage War of Peace: Algeria, 1954–1962.* New York: The Viking Press, 1977.

———. *To Lose A Battle: France, 1940.* Boston and Toronto: Little, Brown and Company, 1969.

Howard, Michael. *The Franco-Prussian War: The German Invasion of France, 1870–1871.* New York: Macmillan and Company, 1962.

Howard, Michael, ed. *The Theory and Practice of War.* Bloomington: Indiana University Press, 1975.

Howarth, David. *Trafalgar: The Nelson Touch.* New York: Atheneum, 1969.

———. *Waterloo: Day of Battle.* New York: Atheneum, 1968.

Hoyle, Martha Byrd. *A World in Flames, The History of World War II.* New York: Atheneum, 1970.

Huntington, Samuel P. *The Soldier and the State: The Theory and Politics of Civil-Military Relations.* Cambridge and London: The Belknap Press of Harvard University Press, 1957.

Irving, David. *Hitler's War.* 2 vols. New York: The Viking Press, 1977.

———. *The Trail of the Fox.* New York: E. P. Dutton, 1977.

Jackson, Gabriel. A Concise History of the Spanish Civil War. New York: John Day, 1974.

James, D. Clayton. *The Years of MacArthur.* 2 vols. Boston: Houghton Mifflin Company, 1975.

Janowitz, Morris. *The Professional Soldier.* New York: Free Press, 1960.

Jomini, Baron de. *The Art of War.* Translated by G. H. Mendell and W. P. Craighill. Westport, Conn.: Greenwood Press, 1974 (1862).

Jones, Archer. *Confederate Strategy from Shiloh to Vicksburg.* Baton Rouge: Louisiana State University Press, 1961.

Kahn, Herman. *On Thermonuclear War.* Princeton: Princeton University Press, 1960.

———. *Thinking About the Unthinkable.* New York: Horizon Books, 1962.

Karsten, Peter, ed. *The Military in America: From the Colonial Era to the Present.* New York: Free Press, 1980.

Keegan, John. *The Face of Battle: A Study of Agincourt, Waterloo and the Somme.* New York: Vintage Books, 1977.

———. *Six Armies in Normandy: From D-Day to the Liberation of Paris, June 6th–August 25, 1944.* New York: The Viking Press, 1982.

Kemp, P. K. *Key to Victory: The Triumph of British Sea Power in World War II.* Boston and Toronto: Little, Brown and Company, 1957.

Kennan, George F. *The Nuclear Delusion: Soviet-American Relations in the Atomic Age.* New York: Pantheon Books, 1982.

Kennett, Lee. *The French Armies in the Seven Years' War: A Study of Military Organization and Administration.* Durham, N.C.: Duke University Press, 1967.

Ketchum, Richard M., ed. *The American Heritage Picture History of the Civil War.* 2 vols. New York: American Heritage Magazine, 1960.
King, Jere Clemens. *Generals and Politicians.* Berkeley and Los Angeles: University of California Press, 1951.
Kitchen, Martin. *The German Officer Corps, 1890–1914.* Oxford: The Clarendon Press, 1968.
———. *A Military History of Germany from the Eighteenth Century to the Present Day.* Bloomington and London: Indiana University Press, 1975.
Kohn, Richard H. *Eagle and Sword: The Federalists and the Creation of the Military Establishment in America, 1783–1802.* New York and London: Free Press, 1975.
Korb, Lawrence J. *The Joint Chiefs of Staff: The First Twenty-Five Years.* Bloomington and London: Indiana University Press, 1976.
Laffin, John. *Fight for the Falklands!* New York: St. Martin's Press, 1982.
Larrabee, Harold A. *Decision at the Chesapeake.* London: William Kimber, 1965.
Leckie, Robert. *Conflict: The History of the Korean War, 1950–1953.* New York: Charles Putnam's Sons, 1962.
———. *The Wars of America.* Rev. ed. New York: Harper and Row, 1981.
Lefebvre, Georges. *Napoleon.* 2 vols. Translated by Henry F. Stockhold. New York: Columbia University Press, 1969.
Lewin, Ronald. *The Life and Death of the Afrika Korps.* New York: Quadrangle Books, 1977.
———. *Rommel as Military Commander.* New York: D. Van Nostrand Company, 1970.
———. *Ultra Goes to War: The First Account of World War II's Greatest Secret Based on Official Documents.* New York: McGraw-Hill Book Company, 1978.
Lewis, Emanuel Raymond. *Seacoast Fortifications of the United States: An Introductory History.* Washington: Smithsonian Institution, 1970.
Lewis, Michael. *The History of the British Navy.* Harmondsworth: Penguin Books, 1957.
Liddell Hart, B. H. *Defence of the West.* New York: William Morrow and Company, 1950.
———. *Deterrent or Defense: A Fresh Look at the West's Military Position.* New York: Frederick A. Praeger, 1960.
———. *History of the Second World War.* New York: G. P. Putnam's Sons, 1970.
———. *The Real War, 1914–1918.* Boston and Toronto: Little, Brown and Company, 1964 [1930].
———. *Strategy: The Indirect Approach.* New York: Frederick A. Praeger, Publishers, 1954.
———. *The Tanks.* 2 vols. London: Cassell, 1959.
Livermore, T. L. *Numbers and Losses in the Civil War in America, 1861–65.* New York: Kraus, 1968.
Longford, Elizabeth, *Wellington: The Years of the Sword.* New York and Evanston: Harper and Row, 1969.
Lundin, C. L. *Finland in the Second World War.* Bloomington: Indiana University Press, 1957.
Luttwak, Edward, and Dan Horowitz. *The Israeli Army.* New York, Evanston, San Francisco and London: Harper and Row, 1975.
Luvaas, Jay. *The Education of an Army: British Military Thought, 1815–1940.* Chicago: University of Chicago Press, 1964.
———. *The Military Legacy of the Civil War: The European Inheritance.* Chicago: University of Chicago Press, 1959.

———, ed. *Frederick the Great on the Art of War.* New York: Free Press, 1966.

Lyall, Gavin. *The War in the Air: The Royal Air Force in World War II.* New York: William Morrow and Company, 1968.

McElwee, William. *The Art of War: Waterloo to Mons.* Bloomington and London: Indiana University Press, 1974.

McFeely, William. *Grant: A Biography.* New York and London: W. W. Norton and Company, 1981.

Mackesy, Piers. *The War for America, 1775–1783.* Cambridge, Mass.: Harvard University Press, 1964.

Mackintosh, Malcolm. *Juggernaut: A History of the Soviet Armed Forces.* New York: Macmillan and Company, 1967.

Macksey, Kenneth. *Guderian: Creator of the Blitzkrieg.* New York: Stein and Day, 1976.

Macksey, Kenneth, and Batchelor, John H. *Tank: A History of the Armoured Fighting Vehicle.* New York: Charles Scribner's Sons, 1970.

Maclear, Michael. *The Ten Thousand Day War: Vietnam, 1945–1975.* New York: St. Martin's Press, 1981.

McNeill, William H. *The Pursuit of Power: Technology, Armed Force, and Society since A.D. 1000.* Chicago: University of Chicago Press, 1982.

McWhiney, Grady, and Jamieson, Perry D. *Attack or Die: Civil War Military Tactics and the Southern Heritage.* Auburn: University of Alabama Press, 1982.

Mahan, Alfred T. *The Influence of Sea Power Upon History, 1668–1783.* New York: Sagamore Press, Inc., 1957 (1890).

Mahan, John K. *The War of 1812.* Gainesville: University of Florida Press, 1972.

Manchester, William. *The Arms of Krupp, 1587–1968.* Boston and Toronto: Little, Brown and Company, 1964.

Marcus, G. J. *The Age of Nelson.* New York: The Viking Press, 1971.

———. *A Naval History of England: The Formative Centuries.* Boston and Toronto: Little, Brown and Company, 1961.

Marder, Arthur. *From the Dreadnought to Scapa Flow: The Royal Navy in the Fisher Era, 1904–1919.* 5 vols. New York: Oxford University Press, 1961–1971.

Markham, Felix. *Napoleon.* New York: Mentor Books, 1966.

Marshall, S. L. A. *Crimsoned Prairie: The Wars between the United States and the Plains Indians.* New York: Charles Scribner's Sons, 1972.

Martienssen, A. K. *Hitler and His Admirals.* London: Secker and Warburg, 1948.

Marwick, Arthur J. *War and Social Change in the Twentieth Century: A Comparative Study of Britain, France, Germany, Russia and the United States.* New York: St. Martin's Press, 1975.

Mason, Herbert Molloy, Jr. *The United States Air Force: A Turbulent History.* New York: Mason/Charter, 1976.

Mellenthin, F. W. *Panzer Battles: A Study of the Employment of Armor in the Second World War.* Translated by H. Betzler. Edited by L. C. F. Turner. New York: Ballantine Books, 1971 (1956).

Meredith, Roy. *Storm Over Sumter.* New York: Simon and Schuster, 1957.

Merrill, James M. *The Rebel Shore: The Story of Union Sea Power in the Civil War.* Boston: Little, Brown and Company, 1957.

Middlebrook, Martin. *The First Day on the Somme: 1 July 1916.* New York: W. W. Norton & Company, 1972.

Miers, Earl Schenk. *The Web of Victory: Grant at Vicksburg.* New York: Alfred A. Knopf, 1952.

Moorehead, Alan. *Gallipoli.* New York: Harper and Row, 1956.

———. *The Russian Revolution.* New York: Harper and Row, 1958.

Morgan, J. H. *Assize of Arms: The Disarmament of Germany and Her Rearmament, 1919–1939.* New York: Oxford University Press, 1946.
Morison, Samuel Eliot. *History of United States Naval Operations in World War II.* 15 vols. Boston: Little, Brown and Company, 1947–1962.
Morris, Donald R. *The Washing of the Spears: The Rise of the Zulu Nation under Shaka and Its Fall in the Zulu War of 1879.* New York: Simon and Schuster, 1965.
Newell, Nancy and Richard S. *The Struggle for Afghanistan.* Ithaca and London: Cornell University Press, 1981.
Nickerson, Hoffman. *The Armed Horde, 1793–1939: A Study of the Rise, Survival and Decline of the Mass Army.* New York: G. P. Putnam's Sons, 1940.
Ogorkiewicz, Richard M. *Armor: A History of Mechanized Forces.* New York: Frederick A. Praeger, 1960.
Oman, Carola. *Nelson.* Mystic, Conn.: Verry, 1967.
———. *Sir John Moore.* Mystic, Conn.: Verry, 1953.
Osgood, Robert E. *Limited War: The Challenge to American Strategy.* Chicago: University of Chicago Press, 1957.
Overy, R. J. *The Air War, 1939–1945.* New York: Stein and Day, 1981.
Padfield, Peter. *The Battleship Era.* New York: David McKay, 1972.
Paret, Peter. *Clausewitz and the State.* New York: Oxford University Press, 1976.
———. *Yorck and the Era of Prussian Reform, 1807–1815.* Princeton: Princeton University Press, 1966.
Parish, Peter J. *The American Civil War.* New York: Holmes and Meier, 1974.
Parkes, Oscar. *British Battleships: Warrior 1860 to Vanguard 1950: A History of Design, Construction and Armament.* London: Seeley, 1958.
Peckham, Howard H. *The Toll of Independence: Engagements and Battle Casualties of the American Revolution.* Chicago and London: University of Chicago Press, 1974.
———. *The War for Independence: A Military History.* Chicago: University of Chicago Press, 1958.
Pimlott, John, ed. *Vietnam: The History and the Tactics.* New York: Crescent Books, 1982.
Plocher, Hermann. *The German Air Force Versus Russia, 1941.* New York: Arno Press, 1965.
Pogue, Forrest C. *George C. Marshall.* 3 vols. New York: The Viking Press, 1963–1975.
Porch, Douglas. *The Conquest of Morocco.* New York: Alfred A. Knopf, 1983.
———. *The March to the Marne: The French Army, 1871–1914.* Cambridge: Cambridge University Press, 1981.
Potter, E. B. and Nimitz, Chester W., eds. *Sea Power: A Naval History.* Englewood Cliffs, N.J.: Prentice-Hall, Inc., 1960.
Prados, John. *The Soviet Estimate: U.S. Intelligence Analysis and Russian Military Strength.* New York: Dial Press, 1982.
Prange, Gordon H. *At Dawn We Slept: The Untold Story of Pearl Harbor.* New York: McGraw-Hill Book Company, 1981.
Preston, Richard A. *Canada and "Imperial Defense:" A Study of the Origins of the British Commonwealth's Defense Organization, 1867–1919.* Durham, N.C.: Duke University Press, 1967.
Preston, Richard A., and Wise, Sidney F. *Men In Arms: A History of Warfare and its Interrelationships with Western Society.* New York: Holt, Rinehart and Winston, 1979.
Quick, John, ed. *Dictionary of Weapons and Military Terms.* New York: McGraw-Hill Book Company, 1973.

Quimby, Robert S. *The Background of Napoleonic Warfare.* New York: AMS Press, 1968 (1957).
Rees, David. *Korea: The Limited War.* New York: St. Martin's Press, 1973.
Reynolds, Clark. *Command of the Sea: The History and Strategy of Maritime Empires.* New York: William Morrow and Company, Inc., 1974.
Ridgway, Matthew B. *The Korean War.* New York: Popular Library, 1967.
Ritter, E. A. *Shaka Zulu: The Rise of the Zulu Empire.* New York: Longmans Green, 1964.
Ritter, Gerhard. *The Schlieffen Plan: Critique of a Myth.* Translated by Andrew and Eva Wilson. New York: Frederick A. Praeger, 1958.
———. *The Sword and the Scepter: The Problem of Militarism in Germany.* 3 vols. Translated by H. Norden. Coral Gables, Fla.: University of Miami Press, 1970–1974.
Robinson, D. H. *The Zeppelin in Combat.* Rev. ed. London: Foulis, 1966.
Ropp, Theodore. *War in the Modern World.* 2nd ed. New York: Collier Books, 1962.
Roskill, Stephen W. *The Strategy of Sea Power: Its Development and Application.* London: Collins, 1962.
Ross, Steven. *From Flintlock to Rifle: Infantry Tactics, 1740–1866.* Cranbury, N.J.: Associated University Presses, 1979.
Rothenberg, Gunther E. *The Army of Francis Joseph.* West Lafayette, Ind.: Purdue University Press, 1976.
———. *The Art of Warfare in the Age of Napoleon.* Bloomington and London: Indiana University Press, 1978.
Ruge, Friedrich. *Der Seekrieg: The German Navy's Story, 1939–1945.* Annapolis: U.S. Naval Institute, 1957.
Salisbury, Harrison E. *The 900 Days: The Siege of Leningrad.* New York and Evanston: Harper and Row, 1969.
Savory, Reginald. *His Britannic Majesty's Army in Germany during the Seven Years' War.* New York: Oxford University Press, 1966.
Schandler, Herbert Y. *The Unmaking of a President: Lyndon Johnson and Vietnam.* Princeton: Princeton University Press, 1977.
Scheer, George F., and Rankin, Hugh F. *Rebels and Redcoats.* New York: Mentor Books, 1957.
Schurman, D. M. *The Education of a Navy: The Development of British Naval Strategic Thought, 1867–1914.* London: Cassell, 1965.
Seaton, Albert. *The Russo-German War, 1941–1945.* New York and Washington: Frederick A. Praeger, 1970.
Segur, Philippe-Paul de. *Napoleon's Russian Campaign.* Translated by J. David Townshend. Boston: Houghton Mifflin Company, 1958.
Sheehan, Neil *et al. The Pentagon Papers as Published in the New York Times.* New York: Bantam Books, 1971.
Showalter, Dennis E. *Railroads and Rifles: Soldiers, Technology, and the Unification of Germany.* Hamden, Conn.: The Shoe String Press, 1975.
Shulman, Milton. *Defeat in the West.* Rev. ed. New York: Ballantine Books, 1968.
Simmons, Edwin H. *The United States Marines: The First Two Hundred Years, 1775–1975.* New York: The Viking Press, 1976.
Simpson, Colin. *The Lusitania.* Boston and Toronto: Little, Brown and Company, 1972.
Singletary, Otis A. *The Mexican War.* Chicago and London: University of Chicago Press, 1960.
Slim, William. *Defeat into Victory.* New York: David McKay, 1956.

Sokolovsky, Vasilii D., ed. *Military Strategy: Soviet Doctrine and Concepts.* New York: Frederick A. Praeger, 1963.
Sommers, Richard J. *Richmond Redeemed: The Siege at Petersburg.* Garden City, N.Y.: Doubleday and Company, 1981.
Summers, Harry G. *On Strategy: A Critical Analysis of the Vietnam War.* Novato, Cal.: Presidio Press, 1982.
Spanier, J. W. *The Truman-MacArthur Controversy and the Korean War.* Cambridge, Mass.: Harvard University Press, 1959.
Speer, Albert. *Infiltration.* Translated by Joachim Neugroschel. New York: Macmillan and Company, 1981.
Stacy, C. P. *Canada and the British Army: A Study in Responsible Government.* Rev. ed. Toronto: University of Toronto Press, 1963.
Stallings, Laurence. *The Doughboys: The Story of the AEF, 1917–1918.* New York: Harper and Row, 1963.
Stein, George H. *The Waffen SS: Hitler's Elite Guard at War, 1939–1945.* Ithaca: Cornell University Press, 1966.
Sternberg, Fritz. *The Military and Industrial Revolution of our Time.* New York: Frederick A. Praeger, 1959.
Stokesbury, James L. *A Short History of World War I.* New York: William Morrow and Company, Inc., 1981.
———. *A Short History of World War II.* New York: William Morrow and Company, Inc., 1980.
Strawson, John. *The Battle for North Africa.* New York: Charles Scribner's Sons, 1969.
Suchenwirth, Richard. *The Development of the German Air Force, 1919–1939.* New York: Arno Press, 1968.
Sueter, M. F. *The Evolution of the Tank.* London: Hutchison, 1937.
Sunday Times of London Insight Team. *War in the Falklands: The Full Story.* New York: Harper and Row, 1982.
———. *The Yom Kippur War.* New York: Doubleday and Company, 1974.
Suvorov, Viktor. *Inside the Soviet Army.* New York: Macmillan and Company, 1982.
Taylor, A. J. P. *A History of the First World War.* New York: Berkeley Medallion Books, 1966.
Taylor, Telford. *The Breaking Wave: The Second World War in the Summer of 1940.* New York: Simon and Schuster, 1967.
———. *The March of Conquest: The German Victories in Western Europe, 1940.* New York: Simon and Schuster, 1958.
———. *Sword and Swastika: Generals and Nazis in the Third Reich.* New York: Simon and Schuster, 1967.
Thomas, Hugh. *The Spanish Civil War.* New York: Harper and Row, 1961.
Thompson, W. Scott, and Frizzell, Donaldson D., eds. *The Lessons of Vietnam.* New York: Crane, Russak and Company, 1977.
Toland, John. *Battle: The Story of the Bulge.* New York: Random House, 1959.
———. *But Not In Shame: The Six Months After Pearl Harbor.* New York: Random House, 1961.
———. *Infamy: Pearl Harbor and its Aftermath.* Garden City, N.Y.: Doubleday and Company, 1982.
———. *The Last 100 Days.* New York: Random House, 1965.
———. *The Rising Sun: The Decline and Fall of the Japanese Empire, 1936–1945.* New York: Random House, 1970.
Trevor-Roper, H. R., ed. *Hitler's War Directives, 1939–1945.* London: Sidgwick and Jackson, 1964.

Tuchman, Barbara. *Stilwell and the American Experience in China, 1911–1945.* New York: Macmillan and Company, 1970.
———. *The Guns of August.* New York: Macmillan and Company, 1962.
Turner, George E. *Victory Rode the Rails: The Strategic Place of the Railraods in the Civil War.* Indianapolis: Bobbs-Merrill Book Company, 1953.
Turner, Gordon B., and Challener, R. D. *National Security in the Nuclear Age: Basic Facts and Falacies.* New York: Frederick A. Praeger, 1960.
Tute, Warren. *The Deadly Stroke.* New York: Coward, McCann and Geoghegan, 1973.
Upton, Emory. *The Military Policy of the United States.* New York: Greenwood Press, 1968 (1904).
Vagts, Alfred. *A History of Militarism: Romance and Realities of a Profession.* 2nd. ed. New York: Free Press, 1967.
Van Creveld, Martin. *Supplying War: Logistics from Wallenstein to Patton.* London, New York and Melbourne: Cambridge University Press, 1977.
Vandiver, Frank E. *Black Jack: The Life and Times of John J. Pershing.* College Station, Tex., and London: Texas A and M University, 1977.
———. *Rebel Brass: The Confederate Command System.* Baton Rouge: Louisiana State University, 1956.
Van Dyke, Jon M. *North Vietnam's Strategy for Survival.* Palo Alto: Pacific Books, Publishers, 1972.
Von der Porten, Edward P. *The German Navy in World War II.* New York: Thomas Y. Crowell Company, 1969.
Wallace, Willard M. *Appeal to Arms: A Military History of the American Revolution.* Chicago: Quadrangle Books, 1951.
Ward, Christopher. *The War of the Revolution.* Edited by John Richard Alden. 2 vols. New York: Macmillan and Company, 1952.
Warlimont, Walter. *Inside Hitler's Headquarters, 1939–1945.* Translated by R. H. Barry. New York and Washington: Frederick A. Praeger, 1964.
Warner, Dennis and Peggy. *The Tide at Sunrise: A History of the Russo-Japanese War, 1904–1905.* New York: Charterhouse, 1974.
Webster, Sir Charles, and Frankland, Noble. *The Strategic Air Offensive Against Germany, 1939–1945.* 4 vols. London: HMSO, 1961.
Weigley, Russell F. *The American Way of War: A History of United States Military Strategy and Policy.* New York: Macmillan and Company, 1973.
———. *History of the United States Army.* New York: Macmillan and Company, 1967.
Weller, Jac. *Wellington in the Peninsula, 1808–1814.* London: N. Vane, 1962.
Werth, Alexander. *Russia at War, 1941–1945.* New York: E. P. Dutton and Company, 1964.
Wheeler-Bennett, J. W. *The Nemesis of Power: The German Army in Politics, 1918–1945.* New York: Compass, 1964.
Whiting, Charles. *Hunters from the Sky: The German Parachute Corps, 1940–1945.* London: Leo Cooper, 1974.
Whitton, Frederick E. *Moltke.* London: Constable, 1921.
Wiley, Bell I. *The Common Soldier in the Civil War.* New York: Grosset and Dunlap, 1952.
Wiley, Bell I., and Milhollen, Hirst D. *They Who Fought Here.* New York: Bonanza Books, 1959.
William, Kenneth P. *Lincoln Finds a General: A Military Study of the Civil War.* 5 vols. New York: Macmillan and Company, 1950–1959.
Williams, T. Harry. *The History of American Wars: From Colonial Times to World War I.* New York: Alfred A. Knopf, 1981.

———. *Lincoln and His Generals.* New York: Alfred A. Knopf, 1952.
Winterbotham, F. W. *The Ultra Secret.* New York, Evanston, San Francisco and London: Harper and Row, 1974.
Wintringham, Tom. *Weapons and Tactics.* Updated by J. N. Blashford-Snell. Harmondsworth: Penguin Books, 1974.
Wolf, Eric. *Peasant Wars of the Twentieth Century.* New York, Evanston and London: Harper and Row, 1970.
Wolff, Leon. *In Flanders Fields: The 1917 Campaign.* New York: The Viking Press, 1958.
Wood, Derek, and Dempster, Derek. *The Narrow Margin: The Battle of Britain and the Rise of Air Power, 1930–1940.* New York, Toronto and London: McGraw-Hill Book Company, 1961.
Woodham-Smith, Cecil. *The Reason Why.* New York: E. P. Dutton and Company, 1952.
Woodrooffe, Thomas. *The Enterprise of England: An Account of her Emergence as an Oceanic Power.* London: Faber and Faber, 1958.
Woodward, E. L. *Great Britain and the German Navy.* London: E. L. Cass, 1964.
Wright, Quincy. *A Study of War.* 2nd ed., abridged. Chicago: University of Chicago Press, 1965.
Wynden, Peter, *Bay of Pigs: The Untold Story.* New York: Simon and Schuster, 1979.
Wynn, G. C. *If Germany Attacks: The Battle in Depth in the West.* London: Faber and Faber, 1940.
Young, Desmond. *Rommel the Desert Fox.* New York: Harper and Row, 1950.
Young, Peter, and Lawford, J. P. *History of the British Army.* London: Arthur Barker, 1970.
Zhukov, Georgi K. *Zhukov's Greatest Battles.* Translated by Theodore Shabad. New York and Evanston: Harper and Row, Publishers, 1969.

Index